MAKING IT UP TOGETHER

CHICAGO STUDIES IN ETHNOMUSICOLOGY

A SERIES EDITED BY PHILIP V. BOHLMAN,
RONALD RADANO, AND TIMOTHY ROMMEN

EDITORIAL BOARD
Margaret J. Kartomi
Bruno Nettl
Anthony Seeger
Kay Kaufman Shelemay
Martin H. Stokes
Bonnie C. Wade

MAKING IT UP TOGETHER

THE ART OF COLLECTIVE IMPROVISATION
IN BALINESE MUSIC AND BEYOND

Leslie A. Tilley

THE UNIVERSITY OF CHICAGO PRESS
CHICAGO AND LONDON

The University of Chicago Press, Chicago 60637
The University of Chicago Press, Ltd., London
© 2019 by The University of Chicago
All rights reserved. No part of this book may be used or reproduced in any manner whatsoever without written permission, except in the case of brief quotations in critical articles and reviews. For more information, contact the University of Chicago Press, 1427 E. 60th St., Chicago, IL 60637.
Published 2019
Printed in the United States of America

28 27 26 25 24 23 22 21 20 19   1 2 3 4 5

ISBN-13: 978-0-226-66113-1 (cloth)
ISBN-13: 978-0-226-66760-7 (paper)
ISBN-13: 978-0-226-66774-4 (e-book)
DOI: https://doi.org/10.7208/chicago/9780226667744.001.0001

Library of Congress Cataloging-in-Publication Data

Names: Tilley, Leslie A., author.
Title: Making it up together : the art of collective improvisation in Balinese music and beyond / Leslie A. Tilley.
Other titles: Chicago studies in ethnomusicology.
Description: Chicago ; London : The University of Chicago Press, 2019. | Series: Chicago studies in ethnomusicology | Includes bibliographical references and index.
Identifiers: LCCN 2019012687 | ISBN 9780226661131 (cloth : alk. paper) | ISBN 9780226667607 (pbk. : alk. paper) | ISBN 9780226667744 (e-book)
Subjects: LCSH: Gamelan music—Indonesia—Bali Island—History and criticism. | Improvisation (Music) | Performance practice (Music)—Bali Island. | Reyong—Performance—Indonesia—Bali Island. | Kendang—Performance—Indonesia—Bali Island.
Classification: LCC ML1251.I53 T55 2019 | DDC 780.9598/62—dc23
LC record available at https://lccn.loc.gov/2019012687

♾ This paper meets the requirements of ANSI/NISO Z39.48-1992 (Permanence of Paper).

Even though they're making up music, they're trying to make it up together. It feels great, like you're having a great conversation with somebody.

Wynton Marsalis

To My Families

CONTENTS

Notes on Pronunciation · ix
Prelude · 1

1. The Complicated Story of Improvisation: Models and Methods, Creativity and Conceptual Space · 21
2. Finding an Unspoken Model: The Boundaries of *Reyong Norot* · 51
3. Analyzing Improvisations on a Known Model: The Freedom of *Reyong Norot* · 89
4. Analyzing Collectivity: Models and Interactions in Practice · 137
5. Unraveling Unconscious Models: The Boundaries of *Kendang Arja* · 179
6. Beyond Generalizations: The Freedom of *Kendang Arja* · 219

Postlude · 265
Acknowledgments · 277
Glossary of Frequently Used Terms · 281
Notes · 291   *References* · 313
Index · 331

A companion website providing supplementary audio recordings, videos, and photographs for this book's two case studies is available at https://www.press.uchicago.edu/sites/tilley/.

NOTES ON PRONUNCIATION

Throughout the text, most non-English words are italicized, though proper nouns in any language, such as village names, are not. While the book aims to be broadly cross-cultural, because its two main case studies address Balinese music, a brief guide to pronunciation in Balinese and Indonesian languages is provided here.

When speaking Balinese or Indonesian, Balinese speakers generally stress either the final or penultimate syllable of each word. In the term *gamelan*, for instance, the *lan* is stressed.

An *e* in the first syllable of a word is generally pronounced as a very short schwa and may be dropped completely. Peliatan, for instance, is pronounced "Pli-a-tan," Pengosekan is "P'ng-o-se-kan," *empat* is "m-pat." The letters *t* and *p*, as in *penyacah* and *batel*, are generally unaspirated. The letter *r* is rolled throughout, particularly at the ends of words; in words like *arja*, it is more of a short flip of the tongue. The letters *k*, *t*, and *p* at the ends of words, for example, "Alit," are stopped, not sounded. A final *h*, as in the word *wayah*, should be sounded.

PRONUNCIATION GUIDE

Balinese and Indonesian	Approximate English equivalent
a	"a" in "father"
e	"e" in "bet"
é	"ay" in "sashay"
i	"ee" in "feeling"
i between two consonants in later syllables of a word (e.g., *ngematin, ngegongin,* Alit)	"i" in "lick" (with rare exceptions)
o	"o" in "rode"
u	"oo" in "food"
c	"ch" in "cheese"
ç (as in *Çudamani*)	"s" in "sunset"
g	"g" in "gorilla"
j	"j" in "juicy"
ng	"ng" in "singer"
ngg	"ng" in "finger"

PRELUDE

"DOWN THE RABBIT HOLE"

The coffee is strong and sweet, a thick layer of grounds settling in the bottom of the glasses that Sudi's[1] mother has brought on a tray with some jajan, *snacks. This happens each day in the middle of our drum lessons, allowing me a brief respite from the pace of Sudi's teaching. My brain feels full, and my arms are burning and will probably be sore tomorrow. But Sudi and I both know that I'll be back for more anyway. I find Balinese drumming far too irresistible. Sitting in the shade of the* balé,[2] *the porch of his house, I gratefully sip the hot* kopi *and turn to investigate the plate of* jajan. *Like most Balinese mothers, Sudi's* ibu *loves to feed her guests. Yesterday she brought us bags of peanuts and shrimp chips with our mid-lesson coffee; today the serving dish is overflowing with pieces of banana wrapped in a sticky rice flour dough. Just one or two pieces will fortify me for another two hours, maybe three if we really get into a groove. Today our good friend Gus Dé[3] has dropped by for a visit, and we are merrily exchanging stories and pleasantries as we enjoy our refreshments. Leaning back against the wall, my coffee in hand, I watch contentedly as the two of them abandon their* jajan, *pick up Sudi's drums,* kendang, *and begin to jam.*

Sudi has been teaching me the drumming to accompany Legong Lasem, *one of Bali's most famous dances. Like all the Balinese kendang playing I have encountered thus far,* kendang legong *is precomposed. Two drums play complementary parts that interlock— like-stroke following like-stroke—creating carefully crafted composite patterns. I have always assumed that, to accommodate this characteristically Balinese aesthetic of interlocking, all of Bali's paired drum genres must be as exactingly composed as the piece I have been learning today. But the rhythms that Sudi and Gus Dé are busting out in the hot July morning, interlocking though they may be, are clearly not. I have never heard Balinese drumming like this before! (See Video 1 on the companion website).*[4]

"What are you two playing?" I blurt out in my excitement.

They laugh and pick up the pace a few notches, each grinning at me whenever they think they've played a particularly cool pattern, one they might call wayah. When they finally stop in a fit of laughter—from a mistake or just the joy of playing together, I'll never know—I ask again: "What IS that?!"

"It's kendang arja," Gus Dé answers simply.

Sudi continues, "In my father's generation, this style of drumming was used for performances of a long sung dance drama called arja. But arja's not very popular anymore, and these days we mostly use the drumming just for fun."

"We're improvising," Gus Dé explains. "We can play whatever we want."

It seems a simple statement of fact. But their drumming demands that I approach this assertion with care. They're playing at lightning speeds, each producing up to 800 drum strokes per minute.[5] Their hands move far too fast for them to be consciously aware of what the other is playing in time to react accordingly. And yet their two parts interlock as though they had been planned in advance. I imagine in that moment that kendang arja, like much improvisation, must be based on a set of guidelines, whether consciously known or not; that while an arja drummer does have freedom when playing, because he must interlock with his partner, it is possible to play "wrong." And that were I to have picked up a drum that day to join in Sudi and Gus Dé's paired improvisation, and played whatever I wanted to play, I probably would have played nothing "right." The curious Analytical Ethnomusicologist in me—and the drummer—needed to understand how they were doing it.

Gus Dé's claim that "we can play whatever we want" evokes a common image of the improviser: a creative genius who, with no forethought or practice, invents extraordinary music, bringing it into existence in the very moment of performance. Jazz guitarist Wes Montgomery once similarly boasted: "I never practice my guitar. From time to time I just open the case and throw in a piece of raw meat."[6] And Bix Beiderbecke declared: "One thing I like about jazz, kid, is that I don't know what's going to happen next. Do you?" Individuals such as these are often held up as arbiters of the improvisatory art, singlehandedly creating moments of unplanned musical greatness. Miles Davis once said, "you can tell the history of jazz in four words: Louis Armstrong, Charlie Parker." These "bald characterization[s] giv[e] a picture of the improviser as an existential hero taking irrational leaps into darkness" (Brown 2000, 114). Yet the reality, as most improvisers will acknowledge, is not that simple. A contrasting image presents a hard-working musician, honing her craft through years of study and collaboration. In words often attributed to Art Tatum, "you have to practice improvisation, let no one kid you about it!" And Wynton Marsalis avers: "Even though they're making up music, they're trying to *make it up together*. It feels great, like you're having a great conversation with somebody." These differing characterizations of the improviser create competing oppositions of spontaneity and preparation, individuality and collaboration, with reality generally occupying a middle ground. Two *arja* drummers, deftly weaving together fast improvised patterns, invite us to grapple with such dualities. How can spontaneous, personal creativity exist in an intertwining communal practice like *kendang arja*? A friend once jokingly told me that he suspected black magic! I suspected something much more human. But how could I reconcile Gus Dé and other drummers' assertions of their absolute freedom in *kendang arja* with my own failed experiments in improvising, which invariably elicited wrinkled noses, bemused head shakes, gentle laughter, and exclamations of "*belum*," "not yet"? Could I pinpoint the unspoken processes and guidelines that allowed these improvising musicians to interlock so elegantly with one another and make manifest the logic behind the magic?

CREATIVITY AS COLLABORATIVE PROCESS

The musicology of improvisation, whether in jazz, Arabic *layālī* and *taqasim*, baroque preludes and cadenzas, or Hindustani *rag*, often depicts the strategies and schemas of individual musicians.[7] But we also understand that that's not the whole story and have begun to comprehend the ways in which improvised practices thrive on group creativity. In *Saying Something* (1996), Ingrid Monson examines the supporting and improvisatory roles of the rhythm section as she discusses interaction in jazz improvisation. Paul Berliner devotes over three hundred pages of text and transcriptions in *Thinking in Jazz* (1994) to collectivity. And Benjamin Brinner's *Knowing Music, Making Music* (1995) explores concepts of musical competence and interaction through the lens of the collaborative and improvisatory Javanese gamelan ensemble (see also Sutton 1993 and 1998; Perlman 2004). From jazz and Javanese gamelan to Shona mbira music and Aka polyphonic singing, many improvisational practices have been shown to rely on the close interaction of multiple musicians, collectively building a structure like Gödel, Escher, and Bach's colony of ants.[8]

Fields as diverse as psychology, management science, and patent law suggest that the most innovative new ideas across various disciplines and practices are bred through collaborative process.[9] As more researchers begin to "view learning and thinking as social process" (John-Steiner 2000, 3) and focus on "the importance of social, cultural, contextual, and organizational factors in creativity" (Paulus and Nijstad 2003, 5), the legend of the lone genius is brought down to size. Fruitful collaborations of partners are well documented: the bicycle mechanic Wright Brothers succeeded in building the first airplane in advance of well-funded scientists through constant collaboration and the reworking of each other's ideas. Picasso and Braque, with their contrasting skills and vision, came together long enough to transform the art world with cubism; and the complementary training and temperament of chemist Marie Curie and her physicist husband Pierre fueled their pioneering work in radioactivity.[10] In such partnerships, productive differences between associates create an environment where revolutionary discoveries and developments are made via a string of small insights, each triggering a new one. What emerges is *group genius* (see Sawyer 2007; 2015). The proverbial "eureka moment" has been overly hyped.

While the genius of the group is perhaps easiest to trace in small partnerships, this same give-and-take can also fuel creativity in larger groups. In improv theater troupes, each player is closely attuned to the actions and utterances of other players, adjusting in response to create a kind of interactional synchrony.[11] It is the interplay between audience suggestions and the equal contributions of multiple improvisers that keeps performances fresh night after night. Pickup basketball players, with no coach, no fixed rules, and no regular practices to perfect strategy, can only succeed "by improvising and collaborating, changing constantly in response to the adjustments their opponents are making" (Sawyer 2015, 31). And though classic group brainstorming techniques have often proven to be relatively ineffective, some companies continue striving to harness the power of group genius.[12] At W. L. Gore and Associates, the company responsible for the invention of GORE-TEX waterproof material, employees are encouraged to spend 10 percent of their working time on speculative new projects, forming ad hoc, self-managed, short-term teams to build, both collaboratively and improvisationally, on new ideas.[13] This brand of group genius can also be fostered across companies, where open, connected networks help to form large *collaborative webs*. The cluster of West Coast computer companies termed "Silicon Valley" succeeded through the 1990s as Boston's competing

Route 128 cluster was declining because the culture in Silicon Valley encouraged free and open collaboration:

> In the bars where everyone in the semiconductor industry hung out, such as the legendary Wagon Wheel Restaurant and Casino in Mountain View, engineers asked each other questions and shared ideas. CEOs thought nothing of calling up a competitor's CEO on the phone and asking for help with a problem. Route 128 companies, in contrast, did not permit their employees to hang out and share information with people from other companies; indeed current and former employees alike knew they would be sued if they shared information. . . . Route 128 was lined with large companies that did everything in-house; Silicon Valley was a network of smaller companies that fostered dense relationships of subcontracts and partnerships. [. . . There,] the vibrant collaborative webs resulted in collective learning and systemic adaptation, both of which made everyone in the web stronger. (Sawyer 2007, 186)

Computer scientists have long touted the advantages of such collaborative work through the development of open-source software and the use of hackathons to generate new ideas and novel approaches.[14] The belief is that, "given a large enough beta-tester and co-developer base, almost every problem will be characterized quickly and the fix obvious to someone. Or, less formally, 'Given enough eyeballs, all bugs are shallow'" (Raymond 2001, 30).[15]

From the creative partnership to the collaborative web, this reframing of concepts of creativity and invention has led to a rethinking of patent law and the various theories surrounding it. Lawyers must now grapple with the reality that invention is a partially social phenomenon; it happens in teams through a constant intellectual back-and-forth and the adaptation of other inventors' work. Rather than a lone genius creating in isolation, most innovations are the result of *distributed invention*.[16]

DISTRIBUTED INVENTION IN PERFORMANCE: THE CONCEPT OF "COLLECTIVE IMPROVISATION"

Human beings, then, are often at their most creative in collaboration; group genius crosses disciplines, cultures, and practices. Yet "there are very few comparative studies of improvised music traditions" (Solis 2012a, 2), and even fewer specifically comparing group improvised practices. I knew lots of terminology and theory to help explain collaborative process in *kendang arja* performance;

statements like "the higher drum is the bus driver" and "the lower drum calls attention to the gong" would guide any analyses I did. But the usefulness of these concepts lessened if I wanted to look at diverse Balinese practices comparatively, even more so if I wanted to compare collaborative processes across music cultures. I would need terminology and categories broad enough to be applicable cross-culturally and, simultaneously, flexible enough to embrace the specificities of each genre and practice. Yet existing terminology on such practices, even at the highest level of abstraction, is diffuse and unstandardized: Turino (2009) talks about *participatory music* while Brinner (1995) and Monson (1996) refer to various kinds of *interaction* and Sutton (1993) discusses simply *variation*. The terms *group improvisation* and *paired improvisation* are generally only used in pedagogical or music therapy contexts and as often refer to drama as music; and the phrase *collaborative improvisation*, alongside its use in educational contexts, is frequently used to describe human-computer interactions.[17] This lack of terminological coherence makes intertextual reference among researchers of improvised musics that much more challenging.[18] While the choice in naming is somewhat arbitrary, the usefulness of a unified vocabulary is clear. To encourage intertextuality, I borrow the umbrella term *collective improvisation* from studies in jazz, which still make up the lion's share of the literature on improvisation.[19] Through analysis and discussion of many genres and practices, the concept will be expanded and subcategorized with an eye to comparative analysis.

In current usage, the term *collective improvisation* refers to practices, like *kendang arja*, in which "some or all members of a group participate in simultaneous improvisation of equal or comparable 'weight'" (Kernfeld n.d., III.2). It is perhaps most commonly used in descriptions of New Orleans jazz, where the three main melodic instruments each idiomatically improvise on the tune, not only one after the other, as in most jazz, but simultaneously. Each weaves its own thread in the aural tapestry, intertwining with but never overpowering the other two.[20] Figure 0.1 is a representative example: the first eight measures of the penultimate ensemble chorus of "Black Bottom Stomp," as recorded by Jelly Roll Morton's Red Hot Peppers in 1926.[21]

George Mitchell takes the main melody on the cornet, adding idiomatic ornaments and embellishments. Omer Simeon on clarinet improvises a fast-moving countermelody in a higher range. The trombone, played by Kid Ory, fills out the lower end of the sonic space, commenting on these other melodies through call and response with slower rhythmic gestures that accentuate harmonic root movement, and later in the performance adding his own fast-moving fills where the higher melody instruments rest. His "characteristically simpler and lower counterline ... dances between two functions, spelling out harmony and making

FIGURE 0.1. Collective improvisation in New Orleans jazz

counterpoint" (Kernfeld 1995, 120).[22] Together these three musicians create a dense improvised polyphony. Behind them, Jelly Roll Morton on piano and the members of the rhythm section (John Lindsay on bass, Johnny St. Cyr on banjo, and Andrew Hilaire on drums) lay down the rhythm and chord changes. Each musician has a role to play in the soundscape and the freedom to innovate within his idiom, allowing individuality in collaboration without chaos.[23]

Other genres that have adopted the term *collective improvisation* include avant-garde, experimental, and free jazz as well as psychedelic and experimental rock and jam band music.[24] As we will see in chapters 1 and 4, the parameters of collectivity in these practices are quite different than in more regimented forms like *kendang arja* or New Orleans jazz, often more concerned with the sonic canvas than with the specifics of moment-to-moment interactions. Practitioners of 1960s free jazz, for instance, "embraced the principle of collective improvisation, but with a more deliberate dismissal of traditional organizational structures," motivated as they were by "a departure from established norms and desire to 'violate almost every academic canon'" (Thomas 2014, para. 20).[25]

Ornette Coleman's 1961 *Free Jazz: A Collective Improvisation* was perhaps the first recording to rely on these broader conceptions. In it, the independent improvisation of two jazz quartets is captured on the two channels of a stereo recording. But their nearly forty-minute performance is not based on small-scale constraints such as chord changes or tune structure. Instead, the alternating solo and collective improvisations that make up its single track take the form of unstructured commentary on a collection of brief, precomposed fanfares. The performers are "improvising on a limited selection of directions" (Hugill 2012, 285), and the result is meant to sound experimental, free, perhaps even chaotic. A similar framework of flexibility is characteristic of the theater productions of Swedish director and teacher Ingemar Lindh. Generally considered the father of collective improvisation in the theater arts, Lindh created postmodern productions that "resist[ed] single authorhood and fixed, predetermined structures" (Camilleri 2008, 84). He workshopped his collective improvisation practices through the 1970s and '80s, creating performances not through preplanned staging and plotlines but through spontaneous "encounters." Lindh taught that "the theatrical moment is born from the encounter between different intentions [and that] such an encounter can create 'fusion' as much as it can create 'collision'" (Lindh 2010, 45). The intention and method behind this sort of performance results in a very different kind of collectivity from that of Jelly Roll Morton and his Red Hot Peppers.

Outside New Orleans jazz, then, it seems that the notion of *collective improvisation* is reserved for group practices with "the maximum freedom for improvisation" (Spector 2016, 158)—performances loosely exploring a structure, not those bound by melodic, rhythmic, or harmonic constraints. Yet as we will see, the concept can be extended and elaborated to find resonance in extremely diverse improvisatory practices, categorized and subcategorized to provide a framework for comparative and cross-cultural study. Each genre or music culture uses collectivity in distinct ways. We can already imagine that a discussion of collective improvisation in Balinese *kendang arja* would require different terminology, tools, and approaches than one on New Orleans or free jazz. And that studies of improvised practices in which the various instruments enjoy differing levels of creative license—such as Anlo-Ewe dance-drumming (Locke 1998) and many jazz genres—could also benefit from an examination of collectivity but would again present separate challenges. Each of these practices employs its own techniques and is sustained by its own oral music theory. Yet in all of them, and many others, there exist similar processes of listening and communication, give-and-take, the filling of musical roles, and the creation of space for one's musical partners—a balancing of individual creativity with group need. Each inhabits its own range of the same continuum, distinct in flavor and practice yet inextricably linked in its underlying motives and methods.

A closer examination of improvisatory processes and the careful typologizing of collectively improvised genres could provide a scaffolding on which different musical practices find common ground, not in the details but in the design. In this book, my own experiences learning and performing Balinese music, and the analyses emerging from those ethnographic interactions, serve as a springboard for a broader cross-cultural inquiry into processes of collective improvisation.

"THERE'S NO IMPROVISATION IN BALI"

Balinese music may at first seem an unusual arena in which to theorize improvisation. Those familiar with the most internationally visible Balinese genre, *gamelan gong kebyar*, will know that its music prizes rhythmic and melodic precision through close player interaction. The twenty-five-piece ensemble's famous *kotekan* techniques for instance, in which an often blindingly fast melody is impeccably shared between a pair of musicians, generally necessitate careful preplanning. While scholarship on the gamelan music of neighboring Java frequently forefronts the variability of different instrument parts and the associated creativity of its players,[26] the narrative of Balinese gamelan is often one of meticulous precomposition. Important early Balinese music researcher Colin McPhee asserted that "other than in solo parts there can be no place for spontaneous improvisation.... Unison in the different parts must prevail or utter confusion results" (1966, xvii). The generation of scholars following McPhee likewise maintained that "improvisation does not exist" in Bali (Lieberman 1967, 275; see also Reich 2002 and 2000).

While most recent studies of Balinese music do touch on improvisation, it is still often portrayed as limited, rare, or both, its techniques seldom discussed in detail. Of two solo instruments often cast as ensemble leaders in *gamelan gong kebyar*, Michael Tenzer (2011a) states: "since the ugal and the trompong are generally not paired ... their players are allowed some flexibility in interpreting the melody." Yet he continues: "Their roles are among the few places where improvisation, albeit within a narrow range, can play a role in Balinese music" (53–54). This despite his thoughtful examination of various improvised drumming forms in his 2000 book *Gamelan Gong Kebyar* (see Tenzer 2000, 288–304).[27] Michael Bakan in his study of *gamelan beleganjur* also examines some instances of drum improvisation, specifically of *batu-batu* drumming, where one musician in a pair maintains a steady rhythm so that the other can improvise "syncopated rhythmic figures [that] tend to create a kind of 'rolling' effect" (1999, 63). But Bakan, too, clarifies: "batu-batu are distinctive by virtue of their emphasis on improvised drumming, which is otherwise relatively rare in two-drum Balinese styles" (1999, 63).[28]

Bali's gamelan music in general, and perhaps its paired interlocking drumming traditions most of all, are rightly celebrated as exemplars of *compositional* ingenuity. Yet an unintended side effect of this, as Nicholas Gray avers, is that "the *significance* of improvisation in Balinese music has often been neglected" (2011, 24, emphasis added). This reality may inadvertently reinforce a mid-twentieth-century trope, expressed perhaps most memorably by anthropologist Clifford Geertz (1973), of Bali and the Balinese as static and unchanging: a place, culture, and people where "theatricality [is] not spontaneous but almost forced," and where "art, religion, and politesse all exalt the outward, the contrived, the well-wrought appearance of things. They celebrate the forms" (400).[29]

The two case studies that comprise chapters 2–3 and 5–6 of this book join a growing body of work examining the role of improvisation in Balinese music and, by extension, supporting a sociocultural interpretation of Bali and the Balinese as spontaneous, flexible, and truly playful in their approach to "the forms."[30] Woven into Andrew Clay McGraw's 2013 *Radical Traditions*, for instance, is a historical narrative of Balinese composers grappling with traditional and foreign ideas on the appropriateness, function, and possibilities of improvisation in *musik kontemporer*, contemporary music. He observes:

> [Composer] Arsawijaya referred to the *virus improvisasi*, . . . improvisation, as a form of complete freedom that appealed to Western forms of non-idiomatic improvisation as opposed to the highly restricted forms of improvisation performed by the *suling* [flute] in *tradisi* [traditional] contexts. . . . In his score for *Geräusch*, . . . Arsawijaya uses an abstract symbol to indicate passages of free improvisation (*improvisasi bebas*) to be performed on the *gong*, using a metal grinder. (156)

Focusing largely on traditional theatrical genres, Edward Herbst (1997) provides insight into flexible dance choreography as well as spontaneously created text in the performance of sung poetry (*tembang macapat*). Exploring among other things the concept of *perkembangan*, "development, creative flowering" (182), Herbst describes how "Balinese theater is generally improvised, using countless shared devices and sources, as well as standardized characterization techniques" (98). He explains:

> [Performer Ni Nyoman] Candri uses her own personal experience of romance, anger, nature, to imagine the scene and create within it. The study

of texts [written or performed . . .] is a vehicle toward the goal of creating
freely: resources built up, not for use in their entirety, or even directly, but
for incorporation within an improvised style. The process of "composing"
each *tembang* [song] must have a smooth, spontaneous quality, as with performing and improvising a story. (56)

My case studies—each traditional, instrumental, and collectively performed—are kin to the *gendér wayang* chamber ensemble studied by Lisa Gold
(1998) and Nicholas Gray (2010; 2011), who show how even Bali's famous interlocking (*kotekan*) techniques can be improvised. Gray quotes *gendér* performer
I Ketut Buda Astra to explain the fixed and flexible connections between two
interlocking musical lines, *polos* and *sangsih*. Here *dong*, *dang*, and *ding* denote
different pitches:

> If we are improvising in *gendér wayang*, what becomes the teacher, the handle,
> the key, is the *jublag* [. . . a slower moving melody line, often considered the
> "basic" melody of the piece] in the left hand. The *kotékan* in the right hand
> is tied by the left hand's striking. The right hand can improvise but . . . in
> the middle of the improvisation it must meet with the *jublag*. For instance,
> if the *jublag*'s final note is *dong*, the *kotékan* can improvise to *dang*, to *ding*, but
> eventually it must fall to *dong*. Here we are tied to the left hand. The *sangsih*
> is also like that. It can improvise following the *polos*. Sometimes it can cross
> over, but it must think "where is the *polos* improvising to?" (Gray 2010, 236)[31]

Both Gray and Herbst cast Balinese improvisation as a balancing of the
fixed with the extemporaneous, a reinterpreting of known forms, devices,
melodic signposts, and motives—a "playing with the form," to repurpose
Geertz's term. As will become clear, this approach is common in many improvised practices, suggesting a breadth of scope and cross-cultural potential,
which is theoretically contextualized in chapters 1 and 4. The book's two in-
depth case studies—of the paired drumming practice *kendang arja* and a collectively improvised melody-making technique used in *gamelan gong kebyar*—are
given preliminary introductions here.

IMPROVISATION IN *GAMELAN GONG KEBYAR*: REYONG NOROT

When people think of composed Balinese music, they are often picturing
gamelan gong kebyar: an early twentieth-century genre of instrumental music

performed by a twenty-five-piece ensemble of bronze metallophones, hand drums, and gongs. The music of the *gong kebyar*, like much Balinese gamelan music, centers on cyclicity. A composition, which can range from three to forty-five minutes or more in length, generally comprises a series of cyclic melodies. Each repeating melody is kept fresh and surprising through subtle and dramatic shifts in tempo or dynamics and changing melodic elaborations in faster-moving instruments. And each contrasting cyclic passage is stitched to the next with varied introductory, transitional, or concluding material, generating a sense of forward motion in this cycle-based practice. Most prominent in the ensemble are an octet of metallophones, called *gangsa*, elaborating the slower-moving melodies of other instruments, at four notes per beat, through a variety of figuration styles. In faster passages, pairs of musicians realize these elaborations by dividing the notes of a melody between them in various carefully prescribed interlocking idioms, often generically termed *kotekan*.

Four musicians simultaneously playing a single long row of pitched gongs, or gong chime—called *reyong*—fill a similar role. Yet while interlocking melodies on *gangsa* are always fixed, in the figuration style *norot*, the four *reyong* players must improvise. This book's first case study reveals how *reyong norot* improvisations are guided by the fixed *norot* melody of their *gangsa* compatriots. They comprise mostly small-scale note-by-note alterations that require an ingenious creativity within tight constraints. I seek to uncover *how* these musicians stretch their relatively fixed model for improvisation, creating variety and fluidity while still maintaining the substance of the model. Through analysis, I ask: what are the more and less flexible components of such a model, and can one delineate the limits of each musician's freedom within it?

IMPROVISATION IN PAIRED DRUMMING: *KENDANG ARJA*

Paired drum traditions in Bali, as we've seen, are also generally cast as fixed, carefully composed practices. Drums—kendang—are often leaders in their ensembles, directing shifts in tempo and dynamics as well as structural transitions with an interlocking akin to *kotekan*.[32] A bass-y stroke on the lower *wadon* drum is usually followed by a parallel stroke on the higher *lanang*; a slap on the *lanang* immediately answered with a slap on the *wadon*, and so on, often at very high speeds. Yet, in the small *geguntangan* ensemble that accompanies the epic sung dance drama *arja*, this paired interlocking is created through simultaneous improvisation.

Arja is one of Bali's more well-known theatrical genres, where a large cast of singer-dancers enacts complex stories of good and evil. The overall structure of its multihour performances is determined by the chosen narrative as well as the in-performance decisions of the singer-dancers. Songs are interspersed with long stretches of improvised dialogue, often humorous and politically topical. Underscoring the singing of each performer, and punctuating their dancing, is a small ensemble of flutes heterophonically complementing the song, a number of incidental percussion instruments marking cycles of varying lengths, and a pair of interlocking kendang. In this context, the kendang players do not closely track the contour or moment-to-moment timings of the songs themselves, nor does their playing affect these musical details. Rather, they improvise a vamped rhythmic accompaniment of sorts, guided by the cycle-marking instruments. They come together with a singer-dancer only to emphasize the end of a sung phrase or important dance movement with a fixed rhythmic pattern. Yet despite the seeming simplicity of this task, even more than *reyong norot*, playing *kendang arja* requires a balance of creativity with control. Each drummer must somehow interlock with his partner while improvising on a large collection of model patterns, many of them only tacitly known. Together they create "shifting shadings" (Gray 2011, 102) of rhythmic intensity and emotion. Thus, "traditional *arja* drumming is considered to be the most complex and subtle [of Bali's drumming practices], relying upon spontaneity and nuance between the two interlocked but fluid drummers and the dancer" (Gray 2011, 102). This book's second case study begins with the challenge of trying to uncover whatever models for *arja* improvisation may be uncovered, and to understand how models for one drum have been constructed to complement those of the other. These explorations prepare answers for deeper questions: what are the boundaries and freedoms of each musician in this improvisation, and how are they complicated by moment-to-moment performance contexts? How much do such constraints vary, and what are the determinate musical and social factors?

The two case studies have goals both focused and broad: on the one hand, they are microexaminations of improvised practices from a music culture long thought of as essentially nonimprovisatory; on the other, they serve as models for the analysis of collective improvisation across cultures and practices.

AIMS

This book aims to explore the practice of collective musical improvisation cross-culturally, rooting its discussions in genre-specific analyses. Central to the project are case studies of the two collectively improvised Balinese practices just introduced, punctuated and complemented throughout by shorter analytical forays into diverse non-Balinese practices. These varied analyses help establish typologies for exploring the dimensions and incarnations of collective improvisation more globally all while testing the boundaries of those typologies.

Chapter 1 proposes general, high-level principles of improvisation. As a widespread human propensity, what are useful ways to comparatively explore its diverse manifestations? Are there improvisatory processes and strategies that can be found across culturally divergent musical practices, and can these be categorized without flattening their individual qualities? Various interrelated cognitive processes foster the individual and collective aspects of improvisation. What disciplinary tools can we use to examine them? To answer these questions, the chapter draws from research in musicology and ethnomusicology as well as studies on creativity in neuroscience, cognitive science, and other fields. Improvisation is characterized as a process that relies on a preexisting *model* and its surrounding *knowledge base*, and through analyses of diverse practices, several general improvisatory processes are proposed.

Chapters 2 and 3 present the first of two analytical case studies exploring these improvisatory processes in action. They examine *reyong norot*, the Balinese practice in which four musicians collectively improvise interlocking polyphonic melodies based on an explicitly known but unspoken model: the single strand of melody played by the *gangsa* metallophones. What are the challenges of collective improvisation when all musicians are working from the same single-voice model? Such models will impose certain kinds of limits on performance practice. What guidelines must musicians follow to idiomatically actualize them? How are these guidelines determined in individual music cultures, and importantly, how can we discover them when such models and knowledge bases are so often unspoken? While analysts of jazz improvisations begin with explicit knowledge of the tune and chord changes, those wishing to analyze improvisations on unspoken or unconscious models must first discover them. Chapter 2 proposes a research method for uncovering unspoken models for improvisation, using my study of *reyong norot* to illustrate. The practice's single-voice model is then introduced, and elements of its broader knowledge base proposed. Throughout, concepts are comparatively applied to improvised practices worldwide, suggesting potential for cross-cultural exploration. Chapter 3 presents an analysis of *reyong norot* performance through the lens of the general improvisatory processes proposed in chapter 1. It considers the many ways that musicians diverge from the *reyong norot* model, borrowing concepts from related Balinese genres and framing analyses in local oral music theory. Close musical examination shows how processes of improvisation are actualized in a specific music culture, while comparisons to other practices point to the widespread applicability of these concepts.

Can we unravel the processes of interaction that make collectively improvised practices like *reyong norot* possible? Chapter 4 zooms out once more to consider the specifically collective aspects of improvisation, exploring cognitive underpinnings, communication techniques, and other conditions that foster successful collective performances. A framework for analyzing the multifaceted aspects of collective improvisation across cultures is developed, elucidating how varying model types—and modes and degrees of interaction—will independently shape musical analysis. Discussions of the effects of musicians' shared histories, as well as explorations into group flow, collaborative emergence, and other theories of creativity, cognition, and interaction, add nuance to the proposed framework.

Collective improvisation based on an unconsciously known model with multiple voices is the focus of the book's second case study, which plumbs the paired interlocking drumming practice *kendang arja*. What social and pedagogical factors engender models for improvisation that are not explicitly known, and how can we uncover their most salient aspects through fieldwork and music analysis? Diverse musical and social relationships are created when different musicians in a collective improvisation work from unique parts of an unconscious model. Again, specific performer hierarchies and roles, musical textures, and individual approaches will emerge. How can we theorize the complex models underlying these practices, untangling each individual voice from the collective whole? And what musical, cognitive, and social factors individualize musicians' approaches to these models? Chapter 5 explores how diverse methods of learning and teaching can generate different "ways of knowing" and how these will unavoidably affect our analytical approaches to improvised practice. Using *kendang arja* to illustrate, the chapter explores how patterns learned in lessons from practitioners can be combined with informal oral music theory to illuminate aspects of unconscious models for improvisation. Guidelines for *kendang arja* improvisation are presented through a blend of analysis and ethnography. In chapter 6, the general processes for improvisation from chapter 1 are again deployed to shed light on *arja* improvisation. Yet this chapter assumes a wider lens than chapter 3, examining how larger structural elements of the music—or the dramatic performance it accompanies—might influence an improviser's moment-to-moment decisions, and questioning how both regional style and personal choices and preferences can shape collectively improvised practice.

The postlude returns to the wide lens of chapters 1 and 4, reexamining questions of comparative and cross-cultural research. How is such an approach useful or compelling in a study of collective improvisation? What are its strengths and potential pitfalls? And can a framework that encourages comparative analysis of collectively improvised forms give new insights into questions of human creativity? A brief comparison of Shona *mbira dzavadzimu* improvisation with the collectivity of *kendang arja* illustrates the potential of a cross-cultural approach. By the end I hope to have made a case for placing the concept of collective improvisation at the center of improvisation discourse and shown how ethnographically informed music analysis—with an eye to comparative thinking—can be a powerful tool for revealing its dimensionality.

METHODS: THE ANALYSIS OF IMPROVISATION

Analysis matters because, through it, we observe at close range the workings of ... musical minds.

(AGAWU 2003, 196)

"Leslie, it's your turn," Taro *grins, picking up the communal glass to fill it with* arak, *Bali's infamous moonshine.*

"Sedikit saja," I *implore. "Just a little." He pours me a moderately sized portion, and the glass is handed around the circle of gamelan musicians until it reaches me. I down it in one gulp, to uproarious laughter and cheering, and slide the empty glass back across the tile floor.*

"But what about the last drummer?" Taro *suggests, resuming an earlier conversation. "I thought his playing was really* cocok, *suited, to the* Jauk *dancer." This begins an animated discussion on the strengths and weaknesses of the last drummer's improvisations and the quality of his interactions with the dancer, as the glass of* arak *makes its rounds. Not the first such discussion tonight, and it certainly won't be the last.*

It's after midnight and I'm sitting with my friends from the Sanggar Çudamani arts collective in Pengosekan village, listening carefully as they dissect today's performance. I've often been privy to this detailed postperformance debrief, but tonight they are generously speaking in Indonesian, not Balinese, so I can follow the conversation with ease. And what I find there is music analysis. Lots of it.

The concept of music analysis is broad and multifaceted. It has meant many things to ethnomusicologists over the decades, and both its use and popularity have ebbed and flowed in the discipline.[33] Literature on the technical procedures of the world's musics is still somewhat scattered, often approached differently everywhere it's practiced. But my anecdotal sense is that when musicians discuss their own performances, they do so articulately and in very specific musical detail. Although they may not use the same terminology that I do, my friends in Sanggar Çudamani are very interested in understanding and debating the aesthetics of a new composition's structure, or the merits and weaknesses of a long improvisation. Likewise, they will frequently comment on—and try to replicate—an individual improvised pattern that was particularly innovative, or lament a moment in the performance where the music did not "feel good" (*tidak rasa enak*) because two improvisers were not communicating well or were playing patterns at odds with one another. My kendang (drum) teachers, too, are all self-aware musicians, cognizant of the existence of different styles of playing in different villages and adept at identifying village style through kendang patterns alone. When I was studying with Anak Agung Raka (Gung Raka) in Saba village, for instance, if the lesson was particularly satisfying we would often hang out afterward, listening to and talking about music. Gung Raka could always identify the origin of any gamelan recording we heard, particularly in the classic dance style *legong*. His determining of the group's training in Saba or Peliatan or Binoh or ISI Denpasar was often based on structural or ornamental differences so subtle that it took me several listenings to find them. He was equally quick at recognizing musical features I showed him in my Western classical and jazz recordings. And like most Balinese musicians, he was able to differentiate good drummers from mediocre ones, and quick to make a distinction between a *wayah*, or great, improvised pattern, a "good enough" pattern, and a nonidiomatic one. Each of these musicians, in his own way, engages in music analysis.

The analytical approaches of my teachers and musician friends inform the current study. It involves analysis at many levels: social, discursive, and cognitive as well as musical. I see music analysis and cultural analysis as mutually supportive. As Gabriel Solis asserts, "musical analysis, itself driven by a body of theoretical thought, [can be] the basis of, and a necessary driving force for, other theoretical findings" (2012b, 536). Marc Perlman likewise argues: "the more detailed our technical analyses, the more opportunities we will have to show how sounds and context are subtly intertwined" (1998, 68). And Ingrid Monson contends that "detailed knowledge of musical practice is crucial in situating music within larger ideological and political contexts" (1999, 33).

With this in mind I return to a fundamental pillar of ethnomusicology: Alan Merriam's tripartite model of concepts, behaviors, and sounds. These overlapping research parameters are still relevant to ethnomusicological study today, particularly when informed by history, social dynamics, individual creation, and communication among performers, composers, and audience members.[34] What do music makers and music consumers say about the music, the musicians, and their interactions? What behaviors and social interfaces can be observed in and around performance, and how might these inform a researcher's musical understanding? Concepts and behaviors are bound by social norms yet are also influenced by individuals' agency and thus susceptible to change. We can gain insight into these phenomena by examining the musical sounds themselves. Yet the term "music analysis" too often seems to evoke this last aspect of Merriam's model—analysis of the music itself—at the expense of the other two. Thus one might mistakenly assume that music analysis in ethnomusicology is necessarily confined to what Arom, after Molino, perhaps naively terms "neutral" analysis.[35] But this is only one component of good analysis, and in most cases all these approaches are deployed in tandem.

In examining improvised musics, the analysis of musical sounds can help a researcher identify and assess the available musical materials of a practice. Performers will evince differing degrees of creative license in relation to musical elements that are more or less changeable. The musical "object" may be segmented into smaller units that can be shown to have relevance within that particular system. Idiomatic combinations of such segments will likely differ among practitioners in the tradition or change over time. And analysis of these sounds in practice can give insight into a myriad of musical questions, basic and complex. What pitch collections or melodic contours are used by musicians in the practice, and do certain motives or progressions stand out? What rhythms are allowable, and which are played most frequently? What spectra of timbres, dynamics, or articulations are acceptable, and what range of ornaments or embellishments? Is there a repeating form or identifiable sections in the music, and if so, how are they delineated? And importantly, how much latitude for variation is there within each of these performance elements? From this cluster of information, we can begin to propose a model that might underlie musical production.

Suggesting a musical model that guides improvised performance prompts investigation into the cognitive processes of composition and improvisation. And unpacking these concepts in a culturally informed way necessitates incorporating the other two branches of Merriam's ethnomusicological research model. Can what the musicians say about their music provide clues into the underlying concepts and processes behind their playing: the reasons for the musical choices they make? Is there local music theory, formal or informal, that shapes idiomatic performance practice?[36] If informal or implicit, as it is in *kendang arja*, such theory is still ascertainable through a blend of interviews, conversations, lessons, and performance postmortems like the one just described. A musician or audience member's differentiating of "good" and "bad" performances or "satisfying" and "unsatisfying" moments in improvisation can likewise help an analyst refine concepts of a model. Here we may find a diversity of opinions with perhaps regional or generational dividing lines. Such local discourses and their variants will give insight into how musicians conceptualize their own practices, both individually and socially. Much can be learned, also, through observation of a musician's behavior. Are there performance rituals or social interactions that can elucidate improvised practice, or observable communication techniques facilitating successful collective improvisation? How, and how much, do these interactions and techniques differ among musicians and across practices? And why?

These many areas for analysis—idiomatic musical materials, promising models, local discourses, cognitive processes, individual behaviors, and social interactions—all must be combined and cross-referenced to piece together the fullest possible picture of an improvised system. This then opens the possibility of comparative study.

As Michael Tenzer has put it:

> Once observed, sound patterns can be mobilized for many purposes: to demonstrate or inspire compositional depth or ingenuity, to discover an archetypical sound-structure model on which a music or repertoire is based, to symbolize or reflect a philosophy, social value or belief (of the analyst, the composer(s), performer(s), or their society), to reveal a historical process of change, to unearth suspected connections to music elsewhere, to embody a mathematical principle. Good analysis demystifies by cracking sound codes, better enabling the ear to collaborate with the mind in search of richer experience. (2006a, 6–7)

In the chapters that follow, I propose categories and techniques for the analysis of collectively improvised musics throughout the world, demonstrating their application via an examination of diverse genres and practices. The musical analyses in my case studies are informed by fieldwork, lessons, practice, observation, and performance as well as local music theory principles learned through interviews and conversations with musicians. Without these ethnographic insights, my musical analyses would be impoverished and uncertain. Yet I believe the opposite is also true. The nature of human creativity—its freedom and its boundaries—makes "the music itself" remarkably well suited to analytical approaches; the resulting insights can in turn deepen social, cognitive, and cultural exploration. In preparation for the book's main case studies, the next chapter delves into theories and methods for the analysis of improvised music across cultures, unraveling cognitive processes of creativity and unpacking the concept of the model in improvised practice.

CHAPTER ONE

THE COMPLICATED STORY OF IMPROVISATION

MODELS AND METHODS, CREATIVITY AND CONCEPTUAL SPACE

THE MYTH OF SPONTANEITY

The band is hot. Thirteen musicians and two dancers packed onto the stage of the Middle East Upstairs in Cambridge, MA's hip Central Square neighborhood. Tonight is a Felabration: a celebration of the life and music of Fela Kuti.[1] Boston's Afrobeat band Federator N°1 is playing to a sold-out room while video screens project footage of the famous Nigerian musician and social activist. In one corner of the room is a Shrine to Fela, if you are determined enough to push your way through a roiling mass of shoulder-to-shoulder dancers to reach it. I grab a beer and join the dancers on the floor, moving to the strong funk groove laid down by the bass and the tight harmonies of the horns. At a signal from the singer, the tenor sax player steps forward and begins to solo, winding a fierce melody up and then down the range of his instrument, highlighting cross-rhythmic gestures. The crowd goes nuts, and the singer signals for him to take another chorus.

A young guy in a plaid shirt and skinny jeans leans toward me with the most enormous grin. "Outstanding!" he shouts over music. "Can you believe he's just pulling this shit out of thin air?"

I nod and smile back; the saxophonist really is very good. But I suspect that what he's actually doing is much more complicated, and much cooler than that!

FINDING THE BOUNDARIES OF CREATIVITY

It's hardly radical to claim that virtually no improvised music is wholly spontaneous. Unlike the bar brawler improvising weapons from chair legs and pool cues, or the intrepid dinner host improvising a new recipe for "tuna surprise" when, thirty minutes before his guests arrive, he discovers he has no tuna, we know that improvising musicians do not simply play slapdash with whatever materials are conveniently available. "You have to know the *dasar*, the basics, first," my *arja* drum teacher Pak Dewa[2] tells me. "You have to *practice* it to *feel* it," his partner Cok Alit[3] adds. The inadvertent side effect of using "the concept of improvisation as a universal cutting across cultural domains" (Nettl 1998, 2) is that the untrained listener assumes that the process is offhand or unconsidered. As Bruno Nettl amusingly but aptly notes: "We probably never should have started calling it 'improvisation'" (Nettl 2009b, ix).

Yet even unplanned acts of drunken violence and improvised culinary art are based on models and structural understandings of the objects and actors involved. The bar brawler would think: "I wish I had something with which to hit this other person. Like a cudgel." Not being a character in a video game and thus having no cudgel handy, she would search for an object that could fulfill the same function. The mind stores concepts as sets of properties and their associated values (see Sawyer 2007, 115). Properties and values of a cudgel would include shape: long and thin; material: metal or other hard substance; function: to hit things. The way in which ideas, memories, and their representations are mentally encoded allows the brain to conjure useful images that relate, in sometimes surprising ways, to current situations.[4] Using what psychologists call *conceptual transfer*,[5] the bar brawler would seek a replacement cudgel based on the values of that object's properties: something well-shaped for gripping, light enough to lift and swing, and hard enough to inflict damage. A pool cue would work (a TV trope for the improvised bar weapon); a pigeon or a chocolate chip cookie would not. The bar brawler may have improvised a weapon off the cuff and with no preparation to the specific situation, but the choice was neither completely random nor a brilliant innovation in a vacuum; her cultural training and life experience had taught her what a good equivalent to a cudgel might be, and, with that knowledge and memory, her mind came up with a useful solution. It is well established among experimental psychologists, neuroscientists, and other scholars examining human creativity that creative acts and ideas, no matter how radical, are grounded in the familiar.

Cognitive scientists have shown that different kinds of creativity require the brain to process information in different ways. *Combinatorial creativity* involves combining familiar ideas in unfamiliar ways, as in visual collage, analogy, and poetic metaphor. A Balinese *tembang macapat* singer uses a comparable process when improvising new texts, mixing and matching familiar "devices and sources" and incorporating "resources built up" over time (Herbst 1997, 98 and 56). Likewise the *gendér wayang* player who has "a collection of small variations to phrases which may be used in alternation" (Gray 2011, 96). Such creative acts, through *conceptual transfer*, involve "projecting a 'source' (a familiar situation) onto a 'target' situation so as to help us learn about or think about the latter, or, if the 'target' does not yet exist, to create it" (Perlman 2004, 33). The bar brawler's improvised weapon also falls into this category.

The other two primary forms of creativity, *exploratory creativity* and *transformational creativity*, are both grounded in specific *conceptual spaces*: structured, culture-based styles of thinking, such as the inherent rules of a genre of music. And both involve a creative mental process called *conceptual elaboration*, in which existing concepts are not simply mixed and matched, as in conceptual transfer, but modified in order to create something new (see Sawyer 2007, chap. 6). In *exploratory creativity*, the innovator comes up with new ideas within the confines of existing conventions, such as creating a new recipe, or reworking an old one, in the French style. A Balinese composer who reworks a *gendér wayang* piece in "fundamental ways, recreating [it] to such an extent that [it] could be said to be [a] new piec[e]" (Gray 2011, 189) is practicing exploratory creativity, as is that same composer creating a brand new composition in a known style, or a performer taking advantage of the "space" (97) in that composition to make alterations to it in the course of performance.

In *transformational creativity*, by contrast, the innovator alters some aspect of the conventions themselves in order to create the possibility of something more radically new.[6] A thirteenth-century musician at Notre Dame Cathedral who maintained that 3rds and 6ths should be consonant instead of 4ths and 5ths could have created music considered impossible at that time, by changing just one defining dimension of the conceptual space of medieval music making. The new compositions would still be rule-bound, but the rules would now be altered. The contemporary Balinese composition mentioned in the previous chapter, in which a performer plays a gong with a metal grinder, is equally transformative. Such novel transformations, though, are extreme and relatively

Table 1.1 The types of creativity

COGNITIVE PROCESS	CREATIVITY TYPE	PREVALENCE
Conceptual Transfer	Combinatorial	Common
Conceptual Elaboration	Exploratory	
	Transformational	Rare

rare; "all artists and scientists spend most of their working time engaged in combinatorial and/or exploratory creativity" (Boden 2013, 8).[7] Yet even the rare transformational kind is based on preexisting knowledge or conventions; new innovations are really just creative reworkings of culturally accepted or system-appropriate norms, patterns, and styles of thinking. Both combinatorial and exploratory creativity, and their associated cognitive processes, are relevant to a discussion of improvisation (table 1.1).[8]

COLLECTIVE CREATIVITY AS COMBINATORIAL AND EXPLORATORY

How do these concepts offer insight into specifically *collective* creativity? We learned in the previous chapter that many of the most original inventions happen through collaboration. Yet group genius need not involve direct contact between participants; innovation often evolves slowly, becoming a web of ideas and adaptations over time. Gottlieb Daimler's internal combustion engine incorporated the hot-tube ignition system design of an English inventor named Watson, improving on Nikolaus Otto's unwieldy four-stroke engine from twenty years earlier, which itself built on a design by Belgian engineer Jean Joseph Étienne Lenoir (see Diamond 1999, chap. 13; Clark 2010; Wise 1974). And "Edison didn't invent the lightbulb; he found a bamboo fiber that worked better as a filament in the lightbulb developed by Sawyer and Man, who in turn built on lighting work done by others. . . . Inventors build on the work of those who came before, and new ideas are often . . . 'in the air' " (Lemley 2012, 710 and 711). This kind of group genius emerges from a sort of invisible collaboration, where innovations from one place and time spread to influence innovators in another, and the combination of their ideas creates something neither could have created alone. The evolution of the mountain bike through the mid- to late 1970s is a case in point. Bikers in several places across the western United States began off-roading only to realize that the design of their road-racing bikes couldn't sustain the terrain of a mountain. Each group started independently altering their bikes to improve the design, coming into contact with one another's ideas over time:

> The Morrow Dirt Club [of Cupertino, California] designed the gearshifter and the new handlebars; the Marin County riders devised brakes that wouldn't burn out; and several riders independently designed custom-made frames that wouldn't break on the big bumps. . . . The mountain bike was the result of a largely invisible long-term collaboration that stretched from Marin to Colorado. (Sawyer 2007, 7)

Whether improvising a recipe in the moment or crafting a new invention over many years, creativity is a cumulative and imitative process, seldom truly cognitively transformational.

The same appears to be true of musical creativity, where invisible collaboration is key to idiomatic performance in well-established genres and styles. *Arja* drummers often attribute elements of their playing to the innovation of others. I Dewa Nyoman Sura of Pengosekan village often spoke to me of the many kendang patterns he had adopted over the years. Whenever he heard a great drummer, he once admitted, he would keep his ears open for notable patterns to incorporate into his own improvisations.[9] "*Dicuri!*" he laughed, grabbing at the air between us with glee. "Stolen!" And Anak Agung Raka of Saba village once bragged to me how *licik*, sly, he was in borrowing other drummers' concepts to then rework into his own playing. He described how he would meet master kendang players at the local *warung kopi*, coffee stand, buy them a cup of coffee, and begin a casual conversation about drumming. He would then encourage them to re-create, through mnemonics, their own patterns. Knowing that I sometimes transcribed his patterns after our lessons, he winked as he told me, "I write their patterns down inside my head, and work them out later on the drum. They don't even realize they've taught me anything!"[10]

Many jazz students similarly "begin acquiring an expansive collection of improvisational building blocks by extracting those shapes they perceive as discrete components from the larger solos they have already mastered and practicing them as independent figures" (Berliner 1994, 101).[11] Tenor saxophonist Sonny Rollins describes his own invisible collaborations:

"Coleman Hawkins," he says, "is my idol." There was also Charlie Parker, who, Rollins says, "Had a profound effect on my life, musically as well as personally." Earlier saxophonists such as Dexter Gordon and Gene Ammons had effected a merger between the tone of Hawkins and the lyricism of [Lester] Young, and Rollins also modeled himself on them. "No one," he says, "is original. Everyone is derivative." (Goldberg 1965, 90)

Innovative though all these musicians may be in their improvising, they are also taking advantage of practices and aesthetics that are "in the air." Whether borrowing specific drum patterns or simply emulating another's stylistic preferences, these musicians are all to some extent "derivative."

THE "MODEL"

In his landmark 1974 article "Thoughts on Improvisation," Bruno Nettl suggests that, far from being opposites, *improvisation* and *composition* are in fact two ends of the same continuum, preferring to think of these processes simply as "rapid and slow composition" (6). Nettl argues that all music performance, whether precomposed or created in the moment, is built from a *model*: a series of preset signposts or "musical macro-units" (6). He describes improvisation not as spontaneous creation but rather as "giving a rendition of something that already exists, be it a song or a theoretical musical entity. And its basic 'table of contents' is set" (9).

This general concept is now well established among researchers of improvised music, though terminology among them varies. Aaron Berkowitz (2010) defines improvisation as spontaneous creativity within constraints. Looking mostly at Western classical traditions, he examines the stylistic (musical) constraints of genre as well as the performer's physical and physiological constraints. Jeff Pressing proposes the term "referent" to denote the "set of cognitive, perceptual, or emotional structures (constraints) that guide and aid in the production of musical materials" (1998, 52). He uses the example of a standard tune and chord changes on which a jazz musician extemporizes.[12] And in his analyses of improvisation in Central African polyphonic traditions, Simha Arom considers the model of a musical object (a piece or repertory) to be "the pattern underlying each of its realisations, the 'skeleton' consisting of all the relevant features of the object, to which its substance can be reduced" (1991a, 168). Here the model concept is used as an analytical tool; modelizing a musical object allows us to understand what individuates it by identifying its distinctive features. Yet it is also considered a culturally relevant categorization: "an ultimate reference and reduction to [a musical object]'s essentials, which can still be identified by the cultural heirs of a musical tradition" (Arom 1991a, 225).[13] *Arja* drummer Pak Dewa would call such a model the *dasar*: the basic form.

Performing experience in diverse genres told me that not all models worked in the same way. Any more than one or two poorly placed bass strokes in my *arja* improvisations were likely to elicit good-natured laughter or an exclamation of "*aduh*," "ouch," from my teachers. My flamenco dance instructors, by contrast, were generally fine with my attempts at improvisation, so long as I didn't confuse a marking step with a cuing gesture. And my brief forays into vocal jazz improvisation, mediocre though most of my attempts were, always seemed to be received on a range from "acceptable" to "good." But I didn't yet understand how this seeming variety in model specificity and flexibility shaped improvisational processes and choices nor, by extension, the profound ways it would influence my analytical approach.

The concept of the model is purposefully broad, encompassing referents ranging from specific motives only conservatively variable to more general guidelines of style conventions and aesthetic intentions. It is the relative distance between fixed points in the model, Nettl proposes, that determines the level of improvisation involved in any musical performance (see Nettl 1974).[14] Said another way, each model has an inherent level of specificity and, by extension, flexibility. Different model types inevitably require different techniques to "fill in the spaces" between fixed signposts, and these demand the use of different types of creativity. A composition, even a meticulously notated one, still requires some spontaneous decision-making in the course of performance. The spaces between its signposts may be objectively small, but the performer will still need to decide on the best interpretation of adagio or mezzo forte, the most appropriate kind of vibrato or suitability of rubato, the precise speed of a trill or angle of a crescendo, and so on.[15] As Laudan Nooshin observes, "the grouping together of quite different forms of music in the category of improvisation and their separation 'from the rest of music making' is increasingly untenable" (2017, 215).[16] Where "composition" can often be used as a foil for "improvisation," these two concepts are also part of the same process, inseparable. We might usefully think of a model—whether the notated score of a Mozart sonata or the desired large-scale contour and idiomatic gestures and ornaments of a Turkish *taqsim*—as the "composed parts" of a performance, and the spaces between its fixed signposts—whether small or substantial—as the "improvised parts." In every composition is an element of improvisation;

in every improvisation a kind of composition. This perspective suggests a flexible continuum between concepts of *improvisation* and *composition, process* and *product*.[17] In each case, the musician begins with a model and adds her own spin. How, and how much, she alters her model is necessarily genre specific.

A brief examination of two very different kinds of music performance—Balinese *kendang arja* and Hindustani *alap*—serves in the upcoming pages as a vehicle for exploring diverse model types and improvisatory processes. As each analysis generates new concepts and terminology, I draw parallels to other practices to demonstrate the breadth and flexibility of the concepts. Woven throughout is a myriad of terms used by both scholars and musicians to describe the act of improvising. Some identify specific processes; others describe degrees of freedom taken or allowed. Berliner, for instance, presents four "levels of intensity"—proposed by alto saxophonist Lee Konitz—for the improvised realization of a jazz tune (see Berliner 1994, 67–71). Yet as we will see, the terms at the more conservative end of Konitz's spectrum—*interpretation* and *embellishment*—describe processes. By contrast, his more "intense" terms—*variation* and *improvisation*—are both assessments of degree. The overlapping array of terminology used to describe improvisation clearly requires unpacking. A comparative exploration of contrasting model types, traditions, and their associated techniques will help to refine a typology of both process and degree. While it may be startling to find such a diverse palette of music and terminology discussed in such a concentrated space, the purpose is to better understand how improvisation has been differently conceived, and to examine what connections we might find between traditions. By seeing improvisation as a human practice distinct in each culture but not bound by any one culture, we are free to engage with these cross-cultural connections through music analysis.

SPECIFIC TEMPLATES FOR FORMULAIC VARIATION

"Begini kita improv." "This is how we improvise," Cok Alit explains, picking up his drum and starting to cycle the 4-beat kendang arja *pattern we'd been working on a moment ago when someone arrived with a tray of coffee. After cycling it three or four times, he begins to alter it, but ever so subtly, somehow creating a stream of new patterns that all contain the essence of the original. I realize in this moment that I have never before really thought about what "improvisation" means. That I've been unintentionally holding on to a tacit definition of the term that now seems narrow: a concept that embraces only the most "intense" of Konitz's creative options. "True" improvisation was free jazz or improv*

theater, or it was the most extreme solos of Miles Davis or Charles Mingus. What Cok Alit is talking about now, the masterful ways he is manipulating this short, relatively simple pattern, is an altogether different kind of improvisation.

I sip my coffee and listen hard as he plays, trying and failing to decipher what makes each pattern feel "changed" yet also "the same." And I imagine a field of grass gently undulating in a soft spring breeze . . .

I slowly come to learn that Cok Alit and other *arja* drummers each have a storehouse of short patterns like this one: models for improvisation that they vary, blend, rearrange, and build upon in the course of performance. Yet this "different" kind of improvisation is not unique to *kendang arja* or to Bali. It happens in improvised practices worldwide, from Shona mbira to old-time American string-band music—a reworking of relatively specific models through "melodic, rhythmic, or harmonic paradigmatic substitutions" (Turino 2009, 104). This approach, which Turino dubs *formulaic variation*,[18] is often used in collective practices, like *kendang arja*, where each musician enjoys a comparable level of creative license; the constraints that models and formulas place on individual musicians allow the collective whole to remain idiomatic. Strategies for interlocking in *arja*'s collective improvisation require additional explanation and will be addressed in later chapters. Here, a short passage of improvisation on just the higher-pitched *lanang* drum reveals some techniques for formulaic variation.[19]

Figure 1.1 shows an excerpt of improvised *lanang* drumming played by I Wayan Tama (Pak Tama) of Singapadu village. Audio for this and many other figures in the book can be found on the companion website. The drum's two main strokes—a high and a low stroke—are transcribed using round noteheads, while [x]-noteheads denote various softer subordinate strokes.[20] The transcription is divided into eight segments for ease of analysis, but these should not be thought of as discrete units of music.

Comparing this improvisation to related model patterns in Tama's arsenal (figure 1.2) reveals several of his techniques for formulaic variation. Tama taught me each of these patterns and a handful of others before declaring "*itu saja*," "that's it. You've now learned all the patterns I play," despite the fact that in his improvisations he plays many others. Notably, lessons with all my teachers seemed to proceed in this way. Because of my good working relationships with these musicians, and their obvious pride in sharing their drumming knowledge, I don't believe they have deliberately hidden other patterns from me. They either consider additional performed patterns paradigmatically equivalent and thus not worth teaching, or have improvised

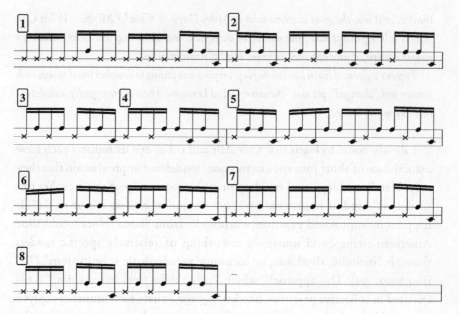

FIGURE 1.1. Excerpt of Tama's improvised *lanang* playing

FIGURE 1.2. Collection of Tama's model *lanang* patterns

them in the moment but cannot consciously replicate them. The question of whether or not it is accurate or appropriate to reify taught patterns as models above other improvised patterns is fraught, and will be addressed in chapter 5. For now, figure 1.2 delineates six of these taught patterns, which I propose as models.

A number of the techniques employed in Tama's improvisation appear to engage combinatorial creativity, and understanding the connections between the improvisation and its model patterns requires a discussion of formulaic variation techniques at several different levels of improvisational freedom.[21] At the more conservative end of the combinatorial spectrum, we have what Lee Konitz terms *interpretation*, where "musicians take minor liberties when orienting themselves to a piece" or model. In jazz performance, "they vary such subtleties as accentuation, vibrato, dynamics, rhythmic phrasing, and articulation or tonguing, 'striving to interpret the melody freshly, as if performing it for the first time'" (Berliner 1994, 67). In *kendang arja* performance, interpretation takes a different form. As in figures 1.1 and 1.2, *arja* drummers always strike their drums continuously, four times per beat. And they do not generally alter volume or articulation on a note-by-note basis. Yet a parallel sort of interpretation emerges when main strokes are incorporated where softer subordinate strokes would generally be played, or vice versa. There are several examples of this kind of interpretation in Tama's improvisation, two of which are shown in figure 1.3. In segment 6, Tama interprets model pattern C by adding an extra high stroke at the end of the first beat; in segment 7 he creates a sparser interpretation of model pattern F by replacing the second high stroke with a softer subsidiary stroke.

Other common manifestations of combinatorial creativity involve a process Berkowitz names *recombination*. In its most basic form in *arja*, recombination determines the large-scale structure of the improvisation itself: Tama has a series of model patterns to choose from and improvise on, and each time he plays, they will occur in a different order. He begins this passage of improvisation with model pattern A, his preferred opening pattern. This he follows with an unaltered version of model pattern B, one of his more commonly used patterns,

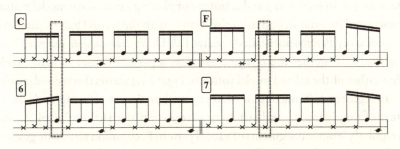

FIGURE 1.3. Interpretation in Tama's *kendang arja* improvisation

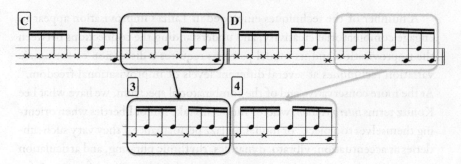

FIGURE 1.4. Recombination of elements from two different model patterns

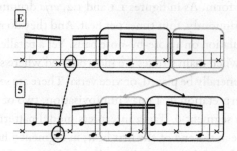

FIGURE 1.5. Complex "micro" recombination

and one of the first I learned from him. The next time Tama begins improvising, he will choose a different combination of patterns. This is equally true of Shona mbira musicians or Balinese *reyong norot* improvisers who also recombine large storehouses of paradigmatic variations.

At this level of recombination, true comprehension of the tradition is not necessarily required, and this simple mixing and matching of model patterns was the first kind of *kendang arja* improvisation that I mastered. More complex recombination, however, also exists. It occurs "at a more 'micro' level, combining and recombining smaller elements to form new musical entities" (Berkowitz 2010, 56). In segments 3 and 4, instead of playing a full 4-beat model pattern, Tama combines the second half of pattern C with the second half of pattern D, a process my Pengosekan-based teacher Pak Dewa calls *campur-campur*: "mixing it up." Together these segments create a passage denser in main strokes than either of the related model patterns. Figure 1.4 shows this recombination.

In segment 5, Tama demonstrates recombination at yet a higher level. Instead of simply mixing and matching patterns or pattern halves, he splices small irregularly lengthed segments of model pattern E, common idiomatic gestures, and rearranges them as in figure 1.5. In *arja*, certain rhythmic gestures recur frequently, and I have come to think of these as idiomatic building blocks for larger patterns. On the *lanang* drum, there is none more ubiquitous than ♫♩, a syncopated gesture designed to begin just after a beat and anticipate the following one with a low stroke, landing a subordinate [x]-stroke together with the beat. Tama's model pattern E begins with a variant on this gesture that delays the arrival of the low stroke by one subdivision; it lands on the beat rather than anticipating it. This results in the much less commonly used gesture ♫♩. In his improvised pattern 5, Tama replaces this unusual first beat with the more common ♫♩ gesture. Placement of the strong low stroke is central to *arja*'s interlocking, making this seemingly small change both noteworthy and risky. Even more so, however, is the second half of the improvised pattern, where a 6-note module and a 4-note module from the model are reversed. This recombination sees the 4-note module, our common *lanang* gesture, freely shifted in relation to the beat. The 6-note module, also reoriented to the beat, is further varied through interpretation: Tama replaces one of the model pattern's low strokes with a subordinate [x]-stroke.

Because of *arja*'s collective nature, this more radical recombination of pattern elements increases the chance of disrupting interlocking. In taking this risk, Tama needs to understand the function of each drum stroke and pattern element, and have a strong sense of how the new whole may interlock with his partner's collection of patterns. Smaller musical modules are "cross-linked by connections at various levels of the hierarchical knowledge structure" (Pressing 1998, 53), and their recombination is indicative of an advanced *arja* improviser. Tama has now crossed over into exploratory creativity. As we can see in figure 1.6, the term *recombination* thus encompasses a wide spectrum of creative choices, more purely combinatorial than *interpretation* on its conservative end—where simple mixing and matching requires little understanding of the genre's conceptual space—but comfortably exploratory in its most radical incarnations.

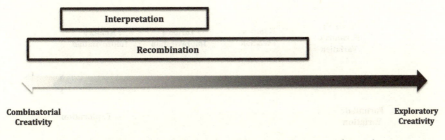

FIGURE 1.6. Creativity type and improvisatory process: interpretation and recombination

"IMPROVISATION" AND OTHER DEFINITIONS

Through the recombination and interpretation in figure 1.5, Tama achieves what Lee Konitz terms *variation*: "transfiguring the melody [or rhythm] more substantially by creating shapes that have greater personality but whose relationship to the original model remains clear" (Berliner 1994, 70). He is perhaps even working in the realm Turino dubs *improvisation*: "instances in a performance where I *surprise myself* with purposeful alterations, extensions, or flights away from the model and habitual formulas" (Turino 2009, 104–5).

Here we come to a terminological conundrum. The "purposeful alterations" in Turino's definition of improvisation appear to describe something akin to Konitz's variation. Turino's "extensions" and "flights away from the model," however, seem closer to Konitz's definition of *improvisation*: "transforming the melody [or rhythm] into patterns bearing little or no resemblance to the original model or using models altogether alternative to the melody as the basis for inventing new phrases" (Berliner 1994, 70). Yet though each requires different strategies, all these levels of "play," from Turino's *formulaic variation* to Konitz's *improvisation*, are "the creation of music in the course of performance" (Nettl 1998, 1), and even the most conservative *arja* drummer would say "*kita improv*," "we are *improvising*," not simply *varying*.[22] Per figure 1.7, each of these overlapping terms falls along a continuum indicating degrees of improvisational freedom. Each part of the continuum presents challenges and opportunities, and creating idiomatic improvisation at one end is not easier than at the other end or at any point in between. To avoid privileging more radical transformations, or reducing processes like recombination to "formulaic in the pejorative sense of the word" (Berkowitz 2010, 177), the term *improvisation* will be used from this point forward exclusively in an overarching capacity. Like *model*, it is an umbrella term encompassing the wide range of possibilities in figure 1.7. The less regimented right side of this continuum I

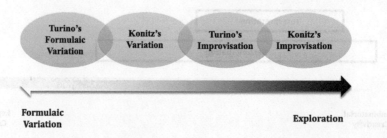

FIGURE 1.7. Continuum of overlapping terms for improvisation

call *exploration*, echoing the idea of "exploratory creativity." Much like *formulaic variation*, exploration embraces a range of freedom and is achieved through diverse improvisational processes, including interpretation and recombination. These processes, though, generally appear to be guided by a different sort of model.

GENERAL SCHEMAS FOR EXPLORATION

My forays into flamenco dance and vocal jazz performance introduced me to a quite different approach to improvisation from *kendang arja*, because the models I was learning provided a different kind of information. Improvisation in these practices seemed guided by a broader structural model with sparser and often more ambiguous or flexible signposts. Friends studying Indian and Arabic solo practices shared similar observations about their models and processes. And I could see free jazz, acid or psychedelic rock, and jam band music at the loosest end of the same model-type spectrum. Chicago's AACM,[23] for instance—an organization that in the 1960s was central to the exploration of free jazz and collective improvisation—practiced a big-picture collectivity with broad musical and aesthetic suggestions as models:

> Lacking a harmonic platform, the musicians work[ed] instead from group example, building their improvisations first from the musical style and the mood that the preliminary written sections or head arrangements set up and, subsequently, in a collective, constructivist fashion, they work[ed] according to the rhythmic, motivic, and stylistic character of the ensemble's collaborative ideas. (Radano 1992, 91–92)

Experimental jam bands similarly improvise on minimal musical elements or ideas in an expansive way: small models approached with breadth and extreme flexibility. Performances often include collective explorations of single notes, chords, or time signatures, where each musician presents new musical ideas as well as expanding on those introduced by his bandmates during improvisation (see Spector 2016). The long-running American jam band Phish puts a unique twist on such models:

> One of Phish's self-devised communication exercises is something called Including Your Own Hey. The idea is that to improve the band's collective improvisation, the members must learn to listen to one another. They do

this by conjuring riffs and patterns from thin air, varying and embellishing them until they're locked in and individually announcing their arrival with the word hey. When they've each "included their own hey," it's onto another round. A variation on the process is Get Out of My Hey Hole, in which the cardinal rule is that one band member's note cannot sustain over anyone else's.

"Mimicry is the lowest, most basic level of communication," explains [bandleader Trey] Anastasio. "These are anti-mimicry exercises: listening to each other, hearing each other, staying out of each other's way." (Puterbaugh 1997, 45)

Here collective improvisation is as much confrontational or competitive as it is interactive. Yet like the AACM, Phish's collective improvisation draws on large structures and aesthetics created over the course of a performance, not specific details of chord changes or interlocking rhythmic patterns to be negotiated in the moment. The musicians stay out of one another's "Hey Hole" as much as possible, and freely take turns presenting new ideas and structures on which to jam as a group. Each improvising ensemble develops its own "collective experimental sensitivities" (Tuedio 2013, 251) over time, learning to listen to one another and allow for give and take. As Howard Brick notes of the AACM, a "commitment to the communal dimension of free self-expression . . . demonstrated that the ideal of personal autonomy need not be corrosively individualistic and that collective action might give vent, and meaning, to the individual's voice rather than suppressing it" (2000, 140). Within this social framework, individuals make decisions that both guide and work independently of group cohesion, and an overarching aesthetic of "experimental," "psychedelic," and "free" is maintained within a loose musical collectivity.

Rather than the moment-to-moment constraining of *kendang arja*'s relatively detailed templates, these more exploratory practices, from flamenco dance to Arabic *taqsim* to Phish, can be theorized in terms of guiding *schemas*: mental structures "consisting of a set of (usually unconscious) expectations about what things look like and/or the order in which they occur" (Mandler quoted in Widdess 2013, 200). Cognitive schemas have been used for analyses of diverse musics, from Indian classical improvisations to Bugandan Amadinda xylophone traditions, oral poetry to hip-hop and country music, and here they are used to describe these looser concepts of a model.[24] A brief analysis of a Hindustani *alap* will examine how general schemas for exploration differ from specific templates for formulaic variation, revealing two additional categories of improvisatory process that round out the creative options generated through interpretation and recombination.[25]

FIGURE 1.8. The opening of Mukherjee's *alap* emphasizes the tonic through embellishment

One of the most ubiquitous forms in North Indian classical music, an *alap* is an unmetered solo improvisation accompanied only by a drone instrument. The musical and structural function of this relatively free style of improvisation is to lay out all the characteristics of a raga.[26] Like a mode or scale, a raga is a collection of pitches, but much more than that, it is a melodic configuration; it governs the relative strength and frequency of the pitches in play, determines their characteristic ornaments, and dictates appropriate melodic contours or motives.[27] The raga shapes many of the overlapping schemas that guide *alap* performance. The two most basic, identified by Widdess (2011a), are pitch schemas determining the relative importance of pitches used, and contour schemas dictating the general melodic progression of the performance. Three figures from Widdess's analysis of an *alap* by sitarist Budhaditya Mukherjee will illustrate how such schemas are actualized.[28]

At a slightly higher level of improvisational "intensity" than *interpretation*, Konitz identifies *embellishment*, where "unique patterns of imagination lend a distinctive character to each artist's practices" (Berliner 1994, 69). Such embellishments may require conceptual transfer and thus combinatorial creativity, or they may employ the conceptual elaboration of exploratory creativity. For a jazz musician, embellishment can include everything from grace notes, mordents, and other idiomatic ornamentation to flexible timing and creative pitch substitutions (see Berliner 1994, 69–70.). A Javanese *rebab* fiddle player might likewise play a melody "similar to the inner [model] melody" but "more elaborate" and "rhythmically varied or active," with flexible timing and added ornaments (Perlman 2004, 134). Figure 1.8 reveals similar embellishment techniques in the opening phrase of Mukherjee's *alap*, whose main role is to emphasize the tonic, pitch "1."[29] Diamond noteheads represent the sitar's drone strings while black noteheads are its melody strings. Lines connecting pitches together indicate the sitar's characteristic glissandi, *mĩds*.

Pitch and contour schemas provide general guidelines for this first phrase. "It is normally considered important that the *rāga* should be identifiable within the first few phrases of an *ālāp*," so this opening phrase must reinforce the tonic

("C") and introduce its intervallic relationships with surrounding pitches (Widdess 2011a, 197). How this is done is open to the embellishment of the improviser. Mukherjee is bound by the pitch hierarchies of the raga (in this case *Rāg Pūriyā-Kalyān*), and the ornaments characteristic to his instrument, the raga, and his pedagogical lineage.[30] But within these constraints, he can play the tonic any number of times at any pace and use any appropriate ornaments; idiomatic embellishments are *recombined*, like *arja* patterns, in each new improvisation. Following a high C from a drone string, Mukherjee opens with the extended 6-1-7-b2-6-6-1 *mīḍ*, exploring the tonic in relation to pitches both above and below. He then unhurriedly strikes the tonic four more times, embellished with different glissandi and interspersed with the plucking of drone strings. This sort of embellishment is equally characteristic of the close heterophony of many group Arabic performances as well as the idioms of several instruments in the Central Javanese gamelan.

While overlapping schemas do determine some moment-to-moment decisions in *alap* performance, they also generate larger-scale structural models. To play a full *alap*, the improviser must slowly work his way up the pitches of the raga, revealing the nuances of each pitch while emphasizing hierarchically important ones, before then much more quickly working his way back down to end on the tonic. This is his basic contour schema. Figure 1.9 shows its realization in Mukherjee's fourteen-minute *alap*. With time on the x-axis and pitch on the y-axis, the gray area represents the range of pitches being used at any given time while the black line indicates the *focal pitch*, the most emphasized pitch in each phrase.

One of the two main pitch schemas that Widdess identifies for *Rāg Pūriyā-Kalyān* emphasizes pitches 1, 3, 5, and 7.[31] And while adhering to the dictates of the contour schema, Mukherjee is also shaping his improvisation on this large scale with guidelines from the pitch schema. As figure 1.9 shows, after a characteristically freer introduction, the focal pitch is only ever one of these four.

This, too, may be seen as a kind of extended embellishment; the improviser is freely and idiomatically adding notes around main goal pitches. But because of the sheer distance between these pitch signposts, there is likely a different process at play. The "fundamental organizational principle of *ālāp*"—this long ascent and fast descent—is known in Indian music theory as *vistār*, "expansion" (Widdess 2011a, 189). And it falls squarely in the realm of exploratory creativity, using a cognitive process I see as a branch of conceptual elaboration, where an innovator "create[s] new things by modifying, stretching, or extending old ones" (Perlman 2004, 29). Called *conceptual expansion*,[32] the cognitive process inspires the name for this last improvisatory process: *expansion*.

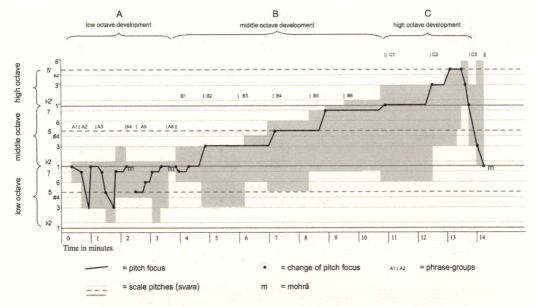

FIGURE 1.9. Large-scale structure of Mukherjee's *alap*, showing range and focal pitch

While expansion in *alap* performance perhaps most obviously guides improvisation on a large structural scale, the same process also determines more localized improvisational choices. Figure 1.10 shows a passage from Mukherjee's *alap* with pitch 3 ("E") as the focal pitch. Here, he expands a motive whose antecedent ascends to the focal pitch while its consequent descends to the tonic. Mukherjee explores this motive through expansion in two ways. In each of several consecutive phrases, he extends the antecedent through "internal scalar expansion to introduce the new, higher pitches ♯4 and 6" (Widdess 2011a, 211). He further expands the antecedent in phrases *a* and *c* through "recursion and repetition" (211), delaying the eventual arrival of the consequent through several iterations of the antecedent. These same kinds of expansion can also be seen in jazz improvisations that expand and embellish on a motive from the tune. Likewise, Karnatak performers will base their *svara kalpana* improvisations on a single motive from a precomposed *kriti*, and each consecutive improvised phrase will often be longer and more complex, delaying the return to the familiar motive (see Viswanathan and Allen 2004, 65–68).

To help visualize the various concepts at play in the preceding discussion, figure 1.11 imagines the four main improvisatory processes proposed in this chapter overlaid onto the interconnected cognitive processes involved in their execution.

FIGURE 1.10. Motivic expansion in Mukherjee's *alap*

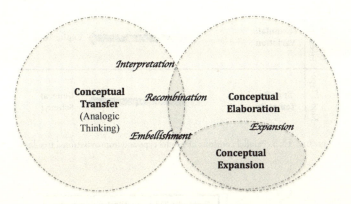

FIGURE 1.11. Overlapping cognitive and improvisatory processes

A UNIFIED VOCABULARY OF IMPROVISATORY PROCESSES

The inherent flexibility of the model concept, ranging from a specific template to a general schema, allows for a continuum of improvisational freedoms per figure 1.12.

The level of specificity or flexibility in a given model encourages the use of its own collection of improvisatory processes, yet these, too, are broad in range and adaptable. Recombination, for instance, can engage both combinatorial and exploratory creativity; it can be employed in the strictest formulaic variation or find its place in more general schema-based exploration; and it can be used in combination with other processes, like interpretation or expansion. The processes themselves also sometimes have blurred borders; where does embellishment end and expansion begin, for instance?

The overlapping shapes in figure 1.13 illustrate these complex relationships. Each process is considered against the continua of creativity type on the x-axis and degree of improvisational freedom on the y-axis. Visualizing these interrelated parameters in opposition serves to clarify the ways in which they differently influence improvisational processes. While the y-axis measures a quantifiable degree of model specificity, or objective musical distance between a model and its improvised realization, the x-axis is a qualitative assessment of cognitive creative process. The easy assumption is that more exploratory creativity is required as the model becomes less specific, or as the distance between the model and the realization increases. Yet as we saw in figure 1.5, a seemingly small formulaic change may require deep knowledge of the practice at many levels and thus engage exploratory creativity. Likewise, a quantitatively large

FIGURE 1.12. Parallel continua of model type and improvisational freedom

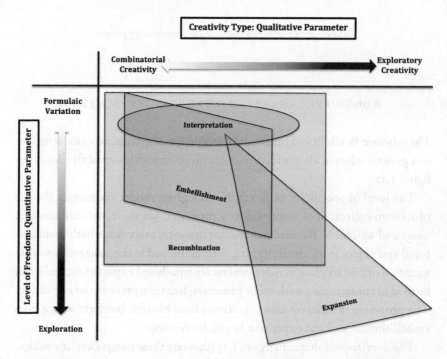

FIGURE 1.13. Relating processes of improvisation to creativity type and level of freedom

divergence from the model may in fact be a relatively simple paradigmatic substitution, thus engaging the most basic combinatorial creativity.

While these two continua are interconnected, then, they do not exist in a linear relationship. Greater latitude for improvisational freedom does not necessarily mean the creativity at play is exploratory, nor are formulaic variations necessarily combinatorial. The diverse shapes in figure 1.13 suggest that each of the four improvisatory processes relates to these continua of creativity and freedom in a different way. Interpretation, for instance, is almost always a small-scale, formulaic variation; the level of improvisational freedom is limited. But its execution may involve either conceptual transfer or conceptual elaboration. Recombination is a flexible enough process that its use in all levels of improvisation may be either combinatorial or exploratory. Expansion, by contrast, appears to demonstrate a more linear relationship between the two continua: the more flexibility allowed in improvisation, the more exploratory expansion becomes.

These four general processes for improvisation can be seen across genres and cultures, in both solo and collective practices. Yet not all genres use every process equally. A Balinese *trompong* player will perform a *gineman* through embellishment, approaching a fixed series of sparse goal tones with free ornamentation in the slow, almost tentative technique idiomatic to that style (see Tenzer 2000, 360–61). The rhythmic rigidity of *kendang arja* improvisation means that *arja* drummers, by contrast, do not use much embellishment. Their improvisations are mostly based in interpretation and recombination, as we've seen, but also make use of expansion. Many Northern Ewe songs are composed and performed through interpretation and other kinds of formulaic variation, where specific model melodies are altered in certain prescribed ways (see Agawu 1990). And a jazz improviser stays within the confines of her instrument's idiom and genre expectations while adhering to the chord changes, melodic material, and desired aesthetic of the tune. As Stan Getz has said of his own improvising: "It's like a language. You learn the alphabet, which are the scales. You learn sentences, which are the chords. And then you talk extemporaneously with the horn" (quoted in Weick 2002, 57–58). Such "talk" involves embellishment, expansion, and other techniques for exploration, while also relying on formulaic variation for processes like interpretation.

To further complicate matters, the appropriate model type and its associated processes can change within a single performance. In Karnatak music, for instance, a *kriti* is precomposed but may be personalized through interpretation and embellishment, sometimes leading to the creation of new *sangati* or variants of the melody. An improvised *niraval* derives its material from a specific phrase in the precomposed *kriti*, but then elaborates on it through embellishment and expansion (see Viswanathan and Allen 2004, chap. 3). And similar to a Hindustani *alap*, other Karnatak forms like *tanam* and *alapana* are bound only by the constraints of the raga. The "distinction is understood to signify different degrees of freedom" (Nettl 1974, 7), as shown in figures 1.7 and 1.12, but all are improvisations on a model.[33]

KNOWLEDGE BASE AND CONCEPTUAL SPACE

So how do musicians faithfully improvise on such diverse models, each of which provides its own level of specificity and demands its own degree of adherence? My abysmal first attempts at *kendang arja* improvisation suggested that, even if I knew the model, I was still missing information. "Thinking outside the box isn't enough to be creative; you have to know *how* to think outside the box" (Sawyer 2007, 88). But how do we learn that? Early twentieth-century Gestalt psychologists tried to understand creative problem solving through thought puzzle experiments. In the so-called nine-dot problem, a test taker is given a series of nine dots arranged in three even rows of three, together forming a square, as in figure 1.14.

FIGURE 1.14. The nine-dot problem

Subjects are then asked to connect all the dots by making four adjoining straight lines without lifting their pencils. Most people struggle with this problem; many find it impossible. The solution to the problem involves literally thinking outside the box. The only way to solve it is by creating lines that extend past the confines of the box of dots, per figure 1.15.

The Gestalt psychologists believed that solving such a problem was hampered by past experience: "First, you're drawn to an obvious solution," which doubtless involves keeping the lines inside the box, "but you quickly realize that it can't work. Yet your mind is already fixated on that solution, and you're blocked from seeing the problem any other way" (Sawyer 2007, 86). They theorized that by overcoming that fixation, the solution would become obvious, in a flash of insight. More modern cognitive studies, however, show that removing the false assumption (by giving hints, for instance) only marginally improves

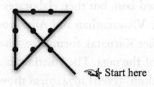

FIGURE 1.15. The nine-dot solution

a subject's chances of solving the problem. Knowing the model, knowing to draw lines outside the box, is still not enough. By contrast, receiving training in similar problem types—joining triangles together by drawing lines outside them, for instance—primed test subjects to think creatively in the right ways and vastly improved their test results on the nine-dot thought problem (see Sawyer 2007, 84–90; Weisberg and Alba 1981). To solve the puzzle with ease, past experience in its specific problem-solving domain was a necessity. Thus, use of a referent, whether musical or otherwise, must be informed by what Pressing (1984) terms a *knowledge base*: a set of ideas, rules, assumptions, and experiences that guides model use. I couldn't improvise *kendang arja* because I didn't yet know how to *use* its models.

To acquire communicative competence in a language, a speaker must be fluent in the many different aspects of its knowledge base, committed to long-term memory through years of practice, analysis, listening, and performance of that language. Elements of a language's knowledge base include:

- Phonology, "sounds and rules for combining them to make words."
- Morphology, "rules governing morphemes . . . [which are] the smallest unit[s] of meaning in a language."
- Syntax, "rules for how to combine words into acceptable phrases and sentences."
- Semantics, the "mental dictionary, or lexicon . . . [The] meaning system."
- Pragmatics, "social rules" for language use (Berkowitz 2010, 100).[34]

A musical knowledge base is similarly multifaceted. Alongside a basic knowledge of the phonology of music—its pitches, intervals, durations, timbres, and so on—it includes:

> musical materials and excerpts, repertoire, subskills, perceptual strategies, problem-solving routines, hierarchical memory structures and schemas, generalized motor programs, and more. It is a cauldron of devices collected and fine-tuned on the basis of optimizing improvisatory performance [. . . and] it encodes the history of compositional choices and predilections defining an individual's personal style. (Pressing 1998, 53–54)[35]

Good, idiomatic improvisation involves much more than mere knowledge of the model. Both the allowable distance from the model and the tool kit of available techniques are bound by conventions of genre—early swing will require a different set of skills and approaches to processes of improvisation than hard bop—and these are informed by the knowledge base within which the musician works. Together the model and knowledge base make up the improviser's *conceptual space*. As Erica Azim says of Shona mbira improvisation:

> As the Shona mbira student gradually becomes familiar with the location of sounds on the instrument through learning basic parts to many songs, he starts to add elaboration drawn from his lifetime collection of memories of hearing the piece performed many times by experienced musicians. Selection of specific variations is inspired by what he is hearing in the music at the moment. (1999, 176)

Paul Berliner notes of jazz improvisers:

> [The] simplistic understanding of improvisation [as spontaneous, intuitive, and "making something out of nothing"] belies the discipline and experience on which improvisers depend, and it obscures the actual practices and processes that engage them. Improvisation depends, in fact, on thinkers having absorbed a broad base of musical knowledge, including myriad conventions that contribute to formulating ideas logically, cogently, and expressively.... The same complex mix of elements and processes coexists for improvisers as for skilled language practitioners; the learning, the absorption, and utilization for linguistic conventions conspire in the mind of the writer or speaker—or, in the case of jazz improvisation, the player—to create a living work. (1994, 492)

And John Coltrane speaks at length about his conceptual space for improvisation on the tenor saxophone, discussing the roots of specific models for musical gestures, the ways in which he acquired a larger understanding of musical structures, and the influences he "felt emotionally" without yet intellectually understanding them:

> I drew from all the men I heard during this period. I have listened to about all the good tenor men, beginning with Lester, and believe me, I've picked up something from them all.... There were a lot of things that Hawkins was doing that I knew I'd have to learn somewhere along the line. I felt the same way about Ben Webster. There were many things that people like Hawk, Ben, and Tab Smith were doing in the forties that I didn't understand but that I felt emotionally.

> The first time I heard Hawk, I was fascinated by his arpeggios and the way he played. I got a copy of his "Body And Soul" and listened real hard to what he was doing. . . . As far as musical influences, aside from saxophonists, are concerned, I think I was first awakened to musical exploration by Dizzy Gillespie and Bird. It was through their work that I began to learn about musical structures and the more theoretical aspects of music. . . . Working with Monk brought me close to a musical architect of the highest order. I felt I learned from him in every way—through the senses, theoretically, technically. I would talk to Monk about musical problems, and he would sit at the piano and show me the answers just by playing them. I could watch him play and find out the things I wanted to know. Also, I could see a lot of things that I didn't know about at all. (quoted in Coltrane and DeMichael 1960)

Building a conceptual space for improvisation involves a heady brew of learning through imitation, understanding the idiom of one's genre and instrument, developing a personal storehouse of motives and strategies that can be expanded on and transformed in the course of performance, and—tempered by all these elements—spontaneously creating new music. Acquiring a knowledge base, as we will see, refines and expands the concept of the model in a continual feedback loop, so that instead of a single template—a tune and chord changes or contour and pitch schemas—the musician has a cluster of related musical and conceptual material to work with. A young jazz trumpeter might listen closely to the solos of Miles Davis or Louis Armstrong, perhaps even transcribing some. She might learn the chord changes of 12-bar blues and practice soloing with notes from blues or altered scales. And she will likely develop a collection of favored licks for certain standards or changes.[36] Because "the novice has a set of techniques that are incomplete in detail and poorly linked, [. . . making them] strongly context-specific" (Pressing 1998, 53), her solos in the beginning might seem either derivative or unfocused. But over time, she will acquire a facility within that conceptual space, developing a personal style that blends her many influences with her own personality and ideas. To become a respected improviser, she will need to demonstrate a deep understanding and embodiment of that tradition's conceptual space as well as a personal creativity and individual voice within it. Similarly, an improvising Javanese gamelan musician "is not considered fully equipped if he merely imitates another in all details. His playing ideally should represent the tradition filtered through his own sensibilities, which . . . are not expected to be precisely like anyone else's" (Sutton 1982, 26). He begins with the model, applies the knowledge base to it, and finally adds elements of himself.

WHEN CONCEPTUAL SPACE IS UNSPOKEN, OR "SOMETIMES IT'S COMPLICATED"

In some improvised practices, the model is explicitly known and discussed, and there are widely recognized ways to build a knowledge base. Jazz improvisers usually work from a standard tune and known chord changes. What's more, there is an accepted canon of great performers, and easy access to their recordings for anyone wishing to build the foundation for a strong knowledge base. Sawyer (2003) describes the jazz knowledge base using a systems model of creativity, which identifies a *field*—the individuals participating in a creative practice who evaluate and collectively filter new offerings—and a *domain*—the products deemed worthy by the field, which then influence future products. He notes: "the [jazz] field would be composed of the musicians, the listening consumer, the magazine critics, and the club patrons, whereas the domain would be the set of albums available, and perhaps books and articles written about performances" (123–24).[37] As we will see in chapters 2 and 3, Balinese *reyong* gong chime players improvising *norot* figuration have similarly overt models; their improvisations are derived from the fixed *norot* playing of *gangsa* metallophones. But the path to a corresponding knowledge base—or domain—is less explicitly laid out; musicians must learn who the good *reyong* improvisers are by watching and word of mouth, and will emulate their style in practice and performance.

In many other traditions, even just discovering the model can be a complicated process. It may be that the model is not explicitly known, or that it is known only by a select few. In Aka polyphonic vocal music, there are various "constituent parts" on which participants improvise with relative freedom (see Fürniss 2006, 168). Yet the musicians may not be able to identify or replicate these models. It is often only when someone strays too far from the constituent parts, and the integrity of the polyphony becomes threatened, that the so-called *master of the song*, the *kònzà-lémbò*, will intervene, making the parts explicit.

In other cases, each musician may have a different idea about what the model is. In Shona mbira music, while models are often named pieces, a single piece may have numerous *versions*. Rather than saying "I am improvising on *Nhemamusasa*," it is more accurate to say "I am improvising on the version of *Nhemamusasa* that I learned from this particular teacher in the summer of 2019." Which moments in an improvisation are idiomatic variations of a single model in the improviser's personal style, and which are borrowings from another musician's version—*their* model of the piece—becomes one of the dimensions of unraveling mbira improvisatory practice.

Even a single musician's model may not be a distinct entity; the model may instead be a constellation of related musical concepts and patterns to be unearthed. In *kendang arja* improvisation, each master drummer appears to know a collection of patterns, which he mixes and matches and freely improvises on within his particular conceptual space. Yet unlike versions of mbira songs or melodies of jazz standards, these model patterns are not overtly discussed. Their defining structural elements are implicit, and details must be discovered through practical study of the drumming.

This becomes one of the major challenges of analytical ethnomusicology. Those of us who delve into the analysis of improvised forms, as we will see in chapter 2, must discover their many dimensions through a combination of casual conversations, interviews, lessons, practical experience on the instrument, recording sessions, transcription and analysis, and other fieldwork techniques. Simha Arom, for instance, discovered what he proposed were models for Central African polyphonic music through multitrack recording, paradigmatic analysis, and asking to be taught the music as though he were a child. He recalls a eureka moment in his study of interlocking Banda-Linda horn music:

> It occurred to me to ask him whether the boys learning to play the horns during their initiatory retreat were not taught first to play simpler figures than the ones performed by more experienced musicians. I thus learned that there is a highly simplified figure for each of the five basic horn parts in each piece of the repertory, which is used for purely didactic purposes. This figure is *minimal* in the sense that nothing more may be removed from it without destroying the structure, and thereby the identity of the piece. This bare figure furthermore has a name; it is called àkɔ̃.nɔ̀ which literally means "the husband, the male." Now the Banda-Linda use the same term to designate the *ultimate reference* or simplest realisation of *each of the constituent parts of any musical entity*. . . . Not only do we have a *model* here, i.e., a fundamental organizational principle to which every realisation of every constituent part in a given piece refers; but moreover, this model is clearly conceptualized by the Linda people themselves. (Arom 1991a, 370)

Thus can a known but unspoken model be discovered through fieldwork. In many traditions, however, we may not be that lucky; there may be no explicitly named model to find even *if* we ask the right questions. In my study of *kendang arja*, just getting beyond the statement "you can play whatever you want" involved taking many lessons with each master drummer and only being given new patterns when my drumming on current patterns was deemed sufficiently *lancar*, fluent. And without overt confirmation from my teachers, I can only hypothesize that their taught patterns may be a kind of model.

Further, as we have seen, finding the melodic, rhythmic, or harmonic model of a piece or performance, explicit or unspoken, only solves a portion of the mystery behind an improvised practice; we also must uncover the rules of engagement with that model—its knowledge base. The components of this, too, are often unspoken or entirely unconscious and must be discovered through fieldwork and hands-on study of the instrument.

Only by discovering both the model and the technical, aesthetic, and social guidelines shaping its idiomatic performance do we reveal the fullest possible *conceptual space* of any improvised practice. This challenge becomes even greater in a collaborative tradition like *kendang arja*, where multiple musicians are simultaneously improvising on their own unspoken or unconscious models and knowledge bases. Turino describes this interactional complexity:

> Improvisations are . . . typically generated in a variety of habitual modes in response to what the people I am playing with are doing. When I play old-time music or sing with mbira music, these modes include inventing contrapuntal lines, interlocking melodic-rhythmic parts with other players or dancers, making imitations that extend or alter things my partners are doing, or shifting my part to create close rhythmic synchrony with, or alternative accents in relation to, other players or dancers. (2009, 106)

Thus, not only models and knowledge bases but also modalities of interaction and mutual inspiration must be taken into consideration in an analysis of collectively improvised practices. In chapter 4, I examine these various modes of communication and interaction, and the cognitive processes guiding them, in order to formulate and refine a more nuanced typology of collective improvisation. But I turn now to the first case study: an exploration of improvisatory process in the collectively improvised *reyong* practice *norot*.

CHAPTER TWO

FINDING AN UNSPOKEN MODEL

THE BOUNDARIES OF *REYONG NOROT*

IMPROVISATION IN GAMELAN, AFTER ALL

The familiar din of happy voices and the tinkling of wood on bronze greet me as I rush down the basement stairs of UBC's Asian Center, characteristically two minutes late for class. I drop my backpack in the corner of the room and kick off my shoes. Not a regular occurrence in most university classes, but after a year of playing Balinese gamelan gong kebyar for credit, it seems as normal as brushing my teeth before bed. Our teacher Alit[1] offers me a quick wave and a smile as I make my way over to the reyong, *a long row of horizontal bossed kettle gongs played simultaneously by four people (see figure 2.1). I sit on the floor at the left-hand edge of the instrument, pick up my two* panggul—*mallets— and wait for Alit to come show us our parts.*

We've been learning a new melody for the famous dance piece Oleg, *and I've predictably forgotten much of what I learned last class, thanks to the traditional oral learning method for Balinese gamelan that I have affectionately dubbed "learn-forget-learn-forget-learn . . . remember!" I should be able to retain this new section by the end of today's rehearsal, though. If only Alit would stop changing my part!*

FIGURE 2.1. Four musicians play the *reyong*. *Left to right*: I Dewa Putu Rai, I Dewa Madé Sakura, I Dewa Putu Berata, I Gusti Nyoman Darta. (Photo by Nicole Walker, 2003. Used with permission.)

This is a new problem, and its cause is a bit of a mystery. The last year of playing has taught me that, though gamelan pieces are learned by rote, they are as precomposed and fixed as any notated composition. Most musicians in the ensemble, including we reyong-*ers, play formulaically composed elaborations on slower-moving melodic lines, and artistic license is not within our purview. So I've been trusting Colin McPhee's claim that "other than in solo parts there can be no place for spontaneous improvisation" in gamelan (1966, xvii).*

All the reyong *playing I've done thus far exemplifies McPhee's assertion to a tee. The ensemble's jack-of-all-trades, we sometimes join a small tray of cymbals in a rhythmic support role, tapping running 16th notes with the brassy clang of wooden mallets on gong rims. In other moments, our playing exudes the fiery unpredictability of* kebyar, *a musical aesthetic meaning to "flare up" or "burst open." In perhaps our most iconic technique, percussive 16th notes are interspersed with syncopated shots exploding in a perfect synchrony of 8-note cluster chords.[2] But my favorite thing of all is playing fast interlocking melodies: sharing a phrase that's been carefully divided into two complementary strands, allowing us together to reach speeds that none of us could alone.[3] In the last piece Alit taught us, the warrior dance* Baris, *these interlocking melodies were as composed and unchanging as our other techniques: two parts meticulously designed to fit together like jagged puzzle pieces. In first position at the* reyong's *left-hand edge, I played the phrase in figure 2.2. My friend*

Jocelyn in third position doubled my part up the octave. I later learned that this reflected a principle of octave equivalence *fundamental to* reyong *performance, where notes in lower octaves are functionally the same as their scalar equivalents in higher octaves.*

Our partners in second and fourth positions interweaved the rhythm in figure 2.3. Together we made a continuous, interlocking melody from four adjacent tones. Shown in figure 2.4, this technique is called ubit empat, *or simply* empat, *meaning "four."*[4]

We eventually discovered that removing the highest pitch, which in empat *figuration always plays in harmony with the lowest, revealed a carefully composed 3-note melody snaking its way around this small range.*[5] *The top staff in figure 2.5 shows this melody divided into its two voices; in the bottom staff, all the notes of the composite melody are beamed together.*

The nature of Balinese interlocking meant that each musician needed to stay true to his or her part in order to maintain the integrity of this melodic composite. Gamelan was not an improvising art. Or that's what I had always believed.

So what in the world was happening now? When Alit teaches gamelan he does it with the assurance of someone who's been playing since he was a small child. He can deftly

FIGURE 2.2. *Baris* interlocking pattern on *reyong*, 1st and 3rd positions

FIGURE 2.3. *Baris* interlocking pattern on *reyong*, 2nd and 4th positions

FIGURE 2.4. *Baris* interlocking *empat* pattern on *reyong*, all players

FIGURE 2.5. Baris interlocking *empat* pattern on *reyong*, composite melody

move from instrument to instrument, switching between vastly divergent parts without the slightest hesitation or memory lapse. But last rehearsal it took him several attempts to settle on figuration for each of the four reyong *players, as though he were weighing alternatives, and today he has forgotten what he taught us last class and seems to be choosing from a whole new set of slightly different options with an out-of-character indecision. This new figuration style*—norot *it's called*—*is not the predictable* empat *we've grown accustomed to! When I finally summon the courage to say, "I don't think that's what you showed us last time," his answer changes everything: "It's ok," he smiles. "You can just improvise on what I've shown you. Go ahead. Try it." And he walks away confidently to help another student.*

My three compatriots and I look back and forth with confusion and some concern, and much less confidence in our abilities than Alit appears to have. Then, seeing no other choice, we begin hesitantly to "improvise." More quickly than ought to be possible, Alit is back. "Not like that," he says, with a pained look. But when we ask what can and can't be done while "improvising," our questions are met with uncertainty; Alit simply knows what sounds right and what doesn't. He can show us idiomatic patterns, but he can't explain what makes them work. It comes from his rasa *he says: his "feeling" developed though years of playing the music in Bali. "OK," he finally concedes. "I'll just show you one for now."*

The combination of Alit's indecision, his pained looks, his verbal instructions, and his Balinese rasa *means three things to me: (1) though Balinese interlocking generally necessitates fixed idioms,* reyong *players have freedom to improvise in* norot; *(2) this freedom is not without its boundaries; and (3) though Alit obviously knows what the boundaries are—he can perform many versions of the* norot *melody and is quick to recognize inappropriate note use in our playing—it's difficult for him to express these things verbally. His conceptual space for* norot *improvisation, it appears, is largely unspoken.*

UNRAVELING CONCEPTUAL SPACES FOR IMPROVISATION

THE IMPORTANCE OF THE MODEL

To understand Alit's conceptual space for *norot*, I first needed to be familiar with the model on which he was improvising. I could not truly grasp the mastery of his performance, appreciate the ways in which he individualized techniques of interpretation, embellishment, recombination, and expansion, or gain insight into his embodied experience without first knowing the foundation for his creative choices. I might still enjoy his performance, of course, but the craft behind his creativity was a more elusive animal. The same is true in the study of any improvised practice. Research in cognition and perception has found that a listener's level of familiarity with a piece and her experience within its musical system work in concert to determine the subtlety with which she can recognize alterations to the piece in different performances.[6] Knowing the musical and aesthetic expectations of a specific raga lends depth to a listener's appreciation of an improvised *alap* in a way that a casual interest in Hindustani music cannot. In much the same way, only fluency in the written and tacit rules of Italian *partimenti* reveals an improviser's often understated choices in that practice. And knowing to listen for creative references to famous recordings in the performance of well-known Brazilian *pagode* songs, or recognizing the new spin that a skilled jazz soloist puts on an old favorite, can allow for fuller insight into each of these musicians' artistries than hearing them improvise on something unfamiliar.[7] Whether or not we are consciously aware of it, our indoctrination into these models as listeners helps us navigate performances to identify moments of particular ingenuity. Like an ornithologist's field guide:

> You can approach [this knowledge] pragmatically to ID particular flora and fauna. Or you can read it for more general tips on how to go a-looking. A field guide can help you figure out how to be ready to go into the woods, can give you a framework for observing once you're out in the woods, maybe even help you get over an inhibition about venturing into the woods. A framework, a chassis, a scaffold, some tips, a dram of encouragement. (Corbett 2016, 7)

Whether a specific template for formulaic variation or a broad schema for exploration, a model contextualizes a performance, allowing real-time access to an improviser's musical processes. Yet this link between model and performance can also present one of the greatest initial hurdles to the analysis of improvised musics. When a model is unconscious, or conscious but unspoken, analysts and uninitiated listeners are often left in the dark. To find the models behind such practices, we cannot simply open a "fake book," as we might to learn the basic tune and changes of a jazz standard, or read a treatise, as we might to ascertain the desired aesthetic of a given raga.[8] Nor will attending many performances by the same ensemble, as Corbett suggests for discovering free jazz models, be sufficient.

I showed in chapter 1 how Simha Arom used a combination of fieldwork and analysis to find the consciously known but unspoken models of Central African polyphonic horn improvisers. An expert *reyong* player likewise wields a storehouse of fine-grained musical knowledge communicated to him through

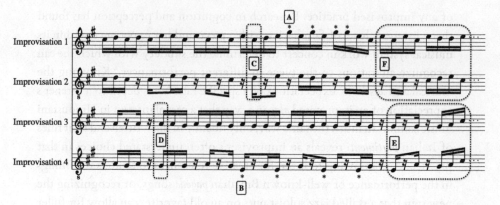

FIGURE 2.6. Four "equivalent" improvised *norot* melodies

practice alone: a collection of very specific musical and aesthetic requirements that nevertheless remain unspoken. In performance, this model and knowledge base are materialized through continuous, varied, rapid-fire choices made in an exquisitely limited musical field of just a handful of tones. Four short *norot* improvisations demonstrate this constrained flexibility. Alit played each of these phrases, marked for analysis in figure 2.6, in different iterations of the same piece, though one might also hear four such phrases played simultaneously by the full *reyong* complement.[9] Thus, like multiple improvised performances of the same jazz tune, these phrases can be considered paradigmatically equivalent.

The concept of musical equivalence is culturally bound and system specific; variations on a model retain perceptual similarity "to the extent that the transformations do not violate the 'grammaticality' of the musical system within which the material has been conceived." This "suggest[s] a close link between comprehension of the musical system and the categorization process that one may hypothesize to operate in the recognition of variations of an original theme" (McAdams and Matzkin 2003, 91). Understanding how Balinese musicians deem these four melodies equivalent involves deciphering unspoken conceptual spaces of cognition and musical expectation, and a preliminary analysis can help define the boundaries of this task. One might first notice that Improvisations 1 and 2 share certain similarities of range and contour, as do Improvisations 3 and 4: pitch use in their first beats is identical, while rests create some variation between them. Yet Improvisations 1 and 4 feature larger ranges: pitches marked with asterisks at A and B are not used in the other two improvisations. What determines these range choices, and when should extra notes be employed? Further, while

Improvisations 1 and 3 use almost continuous 16th-note motion, Improvisations 2 and 4 contain many 16th-note rests, often creating syncopated gestures, as in the third and fourth beats of Improvisation 2. What is the function of these rests, placed seemingly at random throughout Alit's improvisations? Are they a part of the rhythmic quality of the model or do they represent a creative move away from it? Equally curious are instances where, in two similar improvisations, Alit chooses to play different pitches in the same subdivision, as at C and D. Does the model contain both these notes, and if not, is their concurrence considered dissonant? Are there even operative concepts of consonance and dissonance in this practice? Next, even in closely related improvisations, Alit appears to have a relatively wide range of freedom in note placement within his small ambitus. At E, Improvisations 3 and 4 have the same end goal—the 3-note ascending gesture—but the approach to it differs. At F, Improvisations 1 and 2 use the same limited pitch palette, but temporal placement of the tones is different in all but one subdivision. What determines Alit's choices here? Does the model dictate specific rhythmic placement, as might be suggested by the extensive neighbor-note oscillations in beats 3–6 of Improvisation 3? And if so, what are the idiomatic ways of diverging from this rigidity? Finally, how do Improvisations 1 and 2 relate to Improvisations 3 and 4, and what makes them "equivalent"?

Both the unspoken model and the unconscious knowledge base of *reyong norot* are needed to answer these questions, and over the next two chapters I will explore this conceptual space, using fieldwork and analysis to gain insight into the embodied experience of collectively improvising musicians. In many ways, *reyong norot* presents an ideal first case study. Each *norot* improvisation is based on the same specific, unspoken but consciously known template for formulaic variation: a simple set of rules that determines melodic construction for every player in any piece. Unlike in jazz, where each standard has a different melody and chord changes, or in Hindustani music, where individual ragas each have their own musical and aesthetic guidelines, the *norot* model's standardization across the repertoire allows for easy comparative analysis between pieces, eras, villages, and performers. What's more, *gamelan gong kebyar* uses a limited five-tone scale, with each *reyong* player controlling just two to four of those tones. While *reyong* musicians have developed ingenious techniques engendering a virtually infinite number of possible variations on a melody, the model's limited scope and specificity and the instrument's narrow pitch range provide a small pool into which we may dive deeply. They enable comprehensive discussions examining how improvisers diverge from models in performance, and provide relatively straightforward examples of each of the four general improvisatory techniques discussed in chapter 1.

This chapter serves two purposes. At the microlevel, it introduces the specifics of the *reyong norot* model and preliminary knowledge base, preparing the reader to fully appreciate the subtle wizardry of the improvisations in chapter 3. But it begins at the macrolevel with a discussion of research techniques that fuel good analysis—methods for finding unspoken models and formulating culturally relevant hypotheses for their knowledge bases.

SEARCHING FOR A MODEL

Although the process for uncovering an unspoken or unconscious model and effectively analyzing its improvisations will be different in every music culture, in my forays into collectively improvised genres in Bali, I found five general steps to be essential. I present them here in what I consider to be the most useful chronological order, though it will quickly become apparent that each step leads back to the other four in a continual feedback loop of information and inspiration.[10] Along the way, I introduce some of the basics of *gamelan gong kebyar* necessary to an analysis of *reyong norot*. While the research process outlined here may seem obvious to the seasoned ethnomusicologist, I hope that articulating it explicitly will underscore the challenges and benefits of each step.

STEP 1: LISTENING

When Mantle Hood proposed the then-radical concept of bi-musicality[11]—the idea of acquiring performing fluency as an ethnomusicological research method—he opined that the first obstacle to success would be developing "an ability to hear" (Hood 1960, 56). The same is true for music analysis. An English speaker wishing to learn Cantonese, Hmong, or Ewe needs first to become accustomed to hearing the various tones in those languages. In much the same way, to fully understand Arabic or Persian classical musics, for instance, we must learn to hear the quarter tones that an ear trained in Western traditions might be inclined to "equalize." *Gamelan gong kebyar*, too, uses a non-Western tuning system, all the more complex because it is not standardized. Generally referred to using the Balinese solfège syllables *ding-dong-deng-dung-dang* (which I abbreviate i-o-e-u-a), its five-tone scale translates roughly to C#-D-E-G#-A, as in figure 2.7.[12] Perceiving this collection of pitch classes as "normal," and not expecting them to behave as notes in Western scales might, takes time, patience, and exposure. The clangorous timbre and complex overtones of the ensemble's

FIGURE 2.7. The five tones of *gong kebyar*'s scale, with solfège and abbreviations

bronze keys and gongs, as well as the pulsating shimmer of its characteristic paired tuning, equally require acclimation.[13]

Repeated and attentive listening goes much deeper than simple pitch discernment, however. It builds familiarity with a full musical system, from the general swing feel in many jazz styles to a specific musician's favored unfolding of the pitch palette in a Hindustani *alap*. Typical harmonic progressions or melodic trajectories, common structures, appropriate ornaments, characteristic rhythms or riffs—these and many other aspects of a musical language are revealed and made to feel familiar through thoughtful listening.[14] One might initially notice, for instance, that *gamelan gong kebyar* pieces are often cyclic, and that while some instruments play very quickly, others consistently play sparsely. With repeated listening yet more details will come into focus and begin to seem both obvious and expected. This familiarity is even more vital when analyzing improvised traditions. Where each performance of a piece may be quite different from any other, learning to recognize when a performer has reached the boundaries of his or her idiom is that much more challenging. Collectively improvised genres, moreover, demand that we tackle these questions for multiple musicians simultaneously. But "if the spirit, melodies and rhythms of the music are already a part of you," if you have embodied the tradition, "a theoretical analysis or a transcription is more effective" (Blake 2010, 13).

STEP 2: LEARNING TO PLAY

Most ethnomusicologists agree that understanding and embodiment of any form of music can be enhanced through performance.[15] Recent studies in embodied cognition support this notion, proposing that "the human motor system, gestures and body movements play an important role in music perception" (Leman and Maes 2014, 236).[16] This means that "the concepts with which we consciously and verbally make sense of musical experience are likely to be shaped by the structure of our bodies and by our experience of interaction with our environment" during performance (Clayton and Leante 2013, 197).

Finding the unspoken model behind an improvised tradition like *reyong norot* requires fluency both on the instrument and within its larger musical system, and playing the music allows us to understand it "from the 'inside,' so to speak. The structure of the music comes to be apprehended operationally, in terms of what you do, and, by implication, of what you have to know" (Baily 2001, 94).[17]

One need not become a virtuoso in the genre, but basic musical proficiency on the instrument being studied and performance experience in its ensemble context create a baseline of embodied idiomatic knowledge that fosters more culturally faithful analyses. In his call for bi-musicality, Hood argued that this "basic musicianship" would ensure our "observations and analysis as musicologist[s] do not prove to be embarrassing" (Hood 1960, 58). Yet at a more profound level, as Michael Bakan observes, "learning to play" eventually becomes "playing to learn"; we reach a point when we can "productively engage what are often [our] most direct and subjective experiences of the 'alien musics' [we] study, the experiences of music-learning and performing, and in so doing move toward new and deeper musical and scholarly understandings" (1999, 316). In his research into Balinese *gamelan beleganjur*, Bakan's playing experience gave him access to local concepts of trust and partnership in music performance, taking him far beyond the notes on the proverbial page. In my own research in Bali, performance taught me some of the music's fundamentals while also facilitating connections with potential teachers and collaborators and providing insight into traditional pedagogies. It helped me, as Bakan puts it, "inadvertently become more 'Balinese' through the course of my development" (318) as a learner, listener, and player.[18]

Performing and the Fundamentals

When Western-trained musicologists like me analyze Western improvised music genres, we can take so many of the fundamentals for granted. Performing within these and other Western practices has helped us embody basic assumptions about how the music should feel and sound: the make-up of the major and minor scales, the strong pull of the leading tone toward the tonic, the feeling of an accidental or syncopation, a suspension or cross-rhythm, the culturally agreed-on concepts of consonance and dissonance, the location of C on our instrument, or on a treble clef, and so on. The more we perform, the more refined our foundation becomes. We begin to instinctively know which note combinations are idiomatic for a particular style, which contours or gestures most appropriate for a given moment in an improvisation. We begin to internalize idiom, to develop *rasa*, "feeling." But different music cultures have different foundations with different assumptions, idioms, and *rasa*.

At the heart of any *gong kebyar* ensemble, for instance, is a collection of hanging gongs. Many gamelan pieces are built in contrasting sections of cyclic melodies, and strokes on these gongs emphasize important structural points within them.[19] I once played a recording of Bach's chaconne for violin to one of my Balinese drum teachers, a longtime friend and very skilled and curious musician. After a minute or two of intense listening, he looked at me quizzically and said, "It's interesting . . . but where's the gong?" In asking this, he was not actually implying that what Bach had been missing all these years was a good bronze gong; he simply felt the music lacked recognizable structural markers. My indoctrination into Western music allowed me to feel the chaconne's structure through the implied harmonic motion of the violin's melodies; his training in gamelan had prepared him for a very different kind of musical understanding. In Balinese gamelan, the end of a melodic cycle is generally marked by the largest hanging gong: the *gong ageng* or great gong (often abbreviated "G"). Other gongs highlight other important beats. Underlying the 8-beat *Baris* melody from figures 2.2–2.4 is a pattern using the *gong ageng* and medium-sized *kempur* (P) in the following configuration: (G) _ _ _ G P _ P G.[20] Learning to play gamelan helped me understand the importance of such cyclic structures. I quickly learned that if I got lost in the unfamiliar rhythms of my interlocking melody, I could listen to the gongs to find my way again. But I would later discover that their function as structural markers influenced *reyong norot* improvisation too (discussed in chapter 3).

Performing and Traditional Pedagogies

If one is fortunate enough to work with musicians from living music cultures, performance also allows access to traditional pedagogical practices, and these often reveal essential musical concepts.[21] Central to gamelan music, for instance, is an end-weighted metrical system where the stress is felt not at the beginning of each cycle but at its end, and melodies are composed to lead toward strong beats. "This is the exact inverse of tertian harmony where bass provides the harmonic foundation for the material to come (for example, a C chord is played on the downbeat of a bar, followed by a measure of melodic material based on C)" (Steele 2013, 230). As a Western-trained musician, I naturally felt Balinese gong cycles as starting on beat 1, and would count them **gong**-2-3-4-5-6-7-8-**gong**. My Balinese teachers, though, would always count **gong**-1-2-3-4-5-6-7-**gong**.

FIGURE 2.8. End-weighted cycles and beats: the *reyong*'s composite *Baris* melody

To them the *gong ageng* did not begin the cycle but ended it; the strong beat was not 1 but 8. In the *Baris* gong pattern (G) _ _ _ G P _ P G, the first *gong ageng* is notated in parentheses because it actually "belongs" to the previous cycle, and each gong stroke after it is considered to be leading toward the beat-8 *gong ageng* at pattern's end.

Learning gamelan from Balinese musicians also taught me that, when considering the subdivisions of a single beat, the accent likewise falls at its end. Two beats, each divided into four subdivisions, are not thought of as 1-2-3-4-1-2-3-4-1, but rather 4-1-2-3-4-1-2-3-4; accordingly, Balinese musicians almost always begin singing or playing a melody *after* the beat. While beaming conventions of Western staff notation make representing this perception difficult, in solfège notation, I follow each strong tone with a backslash (/) per figure 2.8; each marks not the beginning of a collection of four notes, but its end.

This end-weighted conception of meter and beat influences how melodies, both composed and improvised, are constructed: motives are designed to lead *to* strong beats and subdivisions. Yet only through traditional pedagogies and performance can the proper feeling for this metrical organization be embodied and the appropriate analysis pursued.

Performing and Social Connections

The benefits of performing also reach beyond these technical, aesthetic, and kinesthetic dimensions. When beginning fieldwork, playing experience can "provide one with an understandable role and status in the community, and it can be very useful in early orientation. It explains why you are there and what you are doing" (Baily 2001, 95). Being able to play can help an ethnomusicologist gain the trust and acceptance of potential teachers and collaborators, and may in time unlock access to more advanced musical, pedagogical, social, or philosophical concepts. As Helen Myers observes:

Ethnomusicologists are more fortunate than anthropologists and sociologists because the private feelings we study are publicly expressed in musical performance. Cultural barriers evaporate when musicologist meets musician. There is no substitute in ethnomusicological fieldwork for intimacy born of shared musical experience. (1992, 31)

Ingrid Monson (1996) credits her familiarity with jazz and "considerable professional experience as a trumpet player" (16) as well as her connection to well-known radio producers for opening doors to interviews and lessons with jazz musicians. Yet she also recalls: "in some cases, it took several trips to performances to make arrangements [for an interview], as musicians checked me out" (16). Recounting his experience in Afghanistan, John Baily observes that playing the music "gave me an immediate and large area of common experience with people to whom I was a complete stranger. We were all heirs to a common musical tradition [. . . and] musical relationships form[ed] the basis for social relationships" (2001, 96). And Paul Berliner tells of the many years of relationship building and practical study required to truly gain the trust of his Shona mbira teacher and community, out of which stemmed access to privileged information about the instrument. He notes: "the elders who are the guardians of an oral tradition do not treat their knowledge lightly. Rather, they 'give what they like.' Moreover, they give only the amount of information they believe to be appropriate to the situation and to the persons involved" (1993, 7).

In my research into improvised *arja* drumming, performing *gamelan gong kebyar* in Bali connected me with musicians my own age who could teach me the basics. Once they deemed me sufficiently proficient, they would introduce me to older master drummers they admired. These men, like Monson's jazz musicians, would always "check me out" before agreeing to work with me. When my friend Sudi brought me to meet the Peliatan-based *arja* master Cok Alit, I was offered a cup of coffee while the two of them spoke at length in Balinese (I knew only Indonesian). Cok Alit initially seemed reluctant to teach me, in part because I was a woman looking to learn a man's instrument, and in part because he could not be sure that I was both capable and serious. After what seemed an eternity, he picked up his drum, played a short pattern, and handed the drum to me. Sending silent thanks to my parents for their musicians' genes and my undergraduate professors for their aural perception classes, I played the pattern back to him on the first try. A smile crept across his lips, growing wider and wider until he broke into uproarious laughter. "OK," he said at last. "I'll see you tomorrow at 10:00." Over time it became clear that Cok Alit enjoyed teaching me because I wanted to learn the older classical styles many young Balinese musicians no longer deemed interesting. Our shared interest gave us common ground and brought us closer, both as musicians and as people. As our friendship developed, I gained access to Cok Alit's intimate thoughts and ideas about music, and he seemed to feel excited and proud to play in recording sessions I organized. In our lessons, though, I would only be taught more difficult drumming patterns once I had mastered proper technique on easier ones. To Cok Alit, commitment and potential got me through the door, but playing proficiency, not simply mental understanding, was the key to my advancement. The same was true of my *norot* lessons with Alit. And because each pattern I learned taught me more about models as well as collective improvisation, my playing abilities were essential to my research.

The insights gained through performance, and the questions they raise, lead back to Step 1 for a more nuanced listening experience. But they also inspire a move into Step 3: a fuller immersion into the existing knowledge base of the genre.

STEP 3: IMMERSION

Research in second language acquisition has shown that the most effective approach toward fluency is intensive immersion. In a comparative study of college students learning French in different educational contexts, for example, not only the number of class hours but also, significantly, the consistency with which the target language was used in varied out-of-class activities, affected the acquisition of oral fluency (see Freed, Segalowitz, and Dewey 2004).[22] Learning a musical language likewise benefits from full immersion. Whether this takes the form of the ethnomusicologist's once-standard "year in the field," a collection of shorter, more intense research trips complemented by conversations and lessons over Skype, or many evenings and weekends of research done locally, immersing ourselves into the music cultures we study—improvised or otherwise—is essential to analysis. Even before taking lessons or doing one-on-one interviews, there are dozens of ways to dive headfirst into a music culture. For me, in Bali, immersion primarily meant hanging out with musicians. Lots of them. It meant being a fly on the wall, listening to and participating in as many conversations as I could, even if I didn't always understand what was being discussed or have the background knowledge to make intelligent contributions. So it also meant sometimes feeling awkward or stepping out of my comfort zone. It meant making friends and accepting invitations, letting conversations flow naturally without trying to steer them too much; these were musicians and inevitably music was what they loved talking about most.

It meant attending every performance I could find and watching every rehearsal my musician friends allowed me to (which was all of them) to start getting a sense of different improvisers' styles. It meant actively participating in these events whenever I was invited, whether or not I felt equal to the task. It meant getting permission to record rehearsals, performances, lessons, and performance postmortems. All of these activities helped me better understand the music cultures of *gamelan gong kebyar* and *arja*, confirming, contradicting, or adding nuance to the things I had read and the hypotheses I had begun to formulate.

My first gamelan immersion experience, however, was not in Bali, but rather in the town of El Cerrito, California, the then stomping grounds of the long-standing American gamelan group Gamelan Sekar Jaya. After spending a year playing *gamelan gong kebyar* twice a week at the University of British Columbia (UBC), I'd decided it was time to up the ante. So for two months in the summer of 2001, I rented a room in the home where Sekar Jaya housed their instruments, living downstairs from their artists in residence, radical composer I Madé Subandi and revered dancer Ni Ketut Arini. Each morning, I rolled out of bed and played *reyong* before breakfast, slowly mastering the difficult technique of damping the instrument's bright ringing bronze with one mallet while playing my next note with the other. I took lessons every day, sat in on rehearsals and performances, hung out with Subandi and Arini in the evenings, learned a little Indonesian, and soaked up as much music and culture as I could. It was at a Sekar Jaya rehearsal that I gained insight into one of the most foundational aspects of Balinese compositional process, central to the *reyong norot* model: the "core melody," or *pokok*.

Aside from the *reyong*, I had only tried my hand at one other gamelan instrument: one of a group of eight two-octave metallophones called *gangsa*. Like the *reyong*, these instruments were responsible for the ensemble's fastest-moving melodies. In the last year of playing with my group at UBC, I had noticed that slower-moving metallophones seemed to loosely track these faster melodies, sparsely striking our notes every few beats. Like the early scientists who believed that the sun and stars revolved around the earth, because that's how it looked from their perspective, I assumed that these instruments' melodies were derived from ours. I was wrong.

Tonight I am sitting at a gangsa *in Sekar Jaya's gamelan room learning a melody from the piece* Oleg Tumulilingan (Oleg), *the very same melody that, six months later, will spark my curiosity in* reyong norot. *"OK, here's the* pokok, *the core melody," Subandi begins, singing the tune in figure 2.9 while tapping the beat on his thigh.*[23]

The lead metallophone ugal *begins to trace this core melody, adding grace notes and*

Solfège:	(U)	U	U	U	A	I	o	I	I	A	o	I	A	U	U	e	e	o	o	A	A	U
Beats:	(16)	1		2		3		4		5		6		7		8	9	10	11	12	13	14	15	16

FIGURE 2.9. *Oleg Tumulilingan*'s core melody (*pokok*)

FIGURE 2.10. Learning a new melody on *gangsa*, I Dewa Ketut Alit and Leslie Tilley. (Photo credit unknown, 2001.)

passing tones, and the small horizontal gong, kempli, *joins him, tapping a steady beat with loud, dry strokes. "Just like in* Jaya Semara,*" Subandi calls out, smiling at the woman sitting among the hanging gongs. She nods and begins to play a 16-beat cycle of strokes on the large gong* ageng *(G), medium-sized* kempur *(P), and small* klentong *(t): (G) _ _ _ P _ _ _ t _ _ _ P _ _ _ G. I notice that the three pairs of one-octave metallophones considered "core melody instruments" have also begun to figure out their parts, the* penyacah *playing every beat, the* calung *every two beats, the* jegogan *every four. Subandi watches them for a moment, leans forward to help one guy who seems to be struggling more than the rest, then decides that the others will figure it out on their own. He turns to the* reyong—*peopled with some of the ensemble's senior members, I know—and says "OK,* norot.*" Then, "I'll be back."*

Finally, Subandi turns to us gangsa *players and begins to play face-to-face with the person nearest him, a common pedagogical approach shown in figure 2.10.*

66 · CHAPTER TWO

I crane my neck to see what he's playing, piecing my melody together one beat at a time. But I notice with a blend of surprise and awe that, with just the core melody and the word "norot" to work from, many of the more advanced gangsa players have already figured out their parts. And suddenly, like Copernicus, it dawns on me: perhaps the core melody is not following us. Perhaps the earth revolves around the sun after all; perhaps we derive our melodies from theirs.

I was to call this rehearsal to mind months later, back in my own gamelan ensemble at UBC, when Alit told us reyong *players to just "improvise" our* norot. *Although they would eventually need some help from Subandi, the* reyong *players in Sekar Jaya could clearly formulate* norot *improvisations from the core melody alone. The gangsas, too, seemed to know how to proceed as soon as Subandi said "norot." And the questions began swirling. How did the core melody determine the* reyong *and gangsa parts? Did the gangsas, who were never allowed to improvise, also play a kind of norot? If they did, how was it connected to* reyong *norot? Did the two instruments share a single model, and if so, why did their melodies seem so different?*

Each of these questions was born out of immersion. Immersion let me experience a Balinese style of teaching, watch and record more experienced players working through problems, and gain new Balinese vocabulary to contextualize the things I was learning. It would eventually help me to ask new questions of my teachers in their own musical vernacular and to formulate new, more relevant hypotheses. Although I did not yet fully understand how they had done it, the Sekar Jaya musicians helped me think about the music in more culturally accurate ways. I was now ready to start transcribing the things I had learned.

STEP 4: TRANSCRIPTION

Like analysis more generally, the use of transcription in ethnomusicological research has been the topic of an ongoing negotiation since the mid-twentieth century.[24] The choices we make about what to emphasize, what to omit, and which notation systems to use will unavoidably affect both our analyses and the perceptions of our readers; like the "theoretical cuts" of Seeger's banana, each approach "will yield different visions of what music is" (2002, 189). This is why Steps 1 through 3 are so vital early in the research process; they help us make culturally sensitive decisions about visual representation.

When using staff notation for gamelan, I have chosen to approximate pitch to the Western scale. In a tradition where almost all melodic instruments are

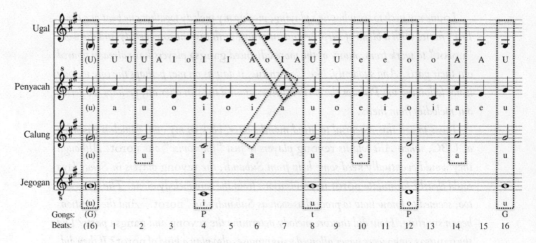

FIGURE 2.11. *Oleg Tumulilingan*'s core melody instruments: stratified polyphony with end-weighted meter

idiophones with no moment-to-moment pitch variability, and individual sets may be tuned quite differently from one another, the clutter of additional pitch detail seemed unnecessary. Instead, I include Balinese solfège in all transcriptions, which allows the material to be played on any set of *gong kebyar* instruments and, importantly, to be accessible to Balinese musicians not versed in staff notation. The audio and video files on the companion website further clarify how the music should look and sound. I have also opted to transcribe both *reyong norot* and *kendang arja* using strict 16th notes, ignoring any nuances of microtiming that may occur in performance. While interesting for a study of player precision and flexibility, or for examining potential subconscious relationships of leaders and followers,[25] this level of detail was not pertinent to the questions I was asking.

What I did consider important was a visual representation of end-weightedness. Because of the limitations of Western staff notation, strong beats in all transcriptions are notated at the beginnings of measures, strong subdivisions at the beginnings of beats. But the first tone aligning with gong (the "gong tone") is placed in parentheses, implying that it belongs to the previous cycle, and each transcription ends with the last gong tone—a single note standing by itself. As in *Oleg*'s various core melody parts in figure 2.11 (to be discussed), there are no bar lines and no repeat signs; the first and last note transcribed are both the gong tone.[26]

Despite the inherent limitations of any notation system, transcription facilitated my research on *norot* models and improvisations in three important ways:

it solidified my understanding of the larger musical context, confirmed and reinforced things learned in lessons and rehearsals, and allowed start-and-stop replay of recorded improvisations from Balinese musicians, thus enabling more detailed analysis.

Transcription for Context

My earliest transcriptions for *norot* research were not yet concerned with the minutiae of improvised patterns; they served instead to better understand the larger musical context of an unnotated ensemble genre in which I played only a single instrument. We learned in the previous section that *gamelan* pieces are built around a *pokok*, a core melody from which musicians on fast-moving instruments like *reyong* and *gangsa* somehow formulaically derive their parts.[27] Thus, discovering the *norot* model first required an examination of core melody, and recording rehearsals allowed me to transcribe what other people were playing, helping to contextualize my own part within the piece as a whole.

The melodic building blocks of *gong kebyar* comprise multiple variants of a single melody running simultaneously at different note densities. The *Oleg* melody sung by Subandi and played by the lead metallophone *ugal* dictates notes for three pairs of core melody instruments, which result in a stratified polyphony characterized by regular vertical pitch class convergences.[28] Each instrument pair interprets the *ugal*'s melody at its own density, coming into pitch class unison every two beats. Shown in figure 2.11, the *penyacah* play at the quarter-note density, compressing the melody into their one-octave range and interpreting off-beat notes in their own idiom.[29] The *calung* play every other note in the *penyacah*'s melody, while the *jegogan* play every four notes, each beginning and ending with the gong tone and maintaining vertical pitch class convergence (circled with dotted lines).[30]

As we will see, the concept of a stratified polyphony based on a single melody also extends to the fast elaborating instruments, and it is only through this core melody that the *norot* model becomes clear.

Transcription for Confirmation and Detail

While my initial transcriptions were mostly useful in providing context, they also aided in retention and clarification. This was especially true of melodies for which I only played half the notes. When interlocking, the eight *gangsas*

FIGURE 2.12. *Polos* part in interlocking *gangsa* melody, *Oleg Tumulilingan*

FIGURE 2.13. Composite *gangsa* melody, *Oleg Tumulilingan*

are divided into two roles: four so-called *polos* musicians generally align more closely with the beat, while four *sangsih* players sound the notes in between. I thought of these respectively as the "easy" and "hard" parts, though their names actually mean "basic" and "complementary." For *Oleg*, I was learning the *polos*, shown in figure 2.12.

I knew that the *sangsih* players filled in the spaces between my notes in a reasonably strict alternation, but I was not at the point where I could focus on this interlocking while playing. Still a relatively new gamelan player, shutting out the *sangsih* when things were fast or difficult was a survival tactic for me. So it was through recording and transcription that I could both confirm my own part and understand the interlocking melody I made with my partner. In figure 2.13, the two parts are shown on the top staff with *polos* stems down and *sangsih* stems up; the bottom staff shows the composite melody formed through their interlocking.

A little research told me that this melody was indeed a kind of *norot*, a figuration style characterized by a "wavering or neighbor-note motion" (Vitale 1990, 5).[31] But although they had the same name, this unimprovised *gangsa* figuration was not the same as *reyong norot*. How were these two elaboration styles connected? Conversation, lessons, and transcription of improvised *norot* would all point to the fixed *gangsa* melody as a model for *reyong* improvisation.

STEP 5: ONE-ON-ONE INTERACTIONS

The first four steps in the research process prepare ethnomusicologists to get the most out of our one-on-one interactions with teachers and collaborators. Performance illuminates the aesthetic and technical challenges of the practice; reading, listening, and immersion foster familiarity and generate useful vocabulary; transcription clarifies musical context and points out mysteries to be solved. These skills and understandings, when combined with relationships formed through immersion, generate the social capital to ask for private lessons, interviews, and recording sessions with master musicians as well as the intellectual and musical frameworks to more fully benefit from them. The full research package teaches us how to think about the music in more culturally relevant ways and thus to better pose questions of musicians whose knowledge of their tradition may be tacit.[32] It introduces us to the scene, exposing us to improvising musicians we might want to take lessons with, interview, or record. And it teaches us something about the most effective ways, socially and musically, to achieve these goals.

Recording Sessions

When analyzing music without readily available recordings, or where the details of improvisation in recorded tracks, as with *reyong norot*, are buried beneath other louder instruments, organizing recording sessions is a must. These will provide the raw data from which our analyses emerge. Particularly when looking at ensemble or collectively improvised music, a high quality recording is essential. The first time I recorded a pair of *arja* drummers, I had only a single handheld recorder placed on the floor between them and no musician keeping a steady beat for reference. I loved listening to this recording, and it offered some sense of the practice's characteristic interlocking. But the speed and rhythmic complexity of the drumming, as well as the abundance of quieter subordinate strokes, made it impossible to transcribe from this recording with certainty. On my next trip to Bali, I brought separate microphones for each of the four drumheads, so that their tracks could be panned in the mix to ease transcription. I also placed a small video camera in front of each drummer, capturing a clear view of both their hands. One additional camera took in the whole scene: drummers, beat-keeper, and cycle-marking instruments as well as the singer they were accompanying. The majority of the recordings I made of *reyong norot*, by contrast, were of a single musician playing alone, accompanied only by core melody. This, of course, made transcription easier, but it created something of a laboratory setting in which I could not truly assess collectivity. When wanting to look at the collective aspects of *norot* improvising, I had only a video recording taken with a single camera. Transcription from this recording was predictably more difficult. The lower end of the *reyong*, louder by nature and closer to the camera, was easy to discern. The top two positions of the instrument—quieter, and in this session played by less experienced musicians—required a great deal of repetition, slow-down, and ultimately transcription as much by visual as aural cues.

Although recording sessions were a somewhat contrived context for music making, I did what I could to make them feel natural. Food, coffee, and cigarettes were provided for the musicians, and we took lots of breaks to hang out, chat, and jam. I set the basic parameters for each session, but then let the musicians lead them. I set up the recording equipment, but in soundcheck asked the musicians to provide feedback on levels. I expressed to the performers my basic goal for a given take, but let them determine its length and structure. My *reyong norot* sessions always began with Alit showing me a core melody to play on the lead metallophone *ugal*. I then cycled that melody while he played *reyong*, improvising for as many cycles as he wished at one position of the instrument before moving to the next. We then played *reyong* together, talking about aspects of coordination and interlocking. My *arja* drumming sessions in Bali were longer and more involved. Two drummers, a singer, and a beat keeper were all required, but other musicians wishing to make music with these masters would inevitably come out of the woodwork to play accompanying instruments like gongs and cymbals. I let this flow naturally without organization. For each take, I requested a particular emotion or character type from the singer—which would result in different gong structures and drumming styles—but left all other details up to the performers. Throughout, the musicians might ask to listen to the recording and make comments on its quality, sometimes suggesting changes in mic placement or asking to play certain songs a second time. The photo in figure 2.14 shows Pak Tama of Singapadu listening to the early part of an *arja* recording session. As he made comments and suggestions, the headphones were passed to other musicians in turn. I hoped this back-and-forth and shared control of the recording session would give the musicians a sense of agency and active participation in the research process.

Interviews

While the formal interview is a time-honored research tool, valuable for gathering certain kinds of data, I found it to be only marginally useful for clarifying details about musical structure, communication, and intention. Often the musicians I was working with struggled to put into words their ideas about music, and I in turn struggled to find ways to ask about abstract concepts like models

FIGURE 2.14. Soundcheck in Singapadu, I Wayan Tama.
(Photo by Chelsea Edwardson, 2011. Used with permission.)

and knowledge bases, idioms and their boundaries. I found guided interviews, where specific recorded musical examples were the focus, to be somewhat more fruitful. Ingrid Monson, in her study of improvisation in jazz rhythm sections, centered her interviews on recorded excerpts from the musician's own catalog (see Monson 1996, 17–20).[33] For a practice like *arja*, where recordings are not readily available, I often interviewed musicians immediately following a recording session, listening back to excerpts from the session and discussing them. Having something concrete and creative to talk about helped focus our conversation. Yet the most important thing, I learned, was to let the musicians guide the discussion. As Monson notes:

> While I had a general plan in mind when I arrived in the interview situation, I played each one by ear: if a musician didn't seem to enjoy hearing an example, or seemed to find some of my questions uninteresting, I tried to listen for topics that were of interest, encourage expansion upon them, and stay out of the way. On some days, not surprisingly, I was better at this than other days. (Monson 1996, 19)

This process could sometimes be frustrating, particularly when I had very specific questions in mind. Yet, though I didn't always get the information I was looking for, this tack often brought surprising new ideas to the fore. What resulted was something closer to a "dialectical ethnomusicology" (see Kippen 1992 and 1985), where musicians could point out moments in an improvisation that worked well and those that didn't, discuss issues that they considered important, and even comment on specific improvised patterns.

Lessons

Insights gained through interviews and sessions still require unraveling. And once basic musical proficiency has been reached through listening, playing, and immersion, private lessons can solidify and expand a researcher's understanding of a practice. As Monson notes, though she was already a proficient jazz trumpeter, "the knowledge [she] gained of drumming from [lessons with jazz drummer] Michael Carvin was absolutely critical to [her] understanding of the rhythm section" (Monson 1996, 17). I found the same to be true in my studies of *reyong norot* and *kendang arja*. Perhaps most importantly, my lessons gave insight into musicians' thought processes about their own music. When we ask improvisers to teach improvisation, we're asking them to make choices: decisions about which patterns or ornaments or variants are the most foundational, or the easiest, or the most important, or the most interesting. We're asking them to show us the things they know consciously about their practice and to think about presenting that practice to a cultural outsider. This process can elucidate unspoken or unconscious models and help unearth the knowledge bases surrounding them.

As useful as the music I learned during my lessons was, it was the dialogue that flowed naturally out of the learning process that provided many of the most profound insights into the collectively improvised genres I was studying.

"But you must be following rules when you improvise, right? I mean you can't really just play anything." I'm sitting at the reyong with Alit, feeling both hopeful and nervous as I ask this question. We're thirty minutes into our first norot lesson, and I can sense him trying to negotiate my direct and analytical questions with his own tacit knowledge of the practice. This is new territory for both of us.

"OK, it's like this," he begins. "When I play norot, it comes from the base. You cannot just go anywhere," he asserts, "not just do what you want. . . . It's from the base, what I give you . . . I feel from that."

"What do you mean by 'the base'?" I ask. This could be the answer I've been looking for!

Alit sits quietly for a minute, characteristically thoughtful as he mulls over this new question. But he finally responds: "I'm sorry. I don't know how to explain."

FIGURE 2.15. The "base," *Oleg Tumulilingan*

FIGURE 2.16. Comparison: composite *gangsa* melody (*top*) and *reyong* "base" (*bottom*), *Oleg Tumulilingan*

"Could you maybe show me the base for Oleg?" I suggest.

"Ya," he smiles. *And from his position at the low end of the* reyong, *he plays the melody in figure 2.15.*

Although Alit's passive knowledge of the tradition means he can't verbally articulate an answer to my question, he's clearly able to show me a concrete example of "the base" in action. It seems there is a consciously known model for this improvised practice after all, unspoken though it may be. And my excitement grows as it dawns on me how similar this "base" is to the gangsa norot melody I'd learned with Sekar Jaya the summer before. The biggest difference, circled in figure 2.16, is likely due to the gangsa's melody going into a range Alit's reyong mallets could not reach.[34]

It occurs to me then, a hypothesis to be tested, that fixed gangsa melodies may provide models for reyong improvisation.

A FIXED ELABORATION PRACTICE: *NOROT* ON *GANGSA*

A QUESTION OF INFLUENCE

One can find examples in many music cultures of known models for one voice or instrument guiding the improvisations of another. Such influence often comprises large-scale formal or aesthetic guidelines, as in traditions where song melodies, lyrics, or structures inform musical choices of improvising instrumentalists. In Balinese *arja*, as we will see in chapter 6, the various cyclic structures used in songs for different character types affect the density of improvised drumming. In Brazilian *pagode* performance, instrumentalists working with well-known melodies and song forms improvise musical figures that emphasize cadences, fill small breaks in sung phrases, and even support lyrical content (see Stanyek and Oliveira 2011, 135–43.). Yet such model borrowing can also occur as small-scale mimesis. *Pagodeiros* will "sometimes vary their characteristic patterns by matching their playing to local rhythms of the vocal melody" (Stanyek and Oliveira 2011, 136). Similarly, the improvising lead drummer of an Ewe dance-drumming troupe will sometimes mimic the rhythm of a supporting drum, or invent a new rhythm that highlights a relationship between two contrasting drums, in order to bring these elements to the forefront of the texture. In each tradition, an improvising musician uses the more fixed idioms of other voices or instruments in the piece for her model. I wondered if *reyong* players drew their *norot* models from *gangsa* melodies in similar ways.

My thinking from this point proceeded as follows. I knew that there were direct connections between *reyong* and *gangsa* figuration. The 4-note *ubit empat* technique used in the warrior dance *Baris* (see figures 2.2–2.4) was often played identically on the two instruments. And I knew also that there were certain figuration styles unique to *gangsa*. *Ubit empat*'s close cousin *ubit telu* uses an interlocking technique that necessitates sharing the middle of its three notes between two *gangsa* players, impossible on a *reyong* where the four musicians use a single instrument. Thus, *ubit telu* is not played on *reyong*. Nor is another interlocking *gangsa* technique called *nyog cag*, where partners cover a much wider range by leaping over each other in strict alternation (see Vitale 1990, 4–5; Tenzer 2000, 216–20). If played on *reyong*, "the disjunct nature of the parts would cause them to cross repeatedly between players' positions. When *gangsa* play *nyog cag* the *reyong* must do something else" (Tenzer 2000, 217). Musicians have not devised new ways to play *nyog cag* or *ubit telu* on *reyong*; they simply do not use them. That both *gangsa* and *reyong* have a style of figuration called *norot* hints at a level of equivalence that would require parallel realizations on the two instruments.

Although Alit could not verbalize his understanding of the *norot* "base," nor confirm or deny a possible foundation in *gangsa* figuration, his pedagogical approach in our one-on-one lessons provided additional insight. After teaching me a new *reyong* pattern, Alit would often move to the lead melodic instrument *ugal*. Playing its elaborated core melody together with my *norot*, he hoped, would help me feel the musical link between the two. But whenever I faltered, forgetting the *reyong* pattern he had taught me, Alit would abandon the *ugal* melody and begin playing *gangsa norot* on his instrument, staring at me with an intensity that said, "Listen to what I'm playing. I'm helping you!" I found the combination of musical and ethnographic evidence for a *reyong-gangsa* connection in *norot* compelling, and it became a working theory. It would be fifteen years before Alit confirmed it.

We're sitting in the World Music Room at MIT, talking about the varied naming practices for Balinese interlocking techniques. Alit has just informed me that, in his village, the term norot *is not in fact used for interlocking* gangsa *melodies. His teachers instead used "noltol"—a Balinese term meaning to pick things up one by one, but which Alit likens to chickens pecking at the ground—to describe the regular alternation between interlocking partners seen in figure 2.13.*

I feel pretty deflated by this casual revelation. Every book on gamelan I've ever read calls this technique norot, *and I've been working for fifteen years under the assumption that these* gangsa *and* reyong *styles must be connected. Does Alit's insistence that* norot *is the wrong term for this gangsa figuration negate that link? Will I need to throw out my hypotheses and go back to the drawing board?*

"What about when it's played slowly?" I ask, referring to a technique where all gangsa *players strike every note in a melody instead of sharing it with a partner. "Did they call it* norot *then?"*

"I don't remember," Alit responds. "But it must be," he continues, before unceremoniously adding, "because that's where reyong norot *comes from."*[35] *A decade and a half after our first conversation about the* norot *"base," I stumble into the answer while looking for something else entirely. The model for* reyong norot *is* gangsa norot*!*

MAKING THE MODEL

If fixed *gangsa norot* melodies provide explicit, consciously known models for *reyong norot*, an overview of just a handful of their particulars can help frame *reyong* improvisation. The reason the Sekar Jaya *gangsa* players were able to figure out their *norot* so easily is that, unlike models in many improvised traditions that are unique to a single piece, the *norot* model is entirely formulaic. It begins with the *calung*, the core melody instrument moving at the half-note density. A *norot* melody, playing four notes per beat, alternates back and forth between the current *calung* tone and its scalar upper neighbor. It alters from this pattern only to prepare for a new *calung* tone.[36]

Every moment in a *calung* melody is defined by one of two possible kinetic qualities. The simpler of the two is the *ngubeng*, or static quality, and occurs between two successive *calung* tones of the same pitch. In such cases, the *gangsa norot* will simply alternate between the core melody tone and its upper neighbor for the full two beats. In the beginning of the *Oleg* core melody, the gong

FIGURE 2.17. Static (*ngubeng*) *norot* on *dung* (u).

FIGURE 2.18. *dung* (u) to *ding* (i) *norot* shift

tone *dung* (u) is followed by another *dung* two beats later, and the *gangsas* follow suit with static figuration. With structural tones that align with *calung* bold-faced and followed by a double backslash, the *gangsas* play (**u**)// a-u-a-u/ a-u-a-**u**// per figure 2.17.

The other melodic quality for core melody motion is *majalan*: kinetic or moving. This occurs in any 2-beat cell between differing *calung* tones, as in the *dung-ding* (u-i) shift following *Oleg*'s static start. The first half of a kinetic cell stems from its first core melody tone, alternating between that tone and the one above it just like a static cell; *norot* for a melody moving from *dung* (u) to *ding* (i), as in figure 2.18, also begins (**u**)// a-u-a-**u**/. The second half of a kinetic cell prepares the new core melody tone, paying no heed to the old one. It will always comprise the new tone twice, its scalar upper neighbor once, and the new tone once more, timed to land together with *calung*. In the same *dung-ding* (u-i) example, this anticipatory pickup gesture of sorts is / i-i-o-**i**//. The rocking motion then begins anew, this time on *ding* (i).

This simple set of rules lays out a single-voice model for *gangsa norot* figuration: a model made from a single strand of melody. Yet, although *norot* on the *gangsa* is a fixed practice, playing it idiomatically still requires indoctrination into a knowledge base. We know that the eight *gangsa* players are divided into four pairs, each musician taking on one of two roles. As we saw in the *gangsa*'s *Oleg* melody in figure 2.13, when the tempo is sufficiently fast, partners work together to create the single-voice model through melodic interlocking.[37] The fixed formula for interlocking *gangsa norot* dictates that the *polos* ("basic") players sound all the current core melody tones while their *sangsih* ("complementary") partners play the scalar upper neighbors. The two share the 3-note anticipation, *polos* playing only the new core melody tone while *sangsih* plays both the new tone and its upper neighbor. This neatly prescribed idiom has the two strands playing identical rhythms offset by one 16th note. For the *dung* (u) to *ding* (i) shift, with rests notated as underscores (_), the *polos* plays (**u**)// _ u _ **u**/ i-i _ **i**//; the *sangsih* interlocks with (_)// a _ a _/ i-i-o _// o. Every note of the model is sounded, either by one or both musicians in the pair, and figuration for both *polos* and *sangsih* players is fixed.

In slower passages, by contrast, the *polos* players do not need help playing the full melody. The function of *sangsih* often then becomes sounding a parallel "harmony" note, called *kempyung*, consistently three scale tones above *polos* per figure 2.19.

The *dung* to *ding* (u-i) *polos* pattern (**U**)// A-U-A-U/ I-I-o-**I**//, for instance, is complemented by the parallel *sangsih* pattern (**o**)// e-o-e-o/ u-u-a-u//. Figure 2.20 shows the full *Oleg* melody in parallel *norot* figuration, with *polos* notated stems down and *sangsih* stems up.[38]

These formulas for actualizing parallel and interlocking figuration become the knowledge base informing idiomatic *gangsa* performance on the single-voice *norot* model.[39] Once a *gangsa* player understands the model and knowledge base—static and kinetic, *kempyung* and interlocking—she may realize any piece without the aid of a teacher; she simply follows the *calung*'s core melody. Yet while *norot* is probably the simplest figuration style to master on *gangsa*, though they use the same model, it is anything but straightforward on *reyong*.

FIGURE 2.19. *Kempyung* parallel "harmony" tones

FIGURE 2.20. *Gangsa norot* in parallel figuration, *Oleg Tumulilingan*

FIXED ELABORATION TURNED FLEXIBLE: *NOROT* ON *REYONG*

Knowing that the strict single-voice *gangsa norot* template is a model for *reyong* players, I examine *reyong norot* by degrees of improvisational freedom. On the more conservative end, it involves combining basic model notes, *kempyung* "harmony" tones, and rests to create a variety of realizations without yet "breaking the rules" of the model. These formulaic substitutions are comparable to the free interchanging of subordinate with main drum strokes seen in *kendang arja* in chapter 1, and thus fall under the rubric of *interpretation*. On the more extreme end are those patterns created from a broadened conceptual space for *norot* figuration delineating idiomatic deviations from the model. These more drastic departures are based on improvisatory processes of *embellishment*, *recombination*, and *expansion*. For the remainder of this chapter, I explore how the particularities of the *reyong* itself create both boundaries and freedom for improvisation, before then seeking to derive a grammar of guidelines for idiomatically actualizing these improvisatory processes in chapter 3.

THE BIG PICTURE

Much of the analysis to follow is cellular, examining 2-beat units of sound at one of four positions on the *reyong*. These must first be understood as part of a fuller picture. As Simha Arom cautions: "Once the diverse elements have been disassociated the one from the others, they may lose their meaning and even their identity. It seems necessary, therefore, to always have at hand a *global image* of the aural document being analyzed."[40] Watching four experienced *reyong* musicians improvise *norot* is aurally and visually exhilarating: a flurry of eight mallets racing together over the twelve kettle gongs of the instrument, playing and damping with the same action. Each musician is at some points playing an independent line, at other moments interlocking with the player above or below, or even with an imaginary partner just outside the instrument's range.[41] Their interconnected streams of music dance across the *reyong* in continuous motion; the global impression is both more intricate and less simply elegant than *gangsa norot*. A careful eye will catch a small 3-note ascending passage being shared seamlessly between two musicians, or an alternation of two adjacent notes distributed between partners, much like interlocking *gangsa* players. And always, *kempyung* tones are an ever-present enrichment of the music's "harmonic" pitch makeup.

FIGURE 2.21. Improvised *reyong norot*, *Teruna Jaya* (2 cycles)

A brief improvised excerpt, played by musicians from the Sanggar Çudamani arts collective in the summer of 2016, will illuminate some general features of *reyong norot*. Figure 2.21 shows two successive cycles from a moderately paced improvisation on one of many cyclic melodies from the dance piece *Teruna Jaya* (see Video 2. Video 3 shows a longer excerpt of the improvisation).

Like *gangsa norot*, *reyong norot* creates a texture of almost continuous motion. Two notable exceptions in this excerpt are the gong tone and the *dung* (U) at the cycle's midpoint, both of which are almost always left empty by all four players. A common technique on the *reyong* also occasionally used by *gangsa* players, this rest creates space for the hanging gongs to ring through the texture, emphasizing their structural importance. Yet what becomes equally apparent is that, unlike *gangsa* players, these *reyong* musicians do not perform fixed rhythms or note combinations; rhythmic variety is central to the *reyong*'s *norot* idiom. "It's not *noltol*," Alit laughs, referring to the *gangsa*'s technique of strict alternation named for its likeness to chickens pecking at rice in the dirt.[42] Thus, each time they play through the *Teruna Jaya* melody, which will be cycled several times before the composition shifts to a new melody, the four

Çudamani musicians all play unique variants on the model. Although partially dictated by instrument idiom, these are also determined by the stylistic preferences of individual musicians. The second position player, I Madé Supasta, prefers denser figuration, filling almost every subdivision in many 2-beat cells. Alit's eldest brother I Dewa Putu Berata in first position, by contrast, employs more rests. And though the principle of octave equivalence means that the first and third position players, and those of the second and fourth positions, play similar figuration, they are almost never identical. The existence of both freedom and boundaries, and the negotiations between idiomatic options and individual preferences and choices are all in play here. These are informed by the physical limitations of the instrument, limitations that necessitate a refining and expanding of the *norot* knowledge base.

AN EXPANDED KNOWLEDGE BASE FOR *REYONG NOROT*

THE INFLUENCE OF INSTRUMENT CONSTRUCTION

Instrument construction and playing technique are central to the knowledge base of any music tradition, improvised or otherwise. Which idioms or common motives may be seen as a choice between equally plausible alternatives; which are necessities or likely eventualities of instrument technology? The limits of an average vocalist's range and the physical challenge of singing large intervals with precision means that many vocal traditions feature stepwise motion and small intervallic leaps in ranges little more than an octave. Construction of the heads for Indian tabla and *mridangam* drums encourages idioms with large timbral palettes; the use of finger strokes in their playing techniques allows for faster rhythmic passages than in Balinese drum genres, where musicians must rely on slower wrist and elbow joints. The construction and playing technique of the Shona *mbira dzavadzimu* likewise determines many of its idioms. Two left-hand manuals an octave apart are played with the left thumb only. The right thumb plucks the first three keys of the higher-pitched right-hand manual, while the remaining keys are played with the right index finger.[43] The physical arrangement of the mbira's keys encourages disjunct melodies as players alternate right- and left-hand strokes, while right-hand fingering techniques dictate a common formulaic variation in which index-finger harmony notes are added three keys above existing thumb notes.[44] Many of the most basic features of *reyong norot* improvisation, too, are artifacts of instrument technology and playing technique.

THE LIMITS OF RANGE

A *gangsa* player is able to realize uniform *norot* figuration on any core melody tone because she has sole control over her instrument's two-octave range. A *reyong* player, by contrast, must share his instrument with three other people, each controlling only a few of the notes in the scale. As shown in figure 2.22, the first position *penyorog* player controls a 3-note range from *deng* (e) to *dang* (a), extending to *ding* (i) only when his neighbor is not using it. This latter player, the *pengenter*, controls the 3-note range from *ding* (i) to *deng* (e). The third position *ponggang* player often has the most abstract figuration, limited to just two tones: *dung* (u) and *dang* (a). Like her *penyorog* counterpart, she can only play the *ding* (i) above when the player to her right is not using it. This last player, the *pemetit*, has control over the widest range of pitches: the four notes from *ding* (i) to *dung* (u).[45]

Setting aside improvisational freedom for a moment, a few observations will clarify the effects of this *reyong* construction and practice. Because of the limited ranges available at each position, unlike on *gangsa* there are no fixed roles in *reyong* interlocking. Actualizing the (**u**)// a-u-a-**u**/ i-i-o-**i**// contour of *Oleg*'s *dung* (u) to *ding* (i) shift requires a different kind of teamwork. Only the first and third position players have access to the *dung* (u) and *dang* (a) required for the first half of this pattern, while their neighbors control the *ding* (i) and *dong* (o) needed for its second half. Other patterns require sharing on a smaller scale, similar to interlocking on *gangsa*. *Norot* figuration for a static melody on *dang* (a) alternates between that pitch and the *ding* (i) above it. While the first and third position players control *dang* (a), it is the second and fourth that play *ding* (i). Performing the (**a**)// i-a-i-**a**/ i-a-i-**a**// rocking motion of the model thus requires alternation between *reyong* partners.

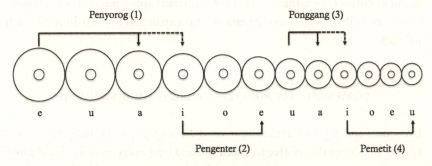

FIGURE 2.22. Ranges of the *reyong*

FIGURE 2.23. Flexible pairings on *reyong*

Yet, unlike in interlocking *gangsa* patterns, no two positions on the *reyong* interlock exclusively with one another. The second position *pengenter* player, for instance, interlocks at times with the third position *ponggang* above, at other times with the first position *penyorog* below. While a (**a**)// i-a-i-**a**/ motion requires the second player's *ding* (i) to complement the first's *dang* (a) below, for an (**e**)// u-e-u-**e**/ contour, her *deng* (e) instead interlocks with the third player's *dung* (u) above. These patterns are shown in figure 2.23 with the two voices not under consideration notated using smaller diamond noteheads.

The octave equivalence so fundamental to *reyong* grammar is equally fuzzy. The low *deng* (e) of the first player and the highest *dung* (u) of the fourth player expand the ranges of these outer parts in relation to their inner counterparts. The fourth player's high *dung* (u) is "often judiciously used in what might otherwise be inhospitable tonal situations as a way to boost the prominence of the *reyong* in the texture and add extra cross-rhythmic vitality" (Tenzer 2000, 216). Yet even while abiding by the model, these extra notes given to the outer players influence the contours of their elaborations. In figure 2.23, the (**e**)// u-e-u-**e**/ figuration necessarily shared between second and third position can be performed alone by either of the other players. The *reyong* players' limited ranges demand creativity, different for each of the four musicians. In the next chapter, I examine how these musicians apply methods of interpretation, embellishment, recombination, and expansion to their limited pitch palettes.

COMPARATIVELY ANALYZING ACROSS THE INSTRUMENT

Even just a cursory look at the improvised *Teruna Jaya* passage in figure 2.21 reveals that, despite the relative freedom allowed *reyong* players in model-abiding *norot*, these musicians are still constantly playing patterns that diverge from the model. In chapter 3, I analyze these more complex patterns in an effort to uncover the conceptual space that guides them. In order to facilitate comparison of idioms across the instrument, each pattern is conceived in something of a moveable *do* system. Because of the end-weighted conception of beats, the second of two core melody tones in any 2-beat cell, regardless of pitch, is labeled 0 (zero). All other notes in the 5-tone scale are labeled 1, 2, 3, or 4, in relation to the second tone and without reference to relative frequency distance or octave placement. The note directly above any core melody tone 0 is labeled 1; the note one scale tone below is labeled 4. Thus a melody moving from *deng* (e) to *dong* (o) is considered a 1–0 shift while one moving from *dong* (o) to *deng* (e) is a 4–0 shift.

Figure 2.24 shows all possible core melody shifts compressed into the one-octave range of the *calung*. Figure 2.25 shows the *Oleg* melody with each of its core melody shifts labeled for analysis, revealing many areas for potential comparison in 1–0 shifts across its range.

FIGURE 2.24. All core melody shifts labeled for analysis

FIGURE 2.25. *Oleg*'s core melody shifts labeled for analysis

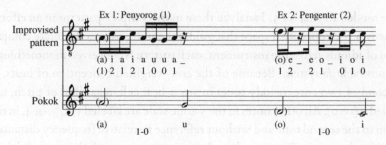

FIGURE 2.26. Comparing improvised cells analytically

This numbering system simplifies analysis by encouraging pattern identification based on the number of scale tones traveled as opposed to the actual pitches used. Because of the "movability" of *norot* contours, I can search for commonalities of design in *reyong* improvisation between players. I know, for instance, that the (o)// e-o-e-o/ i-i-o-i// realization of a 1–0 *dong-ding* (o–i) shift is only possible at the second and fourth positions of the instrument where those three tones fall within range. A more inclusive analytical system allows direct comparison of these patterns with those of their first and third partners on other tones. Figure 2.26 shows two cells from Alit's improvisations using only notes from the model; they are labeled with numbers for analysis. Although seemingly dissimilar, their numbering reveals structural parallels.

IN BROADER SCOPE: WORKING FROM A KNOWN MODEL

From *reyong norot* to Ewe dance-drumming, Karnatak *kriti* to big band jazz, many improvisatory traditions are based on consciously known, overtly conceptualized models. Uncovering these models in oral music cultures can be a complex process, where ethnography plays as important a role as analysis. Once discovered, however, such models allow us to bypass the kind of early stage, trial-and-error hypothesizing I experienced in my search for *kendang arja*'s unconscious models discussed in chapter 5. Our task as analysts, then, becomes to work in partnership with our collaborators within the culture, both to decipher their knowledge bases and to formulate suitable categories of divergence from known or hypothesized models. This research should be approached through a flexible combination of discourse, observation, and musical analysis appropriate to the culture being studied.

In his examination of improvisation on known jazz tunes, we saw Berliner (1994) first being given the concept of "levels of intensity" by alto saxophonist Lee Konitz, generating the insider categories of *interpretation, embellishment, variation*, and *improvisation*. Berliner then delineates the rough boundaries of these classes through examples and descriptions of jazz idioms. David Locke by contrast develops categories for improvisation in the Ewe music and dance form *Gahu* through "a synthesis of the playing styles of [his] teachers and [. . . his] years of exposure to performances of the piece" (Locke 1998, 3). In his 1998 *Drum Gahu*, Locke presents specific processes for generating "improvised variations" on both lead and response drums, proposing his own terminology for techniques he has observed. These include methods of *interpretation*, like "variation by accentuation," as well as techniques of *embellishment*, like "variation by subdivision." Locke also identifies *recombination* techniques such as "isolation and repetition" and *expansion* techniques like "rephrasing" and "metric modulation."[46] Although seemingly quite different studies, both Locke and Berliner begin their analyses with a known model. Musical processes are then discovered, and locally appropriate categories derived through a combination of hands-on experience with the music, conversation with and observation of its practitioners, transcription, and musical analysis.

In the next chapter, I explore the many ways that *reyong norot* players diverge from their known model and its knowledge base in improvisation. Drawing on local music theory concepts, both formal and informal, as well as on my transcriptions of improvised performances, the analyses look to create a culturally relevant grammar of guidelines for *norot* improvisation and provide a test case for identifying and examining improvisatory processes across cultures.

CHAPTER THREE

ANALYZING IMPROVISATIONS ON A KNOWN MODEL

THE FREEDOM OF *REYONG NOROT*

REACHING FOR AN INSIDER'S LISTENING EXPERIENCE

I first met the musicians of Sanggar Çudamani in the summer of 2003. It was the proverbial light at the end of my master's in ethnomusicology's thesis-writing tunnel: an eight-week trip to Bali to collaborate in the premiere of Michael Tenzer's latest composition, this one for two gamelan ensembles.[1] *We were six Canadians new to the island, happy to have Michael there to show us the ropes. Our first stop was Alit's family home: the sanggar's headquarters. With our suitcases in tow, our culture shock yet to set in, the Çudamani musicians treated us to glasses of Balinese coffee, plates of tasty, unfamiliar snacks, and the most outstanding gamelan performance we had ever heard.*

Watching gong kebyar played by Balinese musicians is transformative. Your senses are overloaded; you don't know where to look or what to focus on. Most of us sat on the tile floor facing the gangsas, their showy playing style holding our attention. But I noticed Alit's father Pak Dewa, who had quietly joined us, looking in the opposite direction. And following his gaze I saw, for the first time, what reyong norot *could be.*

A gangsa player likes a partner with solid timing who really feels the interlocking; when the gangsas are in the pocket, it's categorically satisfying. Playing reyong *goes deeper than that. The celebrated musician I Wayan Loceng once suggested that this was the hardest Balinese instrument to master. Alluding to the fearsome abstractness of the third position ponggang part, he asked, "How are you going to play all that music with just two notes?"[2] Yet like the improvised continuo accompaniment unobtrusively complementing the famous soloist, or the intricate patterns of the soft gambang xylophone buried beneath the Javanese court gamelan's louder bronze instruments, the reyong's improvisations are rooted in a specialist's knowledge only fully appreciated by those in the know. In the thick texture and often blinding speed of the gong kebyar, it is the lineaments of the reyong's norot figuration, the small perturbations in topography shaped by its collective improvisation, that excite the expert listener. While my friends looked the other way, enthralled by the louder, flashier gangsas, I followed Pak Dewa's lead. Together we took in the seeming nonchalance of Komin's dexterous playing in first position, the grinning confidence of his brother Ketut beside him.[3] I watched their mallets move across the instrument in elegant synchrony, Ketut's eyes never straying from his brother's face, his unabashed joy palpable. And seeing Pak Dewa's private smile as he sat there watching too, I felt I was somehow peering beneath the surface of the music. Being granted access to the secret code of its connective tissue, malleable and detailed. Listening where the expert listeners listened.*

SEEING BEYOND THE MODEL

In seeking a broader understanding of collective improvisation, I am fortunate that the *reyong* provides this restricted medium, so pared down it enables a microanalysis of the field of action verging on a vanishing threshold of comprehensiveness. Yet, though the scope of *reyong norot* is limited, the characteristic high speed of the music, the abstractness enforced by the very few notes each player has, and the ingenious vocabulary of options that has been invented against all odds combine to push musicianship to deep, nimble fusions of human engagement, feeling, and intelligence. A *reyong* improviser is in a kind of ultimate Balinese space: a finite realm in which we can closely examine wide-ranging concepts of improvisation. Instead of focusing on a single performance of a single piece—often necessary for the analysis of freer improvised genres like jazz or Hindustani *alap*—here I can make observations about the practice as a whole. I can delve with insight into this embodied cognitive-imaginative process, helping the reader to envision herself inside the hands and minds of these collectively improvising musicians, to begin to grasp how they reduce upwards of 1.5 million potential realizations for any two beats of music into a well-defined (and much smaller) subset of idiomatic ones.[4] Along the way, I project the general principles of my findings to other traditions.

Chapter 1 proposed four broad classes of improvisatory process: interpretation, embellishment, recombination, and expansion. Each is flexible enough to find purchase in most practices. Yet in order to identify and discuss these processes in relevant ways, our analyses of any performance must be framed in concepts of improvising and music-making from within its culture. Such insights may arise from diverse intellectual spheres, and part of the point of fieldwork is to hone in on those elements considered most important to the musicians themselves. In his *Unplayed Melodies* (2004), Perlman provided penetrating insight into cognition, theory, and practice in Central Javanese gamelan by beginning with a well-known, yet elusive, Javanese musical concept (the underlying melody, *balungan*) and referencing existing Javanese music theory. A very different kind of knowledge informed Feld's field-defining *Sound and Sentiment* (1982), which showed that the music of the Kaluli could only truly be grasped through an understanding of their natural and spiritual worlds. Different again were the fruits of Monson's fieldwork among jazz rhythm section musicians, where guided interviews revealed a rich oral music theory. The oft-used metaphor of jazz as conversation, for instance, situates Monson's analyses in a realm of interaction where musicians not only play off one another's musical ideas but also use musical allusion and quotation to converse with past performances. And within that social framework, each instrument performs specific roles in the collective whole. The function of the bassist, for instance, "is to ascertain the pulse, the harmony and rhythm all in one.... The rhythmic-harmonic pulsative path that the bass takes serves as a guide toward whatever improvisation . . . is to occur at the time" (Cecil McBee quoted in Monson 1996, 29–30). Such ethnographic insights determined the trajectory of Monson's analyses.

Understanding musicians' expectations of themselves and their partners, then, is vital to a faithful analysis of any collective improvisation, and both formal and informal music theories provide a sharper lens through which we can endeavor to see the music as our teachers and collaborators do. Sum (2011) positions her analyses of improvisation in Gnawa *lila* performances in a discussion of musician *intent* that compares sacred and secular functions and differentiates insider categories of accompaniment and solo playing. Ferreras's 2005 analyses of improvised drumming in Puerto Rican *bomba*, by contrast, consider various regional styles and substyles, motives suggested by improvising dancers, venue type, and so on. And in his studies of variation among Central Javanese gamelan performers, Sutton (1993) hones in on ways that improvisation is shaped by ensemble type, differentiating approaches for specific pieces, instruments, performances, and musicians. While there are multiple fruitful ways to examine and understand any practice, we often need to focus our lenses differently to assess the same things. And only through discourse with musicians can we find culturally appropriate filters. In my musical analysis of *reyong norot*, Balinese concepts of stasis and motion and additional interlocking techniques introduced in the previous chapter, as well as a knowledge of the idiosyncrasies of popular gamelan melodies and a grasp of the complex concept of *wayah* (which will be discussed), are all indispensable pieces of the puzzle.

When diving into the collective improvisations of *reyong norot*, the devil is in the details. These musicians, like *kendang arja* drummers, Shona mbira players, or Aka polyphonic singers, begin with a template for formulaic variation that establishes certain specific requirements and expectations: a model meticulously designed to interlock.[5] Unlike the jazz singer freely scatting over the sparse changes of a 12-bar blues, or the sitarist improvising an *alap* guided by broad schemas of pitch and contour, *reyong* players work from a limited pitch palette in a strict rhythmic idiom, bound musically to the contour of the core melody and aesthetically to the *norot* oscillation. Kin to the *gendér wayang* improvisation examined by Nicholas Gray (2010), where pairs of musicians extemporize on relatively specific melodic models, "the impression is one of a stable framework with micro-changes" (238). Within such a closely contained musical field, creating continually varied patterns demands a subtle use of improvisational techniques given much more latitude in other genres. Careful alterations on a note-by-note basis, almost too fast to catch, create ripples in a constantly shifting landscape, a pattern of raindrops on the surface of a lake. The analyses to follow are detailed and specific, designed to establish categories for a *reyong* player's moment-to-moment deviations from the model in the context of the improvisatory processes established in chapter 1.

The categories I propose, as with David Locke's of Ewe drumming (1998), are my own creation: an "active intrusion of [an] ethnomusicologist, who states, to the best of . . . her ability, what the variations and rules of occurrence are" (Herndon 1974, 248–49).[6] Yet tempered by fieldwork and performance experience, they emerged through the combined *rasa*, feeling, of many diverse insiders: a plural "views" of *reyong norot*.[7] This polyphony of voices has guided the course to answering my research questions:[8] what knowledge, aesthetic desiderata, and strategies enable *reyong* improvisers to weave nonstandard tones into the musical fabric of *gamelan gong kebyar*, tastefully subverting expectations? And can I identify and analyze these changes in terms of the four classes of improvisatory process? In other words, how do I distinguish patterns in seeming chaos?

INTERPRETATION

When alto saxophonist Lee Konitz described to Paul Berliner what he saw as different "levels of intensity" in jazz improvisation, the least radical departure from the model was *interpretation*. Berliner notes:

> At the outset of a performance, players commonly restrict themselves to interpretation. They reenter the piece's circumscribed musical world along the rising and falling path of a particular model of the melody, focusing firmly on its elements and reacquainting themselves with the subject of their artistic ventures. (1994, 67)

He goes on to describe the "minor liberties" a jazz musician might take in performing a model melody, freshly interpreting it through accentuation, articulation, dynamics, rhythmic phrasing, timbral effects, bends, blue notes, and so on. The model itself stays essentially intact, but, as clarinetist Louis deLisle Nelson notes, "you must handle your tone. . . . There are a whole lot of different sounds you can shove in—such as *crying*—everywhere you get the chance. But . . . with a certain measurement and not opposed to the harmony" (quoted in Berliner 1994, 68). It is easy to imagine such subtle alterations used in practices worldwide; they can be employed by any voice or instrument with flexible pitch or varied articulation techniques. A North Indian sarod player makes extensive use of pitch bends; like most Indian classical music performers, she will often not stay at a fixed frequency for more than a fraction of a second. A Balinese singer of *tembang macapat* works within a very wide timbral palette—from nasal to breathy to powerfully throaty—as a way to interpret emotion and character (see Herbst 1997, 25–37). And the various horn players in a funk band play with different articulations and accentuation depending on necessities of emotion and groove in any given moment.

Yet for the concept of interpretation to be truly cross-culturally germane, it must also be applicable to instruments with fixed pitches or minimally variable timbres, or to practices where variability in phrasing and dynamics is not idiomatic. How then do we interpret *interpretation*? Which musical characteristics in an unpitched percussion practice, for instance, may be subtly altered without markedly disrupting the model, which elements considered comparably variable? Again, fieldwork helps us discover what interpretation might mean in each practice. In chapter 1, we saw interpretation in Balinese *arja* drumming take the form of a free interchanging between main strokes and quieter subordinate strokes, an aesthetic that may be considered to parallel moment-to-moment shifts in dynamic or timbre. Similarly, a Cuban bongo player can interpret familiar rhythms in new ways by replacing one stroke type for another. And Ewe dance drummers interpret rhythms by both "variation by accentuation" and "stroke substitution": "altering the intensity/loudness of strokes without changing their timing or timbre [. . . and] changing the timbre of strokes without changing their timing. The motor pattern remains the same, but the shape of the rhythm changes" (Locke 1998, 48).[9] Interpretation on the *reyong*'s fixed pitches and timbres and its relatively strict dynamics and rhythms must be considered along similar lines: what musical elements can be idiomatically interchanged without disrupting the model?

A FREE INTERCHANGING OF ALLOWABLE NOTES: *KEMPYUNG* TONES AND RESTS

In the parallel *gangsa* figuration examined in the previous chapter, we saw *sangsih* ("complementary") players "harmonizing" their partners' melodies three scale tones up; the *dung-ding* (u-i) *norot* model (**U**)// A-U-A-**U**/ I-I-o-**I**// was realized by *sangsih* using the *kempyung* tones (**o**)// e-o-e-**o**/ u-u-a-u// (see figure 2.20). These parallel pitch options become even more important for *reyong* players because of their limited ranges, and a flexibility in their use, as we shall see, comprises a kind of *interpretation* of the model. We know that in a *dung-ding* (u-i) shift, first and third position players can use basic model notes for the first half of the pattern while employing *kempyung* tones in its second half; second and fourth position players will do the reverse. Yet model and *kempyung* tones are also frequently combined on a smaller scale, and different core melody tones necessitate different kinds of *reyong* interaction. First and second position *penyorog* and *pengenter* players necessarily sharing a (**a**)// i-a-i-**a**/ gesture, for instance, could each rest while the other played, performing (**a**)// _ a _ **a**/ and (_)// i _ i _/ respectively as *gangsa* players do. But they might also make use of *kempyung* tones in their ranges to fill out their elaborations, playing (**a**)// u-a-u-**a**/ and (**e**)// i-e-i-**e**/ respectively, per figure 3.1.

To further expand their palette, *reyong* players also frequently make use of the *kempyung* three scale tones *below* model notes, as shown in figure 3.2.

When I asked Alit why *kempyung* below could be used for *reyong* but were not employed by *gangsa* players,[10] he answered simply, "because it's *reyong*"; its players just follow a different set of constraints. Thus, in the same (**a**)// i-a-i-**a**/ melody, the first position *penyorog* player could replace the *ding* (i) outside his range with its lower *kempyung*, *deng* (e), playing (**a**)// e-a-e-**a**/. Or he could

FIGURE 3.1. Using *kempyung* on *reyong*

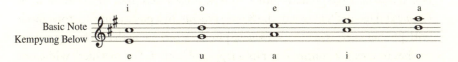

FIGURE 3.2. *Kempyung* below

FIGURE 3.3. Combining model notes with *kempyung* on *dang* (a)

elect to combine *kempyung* above and below with model notes, playing either (**a**)// u-a-e-**a**/ or (**a**)// e-a-u-**a**/.[11] Alongside solfège notations in figure 3.3, these variants are shown with "m" indicating model notes, "h" indicating *kempyung* above or higher *kempyung*, and "b" indicating *kempyung* below. The lower staves in each example show all three available tones for every subdivision, indicating selected tones with a black notehead.

I see these subtle, surface-level individualizations that yet do not diverge from the basic knowledge base as interpretation. Such techniques are common improvisational options on fixed pitch instruments. As previously noted, mbira players frequently interpret melodies by adding right index-finger harmony tones above basic right-hand thumb tones, or completely replacing those thumb notes with higher finger notes.[12] And *kemypung*-based interpretation has very close parallels in Central Javanese gamelan. This is particularly true of the *imbal* techniques used by its *saron* metallophones and *bonang* gong chimes, where musicians employing interlocking to "creat[e], or ad[d] to, the excitement of the piece" (Sumarsam 1984, 285) can often spontaneously choose between two or three predetermined tones. Brinner describes *imbal* between the *bonang* and its smaller cousin, the *bonang panerus*, in a piece using a 5-tone mode with pitches 1-2-3-5-6:[13] "Two *bonang* pitches alternate with two *bonang panerus* pitches to create a continuous rapid ripple of sound. For instance, while one plays pitches 1 and 3, the other plays 2 and 5 (or reverses the order to 5 and 2) in between, resulting in the melody 1235 or 1532" (2008, 69). Two *saron* players may similarly elaborate the core melody by interlocking in a strict back-and-forth *imbal*, each repeating a single note several times in succession, with the off-beat musician playing the note above the on-beat one like a strict *norot*. Yet the on-beat player can somewhat freely substitute the note *above* the off-beat player, changing (1)-2-1-2-1 to (1)-2-3-2-1, for instance. At the same time, her partner can select instead either the note below that basic pitch, in this case the low 6 just below pitch 1, or the one above the variant note, here the high 5 above pitch 3.[14] This collective interpretation of the core melody creates a large variety of possibilities, each generating a unique melodic contour in the moment.

As if constantly juggling three different note possibilities at high speeds was not complex enough, the improvised *Teruna Jaya* passage in the previous chapter (figure 2.21) demonstrated that *reyong* players, though not remotely *metrically* flexible, do have more rhythmic freedom than their *gangsa* counterparts. Rather than playing running 16th notes or sticking to formulaic rhythmic patterns, they freely combine the notes in their ranges with rests. Locke (1998, 61–62) notes the same technique at play among Ewe dance drummers, a process he terms "variation by subtraction."[15] On *reyong* such variation is done partially for practical reasons: constantly playing with one mallet while damping with the other is a difficult technique to sustain, particularly at fast tempi. Yet it is as much done for reasons of variety and thus employed in slower passages also. For a (**u**)// a-u-a-**u**/ contour, the *penyorog* musician in first position could play all model notes, or combine these with the *kempyung* in her range, replacing *dang* (a) with *deng* (e) for a (**u**)// e-u-e-**u** contour. But she would as likely replace one or more of these notes with rests in a variety of interpretations, as in figure 3.4.

Researchers of instrumental traditions across sub-Saharan Africa, from the Shona mbira to the *enanga* harp of the Baganda people, often discuss the phenomenon of *inherent rhythms*: melodic or rhythmic patterns that emerge from the

FIGURE 3.4. Incorporating rests in *norot* improvising

FIGURE 3.5. Inherent patterns

texture through a perceptual recombination of notes in different streams.[16] This concept is particularly germane to collectively improvised polyphonic musics. By cognitively grouping together notes in similar ranges, a listener will often "perceive the melodic parts of a piece differently from the way they are actually played by the performer" (Berliner 1993, 129). Rather than hearing the wide, leaping melody of an mbira player as a single entity, a listener's mind will combine those notes from an mbira pair that fall in similar ranges, creating "a conflict of other rhythms, which are not played as such but arise in his imagination.... The listener does not add any notes, but their grouping in his perceiving mind is often different from the grouping in the musician's hands" (Kubik 1962, 33).[17]

A similar effect is created when *reyong* performers interpret the *norot* model by inserting rests into their patterns, leaving space for another musician's notes to be heard in combination with their own. We know that a (**u**)// a-u-a-**u**/ contour falls within the ranges of the first and third position players while the second and fourth control the *kempyung* above: (**o**)// e-o-e-**o**/. When teaching the UBC *reyong* players *norot* for this contour, Alit had the third position *ponggang* sounding (**u**)// a-u _ **u**/ while the *pengenter* to her left struck (_)// e-o-e _/. The combination of these patterns created space for two distinct inherent melodies to emerge, shown with full noteheads in figure 3.5. If paying attention to the third player's range, a listener would hear (**u**)// a-u e **u**/; one focused on the second would hear (**u**)// e-o-e **u**/.

ANALYZING IMPROVISATIONS ON A KNOWN MODEL · 97

IDIOMATIC GUIDELINES FOR INTERPRETATION

At any given moment, then, a *reyong* player has four options that completely abide by the *norot* model and knowledge base, enabling a large variety of alternatives for any core melody motion: she can play the model note, play the *kempyung* above, play the *kempyung* below, or rest. This ostensibly leaves only two "rule-breaking" options: sounding one of the two remaining notes of the 5-tone scale. Yet a knowledge base in *reyong norot* imposes additional constraints.

Successful improvisation, as we know, lies far beyond any one set of guidelines; there are countless ways to play unidiomatically while apparently "following the rules." Even more complex, as Kippen notes in his study of North Indian tabla patterns, are instances "where an informant says of a variation: 'well, it's not exactly wrong, but I don't think it's very good!'" (Kippen 1985, 10). When Lee Konitz via Berliner established the concept of *embellishment* on jazz standards, for instance, he endorsed ornaments like grace notes and mordents as well as flexible timing and creative pitch substitutions. Yet though these are all idiomatic embellishments, they cannot be played in any manner on any note of any piece; a knowledge base in jazz helps a player decide how, when, and how often to employ these devices to greatest effect. Similarly, knowing how to use *recombination* in appropriate ways necessitates "learning how stylistic elements interact with one another in time [. . . by discovering] transitional probabilities [between diverse musical elements] that reflect the likelihood that a given event will follow another event" in idiomatic performance (Berkowitz 2010, 69). Sanguinetti (2012), therefore, prefaces his exhaustive study of the rules of *partimento* improvisation with a warning: whether or not the *partimento* is figured, one cannot make assumptions about which chord to play above any bass note without understanding its larger musical context, and even the simplest rules are rife with exceptions and conditions.[18] Like all pieces designed for improvisation, *partimenti* "are only potential musical works. Played as they are written, they make no musical sense; their implications need to be unfolded in order to become real music . . . they need to be completed by the performer" (Sanguinetti 2012, 167). In much the same way, strictly following the *norot* model on *reyong* will often generate unidiomatic patterns. Alit claims that teaching *reyong* musicians how to play *norot* directly from the *gangsa* model, "even if it's the right notes," would "make them stupid. I don't think Balinese people are taught that way," he opines. "It's not flexible."[19]

Thus, a model and knowledge base, once established, often need to be refined with a second layer of guidelines. Returning to the improvised passage from figure 2.21 will clarify how I have done this for *reyong norot*. The guidelines outlined here are based on transcriptions and analyses of this and other passages as well as my own embodied experience gleaned through years of listening, lessons, performance, and immersion. Five additional parameters delineate the appropriate nuances of *norot* interpretation.

First, while musicians commonly play a note twice in succession, the same note is never played three times in a row. In the *Oleg* melody's *dung-ding* (u-i) shift, where the first position player controls model tones (**u**)// a-u-a-**u**/ in the first half of the pattern and higher *kempyung* tones / u-u-a-**u**// in the second half, rests or *kempyung* below would be employed to avoid the three successive *dung* (u) of a (**u**)// a-u-a-*u*/ *u*-*u*-a-*u*// realization. Second, and in a similar vein, *reyong* players almost never rest for longer than one subdivision, as much as anything else because this interrupts the kinesthetic running 16th notes of playing and damping so central to rhythmic accuracy at high tempi. (If a player rested for two subdivisions in a row, her hands would cease to move on the second one). This sort of disruption makes fast playing far more difficult and is almost always avoided. In the improvised passage in figure 2.21, exceptions to this guideline from the fourth position player reveal his age and level of experience. A younger player than the other three, he is still struggling with *norot* improvisation and his hesitance and mild faltering are clear in the video.[20] More experienced *reyong* players will generally avoid successive rests completely.[21]

Third, it is rare for a musician to play all eight notes of a single 2-beat cell. Although the moderate tempo of this performance allows the musicians to play many notes in a row, each 2-beat cell in the excerpt contains at least one rest, allowing the *calung*'s core melody tones to be better heard.[22] Fourth, while *kempyung* harmony tones can be freely used, rests are somewhat more common in ranges using *kempyung*, particularly on strong beats. In cells from the improvised passage on *dong* (o), for instance, the first and third position players avoid playing on the beat completely, saving their *kempyung* tones for off-beat gestures. This judicious use of *kempyung* indicates some preference for allowing model notes to ring through.[23] And finally, rests in all ranges are common on structurally important beats, allowing slower streams in the texture to come to the fore. As Alit avers, it is vital that the *reyong* not "get in the way" of important structural markers like gongs or slower-moving core melody instruments.[24]

These five guidelines—no triple note repetitions, no double rests, very few full cells, more rests in ranges using *kempyung*, and a preference for rests on structurally important tones—help musicians shape idiomatic *reyong norot* improvisations without yet truly diverging from the model. A handful of Alit's improvised patterns in figure 3.6 exemplify the reasonably free interpretation that this refined knowledge base allows. Again, transcriptions are marked with "m" for model tones, "h" for higher *kempyung*, and "b" for *kempyung* below. In this and other musical examples, the core melody is labeled using its Balinese name, *pokok*.

As the patterns under analysis become increasingly complex, the reader need not get overly bogged down in which model-abiding tone is used at any given moment to appreciate the wide variety of contours this interpretive process generates. Constantly switching among three pitch alternatives in *norot* does not require radical conceptual shifts. Experientially this process is similar to oscillating between two closely related triads on successive 16th notes, freely making a melody with any of their three pitches. While there are more and less creative ways to craft a melody thusly, an experienced player does not switch cognitive contexts when interchanging model tones and *kempyung* any more than when shifting from root to third to fifth in two alternating chords; a choice of tones simply enriches her musical palette.

FIGURE 3.6. Improvised patterns using model tones, *kempyung*, and rests

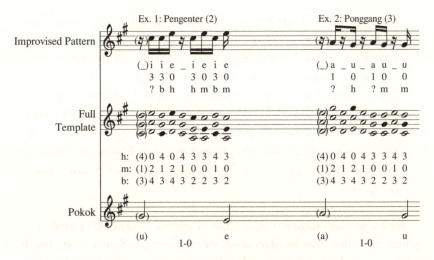

FIGURE 3.7. Improvised cells with nonstandard tones

Thus, through interpretation alone, a *reyong* musician has a myriad of possibilities for any given 2-beat cell of music; taken together, the four available options in each subdivision constitute a more dimensional *norot* template. Only two pitch classes in the gamelan's scale fall outside this template; the scalar neighbors above and below each model tone may be considered nonstandard notes. Yet generously peppered through Alit's improvisations, and those of other musicians, are nonstandard tones of every pitch, on every subdivision, in every melody, at every position on the *reyong*. Figure 3.7 shows a pair of patterns that diverge from the model in various ways to be discussed, their nonstandard tones notated with question marks.

With careful comparative labeling, connections between improvised patterns can be seen, and isolating divergences is simplified. As a result, the task of discovering the function of nonstandard notes and gestures, and thus the expanded knowledge base that guides them, becomes that much more manageable. I puzzle out these more radical departures from the model in terms of embellishment, recombination, and expansion.

EMBELLISHMENT

Chapter 1 established the term *embellishment* to describe slightly larger digressions from the model that include flexible timing, idiomatic ornaments, and creative pitch substitutions. As Berliner notes, in jazz:

Even at the level of subtle embellishment, unique patterns of imagination lend a distinctive character to each artist's practices. A player can append grace notes to the melody's important pitches.... Some routinely favor the use of a single ascending chromatic grace note at the beginnings of phrases, but others use the same embellishment only sparingly or favor descending grace notes.... Inventive pitch substitutions, and occasional chromatic fills added between consecutive melody pitches, are also common. Additionally, soloists can rephrase the melody subtly by anticipating or delaying the entrances of phrases or by lengthening or shortening particular pitches within them. (1994, 69)

Again, we can imagine similar kinds of embellishment being used in many genres and styles, from Sundanese *suling* flute playing to flamenco singing, Irish fiddling to rock 'n' roll guitar solos. But how can we talk about flexible timing or rhythm-based ornaments in practices where models are rhythmically restricted? Moreover, what constitutes an idiomatic "inventive pitch substitution" in any practice? Examination of flexible timing, ornamentation, and creative pitch substitutions in *reyong norot* elucidates how these questions can be answered through a combination of fieldwork, playing experience, and transcription.

FLEXIBLE TIMING

Rhythmic flexibility is central to embellishment in many improvised practices, from the rubato of a jazz ballad or the elaborate improvised rhythms of a Central Javanese *gendér* performer to the unmetered quality of a Hindustani *alap* or Egyptian *taqsim*. Such flexibility, however, must be differently conceived in genres like Balinese gamelan where all but a handful of solo instruments follow fixed rhythmic idioms. In interlocking melodies, as we've seen, consistent onsets at the minimal rhythmic value are the norm (running 16th notes, in Western notation). While flexible timing is a key feature of gamelan music at the ensemble level, where both subtle and dramatic tempo shifts create wavelike qualities, this freedom does not trickle down to the individual.[25] Given that fact, can I consider flexible timing an appropriate class of embellishment for *reyong norot* analysis? Framing the conversation in two central principles of Balinese music performance and reception—*rasa* (feeling) and the complex concept of *wayah*—reveals that Alit and other *reyong* players do indeed consider rhythmic flexibility idiomatic to *norot*.

RHYTHMIC FLEXIBILITY AS STRUCTURE MARKING

One of the first things I noticed in my one-on-one lessons with Alit was that he seldom began a *norot* melody together with gong, often preferring to rest. End-weightedness, I thought, explained this idiosyncrasy. Of course Alit would not begin on gong; that note belonged to the previous cycle. What perplexed me, however, was how often the note directly following this rest deviated from the model; Alit frequently sounded the tone he had skipped—the current core melody tone—in this subdivision purportedly reserved for a scalar upper neighbor. This technique is seen in the two patterns on the top staff of figure 3.8. Each is juxtaposed against their full template in the second staff, black noteheads indicating those pitch classes used in the improvised pattern, while the third staff shows the nearest template-abiding variant. Here and in subsequent musical examples, vertical gray bands and question marks highlight nonstandard tones, while asterisks mark other relevant subdivisions.[26]

The ubiquity of this technique in Alit's playing, and in the improvisations of other *reyong* players I watched, told me that this was a fundamental improvising idiom. But why did they do it? Alit often stressed that a gamelan's elaborating instruments should emphasize the gong tone, but that to do so simultaneously with gong was not good *rasa*, not good feeling. To trace a core melody with the gong tone *deng* (e), he notes, "it is good feeling to stop when the gong plays, and play *deng* after."[27] Accordingly, *reyong* players will often rest as the gong sounds, then play the gong tone late, as in figure 3.8. Thus does large-scale structure

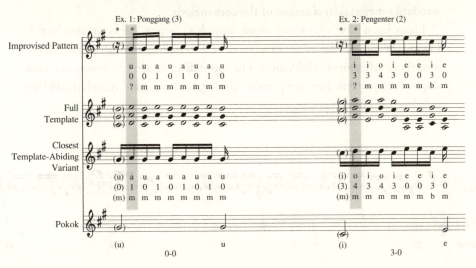

FIGURE 3.8. The effects of resting on gong (delayed unisons)

ANALYZING IMPROVISATIONS ON A KNOWN MODEL · 103

shape small-scale strategy; an aesthetic need to emphasize the gong tone without masking the gong itself creates this small ingenious change.

Yet this nonstandard usage is not reserved for gong tones alone; Alit often proceeds likewise for other tones of the *calung*'s half-note core melody. One early spring afternoon, while discussing the finer points of improvisation over a clove cigarette, he informs me: "sometimes you make *wayah* with the melody.... When *jegogan* [the whole-note core melody instrument] or *calung* go to *dong*, you go early to *dong*, sometimes late."[28]

"What do you mean *wayah*?" I ask, hoping this new word might shed some light on old questions. Little do I know I'm leaping head first down the rabbit hole of all rabbit holes. For most of my teachers, trying to translate this word is something akin to describing *love*: you just know it when you feel it. To dancer and scholar I Madé Bandem it relates to something "venerable," and Tenzer translates the term as "deep or profound."[29] Alit finally settles on the word "great."

Back in the gamelan room I initiate the conversation once more. "So, to make my *norot* more 'great,' I *shouldn't* arrive at the next core melody note with the core melody?" I ask, a bit confused. "Exactly," Alit replies. To clarify, he has me cycle a short melody on the *calung* as he sits at the *reyong* striking just my sparse tones. At first he plays precisely together with me, but he soon starts shifting his timing, arriving to my core melody tones slightly early or late. Then he puts the technique into practice. In the improvised excerpt in figure 3.9, Alit rests as the core melody sounds on four occasions marked with asterisks. He then strikes those core melody tones late, diverging from the template in the weak first subdivisions of the new cells. I think of these nonstandard tones as *delayed unisons* of the core melody.

I later learn how a yet more *wayah*, complex, pattern can be created by following these nonstandard tones with a rest, forestalling resolution back to the model one additional subdivision. The top staff in figure 3.10 shows one such improvised pattern. For comparative clarity, the associated template-abiding cell does not contain rests.

FIGURE 3.9. Delayed unisons, *Oleg*

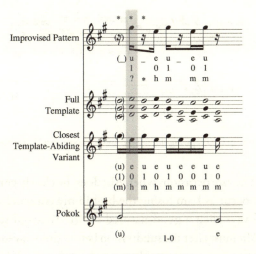

FIGURE 3.10. Delayed unison followed by a rest is more *wayah*

When Improvisation Inspires More Improvisation

Sometimes one improvisational choice implies or even necessitates another. A jazz soloist wanting to hint at an alternate chord in a set of changes, for instance, might need to differently conceive her melodic approach to or movement away from that chord. And returning to the head with a descending scale would first require bringing her improvisation into a higher octave. Likewise, each time Alit plays a delayed unison with the core melody, he needs to decide how to approach it. To further emphasize the nonstandard tone, he may choose to rest in the final strong subdivision of the preceding cell, as on the *calung*'s *dung* (u) in the first example of figure 3.11.

Yet a problem arises if he elects not to rest, as in the theoretical pattern in Example 2. We know that *reyong* players do not sound the same tone three times

FIGURE 3.11. The danger of delayed unisons

ANALYZING IMPROVISATIONS ON A KNOWN MODEL · 105

FIGURE 3.12. Preparing the delayed unison: upper-neighbor suspension

in succession. The rare occasions when Alit does, he clearly considers mistakes; they generally occur as I am losing the beat in my core melody playing, and they almost always elicit a good-natured scowl. To avoid such unidiomatic playing here, Alit must alter the subdivision before the delayed unison. He does this through *suspension*, repeating the preceding upper neighbor tone instead of immediately resolving it. Together with the delayed unison that follows, this upper-neighbor suspension creates a pair of doubled notes, circled in figure 3.12, that contrasts the strict alternation of the *norot* model.

Alit's description of flexible *wayah* timing, however, suggests that a *reyong* player may arrive at a core melody tone not only late but also early; just as there are delays there can be anticipations. Such a technique again requires multiple nonstandard tones. The musician arrives at the new core melody tone not in the eighth (final) subdivision of a cell, but in the seventh, where the upper neighbor tone is generally played. Essential to the pickup gesture, this latter tone cannot simply be removed; it is an aural marker of the new core melody tone to come. When Alit sounds the core melody tone early, he shifts the upper neighbor ahead to the sixth subdivision. He may follow these two nonstandard tones with a rest or create yet another note doubling with the end unit /0-1-0-0//. Figure 3.13 shows these two possibilities.

Alit can further vary anticipations or delayed unisons by incorporating rests or additional *kempyung* into his patterns, as in figure 3.14.[30]

EXTRAPOLATING IMPROVISATORY TECHNIQUES: STRUCTURE-MARKING GESTURES REVISITED

During our recording sessions, Alit would often stop in the middle of improvising and say "that one was very *wayah*," very great, or "that was more *wayah* than the last one." At the time I didn't understand; I was so concerned with my own playing that I wasn't truly taking in the subtleties of his improvisations.

But when I began transcribing, these comments revealed recurring patterns offering clues into *wayah norot* construction.

In the mid-1970s, linguists Walt Wolfram and Ralph Fasold studied the phenomenon of final stop deletion in consonant clusters—as in the omission of the *d* in the word *cold*—among Black residents in Washington, DC. Although

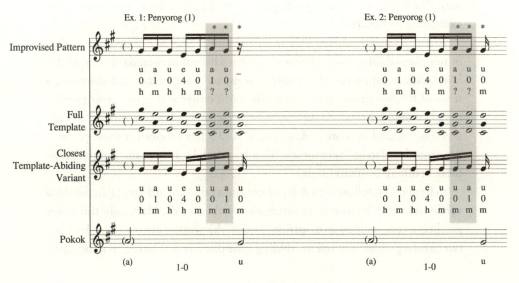

FIGURE 3.13. Core melody anticipation

FIGURE 3.14. Core melody anticipations with *kempyung* and rests

the incidence of deletion in different sentences initially appeared random, a pattern eventually emerged: the letters both preceding and following the final stop in question determined the consistency of its deletion. While only 25.2 percent of test speakers deleted their final stops after a nonsonorant and before a vowel, as in the first *t* of "lift it," 83.3 percent did so after a sonorant and before a consonant, as in the *d* of "sand castle" (see Wolfram and Fasold 1974, 104). The letters surrounding a linguistic variable, therefore, were essential in explaining its variation.

Analogies may be drawn here to Alit's musical language, where the pitches of template-abiding tones appear to govern adjacent nonstandard ones. In delayed unisons, upper-neighbor suspensions, and core melody anticipations, a sense of flexible timing is achieved when Alit either anticipates or suspends a template-abiding tone, disrupting *norot*'s regular pitch alternation with note doubling around the core melody onset. And when I looked at those patterns Alit considered to be "very *wayah*," they too used doubled notes. But they used them in different subdivisions.

In figure 3.15, following a delayed unison, a nonstandard *dang* (a) in the third subdivision may be seen as an *anticipation* of the fourth. Metrically this usage parallels a core melody anticipation, but on the weaker quarter-note beat between *calung* tones; a template-abiding tone directly on the beat is anticipated

FIGURE 3.15. Anticipation

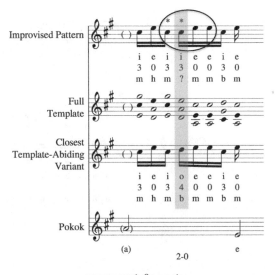

FIGURE 3.16. Suspension

through note doubling in the preceding subdivision. Alit similarly parallels upper-neighbor suspensions on these weaker quarter-note beats. In figure 3.16, a template-abiding *ding* (i) in the third subdivision is suspended into the fourth. Combining this gesture with the two *deng* (e) of the pickup gesture to follow (circled) parallels the two successive note doublings we saw in figure 3.12.[31]

Such note doublings can also be applied to the pickup gesture itself: an anticipation of its upper-neighbor tone changes the characteristic end unit /0-0-1-0// to /0-1-1-0// per figure 3.17.[32]

Alit's assertion that each of these patterns is "more *wayah*" helps to illuminate the concept. Greatness is about improvising a pattern that, unlike the models we learn at the beginning, subverts our expectations. It is a pattern that subtly breaks inherent rules governing accepted idioms to achieve a prioritized aesthetic aim, such as inserting note doublings into a practice built around strict single-note alternation. When comparing a *wayah* with a non-*wayah* pattern, I Wayan Sudirana claims that the latter makes a musician sound "*seperti anak kecil*" (like a small child); only advanced musicians play truly *wayah* patterns.[33] Similarly, a great jazz improviser or Hindustani musician is always seeking new ways to push the envelope, subverting listener expectations while still staying true to the fundamental idioms of instrument, tune or raga, and genre. As Miles Davis notes:

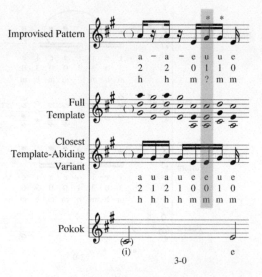

FIGURE 3.17. Anticipation of the pickup's upper neighbor

If you put a musician in a place where he has to do something different from what he does all the time, then he can do that—but he's got to think differently in order to do it. He has to use his imagination, be more creative, more innovative; he's got to take more risks. He's got to play above what he knows—far above it—and what that might lead to might take him above the place where he's been playing all along, to the next place he's going, and even above that. So then he'll be freer, will expect things differently, will anticipate and know something different is coming down. I've always told the musicians in my band to *play what they know and then play above that*. Because then anything can happen, and that's where great music happens. (1996, 243–44)

Alit makes great music by combining and recombining his various embellishment techniques, creating surprising patterns that seem to stand in complete opposition to the *norot* model's strict rocking motion. The first example in figure 3.18 shows a pattern made entirely of doubled notes. The first and eighth subdivisions demonstrate a delayed unison and upper-neighbor suspension respectively; the fourth tone is a suspension of the third. In the second example, a combination of high and low *kempyung* tones in the first half creates the note-doubling aesthetic of a suspension on *dang* (a). The pattern's second half exhibits three nonstandard tones; core melody anticipation in the sixth and seventh subdivisions is made more *wayah* with an upper-neighbor anticipation in the fifth.[34]

Analyzing Flexible Timing at Its Most Wayah

Both suspensions and anticipations can be obscured and thus made increasingly *wayah* through careful use of *kempyung* tones or rests. Alit will sometimes play what appears to be an anticipation, as in the first example in figure 3.19, but then rest in the subdivision that follows, per Example 2. Resolution to the template is forestalled and, like rests after delayed unisons, Alit considers this to be more *wayah*.

But should I consider this *wayah* pattern a kind of anticipation, despite its lack of note repetition? Alit's larger-scale improvisational logic can offer insight. In improvising traditions based in cyclic formulaic variation, musicians will often play similar variants back-to-back, changing small elements on each iteration. An Ewe drummer may begin with a known pattern then methodically alter it with ornamentation, accentuation, and stroke substitution over several cycles. A Karnatak singer improvising *sangati* (variations) in a *kriti* will often progressively modify the melody on each repetition to slowly reveal aspects of the raga (see Morris 2001).[35] And a Shona mbira player might shift between two known but relatively dissimilar versions of a piece over many cycles, gradually morphing from one to the other. In each case, the process reveals formulaic equivalences and variation techniques.

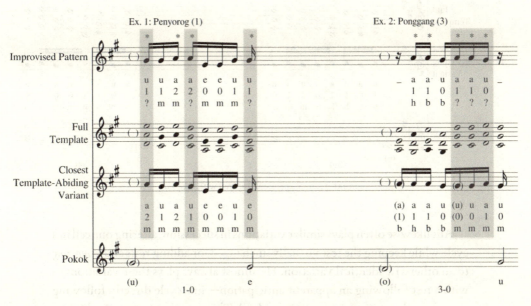

FIGURE 3.18. Embellishment techniques recombined

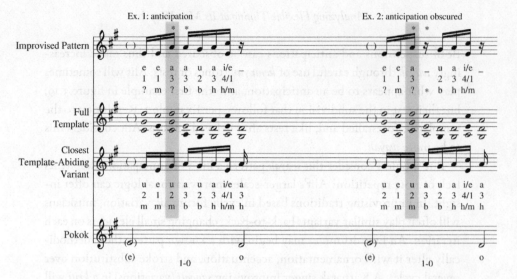

FIGURE 3.19. Anticipation obscured with a rest

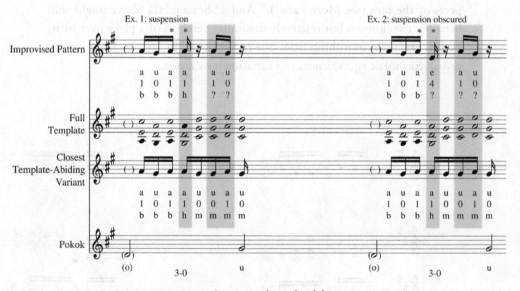

FIGURE 3.20. Suspension obscured with *kempyung*

Alit likewise often plays similar variations in succession, altering one cell in a cycle while keeping the rest virtually unchanged, or adding rests and *kempyung* to an otherwise identical variation. He almost always plays these variations—with a rest following an apparent anticipation—in a cycle directly following one where the same anticipation is resolved. This consistent proximity hints at equivalences between these patterns; although the essential "resolution" notes are not sounded, these more *wayah* gestures still *feel* like anticipations.

The suspension aesthetic becomes obscured in a different way when Alit combines model and *kempyung* tones in the suspension itself. The single non-standard *deng* (e) in the second example of figure 3.20 does not alter any of the surrounding tones, nor is it resolved through note repetition. But, as the higher *kempyung* of *dang* (a), this *deng* may be seen as the template-abiding suspension from Example 1 made more *wayah* through interpretation.[36] (These patterns also contain anticipations of the core melody, marked by wider gray bands.)

CONCLUDING THOUGHTS ON FLEXIBLE TIMING

Each of these embellishment techniques creates a sense of flexibility in a strict rhythmic idiom by incorporating doubled notes into a framework of one-to-one note alternation.[37] Figure 3.21 juxtaposes Alit's various flexible timing techniques, their new note-doublings marked with asterisks.

Category	Definition	Subdivisions Affected	Transcription	*Wayah* Variants
Model	Follows the *gangsa norot* model	n/a	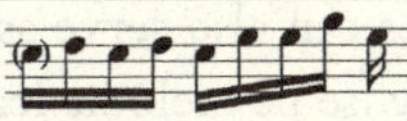 (8) 1 2 3 4 5 6 7 8	Add *kempyung* and rests
Delayed unison	Core melody tone one subdivision late	1st	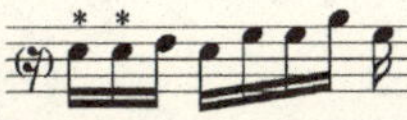 (8) 1 2 3 4 5 6 7 8	Rest in 2nd subdivision
Upper-neighbor suspension	Suspension of pick-up gesture's upper neighbor	8th	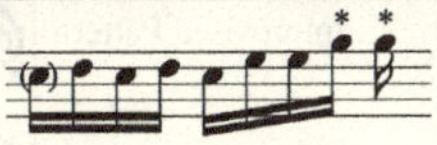 (8) 1 2 3 4 5 6 7 8	n/a
Anticipation of core melody tone	Core melody tone and preceding upper neighbor one subdivision early	6th and 7th	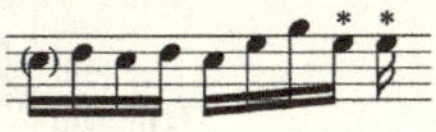 (8) 1 2 3 4 5 6 7 8	Anticipation before upper neighbor
Other Anticipation	Create note doubling by anticipating a model note	Variable, often 3rd or 6th, sometimes 5th	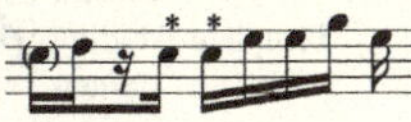 (8) 1 2 3 4 5 6 7 8	Rest on model tone, only play anticipation
Other Suspension	Create note doubling by repeating a model note	Variable, often 2nd or 4th	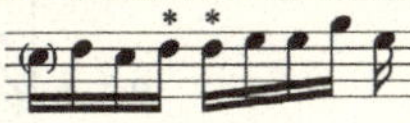 (8) 1 2 3 4 5 6 7 8	Combine model and *kempyung* tones

FIGURE 3.21. Embellishment techniques for flexible timing

These make up the lion's share of Alit's *norot* embellishments. However, he does also employ limited techniques of ornamentation and creative pitch substitution.

WHEN CATEGORIES ARE NOT A GREAT FIT: ORNAMENTATION

Comparative analysis relies on broadly applicable categories and concepts, and terms can often be reimagined to increase their usefulness. Yet it is also important to recognize when a category is not appropriate for a specific practice so that we don't risk flattening or misinterpreting some aspect of that practice through a square-peg, round-hole maneuver. The *reyong*'s strict 16th-note idioms leave little space for embellishment through ornamentation, as in the grace notes, mordents, and other jazz ornaments Berliner identified. It is a category that cannot (and should not) be stretched to accommodate most *reyong* playing. There are only two small ways that Alit incorporates ornaments into his *norot*, both through a limited use of 32nd notes. In one, the ornament takes the form of a neighbor-note mordent, separating two repeated notes as in the pattern in figure 3.22. This first position *penyorog* cell also features a delayed unison in the first subdivision and an upper-neighbor suspension in the eighth.

Ornaments can also serve as double passing tones, smoothing out what would otherwise be melodic leaps. The fourth-position *pemetit*'s 32nd notes in figure 3.23 help create a 4-note stepwise contour in three subdivisions. This

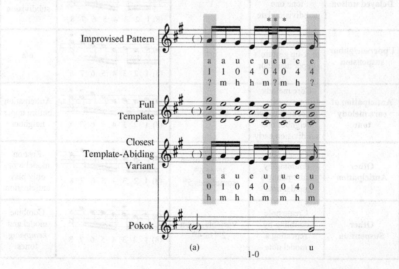

FIGURE 3.22. Ornamentation: mordent

FIGURE 3.23. Ornamentation: double passing tone

passage ends with an upper-neighbor suspension on the *calung*'s *deng* (e) and also contains three other nonstandard tones that can be categorized as either creative pitch substitutions or recombinations (discussed in later sections).

As in these two examples, Alit generally places his 32nd-note ornaments on the weak first or fifth subdivisions of a cell—those directly following the *kempli*'s quarter-note beats. As the only deviations from a strict 16th-note framework, these embellishments are prominently audible. However, they are relatively uncommon, and their importance to the practice should not be overstated.

CREATIVE PITCH SUBSTITUTION

Because of the limited pitch palette of *gong kebyar*, and the nature of the strict *norot* model, creative pitch substitutions are also relatively rare embellishment devices. With only five pitch classes to choose from, three of which are allowable through interpretation, it seems not that useful a category. However, when I began analyzing Alit's *norot* figuration, I discovered many instances in which two nearly identical variations differed in their weak first and third subdivisions, one or both of which were moved up a scale tone, as in the patterns in figure 3.24.

The two nonstandard *deng* (e) in the second cell are mysterious; like the very *wayah* suspension in figure 3.20, they alter none of the surrounding tones and

FIGURE 3.24. Creative pitch substitution

FIGURE 3.25. Interlocking with creative pitch substitution

are not resolved through note repetition. Nor do they borrow idioms from other gamelan interlocking techniques or play on elements of the underlying structure, as in the recombination and expansion techniques discussed further on. So when is it idiomatic to use these creative pitch substitutions, and how do they work?[38] While not a question Alit can answer directly, he offers insight in a different way: "when your partner plays here," he says, hitting *ding* (i), "you can't play here." He strikes the adjacent *dong* (o), then plays the two notes several times together on *gangsa* to underscore their clashing. "Others are OK," he concludes, striking *ding*'s lower *kempyung deng* (e) to illustrate.[39] If we extend the sentiment of Alit's claim—that one has a variety of options provided two adjacent clashing tones are not played simultaneously—the two nonstandard *deng* (e) in figure 3.24 become logical creative note substitutions. In *norot* on *ding* (i), a second-position *pengenter* musician playing (i)//o-i-o-i/ knows that his *penyorog* partner below him will likely play some variant of (_)//a _ a _/. Thus, playing (i)//e-i-e-i/ instead is a calculated risk. In either case, the pitch relationship with his partner remains idiomatic, as in figure 3.25. Only the harmonic flavor of the cell is altered, and this only on weak subdivisions. As Alit avers, "what's important is the destination: the *pokok* [core melody] or the [sparser] *jegogan*."[40] The path to this destination is unchanged by a creative pitch substitution that simply creates a brighter, more open dyad in the pattern's first few subdivisions.

From flexible timing and ornamentation to creative pitch substitutions, each of these embellishment techniques generates a small-scale adjustment of just one or two tones. Through processes of recombination and expansion, while still improvising at the note-to-note level, Alit is also able to make larger-scale structural changes.

RECOMBINATION

The idea of creating something new through the combination of familiar elements is long-standing and widespread. "We screw in light bulbs today because one of Edison's lab assistants saw Edison cleaning his hands with turpentine; when the inventor unscrewed the metal top of the metal can, the assistant had the idea of a screw-in lamp base" (Sawyer 2007, 110). Artistic creation works in much the same way. In his first-century histories of ancient Greece, Pliny notes that by Aristotle's time "all the literary resources required for composing a tragedy had been developed. Fourth-century [BC] tragedy was, according to this model, merely the variable recombination of all the given elements" (Tanner 2006, 243). A related concept gains traction in Europe through the second millennium, when the notion of *ars combinatoria* suggests "using combinatorial principles [to] create new knowledge through the combination of elements from the inventory of pre-existing knowledge" (Berkowitz 2010, 64). Through the seventeenth and eighteenth centuries, *ars combinatoria* becomes a popular approach for music pedagogy, as the idea of generating new music by idiomatically recombining existing musical elements finds its way into several treatises on improvisation (see Berkowitz 2010, 64–67).[41] Cowdery, in his work on traditional Irish song, refers to such musical elements "not as a fixed chain of events, but more a *system of potentialities*" (Cowdery 1984, 499, emphasis added).

This modular approach to a system of potentialities pervades improvised practices. In chapter 1, we saw improvising musicians with flexible schemas or multiple model patterns using recombination to mix and match their many options. Like the lead drummer in an Ewe dance-drumming troupe, Pak Tama in his *kendang arja* improvisations recombined small elements from multiple model patterns to generate new variants (see figure 1.5). He also used recombination on a larger scale, reordering these variants each time he played. Shona mbira musicians likewise recombine models learned from multiple teachers throughout a performance. Hindustani classical musicians, who must constantly keep in mind the musical and aesthetic restrictions of the *tala* or metrical cycle, "possess a number of long and short composed pieces (either handed down from their teachers or evolved during practice), which can then be introduced at the proper moment. These composed pieces, together with the beating of the tāla and a sound familiarity with both processes, enable the artists to improvise freely" (Meer 1980, 46). And jazz musicians mix and match prepared licks with freer improvisation and play off well-known riffs from famous performers. When asked "how he played 'those long, long lines that just keep going,' [jazz pianist Walter] Bishop [Jr.] replied that it was 'easy really; you just string together lots of smaller melodies'" (Berliner 1994, 184).

Much as with interpretation and embellishment, recombination in each practice happens at different scales and through different techniques, and both ethnography and analysis can help illuminate each one's idiomatic methods. We have already seen recombination in *reyong norot* in the mixing and matching of numerous interpretation and embellishment techniques within a single phrase. But Alit also creatively recombines static with kinetic elements as well as incorporating techniques from alternate figuration styles into his *norot* improvising.

INTERCHANGEABLE AESTHETICS: STASIS AND MOTION

In the previous chapter, I showed how a core melody's kinetic quality shapes *norot* figuration; while a kinetic (*majalan*) cell uses the technique's characteristic pickup gesture, a static (*ngubeng*) cell does not. One of the simplest ways that Alit creates variety in *norot*, then, is by subverting this expectation, playing a static cell with a pickup gesture or a kinetic cell without one.[42] The two patterns in figure 3.26 each realize kinetic cells as though static, with no break from the regular neighbor-note alternation to anticipate the new core melody tone.

The examples in figure 3.27 combine rests, *kempyung*, and various embellishment techniques with static-kinetic switches to create more complex, *wayah*, patterns. The first example uses nonstandard tones in four of its eight subdivisions: the *dangs* (a) in subdivisions 1 and 8 are a delayed unison and upper-neighbor suspension respectively, while the *dung* (u) in subdivision 4 suspends subdivision 3. The fifth subdivision *dang* (a) forms a static-kinetic switch, its characteristic /1-0-1-0// contour obscured by the upper-neighbor suspension to follow. In the second example, a static pattern turned kinetic, Alit uses a

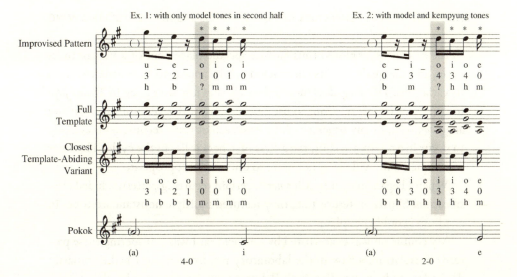

FIGURE 3.26. Static-kinetic switch

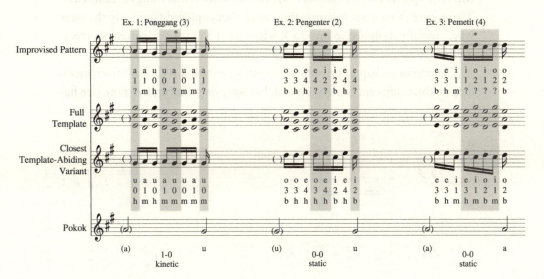

FIGURE 3.27. *Wayah* patterns with static-kinetic switch

fourth subdivision suspension, an eighth subdivision upper-neighbor suspension, and a static-kinetic switch with *kempyung* tones. In the static cell in Example 3, a suspension embellishes the pattern's first half, while the switch to a kinetic /o-o-i-**o**// end unit is further embellished with a core melody anticipation, generating /o-i-o-**o**//.

LIMITS ON HOW TECHNIQUES ARE USED: CROSS-FIGURATION BORROWING

In the categories explored thus far, the specific placement of a variant in its cycle, and the quality of its core melody shift, appear to have little effect on its variations. The *dung-dang* (u-a) shift occurring just after gong in *Teruna Jaya* has no more or less freedom to use suspensions or delayed unisons than any *dung-dang* cell, or any other 4-0 shift. And each of these techniques is as likely to occur in a 0-0 or 3-0 shift, regardless of where it lies in the cycle. This next technique, as we will see, is not quite so universally appropriate.

When I began analyzing Alit's *norot*, certain recurring patterns eluded classification. Shown in figure 3.28, they featured multiple nonstandard tones in an idiom I couldn't explain.

My confusion was exacerbated by the fact that I was considering these patterns in isolation, a flaw in the laboratory research setting I had necessarily devised to study *norot* with a single Balinese musician. It was only when I asked Alit how a partner could interlock with these patterns that things became clear. These weren't random variants; they were always played in exactly the same way, carefully designed to interlock with an equally specific pattern to create the composite melodies in figure 3.29.

The previous chapter introduced *empat*: a figuration style built from melodies on three adjacent tones with a higher *kempyung* "harmony" note (see fig-

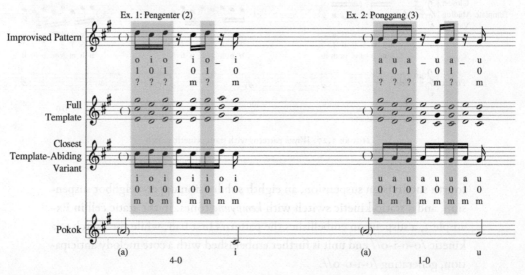

FIGURE 3.28. Unexplained nonstandard tones

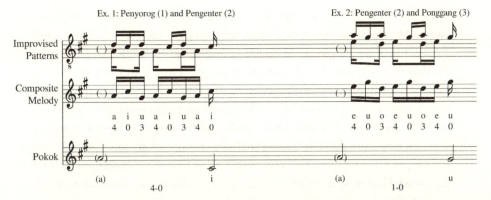

FIGURE 3.29. Unexplained nonstandard tones interlocking (*empat* substitution)

ures 2.2–2.4). The most basic composite melody for *empat* follows a //4-0-3-4/ 0-3-4-0// rising contour with the added tone 1 playing in parallel with tone 3. A closer look at the patterns in figures 3.28 and 3.29 shows Alit is not somehow varying the *norot* contour; rather, he is directly borrowing a cell of *empat*. This is something he does often in his improvising, as do many of the other *reyong* players I've watched. Yet there appear to be strict limits on when *empat* substitution is enacted. This recombination technique seems to be reserved for core melody shifts between adjacent scale tones, and only in cells leading either to gong strokes or to the whole-note core melody of the *jegogan* metallophones.

It their study of Brazilian *pagode*, Stanyek and Oliveira identify section-marking tactics they call "cadential variations." Instrumentalists may anticipate a cadence by playing comparatively elaborate figuration or, conversely, suspending the regular rhythmic flow through a "drop-out," or they may simply employ a pattern "used commonly at key structural moments" (see Stanyek and Oliveira 2011, 139–41, quote on 141). Whatever the chosen method, cadences in *pagode* are marked by a change and meant to be noticed. Alit's use of *empat* to mark gong or *jegogan* strokes similarly denotes structurally important moments through change. But why use this interlocking technique specifically? Part of the reason is simple. *Empat* substitutions follow a strict formula where a //1-0-1 _/0-1 _ 0// contour always interlocks with //4 _ 3-4/_ 3-4 _//. This absolute stability likely increases *empat*'s usefulness as a structural marker, a parallel to the use of common cadential formulas in *pagode*.

To understand the other possible reason for using *empat* as a structural marker, I return to the concept of *rasa*, feeling. Like many aspects of Balinese music, from the chosen gong structure to the specific drums being used, figuration styles each carry their own feeling. *Norot* is considered to be *manis*, sweet. Alit sees it as "romantic," "not very strong," and certainly "not good for a big man walking or a big demon. . . . *Norot* gives a different feeling for the dance from *empat*. The dancer [portraying a warrior] would think *norot* is not good spirit, not good feeling."[43] *Empat* figuration is constructed in rhythmic groups of 2+3+3, its [4-0]-[3-4-0]-[3-4-0] contour creating a cross-rhythm with the main beat. The continual tension and resolution of these 3-against-4 rhythms intensifies the flow leading to the next core melody tone, giving *empat* a strong *rasa*. By momentarily replacing *norot* with *empat*, musically substituting its neighbor-note alternation with *empat*'s prominent 3-note gestures, *norot*'s sweet feeling is temporarily replaced with a strong one. *Empat*'s combination of stability and strength, I hypothesize, leads Alit to use this recombination technique in structurally important moments almost as frequently as all other techniques combined.

EXTRAPOLATING THE *EMPAT* AESTHETIC

We have seen in these analyses how gestures developed with one function in mind may then be repurposed. The delayed unisons devised to bring important structural features to the fore generate note-doubling in a texture of otherwise strict alternation; this idiom then sets precedent for other kinds of anticipations and suspensions. The stepwise ascending gesture characteristic of *empat* substitution could be said to be another case in point. *Reyong* players will often make use of a variety of *kempyung* tones to reinterpret the characteristic kinetic pickup gesture with a similar aesthetic. The three improvised patterns in figure 3.30 show Alit combining lower with higher *kempyung* as well as model tones to create a sweeping stepwise approach to his partner's tone "o" (zero).

Kempyung in a static-kinetic switch may be similarly employed to create a stepwise ascending pickup gesture to a goal tone within the player's range, turning the 1-0-1-0 end unit into 4-0-1-0, as in the patterns in figure 3.31.[44] Note that, as a rethinking of aesthetics from other improvisatory types, these extrapolations may involve processes of expansion rather than simply recombination and interpretation.

Of the techniques examined thus far, *empat* substitution effects objectively the biggest change on the model. Affecting an entire cell of music at an important point in the cycle, it is as much structural as it is surface level. Through various expansion techniques, Alit creates more large-scale and structure-based *norot* improvisations.

FIGURE 3.30. Extrapolating the stepwise aesthetic of *empat*

FIGURE 3.31. Stepwise *empat* aesthetic in static-kinetic switch

EXPANSION

In chapter 1, we saw Hindustani musician Budhaditya Mukherjee improvising an *alap* through *vistār*: creating something new by "modifying, stretching, or extending" something that already exists (Perlman 2004, 29). The level of intensity Lee Konitz terms "improvisation" likewise sees jazz musicians "transforming the melody into patterns bearing little or no resemblance to the original model" (Berliner 1994, 70). Each of these is a kind of *expansion*. Because such approaches are often more extreme than other improvisatory processes, it can become necessary to examine expansion techniques on a case-by-case basis, analyzing each piece and performance for its own particularities, as did Hodson (2007) in his study of jazz interaction and interplay, Widdess (2011a) in his analysis of schemas in Hindustani performance, or Sutton (1993) in his detailed musical analyses of Central Javanese variation. That said, certain generalizations within individual genres can often be made, even at this level of transformation. While in schema-based exploration, expansion often involves developing and extending motives, or improvising on temporally distant pitch signposts, expansion in formulaic variation takes a different form.

THE ULTIMATE FREEDOM OF STASIS

We have seen Alit mix and match multiple techniques of interpretation, embellishment, and recombination in a single cell, creating complex variants on the *norot* model (see, e.g., figures 3.18 and 3.27). Such freedoms, he claims, are even greater in static cells, where the underlying stability provides a framework of predictability on which a player can improvise more radically. When the core melody "is *dung* and goes to *dung* again," he notes, "you can go where you want in the *reyong*, like, make melody from your heart, with your partner. Because if you practice with your partner you will have the same feeling. You know you will go to *dung* again . . . you have a long way to go to *dung*. . . . You have more improvisation with *ngubeng* [stasis] because it is very easy to feel just one note."[45] Berliner has observed the same freedom among jazz musicians. He notes that some of the wildest improvisation occurs "in such static areas of tunes as rests or sustained pitches at the ends of phrases" as well as in freely added introductions and cadenzas or "short 'break' passage[s], during which the other players suspend their performance" (Berliner 1994, 70). Not tied to a kinetic harmonic or melodic progression in these time spans, a jazz improviser has even more freedom.

The *dung-dung* (u-u) static cells in figure 3.32 demonstrate this same freedom of structural statis on *reyong*. Particularly noteworthy is Example 3, where Alit has actually extended the third-position *ponggang* range to *ding* (i). Usually reserved for the fourth-position *pemetit* player in all but *norot* on a *dong* (o) core melody, this usage (marked with asterisks) prioritizes practiced communication between partners, particularly at high speeds.

PLAYING WITH THE UNDERLYING STRUCTURE

To credibly analyze variations on specific elements of any language, one must first be familiar with its wider characteristics. In order to make salient observations about speech patterns among DC's Black residents, Wolfram and Fasold

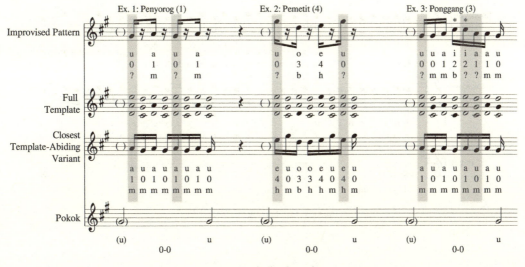

FIGURE 3.32. The freedom of stasis

first needed a foundation in the language standards of English pronunciation. Similarly, knowledge of the larger structural aspects of *gong kebyar*'s musical language adds meaning to Alit's techniques of expansion in *norot*, the modifying or stretching of which often occur at the level of the core melody. We learned in the previous chapter that elaborating instruments like *reyong* and *gangsa* base their figurations on the core melody, converging with the *calung*'s tones every two beats. Yet, though central to *gong kebyar* performance, this is only a partial truth. Sometimes a composer will specify a more static figuration that has elaborating instruments shifting to new core melody tones less frequently, lining up with the *jegogan* every four beats for instance. This structural flexibility in fixed figuration carries over into *norot* improvisation.

DECREASES IN PERCEIVED STRUCTURAL MOTION

Oftentimes in our lessons, Alit would tell me things I didn't understand at the time, but which proved insightful when examining his improvisations. One such cryptic clue emerged as we worked one day on a core melody containing a (i)-o-a-u-i progression. Alit was playing at the *reyong*'s second position when he told me "sometimes you can just stay on *ding* (i) and *dong* (o) instead of going to *deng* (e)." He then played the two realizations in figure 3.33.

FIGURE 3.33. "Staying on *ding* and *dong*"

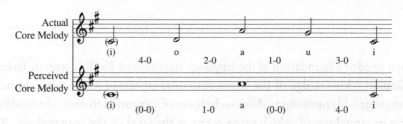

FIGURE 3.34. Actual versus perceived core melody

Alit's first variation adheres almost perfectly to the template, combining model notes, *kempyung*, and rests with a core melody anticipation leading to *dong* (o), a delayed unison on *dung* (u), and a static-kinetic switch leading to *ding* (i). The second pattern, staying on *dong* (o) and *ding* (i) as Alit suggested, is more problematic. It seems far too static. But what if we imagine that Alit is tracing a sparser core melody that only shifts every four beats, per figure 3.34?

Seen in this light, the second example in figure 3.33 makes perfect sense. The first cell is simple static *norot* on *ding* (i), while the next leads idiomatically from *ding* (i) to *dang* (a). The following two beats are more subtly static, Alit's varied use of *kempyung* and rests crafting a slightly less repetitive contour. But again, instead of a kinetic progression from *dang* (a) to *dung* (u), Alit plays a static cell on *dang* (a). The final two beats display the characteristic //1-0-1 _/ 0-1 _ 0// contour of an *empat* substitution, allowable now in the 4-0 shift from *dang* (a) to *ding* (i). This new interpretation is shown in figure 3.35.

INTENSIFICATION OF PERCEIVED STRUCTURAL MOTION

Just as Alit may imply decreased core melody motion through static elaboration of a kinetic melody, so too may he intensify perceived motion through increased core melody tone preparation. In figure 3.36, two first-position *dengdong* (e-o) cells played for the piece *Kebyar Jaya Semara* will elucidate.

While the first example is template-abiding, the second shows three nonstandard tones not easily explained. But the quarter-note core melody for this piece, played by the *penyacah*, offers fresh perspective. An 8-beat melody

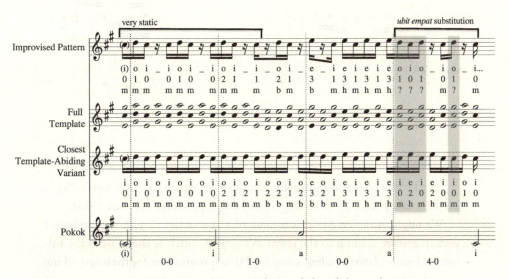

FIGURE 3.35. Improvisation on perceived core melody with decreased motion

FIGURE 3.36. "Rule-breaking" in *Kebyar Jaya Semara*

FIGURE 3.37. *Kebyar Jaya Semara* melody for increase in perceived core melody motion

FIGURE 3.38. Interlocking with increased core melody motion

repeated twice over a 16-beat gong structure per figure 3.37, it features *ding* (i) on the weaker beats between *deng* (e) and *dong* (o) (marked with asterisks).

We might now see Alit's nonstandard a-u-a in figure 3.36 as a midpoint pickup gesture leading to the *penyacah*'s *ding* (i), much as the u-a-i in the following beat leads to the *calung*'s *dong* (o). His improvisations for the interlocking second-position *pengenter* support this interpretation. Close to 50 percent of Alit's realizations for this cell contain *ding* (i) in the fourth subdivision, as in the first example in figure 3.38. Seen from this perspective, the nonstandard a-u-a played in first position is simply tracking increased core melody motion, supported by his *pengenter* partner as in figure 3.38's Example 2.[46]

As with *empat* substitutions, Alit does not create perceived increases in core melody motion in just any cell; like in *Kebyar Jaya Semara* they generally occur directly before gong strokes. Intensification of activity before cadences or other important structural markers is common in many musical traditions, both composed and improvised. Sometimes it involves specific cadential formulas, as in the *tihai* and *mora* of North and South India. At other times, it is simply a matter of note density or activity. Many Balinese gamelan melodies are composed to be more static directly after gong and to become increasingly kinetic as the cycle progresses (see Tenzer 2000, chap. 6). A Karnatak singer improvising a *niraval* or *svara kalpana* will often intensify improvisation leading back into the familiar motive from the *kriti*, much as an *arja* drummer, as we will see in chapter 5, may increase main stroke use approaching a cycle's final gong. In each case, the musical choices "surrounding a cadence present an opposition of densities: intense activity leading in, followed by relative calm" (Stanyek and Oliveira 2011, 139). Again, a piece's large-scale structure determines the relative appropriateness of different improvisatory choices.

PLAYING ON A MELODY'S PARTICULARITIES

While many improvisatory techniques are broadly idiomatic to a genre or instrument and thus appropriate for use in any of its performances, some techniques are specific to individual pieces. This is most often true of expansion techniques. We know that Brazilian *pagode* instrumentalists, for instance, use standard cadential formulas and improvisatory techniques that cross pieces and performances. Yet improvising in this "radical reformulation" of samba also involves a constant negotiation between the live-ness of the *roda* events at which it is performed and the underlying influence of famous recorded performances. As Stanyek and Oliveira (2011) note of the *chamadas* or "calls" used to cue new sections of text: "in theory *chamadas* are improvised in the moment, but often, in practice, they are taken from the first (or most well-known) recording of a particular song; in other words, what was the meta-textual call of a soloist becomes so iconic that it literally becomes part of the text of the song" (110). Much like these calls remain bound to specific songs, certain expansion techniques in *norot* are only appropriate for particular pieces. Examinations of two piece-specific variants illustrate how *reyong* players tailor their improvising to the idiosyncrasies of individual melodies.

AMBIGUITY IN THE CORE MELODY

The first time Alit taught me the *Oleg* melody introduced in figure 2.11, he played not the commonly accepted contour with its *dung-dung* (u-u) static start, but an alternate version that opened with a kinetic *dung-dang* (u-a) cell. Both versions are shown in figure 3.39, the alternate melody on the bottom staff.

While his *reyong* improvisations generally tracked the standard (u)-u-i opening contour despite the fact that I was accompanying him with (u)-a-i, Alit also played on the ambiguity introduced by this variation. Its stepwise smoothing of a 0-0 and 3-0 shift into two 4-0 shifts, for instance, allowed the use of *empat* substitution leading to the *kempur* (P) stroke on *ding* (i), and Alit employed this variant more often than not at all four positions on the *reyong*. Figure 3.40 shows two improvisations of the melody's first eight beats. Interestingly, both trace the static *dung-dung* (u-u) start of the standard melody, only hat-tipping the alternate melody with their *empat* substitutions leading to *ding* (i). The first

FIGURE 3.39. *Oleg*'s alternate core melody

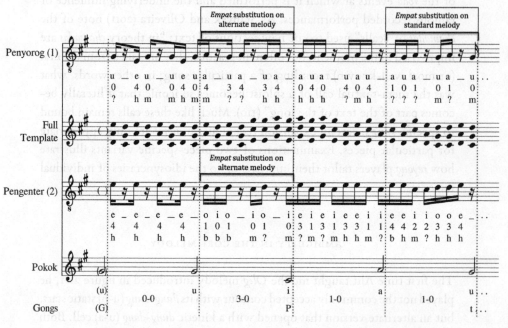

FIGURE 3.40. *Empat* substitution referencing *Oleg*'s alternate core melody

FIGURE 3.41. Parallelism in the core melody for Alit's new composition

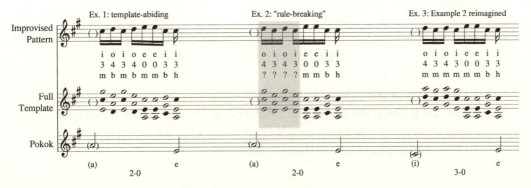

FIGURE 3.42. Improvising on parallelism in the core melody

position *penyorog* pattern on the top staff also features a second *empat* substitution in the 1-0 *dang-dung* (a-u) cell leading to the *klentong* (t) stroke.

PARALLELS IN THE CORE MELODY

Another piece-specific strategy for variation can be seen in a new composition that Alit created during our lessons. Its irregular 40-beat melody, shown in figure 3.41, features interesting almost-parallels: the tones from gong to beat 16 are almost repeated, but expanded, in the remaining 24 beats.

In his *reyong* improvisations, Alit plays on the melody's parallels, particularly the *dang-ding-deng* (a-i-e) contour in beats 12–16 and its parallel *dang-dang-deng* contour in beats 28–32. The first two realizations in figure 3.42, played for the *dang-deng* shift leading to beat 32, will clarify.

Where the first pattern uses only model tones and *kempyung*, the opening o-i-o-i of the second pattern is entirely "rule breaking" with no immediately obvious explanation. It is only when considering the cell in the context of the piece that we see the genius in what Alit is doing; this would be a perfect template-abiding pattern in the corresponding *ding* to *deng* cell leading to beat 16, per Example 3. By interchanging figurations for these beats, Alit may be commenting on the similarity between the two halves of the melody.

ANALYZING IMPROVISATIONS ON A KNOWN MODEL · 131

Clearly, while the categories described in the preceding pages can explain general strategies for *reyong norot* improvisation, musicians also develop techniques for commenting on the characteristics of individual melodies. Thus, as Sutton (1993) shows us, even genres based around formulaic variation must be considered in the context of specific pieces, performers, and performances.

A SUMMARY OF TECHNIQUES

Table 3.1 summarizes the many improvisatory techniques Alit uses in his *reyong norot*. Each affects the playing on a different scale—with its own particular level of freedom—and each creates opportunities to clash with partners, or, conversely, inspire change in their playing in turn.

Table 3.1 Techniques for reyong norot *improvisation*

TECHNIQUE TYPE	TECHNIQUE SUBTYPE	SPECIFIC PROCESS	SCALE OF CHANGE	SCALE OF FREEDOM
Interpretation	n/a	kempyung	1 subdivision, any location	small
		rests	1 subdivision, any location	small
Embellishment	*Flexible timing*	delayed unison of core melody	1 subdivision, 1st	small
		upper-neighbor suspension	1 subdivision, 8th	small
		core melody anticipation	2 subdivisions, 6th and 7th	small
		other anticipation	1 subdivision, various locations	small

(cont'd on next page)

132 · CHAPTER THREE

Table 3.1 (Continued)

TECHNIQUE TYPE	TECHNIQUE SUBTYPE	SPECIFIC PROCESS	SCALE OF CHANGE	SCALE OF FREEDOM
		suspension	1 subdivision, various locations	small
	Ornamentation	mordent	1 subdivision, 1st or 5th	small
		double passing tone	1 subdivision, 1st or 5th	small
	Creative pitch substitution	creative pitch substitution	1–2 subdivisions, 1st and/or 3rd	small
Recombination	*Interchanging stasis and motion*	static-kinetic switch	1 subdivision, 5th	small
	Cross-figuration borrowing	empat substitution	1 cell	small, aesthetic also extrapolated
Expansion	*Ultimate freedom of stasis*	freer in static cells	varies	large
	Playing with underlying structure	decrease in core melody motion	2 or more cells	large
		intensification of core melody motion	1 cell	medium
	Playing on a core melody	melodic ambiguity	varies	large
		parallels in core melody	varies	large

IN BROADER SCOPE: HOW WE MAKE IT UP TOGETHER

With few exceptions, the analyses in this chapter have focused on the strategies of individual musicians within a collective improvisation. But of course the thrill of collectivity lies in how co-performers come together, balancing individual creativity with group goals and shared agency. As David Borgo notes: "one of the particular joys of improvising music together is not knowing precisely the relationship . . . between one's actions and the actions of others" (2016, 93). Like ants "secretly communicat[ing] with each other, solving complex problems together," improvising musicians still "most often . . . appear to follow their own agenda" (91). This individual agency is part of what makes collective improvisation feasible; *reyong* musicians couldn't possibly react to every minutia of their partners' patterns at speed. While some moment-to-moment interlocking may be the result of real-time reactions, as Alit jokes, "by the time you think about *ding* (i), it's already too late."[47] Instead, these musicians understand their own boundaries and make idiomatic music together by playing within them, developing a group feeling, *rasa*, over time. The flexibility of their idioms means a *penyorog* musician can play *dung* (u) in first position, and the third position *ponggang* simultaneously play *dang* (a), without their coincidence being considered dissonant. Or the *ponggang* player can perform an *empat* substitution meant to interlock with the *pengenter* below her without him necessarily following suit. Like Ewe drummers or Shona mbira players improvising within the confines of their particular instruments' idioms, a *reyong* musician's range of possibilities is built to suit her partners'. The focus is less on the moment-to-moment interactions, too fast to control, than on the overall aesthetic of loose interlocking.

That said, close interaction and group *rasa* is what separates good *reyong* partners from great ones. It is the reason why Alit, while in Massachusetts in 2016, did not feel comfortable recording *norot* with other Balinese musicians in residence on the East Coast. All great players in their own right, their improvising would not have been *cocok*—suited—because they did not have a shared *rasa*. Each musician has preferred patterns and idioms, characteristic ways of reaching any musical "destination." Alit notes, for instance, that first position *penyorog* players generally approach *dung* (u) from above, creating a *ding-dang-dung* (i-a-u) contour with their partner. But "the old style in Pinda [village] comes from the low notes," he says, adding, "Komin plays that way too." Komin's brother Ketut, having played with him a long time, would anticipate this preference in a way other musicians don't, thus creating more satisfying connections in second position.

FIGURE 3.43. Improvised *reyong norot*, *Teruna Jaya* (analyzed)

These personal interactions and preferences are where music analysis alone falls short; analysis can provide explanations for idiomatic playing techniques but it cannot truly unpack cognitive process. As we've seen, interdisciplinary approaches are central to good analysis; combining ethnography with musical analysis and incorporating theories both anthropological and scientific gives us our best chance at a complete picture of interaction in collective improvisation. And while intent is difficult to ascertain even with ethnographically informed analysis, the varied musical interactions that emerge from these collective improvisations are relevant and compelling. Returning to the improvised *Teruna Jaya* melody from the previous chapter (figure 2.21), we can begin to understand how a *reyong* musician balances individual creativity with group cohesion. Figure 3.43 shows the first eight beats of the improvisation, now marked for analysis.

Each musician makes creative use of *kempyung*, rests, and nonstandard tones (notated as X-circles), tailored to his personal taste. Yet equally diverse are the ways in which the four players interact. In the first quadrant—a *dung-dang* (u-a) cell—players 1 through 3 work together to create a 6-note stepwise ascending approach to the core melody's *dang* (a). I Madé Supasta (Pasta) in second position begins the second-quadrant *dang-dong* (a-o) shift that follows with a simple oscillating (o)-e-o-e. This pattern is relatively unusual for its complete adherence to the *norot* contour on *kempyung* tones, where a player would generally incorporate a larger variety of notes and rests to contrast the model's strict alternation. I Dewa Putu Berata in first position begins by interlocking with *dung* (u) and *dang* (a), and might easily have stayed on just these two pitches through to the pickup gesture. Yet perhaps hearing Pasta's uncharacteristic approach to the cell, or perhaps simply by chance, he dips down to *deng* (e), coming into parallel octaves with his partner and further emphasizing this off-beat *kempyung* tone (circled). The two end the cell with the archetypical stepwise pickup to *dong* (o). In the third quadrant—a *dong-dang* (o-a) cell—the third and fourth position players blend model notes and *kempyung* to create 3-note *empat*-like gestures between those two tones, ascending to *dong* (o) at the cell's midpoint before descending to the core melody's *dang* (a).

While each of these shared motives intimates close communication between players, there are also times when the interaction works less well. In the final quadrant, Pasta in second position takes advantage of a 1-0 shift from *dang* to *dung* (a-u) to play the //4 _ 3-4/_ 3-4 _// contour of an *empat* substitution. Yet the third position player to his right does not do likewise; perhaps he is listening to the fourth player above him in this moment, perhaps he is simply doing his own thing. His chosen combination of nonstandard and template-abiding tones, instead of neatly interleaving //1-0-1 _/ 0-1 _ **o**//, results in a rhythm and contour completely parallel to Pasta's. In a style that prizes interlocking and leaving space for one's partners, this moment in the interaction is far from *wayah*.

Collective improvisation is inherently unpredictable because of its reliance on interaction; each performance is constructed intersubjectively, through the moment-to-moment combination of multiple simultaneous intentions. Sometimes it fails because "performers have to negotiate their intersubjectivity *while* enacting the performance" (Sawyer 2003, 10, italics added). Each *reyong norot* performer must interpret her partners' signs while simultaneously creating her own. The emergent process is a result of individual choices within a shared knowledge base, communicated in the course of performance to become group creation. Interaction is complex and imperfect, and this is part of what keeps the music fresh and exciting. As we will see in the second case study, these social and musical negotiations become yet more complex when each musician is working from a different, unconscious model for improvisation. First, however, I turn to a fuller exploration of collectivity in an attempt to understand the nuanced interactions that engender it and the cognitive and communicative processes that facilitate it.

CHAPTER FOUR

ANALYZING COLLECTIVITY

MODELS AND INTERACTIONS IN PRACTICE

KNOWING WHEN "THE RIGHT WAY" ISN'T

Don't be thrown by the enormous sign hanging from an upstairs window, its only English-language words loudly declaring "Vancouver Table Tennis Club."[1] This ragged orange building in the heart of Strathcona houses the Hastings Dance Studio. Walk up the narrow concrete stairs, past a dozen simultaneous ping pong games and a poster imploring "no dance shoes in the bathroom, please!" and you'll find the studio. This is where I've been taking flamenco classes for the last month and a half, and tonight, for the first time, we'll be dancing with live musicians. As I strap on my shoes, I see a small gray-haired man settle into a chair at the front of the room. A younger man, guitar case at his feet, sets up microphones.

Tonight we'll be dancing Soleá, a slow form in a 12-beat compas *or rhythmic cycle. After spending a month learning the choreographed partner dance Sevillanas, Soleá has been a chance to dip our toes into the improvisation so central to flamenco.[2] We've learned it as a kind of mild formulaic variation, where song structures and their associated dances are largely fixed, but a dancer may mix and match certain movement types within them. Our teacher Michelle has shown us several variants for the basic marking step* marcaje *and two different ways to emphasize a short break in singing with the strong stomps and claps of a* remate.[3] *We've also learned a dramatic series of movements called* llamada—*the call—that flamenco dancers use to cue important structural shifts. Over the last two classes, Michelle has composed a mini dance sequence for us. A perennial academic, I keep a checklist in my head as we dance, relating each movement back to the 12-beat* compas:

Step 1 · *Get center stage: 2* compas
Step 2 · *Dance in place using any* marcaje *(marking steps): 1* compas
Step 3 · Llamada *(call) to cue singer: 1* compas
Step 4 · *Singer begins. Marcaje for 8 beats*
Step 5 · *Singer pauses mid-phrase. 4-beat* remate
Step 6 · *Singer continues. Marcaje for 4 compas. End with 4-beat* remate

We've carefully memorized this sequence and hope the musicians will be suitably impressed. But there's one important detail about flamenco we haven't yet learned . . .

Steps 1 through 4 go precisely as planned. When the singer begins, we mark time for eight beats then execute our first remate. *Everything stops.*

"No, no, no," the singer chuckles, shaking his head and arching an eyebrow toward Michelle. She offers up a little shrug and the guitarist flashes her a wry smile. But the rest of us aren't in on the joke.

"So, remember how I said that flamenco is improvised?" Michelle explains. "This is what I meant. The song won't always stop in the same place; you need to listen to the singer to know where to put the remate.*" Her explanation is met with a sea of confused faces. "I'll show you," she offers, and the musicians begin again. While her movements are familiar—*marcaje, remate, llamada—*nothing happens exactly where we expect it to. Yet there seems to be an unspoken agreement between the three of them: a conversation we're sure they never had about where to increase intensity, stretch the tempo, place an unplanned* remate. *Both musicians somehow instinctively know where Michelle wants to take the dance, the guitarist's strumming patterns and singer's throaty melodies rising to meet an upraised arm or digging deep into an intense bit of footwork. At the same time, her movements seem shaped by the raw emotion of the song, the fluctuating strength of the guitar. The three of them reach new levels of grief, anger, power, and passion. Together.*

DEFINING COLLECTIVITY

We learned in the prelude to this book about the theory of distributed invention, where the most innovative technological developments and works of art are crafted not by a lone inspired genius but rather by the collaborative dynamic of social networks and creative teams. In a flamenco performance, each member of the ensemble knows the model and knowledge base on which she is improvising and each has a storehouse of favored licks, ornaments, elaborations, and so on. Yet when the group comes together, there is a give-and-take that cannot be preplanned. The singer must listen for the dancer's calls—*llamada*—to know when to enter the texture or move to a new section; the dancer must perform her *remate* in places that will enhance the song without overpowering it; the guitarist must alter his plucking and strumming patterns to match the intensity of the singer and the footwork of the dancer; and each group member must be sensitive to the idiomatic style, emotion, rhythmic density, relative metric flexibility, and motives of her partners. I knew from my time in Bali that *reyong norot* performers interacted in similar ways, though the two experiences also felt quite distinct. The sheer speed of the interlocking patterns I made with my *reyong* partners, for instance, necessitated relative independence in our moment-to-moment decisions. I *couldn't* draw direct inspiration from them in these note-by-note details the way a jazz soloist might in trading fours. Yet, given a second or two of lead time, I could react to a shift in intensity or groove, a cue from the *ugal*, or a larger structural transition. Although our playing remained separate in certain fundamental ways, we still shaped the performance collectively.

Most improvised practices rely at least to some extent on this kind of dynamic interaction between simultaneous improvisers. The *dabakan* drummer in a Philippine *kulintang* ensemble will "variegate" accents and rhythmic patterns to complement the *kulintang* soloist's level of ornamentation (see Onishi and Costes-Onishi 2010, 22). And while the musical roles in a standard jazz combo are often relatively fixed—a walking bassist, a "comp"-ing pianist, a soloing horn player, a drummer establishing meter and groove—performers flexibly negotiate their realizations. Coming to the table with a firm model and rich knowledge base is essential, but coming with a rigid plan, as I learned that day in the dance studio, will at best result in a lackluster performance and at worst end in failure. Performers in collective improvisations cannot only imagine their role as one of storytelling, personal and self-reflexive; they must blend *reflective* with *reactive* processes to engage in a conversation or embark on a journey with one another and with the audience.[4] As jazz bassist Cecil McBee observes:

> When we approach the stage . . . we are collectivized there. . . . This energy proceeds to that area and it says, "all right, I'm here, I will direct you and guide you. You as an individual must realize that I am here. You cannot control me; you can't come up here and say, 'Well, I'm gonna play this,' " . . . You can't go there and intellectually realize that you're going to play certain

> things. You're not going to play what you practiced. . . . Something else is going to happen . . . so the individual himself must make contact with that and get out of the way. (Monson 1996, 67)

While the idioms of each genre dictate how—and how much—an improviser influences her co-performers in real time, what emerges in each case is the kind of performance "governed by *relationships among performers*" that Pelz-Sherman terms *heteroriginal* music (1998, 9).[5]

I wanted an analytical model that spoke to the complexity of that experience. One that considered the very different ways that my *reyong norot* or *kendang arja* teachers and my flamenco teachers interacted in performance. But if I hoped to comparatively analyze collective processes across genres and cultures, I would need useful categories for analysis. In his close examination of polyphony, Tenzer (2018) asks: "how many ways can two sounds (or groups of sounds) be oriented with respect to one another in time? We can respond with a *typology*, a classification of all possible kinds of things specified within a certain *parameter*, possessing a particular *trait*, and sorted by a consistent *criterion*" (7). How we choose to typologize, though, depends very much on what we hope to examine; improvised practices, for instance, can be classified based on elements of musical structure, mode of interaction, model type, and so on.[6]

Once a typology is chosen, and criteria and parameters defined, individual practices can be categorized through specific traits. Yet in trying to narrow down a typology of collective improvisation, I found whichever way I trained my lens seemed to obscure from view other equally important factors. My first attempt at classification neatly categorized practices by their musical textures: a practice with a parameter of two or more improvised musical strands and a criterion that they differ from one another could be subcategorized through the combined traits of each strand's vertical and horizontal relationships to one another: heterophonic versus melody with accompaniment versus multiple melodies of equal weight then subcategorized into interlocking versus noninterlocking polyphonies, and so on. While this approach yielded relevant comparative possibilities, it necessarily *didn't* privilege other parameters: different modes or degrees of interaction, for instance.

Instead of a systematic phylogenetic chart of factors moving from the general to the specific along one axis of observation, I began imagining an interconnected web of musical and interactional considerations. I left a sheet of paper on my desk with a line drawn down the middle, "Musical Factors" written on one side, "Interactional Factors" on the other. Over the ensuing days and weeks, I added to it whenever a pertinent idea or question arose (which often

Musical Factors	Interactional Factors
- Is it useful to sub-categorize collective improvisation types according to texture? → (heterophonic, interlocking, chords/harmony...)	- Do improvisers really influence one another in real time? (if so, how do arja drummers interlock so fast?!)
- Does it matter if the model has one or multiple musical lines? (comparing reyong norot vs. New Orleans jazz?)	- Are there different *kinds* of interaction and influence? (musical and/or social)
- How is collective improvisation impacted by a model's specificity and/or flexibility? (**are these actually the same thing?)	- How do the musicians communicate their ideas with one another in real time?
- Is the model consciously known?	- What's happening inside their minds when they play together? (consciously? subconsciously?)
- ...	- ...

FIGURE 4.1. Brainstorming musical and interactional factors of collective improvisation

happened at inopportune moments, like while trying to sleep or while in the shower). A few of my preliminary musings are shown in figure 4.1.

I hoped this sort of multidirectional inquiry would allow me to pinpoint, across diverse arenas, underlying similarities in different practices and divergent approaches to seemingly similar ones. The discussions in this chapter help shape this more nuanced and multimodal analytical model for collective improvisation, plumbing theories of cognition and communication as well as examining the interactional and social dynamics of improvised performance. Each angle and theory addressed proposes different approaches to thinking about interaction in improvisation, suggests preconditions for effective collective performance, and points to ways of conceptualizing and refining an analytical framework.

MUSICAL CONSIDERATIONS

In chapter 1, I introduced the concept of the "model": a series of fixed musical signposts, learned in advance of performance, on which improvising musicians base their improvisations. My contrasting experiences improvising *reyong norot* and flamenco dance hinted at several ways this concept could be refined to facilitate useful comparison across genres and cultures. In trying to assess those very different experiences through similar lenses, several model-related questions became particularly salient: (1) How specific is the model for each practice, and how flexible? (2) How consciously known is it? (3) How does it dictate performed realizations: what musical interactions and textures are idiomatic? I wanted to understand how each of these factors might shape the collective aspects of improvisation. How might both the specificity and the flexibility of a model, for instance, affect the tenor of a group's interactions, and how should these two interrelated but separate parameters inform my analyses?

SPECIFICITY AND FLEXIBILITY OF THE MODEL

The preliminary analyses of *kendang arja* and Hindustani *alap* performances in chapter 1 prompted a bifurcation of the model concept. Differentiating relatively strict templates for formulaic variation from relatively flexible schemas for exploration illuminated the quite separate model types—and thus the distinct, though related, improvisational approaches—guiding performers of these two practices. Most improvisers, as we saw, draw from models somewhere between the two extremes; while the *reyong*'s *norot* model is a relatively strict template, flamenco models lie somewhere in the middle. The resulting continuum of model specificity and flexibility, Sawyer would argue, creates a spectrum of

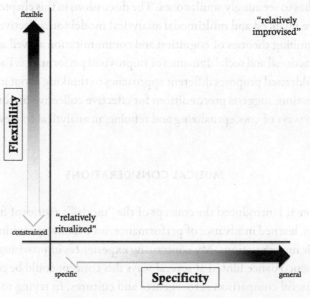

FIGURE 4.2. Specificity-flexibility scale

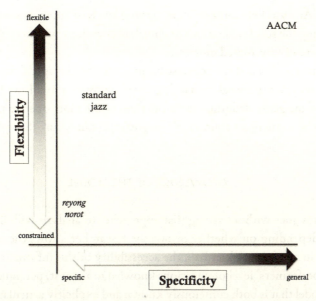

FIGURE 4.3. Specificity and flexibility of AACM, *reyong norot*, and standard jazz

predictability from the "relatively ritualized" to the "relatively improvised" (see Sawyer 2003, 6–8, 81).[7] Yet my own performing experience told me that, while factors of specificity and flexibility are related, they are not equivalent, and I imagine these two parameters rather as opposing axes on a graph, per figure 4.2.

Each area on the specificity-flexibility spectrum demands a different kind of group creativity. At one extreme is *reyong norot*, where four polyphonically interlocking musicians collectively improvise on a model that is specific down to the note and offers limited flexibility for alteration. My analyses of *norot* performances needed to be fine-grained; only examination on a note-by-note basis could reveal how such seemingly constrained musicians exert creative license. On the other extreme is the relatively free improvisation of psychedelic or acid rock bands, jam bands, or free jazz ensembles. Here, models take the form of very broad schemas for exploration that encourage almost unlimited creative flexibility. They offer guiding principles for a performance, like "a general sense of mood, length, contour, or dynamic," or suggest concepts to explore like "difference tones, or 'vertical' or 'sharp' tones" (Borgo 2005, 7).[8] Analyzing this kind of collective improvisation requires a zoomed-out lens, observing large-scale motives or moods as often as note-by-note details.

Spanning a broad middle ground in the specificity-flexibility spectrum are various flamenco and jazz practices, where the tunes and chord changes of models are generally specific but the degree of creative flexibility within them is great. Analysis here must occur at varying levels of zoom, at some moments examining the subtle alterations of chord substitutions, at others, the slow development of improvised motives.

Figure 4.3 charts three contrasting practices on the specificity-flexibility scale. Analysis can reveal "what degree of innovation is allowed, what elements of the genre definition are more rigid or are more open to negotiation, and in which emergent contexts the negotiation can occur" (Sawyer 2003, 58).

KNOWLEDGE OF THE MODEL

It perhaps goes without saying that approaches to analysis will differ significantly depending on whether or not the researcher knows the model. As I learned in my fieldwork in Bali, the accessibility of this information depends on the performers' level of conscious knowledge about it, per figure 4.4.[9]

A model that is both consciously known and explicitly articulated by practitioners, like the chords and melody of a jazz standard, provides the most straightforward foundation for ascertaining elements of a knowledge base and appropriately analyzing improvised realizations in its varied idioms. While models in many other improvised practices are traditionally unspoken, if consciously known by practitioners, they can still be discovered through fieldwork. This was how my research into Bali's *reyong norot* practice unfolded. Once I learned the details of its model, explicitly known though unspoken, it

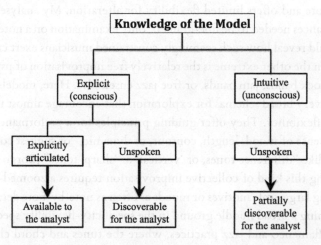

FIGURE 4.4. Level of conscious knowledge of the model and its impact on analysis

became, like a spoken model, a specific road map for analysis. Yet in many aural music cultures, models for improvisation are not just unspoken but unconscious, and thus to some degree unknowable to the analyst. As I discovered in my *kendang arja* research, guiding principles of such models may be unearthed through fieldwork, performing experience, and music analysis. But, unlike the specific information offered by known models, unknown models, like knowledge bases, require additional interpretation by the analyst. They provide clues to analysis but few irrefutable answers.

REALIZATION OF THE MODEL

As my initial attempts at a typology of collective improvisation revealed, models often dictate specific interactional and textural guidelines, and this too can help analysts classify improvisatory type. Fundamental dissimilarities between my two Balinese case studies provided a first branch in this typological tree. While models for *kendang arja*, like flamenco models, contain multiple discrete strands of music as we will see, the *reyong*'s *norot* model comprises a single strand of melody differently realized by each musician. This suggests a useful analytical distinction between single-voice and multi-voice models for improvisation. Each can be realized in a variety of musical textures and interactional relationships.

Much Hindustani classical music, for instance, turns a single-voice melodic model into a flexibly improvised solo over a drone, while some American folk revival music improvises such a model through gentle embellishment and idiomatically improvised vocal harmonies. A single-voice model might equally be rendered in simultaneous variation. The closer heterophony often preferred for Egyptian classical music, for example, sees most musicians playing the same melody in similar rhythmic densities but varying timing and ornamentation. In the stratified polyphony of a Central Javanese gamelan, by contrast, performers simultaneously improvise a single melody in different rhythmic densities.[10] As we saw in the first case study, single-voice models can even be realized as tightly interlocking polyphonies, like in *reyong norot* or, in a very different way, Inuit singing games. These various realization types, illustrative rather than exhaustive, create the range of options in figure 4.5.

While the same single-voice model could theoretically be realized through any of these varied approaches, realizations of multi-voice models appear to depend to a larger extent on the nature of the model itself; idiomatic performances of *kendang arja* and flamenco are at least partially dictated by their distinct model types. Some multi-voice models, like the melodies and changes of

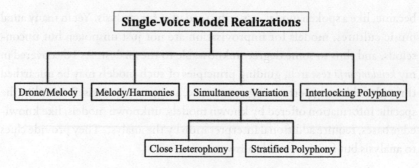

FIGURE 4.5. Realization types for single-voice model melodies

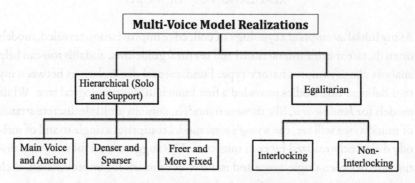

FIGURE 4.6. Realization types for multi-voice models

a jazz standard or the solo and supporting drums of an Ewe dance-drumming troupe, suggest hierarchical realizations. Others, like the interlocking models for Shona mbira or *kendang arja*, or the loose polyphonic schemas of free improvisation, suggest a more egalitarian distribution of musical material. Thus, multi-voice models can be realized as relatively equal polyphonies, either interlocking or noninterlocking, or they may take the form of a solo-and-support-style polyphony.[11] Such solos and supports may manifest as a main voice with anchoring voices—as in chordal harmonies against melodies—or as simultaneous strands of sparser and denser rhythms. They may also be achieved through what Monson terms the *liquid* and *solid* relationships of relatively free and relatively fixed playing: more active or changeable streams over more stable motives like ostinati. Figure 4.6 shows these various possibilities, again offered in a provisional spirit.

While some practices rely exclusively on one realization type, others combine several. Different groups of musicians may relate to one another differently, or approaches may shift throughout a performance. In standard jazz, for instance, the musicians of the rhythm section often form a so-called agent system, supporting the soloist with sparser chords or ostinati.[12] Yet, among themselves, their realizations are closer to an equal interlocking polyphony, and each may at times create equal polyphony with the soloist. It will often be necessary to examine realizations of individual musicians or agent systems separately, or to consider a shifting of realization types over time.

THE MODEL IN PRACTICE: COLLECTIVITY AS SHARED KNOWLEDGE

While each of these musical parameters enabled insight into my research questions, categorization alone couldn't explain *how* flamenco or *reyong norot* performers collectively implemented their models. But a detour into more qualitative explorations of shared knowledge and the cognitive processes that shape it added depth to my understanding of these different models in practice, elucidating successful collective performance. When an improvising ensemble is performing at its peak, it can feel like an impossible kind of magic: musicians coming together to create something somehow greater than the sum total of their separate contributions. Their interplay is often likened to a *complex system*, like the human brain, the financial market, or the earth's climate, where action is unpredictable because "the group as a whole will behave in ways not conceived by any of its individual members, as a result of the pattern of interactions between those individuals" (Clayton, Dueck, and Leante 2013, 18; see also Borgo 2005). As with on-ship navy navigation teams collectively steering large vessels into harbor, the unpredictability of the interaction itself can foster group genius (see Hutchins 1995).

Playing on a "sink or swim" analogy, Borgo has coined the expression "sync or swarm" to refer to "the delicate and exquisite dynamics that can emerge in complex systems" (Borgo 2005, 9). Yet, for collective improvisers, such dynamics are not an inevitable outcome of the system; my many failed attempts at *reyong norot* and *kendang arja* improvisation showed that some collective improvisations were neither delicate *nor* exquisite. Rather, these dynamics emerge "only under certain conditions that require intense communication and cooperation and a shared history of interactions" (Borgo 2005, 9). Competence must reach beyond models into knowledge bases, and these must not only be embodied, but *shared*. In order for a jazz musician to recognize a great musical idea in her partner's performance, and to run with it, "everyone involved must have the same idea about what the better [thing] looks like, a common criterion for knowing it when it appears" (Becker 2000, 175). Shared knowledge enabled the Vancouver flamenco musicians to follow my teacher through her dance improvisations, and she in turn understood how to best complement them. While improvised music will always be unpredictable, collective knowledge allows performers to more easily negotiate their interactions in real time. It enables *elastic coordination*, where groups achieve increased creativity by alternately integrating and de-integrating, balancing individual autonomy with group constraint.[13] As jazz musician Howard Becker recalls:

> The agreement to keep some things fixed and vary others made it possible for a group to sound like it knew, collectively, what it was doing: to not get lost, to have some idea of what might be coming next, to interpret what the others did as hints of a direction the collective effort might take. (2000, 173)

One modern dancer similarly notes: "to give somebody freedom, you actually have to give them really clear guidelines" (Harrison and Rouse 2014, 1263).[14] Comparable shared conceptions allow dancers and drummers in Martinican *bèlè* to loosely coordinate specific rhythms and gestures. Although *bèlè* performers often cue one another to transition between contrasting gestures, they may sometimes perfectly coordinate a transition with no cue, "guided by their knowledge, expectations, and readiness" (Gerstin 1998, 142). A drummer who sees a dancer perform the climactic and tiring *détaché* movement twice in a row may mark a transition out of it on the next downbeat without exchanging a cue with the dancer; he has made an educated guess that she, too, will be ready to move on. Observers impressed by the seeming ESP of dancer and drummer marking the unplanned transition in concert fail to realize that "while it might not have happened, [it] was more than a coincidence [... The drummer] knows what [the dancer] knows" (Gerstin 1998, 142). As Clayton and Leante aver: "We understand another individual's intentions ... because they are expressed in the other's embodied actions and mirrored in our own capabilities for action" (2013, 192–93). The opposite can also be true. Balinese *arja* drummer Cok Alit recalls an unsatisfying collaboration with performers trained in a contrasting village style: the drummers' lack of shared knowledge left them unable to interlock while improvising, and Cok Alit had to resort to repetitive and predictable motives to keep the performance together. "*Rusak! Apa lagi, bosan!*" he complains, with a characteristically joyous chortle. "Broken! And what's more, boring!"[15]

Some genres, like postjazz or improvised Western contemporary art music, have very few genre-specific constraints. In such practices, as we saw in chapter 1, co-performers will often consciously impose constraints to generate a shared vision. Here, "the gradual establishment of a certain kind of culture, a customary way of doing things and collaborating" comes "out of the history of the group" (Eteläpelto and Lahti 2008, 228). Co-performers in the avant-garde jazz group Art Ensemble of Chicago, for instance, generate a shared knowledge of "characteristic Art Ensemble interactive frameworks" through "demanding periods of rehearsal" (Steinbeck 2008, 409 and 405). These frameworks, which include such broad concepts as "cymbal-and-gong-orchestra interactive frameworks" and "intensity structures," allow musicians "to 'negotiate' where to go next, when to leave, and how to get there" (Steinbeck 2008, 409 and 410). Similarly, in the Grateful Dead's collectively improvised song "Dark Star," each new performance strikes a balance between established themes or "maneuvers" and new musical ideas. "The numerous iterations of 'Dark Star' endure as an intertextual mass" that guides subsequent performances (Pettengill 2013, 40 and 41). This becomes the shared history: the group's unique model of the song.

In each of these contexts, " 'knowing' is reconceived as the ability to participate appropriately in . . . shared cultural practices" (Sawyer and DeZutter 2009, 83). And shared expectations about both music and interaction emerge from this shared knowledge and history. I wanted to understand *how* such shared conceptualizations are actualized in real time.

WHAT'S HAPPENING IN THE BRAIN?

In cognitive science, human behavior is often analyzed through a three-phase information-processing model. In the first stage, *sensory input*, incoming sensory data is encoded and perceived by the sense organs. Next is *cognitive processing*, where the central nervous system evaluates sensory data with the help of structures activated in memory, and an appropriate course of action is determined.[16] Finally, through *motor output*, the muscles and glands of the body execute the chosen action (see Pressing 1988, 129–31; Johnson-Laird 2002).[17] While in longer-term creative projects, we may see these three phases of information processing unravel sequentially, in improvised performance they proceed in repeating and superimposed loops in real time. A musician hears and sees elements of the ongoing performance (sensory input) while simultaneously accessing and manipulating the model and knowledge base (cognitive processing) in order to contribute idiomatically to the musical whole (motor output).

The more automatic these steps, the more fluent the action.[18] I can walk without thinking about it because I practiced, concentrating hard and failing until I succeeded countless times as a child. Our brains categorize sensory inputs by type: face, kissing, happiness. And "when multiple instances of the same category are encountered, they tend to activate similar neural patterns.... Over time, this population of conjunctive neurons integrates modality-specific features across category instances and settings, establishing a multimodal representation of the category" (Barsalou et al. 2003, 67). This mental representation, which Barsalou (1999) terms a *simulator*, enables us to recognize and interpret new tokens of a category, to re-create a token in our minds (*simulation*), and to generate tokens by mixing and matching elements from various previously experienced or imagined ones (see Barsalou et al. 2003, 63–70). Through years of rehearsal and collaboration, improvising performers develop simulators for both the broad and specific categories most relevant to their practice. In standard jazz, these might include "improvising on a II-V-I progression," "Monk's piano style," "transitioning to the B section," "My Favorite Things," "walking bass," "ballad," "riffing on the blues scale," "2-beat fill," and so on. In *reyong norot* they would comprise an understanding of idiomatic transitions between different scale degrees, idiosyncrasies of individual pieces and *rasa* (feelings), and the individual preferences of particular partners.

The social situations we repeatedly experience become entrenched in memory, our simulators guiding new interactions in similar situations. What emerge are *entrenched situated conceptualizations* that allow for dynamic, flexible, situation-specific responses. We do not interact with an angry child, an unwanted suitor, or a surprise visit from a friend in the exact same way each time these things occur; entrenched conceptualizations are not "a single simulation but rather the ability to produce many related simulations" (Barsalou et al. 2003, 76). Likewise, an improviser well-versed in model and knowledge base acquires entrenched situated conceptualizations of various pieces and styles. She can then engage dynamically with new instances of them in performance. And when co-performers share common simulators and entrenched conceptualizations, they are able to develop, in real time, a "cognitive representation of all previous event clusters produced by the other performers and any expectations of their likely future actions" (Pressing 1988, 154). A *compatibility effect*, where what musicians are hearing agrees with their cognitive representations of the style, enables quick motor response by reducing the cognitive load of interpretation.[19] Because of the human "propensit[y] to ... anticipate experiences and perceptions, ... only the differences from expectation need to be processed" (Borgo 2005, 44).[20] Musicians are then able to play in an "as-if" mode, "aniticipat[ing], with considerable sophistication, what [o]ther player[s] will do" (Hagberg 2016, 492). Condon and Ogston (1971) term such close mutual attunement *interactional synchrony*; Martinican *bèlè* musicians call it *réciprocité* (see Gerstin 1998).[21]

Underlying such *réciprocité*, some scholars have argued, is a kind of *distributed cognition*, where "one's cognitive abilities are not bounded by the limits of one's own mind." Rather, "the understanding of a problem and its potential solutions reside . . . also in the larger scheme of the combined understanding of the group" (Wiggins 1999/2000, 67; see also Burrows 2004; Theiner and Sutton 2014). While it may be impossible to truly know if cognition crosses the boundaries of individual minds, we can perhaps see the ways in which "the nature of [the] interactions changes both the teams and their outputs" (Harvey 2014, 338).[22] My understanding of these complex exchanges was enriched by considering them through the lens of *flow*.

IMPROVISATION AS FLOW

> It doesn't happen to groups every single night, even though they may be swinging on every single tune. But at some point when the band is playing and everyone gets locked in together, it's special for the musicians and for the aware, conscientious listener. These are the magical moments, the best moments in jazz.
>
> (FRANKLIN GORDON QUOTED IN BERLINER 1994, 388)

It may not happen every night. But in those moments when "everything clicks," the performance becomes much more than we expected, the music seeming to "flo[w] out spontaneously, without obstacles" (Biasutti 2017, 3). Improvising actors and jam session musicians describe such experiences:

> Our conventional suits were cast off. . . . Improvisation swept us into another realm, another consciousness. . . . One day it becomes something you can feel—a learned faculty—and something easy comes about: You forget yourself as the process takes hold. You sort of become part of the form itself. It's suddenly so natural, like going from crawling to walking. (Actor Barbara Harris quoted in Sweet 1978, 66)

> You're like wow did I actually get that, like how did that come out of me like, where did it come from you know. It's very hard to understand when

you snap out of it where it came from. (Musician, quoted in Hart and Di Blasi 2015, 283)

My Balinese teachers might say that each of these performers has moved beyond technical skill and found *taksu*: that ineffable state of spiritual power, artistic inspiration, and magnetic charisma that truly moves audiences, both human and divine (see Heimarck 2003, 113).[23] As I Wayan Sudirana explained to me in an extended conversation over text: "Taksu is not something physical. It's something embodied within the physical/material elements like movements, sounds, and skills. . . . The audience is usually amazed and says the dancer/musician looks different from his/her daily life. This is usually associated with extraordinary movements or playing techniques." He continues: "It comes from you and your beliefs. You will get it if you are serious in doing what you are doing. Everyone has Taksu. For me, Taksu is not coming from 'out of space' and It has nothing to do with Divine beings.[24] You are the Divine being. Everything is actually housed in you. You just need to excavate your best ability to work and to produce. You have the Taksu with you!"[25]

When a performer's skill level and the challenge of the task are balanced, when she has clear goals, unambiguous feedback, and the freedom to focus completely, she can enter a state where she feels competent and in control, abandons self-consciousness, and, in throwing herself into the task, loses all sense of time.[26] This, psychologist Mihaly Csikszentmihalyi posits, creates a *flow state* where both optimal performance and optimal enjoyment occur (see Csikszentmihalyi 1996).[27] We've all experienced this feeling while making music or art, playing chess or sports, writing, rock climbing, or working on a challenging problem in our chosen field. Whether "in the zone," "on the ball," or "in the groove" (Biasutti 2017, 1), we reach a highly focused mental state: an otherworldly feeling of limitless ability and unencumbered creativity, of inspiration, energy, clarity, and ease. Suddenly afternoon has become evening and we don't really remember how we got there:

> In the flow state, action follows upon action according to an internal logic that seems to need no conscious intervention by the actor. He experiences it as a unified flowing from one moment to the next, in which he is in control of his actions, and in which there is little distinction between self and environment, between stimulus and response, or between past, present, and future. (Csikszentmihalyi 1975, 36)

Collective Improvisation as Group Flow

In his seminal *Group Genius*, Sawyer suggests that flow, while often seen as an individual experience, may in fact also occur as a group phenomenon.[28] Borrowing from Csikszentmihalyi, he proposes ten conditions that foster group flow, shown in figure 4.7 (see Sawyer 2007, chap. 3).

Each of these conditions in its own way is essential to successful collective improvisation. The model and knowledge base provide a *group goal*, and a fluency in them allows each player to *be in control* through inevitable unpredictability.[29] *Close listening* and effective *communication* (discussed in more detail further on) enable the sensitive cognitive processing of sensory inputs, while a *blending of egos* encourages players to attend with *complete concentration* not just to their own contributions but also to the collective intention.[30] A semantic interconnection between musicians' intentions arises, such that "the specific content of my shared intention, as it unfolds, will in part be determined by my linked intention that your intention also 'be realized in the right way'" (Hagberg 2016, 485). Performers will not have identical goals or interpretations of the performance. But a desire for *equal participation*, where "members are relatively equal in power and status" (Harvey 2014, 336) creates what Gaggioli and colleagues term a "collaborative zone of proximal development" (2015, 157). The needs of the individual are balanced with those of the group; mutual trust and empathy develop as participants temper their own intentions with an understanding of the intentions of others.[31] This creates space for *moving it forward*: taking a co-performer's suggestion and expanding on it. And it encourages risk taking as musicians look to challenge their co-performers' creative limits. Risk then provides the *potential for failure* that balances the challenge

---

Conditions for Group Flow:
1. group goal
2. being in control
3. close listening
4. communication
5. blending egos
6. complete concentration
7. equal participation
8. moving it forward
9. potential for failure
10. familiarity

FIGURE 4.7. Conditions for group flow

of the task with the performers' level of skill, allowing each to achieve individual flow.[32]

Yet, while every one of these factors is vital to successful collectivity, my playing experience suggested that true success most often hung on Sawyer's final condition for group flow: *familiarity*. As Bakan observes of his experiences drumming in Bali:

> In the musical relationship Sukarata and I shared through beleganjur drumming, every success and failure, every effective strategy employed, every misguided decision and mishap, every joy and frustration, accommodation, misunderstanding, incomprehension, acceptance, rejection, reflection, and disorientation had meaning, and each contributed to the realization of a musical understanding and the construction of a shared musical world. (1999, 333)

Balinese musicians often refer to the concept of *pasangan*: the partnership of long-term co-performers. It is a term often reverently evoked when *reyong* or *kendang arja* partners from the old generation play together. During a recording session I organized between Cok Alit and his longtime *arja* partner Pak Dewa, held rapt by the beauty and subtlety of their improvised interlocking, a drumming friend exclaimed: "*Wah! Luar biasa! Karena dekat sekali. Pasangan, mereka.*" "Wow! Extraordinary! It's because they're very close. They're *pasangan*." "*Ya, itu 'dah!*" several people agreed without hesitation. "Yes, that's it." On a practical level, familiarity allows groups to establish common riffs and patterns and to effectively play on them in improvised performance (see Sawyer 2003, 61–63). But it's also about knowing one's partners' personal preferences and idioms. In the Art Ensemble of Chicago, for instance, Joseph Jarman's "redoubtable 'energy sound'-style playing is one of his improvisation specialties and an interactive role in which he is often cast" (Steinbeck 2008, 422). His longtime bandmates have learned to expect this style from him; they can call on it, recognize it when it occurs, and react accordingly. Martinican *bèlè* drummers similarly "assiduously hone their own 'sound,'" which dancers can learn to anticipate (Gerstin 1998, 134). If a group improvises together long enough, "a general style peculiar to the group will usually develop" (Tom Nunn quoted in Borgo 2005, 24).

Yet even more than mutual style, *pasangan* helps to develop mutual trust.[33] As bassist Ron Carter notes:

> In order for it to succeed each guy has to trust the other guy's sense of it all. If I play a note, [guitarist] Jim [Hall] has to know that I mean that note to be there. If he plays a chord, I know he expects me to find a note to enhance that

chord because I know he means that chord to be there. And without this level of trustworthiness, in spite of talent, it's not going to be successful musically. (Quoted in Monson 1996, 175)

Trust that one's partners will abide by the "moving it forward" rule helps to cultivate "as-if" playing. Pianist Roland Hanna observes of bassist Richard Davis:

> When you're talking about having been around somebody for thirty years . . . you're close to the way they think. Now maybe I don't know exactly . . . the way he thinks, but I am close enough to what he has been thinking in the past to have an idea of what he *might* play from one note to the next. If he plays a C at a certain strength, then I know he may be looking for an A-flat or an E-flat or whatever direction he may go in. And I know he may be making a certain *kind* of passage. I've heard him enough to know *how* he makes his lines. So I may not know exactly what note he's going to play, but I know in general the kind of statement he would make, or how he would use his *words*, you know, the order he would put his words in. (Quoted in Monson 1996, 49)

This level of *pasangan* seems to go beyond a shared knowledge base, group riffs, and familiarity of preferences. There are some musicians with whom playing together simply feels easy; Cok Alit says that he creates great music with Pak Dewa because they are *cocok*, suited to each other. Likewise, *bèlè* dancer Etienne Jean-Baptiste says of drummer Paulo Rastocle, "Me, he follows me like the shirt and the skin. I do the least little thing, he's already seen what I did" (quoted in Gerstin 1998, 138). One jam band musician reports similar experiences: "It's almost like telepathy[;] there is definitely a sense that you both know something that you can't talk about" (Hart and Di Blasi 2015, 284). And jazz drummer Ralph Peterson once said of pianist Geri Allen that if she were unavailable for a gig, "I'd rather have another instrument. I feel that strongly about her playing" (quoted in Monson 1996, 80). Jazz musicians and improv theater performers often refer to this symbiosis, or *cocok*-ness, as *chemistry* (see Berliner 1994, 395).

THE MODEL AND KNOWLEDGE BASE AS DYNAMIC

Concepts of group flow and entrenched situated conceptualizations suggest that models and knowledge bases should not only be seen as stable frameworks for improvisation. Group constraints and shared expectations can also be established in the course of a single performance through chemistry and *pasangan*, forming temporary, localized guidelines for collective improvisation. Here, the common history of model and knowledge base helps performers shape an interpersonally shared history, the *domain* of Csikszentmihalyi's systems model of creativity inspiring a *microdomain* for a single performance.[34] Free improviser Ann Faber explains:

> Our aim is to play together with the greatest possible freedom—which, far from meaning without constraint, actually means to play together with sufficient skill and communication to be able to select proper constraints *in the course of the piece*, rather than being dependent on precisely chosen ones. (Quoted in Borgo 2005, 19)

Thus, improvised musical interaction, like spoken dialogue, "reflects a dynamic process which develops and changes as the participants interact" (Gumperz 1982, 131).[35] The performance and its meaning develop in real time through a shared decision-making process:

> Everyone (or almost everyone) involved in the improvisation is offering suggestions as to what might be done next, in the form of tentative moves, slight variations that go in one way rather than some of the other possible ways. As people listen closely to one another, some of those suggestions begin to converge and others, less congruent with the developing direction fall by the wayside. The players thus develop a collective direction. (Becker 2000, 172)

This defining and redefining of interaction and meaning seem the ever-present reality of collectively improvised music. Two short excerpts from a 1965 performance of "Bass-ment Blues" by the Jaki Byard Quartet, transcribed and analyzed by Monson (1996), illustrate how musical ideas are suggested and adopted in the course of performance. Figure 4.8 shows the opening of the first chorus. It begins with drummer Alan Dawson and bassist George Tucker establishing tempo and groove through simple quarter- and eighth-note rhythms, but almost immediately Tucker introduces a triplet motive. Dawson picks it up in his 2-beat fill at the end of the first staff system, and it becomes a major rhythmic characteristic underpinning the performance.[36]

At a moment of high intensity several minutes later, Tucker plays a triple-stop gesture on the bass and Dawson responds with a roll on the snare. Byard then adds a complementary chordal motive on the piano "resembling a shout chorus-style riff figure" (Monson 1996, 171). This engages Tucker in the high-energy call and response shown in figure 4.9.

FIGURE 4.8. Musical interaction in jazz improvisation, triplet motive

FIGURE 4.9. Musical interaction in jazz improvisation, call and response

Each of these moments could have gone a different way had Dawson or Byard not picked up on Tucker's suggestions or had they responded instead with contrasting motives. In this dialectical process, "it is the connection between members' ideas that is creative" (Harvey 2014, 330).

INTERACTIONAL CONSIDERATIONS

Thinking of the knowledge bases of my *arja* and *reyong* teachers, and those of my flamenco dance instructors, as something dynamic and dialectical brought to the fore the interactive components of collective improvisation, hearkening back to questions of how—and how much—collectively improvising musicians draw influence from one another in the course of performance. I suspected the answers varied greatly. Again, I wanted to address these questions via the more quantitative, analyzable factors of interaction as well as the relatively qualitative sine qua non of successful collectivity.[37] Out of infinite possibilities, improvisers create specific collective products. And from the myriad of these, music analysts are drawn to the subset of performances we consider most interesting or moving, cool or unusual. The musical considerations just discussed offered insight into how I might analyze my teachers' performances. Yet only by exploring the processes of communication and interaction that generated them—quite different for *reyong* and *arja* than for flamenco—could I truly understand what made each one successful. These interactive processes seemed central to an analytical model of collective improvisation.

COLLECTIVE IMPROVISATION AS INTERACTION AND COMMUNICATION

"I haven't played this set of tunes in years," the fiddle player admits with a feigned sheepishness. "So there'll be lots of mistakes."

"Those are called variations*," the whistle player tosses back with a grin. What follows is a rousing set of reels with fantastic arrangements, impeccable tempo shifts, and variations aplenty, but no mistakes that I can discern.*[38]

A show by the traditional Irish instrumental group Lúnasa always promises a blend of incredibly high-level musicianship with an easy and amiable group dynamic. Between tunes, whistle player Kevin Crawford does the lion's share of the talking, introducing each new set and entertaining the audience (and clearly his bandmates also) with hilarious anecdotes and antics; in this way, he seems to assume a leadership role in the ensemble. But when they begin to play, everyone becomes both leader and follower. Their tight transitions and inventive musical interactions are the result of a lifetime of playing this music together, but it is their communication in the moment that ensures a successful performance. In one tune, Crawford playing the main melody suddenly turns his body toward the upright bass and guitarist, changing his gentle foot tapping into a forceful stomp and beginning to improvise a fast, intricate variation. The guitarist, in almost the same instant, increases the density and intensity of his strumming and the bassist shifts to a fast, regular walk. Everyone gets so into the tune that, at the end of the chorus, Crawford actually stops playing his whistle long enough to shout "Again!," and the group adds on another chorus. A "whoop!" at the end of the next chorus tells them to go around one more time.

By contrast, uilleann pipe player Cillian Vallely, shy and quiet, and the only performer who sits as he plays, seems to command attention through his introspection. When the melody falls to him, every other player in the room turns subtly toward him, watching his face or hands out of the corners of their eyes. Likewise, when playing a slow air as a duo, the bassist stares intently at the guitarist's face, seemingly capturing the latter's flexible timing with his eyes alone. And playing a set with just guitar and bass, the fiddle player locks eyes with the guitarist for much of the first tune. But when things really start to rock, he breaks eye contact and stares into the distance. Perhaps he needs an inward focus to complete a more challenging variation or to listen more fully; perhaps he's simply savoring the moment.

Improvisation, Smith argues, is a "dynamic communication process" (1999, 35), and ensembles of musicians communicate in many ways and for many purposes. A new lick to be developed, a new musical direction to take, a change in the preplanned structure of a piece or performance, an increase in intensity, a shifting of roles. These and other suggestions must be not only generated but also communicated on the fly, via performer interaction.

MODES OF INTERACTION

Humans don't always interact in ways that are conducive to creating a collective product or experience. We can be competitive or combative as often as cooperative or collaborative, and often we occupy the gray areas in between. Couch (1986) identifies eight basic forms of human interaction: autocratic action, chase, conflict, competition, social panic, accommodation, mutuality, and cooperation. Collective improvisation can at times demonstrate elements of all these modes. Most improvisers have experienced a moment of near disaster that evokes social panic, an ensemble dynamic where autocratic tendencies emerge, or the conflict or competition of opposing desires often resolved through accommodation. While more seemingly destructive interactive modes may sometimes enhance collective creation,[39] studies of musical improvisation suggest that too many "conflictive group characteristics and a dominant leadership style reduc[e] the level of small group creativity" (Hsieh 2012, 160). In order to interact successfully, Becker maintains, "people must have a real shared interest in getting the job done, an interest powerful enough to overcome divisive selfish interests" (2000, 175). *Cooperative* interaction, then, seems to provide the best framework for understanding successful collectivity.[40] A shared social objective attended to with shared focus and mutual responsiveness leads to what Miller, Hintz, and Couch (1975) term *openings*: shifts from a state of independence to one of interdependence. I wondered if looking at musical, verbal, and physical communications among musicians could lend insight into this interdependence, providing quantifiable fodder for analyzing their interactions.

COMMUNICATION CODES

Just as a knowledge base gives musicians a tool kit of motives and improvisatory techniques, what Bastien and Hostager (1992) call "structural conventions," so too does that knowledge base inform the "social conventions" of *communication codes*.[41] I knew from years of watching and playing with other improvisers that such codes could be verbal, musical, or physical. The nature of performing arts dictates that aside from occasional one-word instructions—Lúnasa's whistle player shouting "Again!" during his solo—most verbal communication takes the form of preperformance preparation or postperformance debrief. Such communication can be simply instructional, but is often cooperative or collaborative.[42] Verbal communication codes frequently include genre-specific expressions and verbal shorthand, like "going to the head" or "taking a chorus" in jazz parlance, and, as we've seen, provides copious clues for the analyst.

Musical communication codes, by contrast, happen almost exclusively in the course of performance, as cues embedded into the music itself. Martinican *bèlè* drummer Georges Dru might play an "ending variation" to alert dancers to an upcoming change; Grateful Dead guitarist Jerry Garcia could execute a series of arpeggios to signal a transition.[43] I had learned to recognize and analyze such cues in the *kendang arja* and *reyong norot* performances of my teachers, indoctrinated as I was into each tradition's idioms. Yet I knew from my own playing experience that musical communication is as often invitational as instructional: suggestions contingent on co-performers' reactions, like the jazz interactions in figures 4.8–4.9. A call asking for a response, an intensity shift asking to be matched, a motive asking to be repeated or developed. In a 2011 recording session, *arja* drummer Cok Alit increases the number of bass strokes he uses to match the singing of an angry character, and his partner Pak Dewa follows suit. Likewise, in a 1972 performance of the Art Ensemble of Chicago, as one structure for improvisation "dissolves into a loosely organized march-style interactive framework," bassist Malachi Favors plays a faster vamp that has "an immediate, galvanizing effect." Lester Bowie on flugelhorn responds with a "soaring melody," and drummer Don Moye centers the new texture with a "backbeat flam pattern" (Steinbeck 2008, 411). In each case, one musician communicates a suggestion and his co-performers receive and respond to it.[44] Musical communication codes manifest in tighter, more internally coherent improvised interactions; as we will see later in the chapter, they guide both large-scale stylistic choices and moment-to-moment adjustments (see Berliner 1994, 348–79).

Nonverbal Communication

Alongside verbal and musical codes, collectively improvising musicians also use gestures, facial expressions, gazes, body direction, and physical proximity to convey intentions or instructions.[45] I felt these interactions each time I played with musicians in Bali, and I saw them in the videos I took of recording sessions, lessons, and performances. Nonverbal interaction is a tricky animal. "Tacit knowledge difficult to articulate and share" (Marchetti and Jensen 2010, 1), it is open to multiple interpretations and misinterpretations. Yet it is also vital to any successful communication and may thus enhance our analyses of collective improvisations. We have learned to interpret such cues subconsciously through a lifetime of conversational interaction, and "almost all musicians communicate important information through bodily movement, even though they themselves might not be aware of this" (Pelz-Sherman 1998, 77).[46] Like musical and verbal communication, bodily cues can tell other participants what to do or expect. Some physical communication codes, such as nodding for emphasis, increasing movement to attract attention, or smiling to indicate satisfaction (or acknowledge a mistake), are relatively universal. Others are style specific, like tapping one's head to indicate a return to the head in jazz. And yet others are specific to a single musician, piece, or performance, "given communicative meaning by their shared referential content and by the environment in which they occur" (Smith 1999, 58). Folklorist Erving Goffman uses the term "impression management" to describe how such cues "shape moment-by-moment reception by other participants" (Smith 1999, 36).

Because of the variance of physical cues between genres and cultures, and their multivalent nature even within a single style, my goal here is not to pinpoint meanings behind specific gestures. Rather, a handful of examples will draw attention to the prevalence of nonverbal communication, both conscious and unconscious, in improvised performance, thus elucidating widespread patterns of interaction. These suggest potentially rich arenas for *interactional analysis*, where videotaped performances can be analyzed for their interactions (see Sawyer and DeZutter 2009).

Example 1, Balinese *arja* drumming:

> When given the chance, Pak Dewa and Cok Alit sit facing each other with only a foot of space between them. They stare directly into each other's eyes as they drum, seeming to read cues from slight motions of head, shoulders, or hands . . . from smiles, from breath. When Cok Alit wants to cue an *angsel* [an accented rhythmic break, structurally significant], he leans in and increases his hand movements, bouncing up and down a little. His gaze intensifies and his smile deepens, like he might burst out laughing at any moment. (Personal field notes, 2011)

Example 2, jazz:

> As his first solo came to an end, Freeman started to become more active physically, then turned to Hodes two beats before the end of his solo. . . . Throughout his first song, the musicians backing him up watched him attentively. At the end of Hodes' solo, Freeman again became more active (thereby attracting the attention of the others) and invoked the agreement with bass and drums for "fours" (four bar breaks) with a questioning look. Both Smith and Bastien nodded in response. (Bastien and Hostager 1992, 98)

You see, if something is not right with Frank [Sinatra] as far as the tempo, he'll start patting his foot and give it to you. . . . Or Frank will give a special hand signal which means: "Come on! Let me have a little more of you, I can't hear." Sounds like a coach, you know, giving signals. (Drummer Louis Bellson, quoted in Pelz-Sherman 1998, 139)

Example 3, Irish traditional music:

Tunes repeat: they are played at least twice, or maybe three, four times; then the players generally change to another tune. Getting "the change" is a skill; it has to be watched for, and listened for [. . .] If the repeats have not been predetermined, the players will use body language to communicate the change—eyes, shoulders, elbows, knees, feet and hands may be deployed. Hence, the manic widening of the flute-player's eyes at the end of the first tune the third time round, or the shaking of her head which means you play that first tune again. . . . Or maybe someone is inspired to form a new set there and then, or maybe someone else is bored, and craves a new experience. On such occasions silent questions will be asked by the participants: an eyebrow raised, a finger pointing to the heart, a deferring nod in someone else's direction. (Carson 1996, 29)

Example 4, psychedelic rock, Grateful Dead

As lead guitarist Garcia and bassist Lesh play the unison opening riff of "Dark Star" . . . we see Garcia attentively facing Lesh and making rhythmic leg movements as the rhythm and tempo of the song's introductory elements stabilize. His repetitive movements establish a short-lived ambiance of calm, stability, and consistency. But within seconds, as Garcia begins his improvised lead work, . . . he assumes his default physical position onstage: his body faces toward the audience but his attention is focused almost entirely on the fretboard . . . of his guitar. (Pettengill 2013, 42)

In each of these practices, nonverbal communication conveys intent, instruction, confirmation, goals, emotions, and desires. Jazz musicians and *arja* drummers use increased physical activity to call attention to themselves and give instructions. Eye contact in Irish music and *arja* communicates intent or a change of plans. Hand signals in jazz and rhythmic leg movements in rock express musical goals—for more stability, for more energy. Body position reflects a player's desired level of interaction; the *arja* drummers' proximity and mutual gaze indicate a need for close communication, while the guitarist's move from facing co-performers to facing the audience and watching his own hands communicates a shift from interaction to introspection. Yet these cues are only meaningful if received and understood. A questioning look in both Irish music and jazz asks for confirmation, while a nod is offered in response, a marker of reception that conversation analysts call *uptake*. This lets the cuing musician know "it is safe to proceed" (Smith 1999, 42).

Interpreting the cues and uptakes of this nonverbal language while simultaneously improvising requires "attentiveness, care, and willingness to give ground and take direction" (Becker 2000, 173). But it is also "contingent upon participants' expectations within the given performance, based upon their individual and collective prior experience in similar contexts" (Smith 1999, 6). Because of the complexity of this process, physical and musical communication codes are very often employed in tandem, as when Lúnasa's whistle player combines body position and direction, size of physical movements, and increased musical activity to cue an intensity shift. This redundancy of messages improves musicians' interpretation of their co-performers' actions, enabling them to disentangle meaningful from incidental information. It also provides clues for the analyst, drawing attention to important or distinctive moments in a performance.

Nonverbal Communication as a Marker of Interactional Roles

"One of the main ways in which people channel expectations in social interactions," Brinner observes, "is by taking roles—patterns of behavior and status in relation to others—and by anticipating and interpreting others' actions and stances in terms of roles" (1995, 287–88). The collectively improvising musicians I worked with, and those I read about, seemed to assume general *performative* roles as well as more specific *musical* roles, each defined by practice-specific norms of musician or instrument function within their ensemble. In jazz, flamenco, or Brazilian *pagode*, for instance, each musician filled a performative role of either soloist or accompanist. Among accompanists, there were more specific musical roles for holding down harmony, supporting rhythm and groove, and so on.[47] While such roles could be flexible or become blurred—an accompanist taking a solo, for instance—most practices appeared to have commonly held expectations guiding performance.

Musicians' *interactional* roles, by contrast, often seemed more mutable and moment-specific, conveyed, clarified, and reinforced through nonverbal communication. During improvised performance, Pelz-Sherman proposes, each musician is "constantly both sending and receiving varying amounts of information, but acts at a given moment primarily as either a *sender* or a *receiver*" (1998, 131). While a sender initiates new musical ideas, a receiver responds with complementary ideas. These interactional roles or *communication states* are often reflected in musicians' nonverbal interactions. In her study of co-regulation and communication between North Indian tabla and sitar players, Moran (2013) posits that the direction of a musician's face communicates her availability for sending or receiving information. "We make our world into what it is by selectively attending," argues Hagberg, "and the composite result of any such act of selective foregrounding against massive backgrounding is our perceptual world in that moment" (2016, 489). Our limited cognitive load capacity means that we constantly need to decide where to place our attention.[48] Like a spotlight, this attention can be narrowly directed and strong, or diffuse but more broadly encompassing.[49] A collectively improvising musician may at times be focused inward, fully engrossed in the task at hand. At other times, she will give one co-performer her full concentration; at yet others, she will attend with less perfect focus to the interactions of the group as a whole, or find a middle ground of *prioritized integrative attention*, where various higher and lower priority actions are given unequal cognitive strength.[50]

Moran found that Indian classical musicians tended to look in one of four places—at their own hands, at their partner's hands, at their partner's faces, and into the distance—but that where they looked at any given moment was linked to both communicative state and attentional need. Sitar soloists spent much more time looking at their own hands than did tabla accompanists, who looked most often at soloists' hands or faces.[51] Open-eyed mutual gaze occurred only rarely, and only at structurally important moments where both musicians wanted to ensure perfect coordination.[52] Further, when sitarists looked at their accompanist's faces, or looked away, tabla players would often perform an expressive gesture within a few seconds. Whether conscious or not, this likely indicates uptake. As Moran notes: "A well-timed expressive gesture may, perhaps, be less demanding than a full mutual gaze, but could still provide acknowledgement by accompanists of their ongoing engagement with the soloist's musical output" (57). Where performative roles are relatively unidirectional, the looking and gesturing behavior of tabla players reflects the consistency of their communication state as receivers.[53]

Interactional roles are similarly expressed across genres and cultures. Improvising Balinese *reyong* players will often watch the hands or face of the strongest performer, while *arja* drummers often alternate between a full mutual gaze and a far-off look. And flamenco guitarists, regularly cast as receivers, routinely watch the dancer's feet or singer's face.

HOW INTERACTIONAL ROLES INFORM ANALYSIS

Interactional roles necessarily influence the improvisational choices of each musician in a collective, and here I see a useful distinction between more equal and more hierarchical interactions. In free improvisation, whether jazz, Western classical, or theatrical, the goal is generally a hierarchy-less encounter where each participant contributes equally to the emerging performance. The same is true of certain stricter-form practices of formulaic variation like *reyong norot*, where the four simultaneously improvising musicians, each of equal importance, together create an interlocking melody. Similarly, in Aka polyphonic singing, any number of participants can add to the texture any way they see fit, each complementing the whole without hierarchy and as likely to send as to receive. Yet as we've seen, many improvised practices, like flamenco, are not truly egalitarian; the existence of stable or shifting leaders, the given or assumed roles of soloist and accompanist, and the copresence of Monson's liquid and solid musical elements all contribute to interactional hierarchies. While a jazz rhythm section or the supporting drummers of an Ewe dance-drumming troupe may interact in a relatively egalitarian fashion among themselves, each musician equally free to improvise within her idiom, this group of musicians exists as an agent system against which a soloist is given more freedom. Such practices are no less collective, but interactional roles necessarily shape improvisational options.

Despite the inherent hierarchizations of many collectively improvised practices, however, none of my teachers ever suggested that certain strands were less central to their music than others, or that improvisation in more *solid* parts was less important.[54] Indeed, many studies of group improvised musics show that the improvisatory freedom of co-performers must manifest itself in inverse relationships.[55] As Monson notes of jazz rhythm section musicians:

> Solid time is the relatively stable element against which a soloist phrases even more offbeat melodic and harmonic ideas. The stronger the time feel, the easier it is for a soloist to take risks with solo phrasing. As [drummer] Michael Carvin put it, "Gravy is nice, but you have to have something to put it on."
>
> At a drum lesson during which I was paying more attention to interjecting

soloistic ideas than to keeping time, Carvin stopped me and remarked that he heard the gravy, "but where's the dinner?" (1996, 28)

Players recognize the "fundamental interdependence of the musical roles fulfilled by the instruments [. . . and] it is the balance of these complementary musical roles that contributes to ensemble cohesiveness" (Monson 1996, 51). As we will see in this book's second case study, understanding musicians' roles—stable and shifting, performative, musical, and interactional—is essential to deducing how each performer differently employs processes of interpretation, embellishment, recombination, and expansion.

COLLECTIVE IMPROVISATION AS COLLABORATIVE EMERGENCE

My desire to unpack how performative, musical, and interactional roles might jointly inflect collective improvisation across genres prompted investigation into two posited features of group creativity: *intersubjectivity* and *emergence*.[56] The former claims that we cannot truly understand the action of any participant in a collective improvisation until it has been interpreted and responded to by other participants. Through this "retrospective interpretation" (Sawyer 2003, 8), co-performers establish a mutual (and mutually constructed) understanding of each individual's actions. The latter, related concept claims that we cannot predict the shape or direction that any improvised performance will take because it does not exist in the mind of any one performer; rather, it *emerges* from the actions and intentions of the group, and from the *interactions* of those actions and intentions. Like a complex dynamical system, the whole is always greater than the sum of its parts. Analyzing an improvised performance after the fact, it can be easy to miss these two defining characteristics because we only see the things that *actually* occurred, never truly being privy to those that *might have* occurred.

Dialogue from a sketch by the improvisational comedy group Upright Citizens Brigade exemplifies intersubjectivity and emergence. Because spoken improvisation is almost purely turn-based, its performers improvising consecutively rather than simultaneously, improv theater offers straightforward examples of both processes.[57] The existence of these processes in the more simultaneous improvisations of many musical practices is partial, mitigated by additional factors addressed later in the chapter.

An Upright Citizens Brigade show centers on improvised monologues inspired by one-word audience suggestions, then used "as fodder for a series of high octane, balls-to-the-wall improvised sketches."[58] The result is an irreverent, sometimes offensive, always no-holds-barred illustration of collaborative emergence. The 2005 televised show "A.S.S.S.C.A.T.: Improv" opens with comedian Tina Fey riffing on the audience-suggested word "ham" while eight other improvisers sit in chairs behind her, listening and waiting.[59] Her monologue bounces wildly from "ham salad" to the discovery of Broadway's first "little orphan Annie." As Fey winds down, several improvisers hop out of their chairs. One man stands downstage, next to a door, and indicates with his hand to another man, beginning the first scene.

> MAN 1 Why don't you just have your daughter sign the sign-in sheet and, uh, she'll just, uh, she'll be in line to audition same as everybody else.
> [short PAUSE. Woman 1 steps downstage, marching like a young, excited kid]
> MAN 2 OK . . .
> WOMAN 1 . . . He said I could sign up, Daddy! [grins at Man 2]
> MAN 2 I know [touches her shoulder]. Go ahead [directs her toward an imaginary table]. Keep "turned out" while you sign.
> [Woman 1 mimes signing paperwork with prim manner and feet turned out like a dancer]
> MAN 2 [to Man 1] So, uh, I manage my daughter's career.
> MAN 1 Oh, oh, well, that . . . that's gr . . . [distracted by Woman 1 doing a little tap dance]. That's great. I . . .
> WOMAN 2 [enters scene through downstage door, interrupting Man 1 and delivering her line back through the door in a loud, jovial voice] Hahaha! Thank you! I had a good time too! [shuts door and walks across the stage in front of Woman 1 and Man 2]
> [8-second PAUSE as they all watch Woman 2 walk away, and laughter dies down]
> MAN 2 [to Man 1, in a serious tone] Look, I know a lot of these roles are won by, uh, casting-couch hanky-panky, and I wanna let you know . . .
> MAN 3 [enters scene through the same door, interrupting Man 2] You know, stop the audition. That little kid in the thong is dynamite![60]

This excerpt is built from both intersubjectivity and emergence. Fey's monologue has given the improvisers plenty of ideas, and from these many options the first speaker sets the scene, also creating roles in his first line for two other characters: the father and the daughter. The next few exchanges build the scene and flesh out the characters, first creating an "explosion of combinatorial possibilities" and then constraining them as each performer seeks to "contribute utterances which retain coherence with the emergent" (Sawyer 2003, 12 and 88). Like the bassist's triplet gestures and triple-stops in figures 4.8 and 4.9, the import of each utterance is contingent on its reception and interpretation by co-performers, and the shape of the full performance emerges from this collective decision-making process. Potential paths not taken become closed.[61] The giddiness of the second woman as she leaves the casting studio, for instance, could have meant many things: that she was happy with her audition, that she had been offered the part, that she was an old friend of the casting director, and so on. It is her co-performers who determine the significance of her behavior, which in turn influences the next steps in path as it unfolds.

The same is often true of musical collectivity. In a 2007 performance of Boston's free improv group BSC, transcribed and analyzed by Bunk (2011), musicians collectively draw from one another's pitch and timbre choices to create an intersubjective, emergent performance. The 12-minute improvisation begins with a sustained A4 on the trumpet. The saxophone responds 30 seconds later with a detuned A4, also sustained, retrospectively giving meaning to the trumpet's pitch and rhythmic choices through imitation and variation. About a minute into the performance, per figure 4.10, the bass on the bottom staff offers up a new motive: a snap pizzicato (circled in black). Had the bassist's co-performers not reacted in kind, this could have remained an isolated gesture. Instead, the saxophone and trumpet fade out in response (circled in gray), and the tape player adds complementary spins, joined a few seconds later by short crackles on the circuit-board (both circled in black). Recognizing the impetus for change, the trumpet player opens up the pitch palette with a sustained D#4 (circled in black), and the "composite event" (238) of *pizz.*, spins, and crackles fades out in turn (each circled in gray). The performance as a whole is unpredictable, the meaning of each event nebulous until defined in retrospect by subsequent events.[62]

Of course, co-performers will not always have a unified vision of where the performance is going, or even similar mental representations about what's happening in any given moment. Action must be thought of as "a process of coordination of individual contributions to joint activity rather than as a state of agreement" (Matusov 1996, 34). In fact, a dialectical model of creativity states that it is the "inconsistencies between competing views" of a situation that "create the opportunity for novelty to emerge" (Harvey 2014, 329).[63] Such inconsistencies allow performers to inspire one another with fresh ideas and perspectives, pushing the performance in directions none of them could have predicted.[64] As one Chicago jazz musician notes:

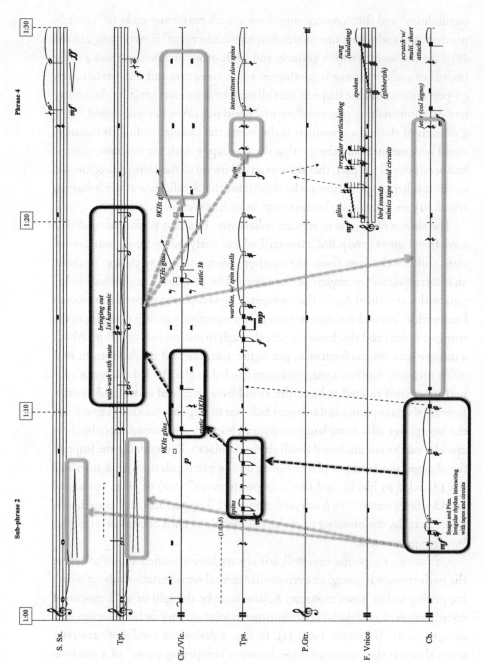

FIGURE 4.10. Intersubjectivity and emergence in free improv

> By talking to people up on stage through your music, you can start working on stuff you've never heard and never done . . . you need people to play with . . . when I do it, I'd find that there are these things coming out of myself, which I didn't even know were there, I'd never heard them, I didn't know where they came from. . . . but playing with the others triggers it, so maybe consciously or subconsciously you'll hear that thing, that you're trying to find . . . by listening to what other people have to say, and by talking to them about it. (Sawyer 2003, 28–29)

In the transcribed theatrical scene, whatever the second woman's own interpretation of her entrance, when the father makes the "hanky-panky" comment he suggests an interpretation to the group. A moment later, following the cardinal "Yes, and . . ." rule of improv theater—that one should accept any suggestion, no matter how wild, and then add to it—the casting director joins the scene, confirming the father's suspicions.[65] Thus "ensemble behavior builds incrementally out of individual agents' actions and reactions. Achievement of the 'goal' is not the specific product of a deliberate, provably correct process, but an emergent and uncertain epiphenomenon of the agents' real-time interactions" (Hayes-Roth, Brownston, and Gent 1998, 145).

Reading the scene's transcript after the fact, we might almost imagine that its trajectory was preplanned; each turn of dialogue coherently follows from the preceding one. The same could be said of the Jaki Byard Quartet and BSC examples noted previously. But in fact each spoken line or played gesture in a collective improvisation suggests a myriad of choices, any one of which might take the performance in a completely different direction.[66] As Ricoeur's theory of narrative avers: "There is no story unless our attention is held in suspense by a thousand contingencies. . . . Rather than being predictable, a conclusion must be *acceptable*" (1981, 277). Every moment in an improvised performance marks infinite possibilities not realized as one decision is made. And at any time, a current activity "can force a reinterpretation of previous moments" or "trigger transformations in the music and its reception" (Borgo 2005, 68). Such suggestions, contingencies, and reinterpretations are the bread and butter of collective improvisation.

COMPLICATING EMERGENCE FOR MUSICAL ANALYSIS: DEGREES OF INFLUENCE

While emergence and intersubjectivity seemed particularly salient to concepts of collectivity, my analyses and performing experience of both *reyong norot* and *kendang arja* warned against blindly overstating their centrality. Collective improvisation, particularly in these more simultaneous interactions, also seemed to succeed because each participant was independently knowledgeable and sensitive to the needs of the performance. Assuming collective intentions and a cooperative mode of interaction revealed neither the *quality* nor *frequency* of co-performers' direct influences on one another.

> Players are constantly doing something with their musical utterances, responding or not responding to particular musical events in the flow and finding that what they play may have both intended and unintended consequences to other players and audience members, as well as to the space of participation (or lack thereof) that is created in the process. (Monson 1997, 102)

Different practices or moments in a performance, then, are governed by different styles of interaction, and these shape the level of emergence and intersubjectivity: the relative degree of moment-to-moment co-performer influence. In his study of jazz interaction, Rinzler is careful to differentiate performances in which the music emerges specifically through creative interaction from those in which players "lay down their part as effectively and tastefully as possible," perhaps even "radically depart[ing] from clichés and standard patterns," but without specifically interacting with the musical offerings of co-performers (1988, 156). These two styles of interaction, which Pelz-Sherman (1998) terms *sharing* and *not sharing*, may be more usefully imagined as a continuum. Collectively improvising musicians, always working with what Searle (1990) terms *we-intentions*, still frequently alternate between sharing and not-sharing or play simultaneously with elements of both.[67]

The distinctions drawn by Rinzler and Pelz-Sherman are not intended as value judgments; sharing does not necessarily create superior music to not-sharing, and often not-sharing is essential, or the two must work in alternation or combination. In the mostly simultaneous improvisation of fast interlocking *reyong norot*, for instance, intersubjectivity operates in a narrower range than in those practices with elements of longer-term or turn-based interaction; when polyphonic interlocking must happen in the moment, there is sometimes no possibility for small-scale sharing. And some "jazz musicians have expressly stated that interactive musical processes can at times be undesirable or even creative hindrances"; that "sometimes it is best for jazz players to adhere to conventional ensemble roles without immediately responding or otherwise adapting to one another's spontaneous flights of interaction" (Givan 2016, paras. 5 and 6).

It becomes useful, then, to think about interaction at different levels of specificity. In any ensemble performance, improvised or not, musicians must be in sync at the fine-grained level of groove, tracking subtle shifts of tempo and dynamics through what Givan terms *microinteraction*.[68] Collectively coordinating the coarse-grained *macrointeractions* of "unified (or at least compatible) stylistic idioms" played at "mutually coherent intensity levels" is also vital (Givan 2016, para. 10). But the *motivic interaction* we so often think of when characterizing jazz or improv comedy is not always possible, or even desirable. Many jazz performances, in fact, employ next to no motivic interaction. Much mainstream post-bop, for instance, involves long passages "where musicians focus on fulfilling individual roles, adhering to a predetermined formal road map, staying rhythmically coordinated, and providing one another with a mutually agreeable, effective macrointeractive playing environment" (Givan 2016, para. 17). An interaction in which a musician adopts and adapts a motive introduced by her partner is different from one in which she responds, in broad ways, to the peaks of her partner's solos; different again is one in which she simply plays simultaneously in a complementary idiom. This final performance is no less *collective* than the other two; it is simply less *contingent* because "what is mistaken for a very subtle interplay between musicians may really only be several members independently fulfilling their own musical function in a creative way" (Rinzler 1988, 156).

The nature of the interaction itself, whether turn-based or simultaneous, to some extent dictates interactional style. In practices like jazz, both the large-scale turn-taking of consecutive solos and the more localized back-and-forth of "trading fours" enable musical influence over time. However, unlike the almost exclusively turn-based dialogue of improv theater, jazz interaction is not purely diachronic; soloists and rhythm section members also improvise simultaneously. Because jazz musicians often think of their musical contributions in motives, phrases, or even full choruses, there is frequently time for co-performers to draw short-term diachronic influence, responding to motivic and stylistic suggestions as we saw in figures 4.8–4.10. However, negotiating these simultaneous interactions also relies on the existence of preordained roles that establish complementary idioms for different musicians in the collective. Such musical roles become even more central in the almost purely synchronic interactions of *kendang arja* or Shona mbira players, for instance, where the need for moment-to-moment interlocking reigns supreme. "Unexpected sensory changes requiring significant voluntary compensations require a minimum time of about 400–500 ms . . . and this is therefore the time scale over which improvising players in ensembles can react to each other's introduced novelties"

(Pressing 1988, 138). As we will see, *arja* drummers, whose strokes interlock a minimum of twice that speed, must, to some extent, have predetermined musical roles dictating who can play what when. Similarly, improvisation in *bèlè* drumming and dance "is (among other things) a learned skill of combining constituent bits so that they appear integrated and directed as they emerge in the performance" (Gerstin 1998, 158). Here, macrointeraction, more than motivic interaction, is key.[69]

A reference to a motive from five minutes earlier, a response to a call from three seconds ago, a simultaneous selection and alteration of motives formulaically designed to interlock; each of these demands a different kind of analysis. The more purely synchronic the interaction, the more we must rely on discovering practice-specific performative and musical roles or idiomatic guidelines for interaction as opposed to analyzing direct dialogic exchange. The role of the analyst is not to judge each performance's relative collectivity but rather, through understanding the differences between motivic and macrointeractions, to be better equipped to analyze collective improvisations of many stripes.

CONTINUA FOR ANALYSIS: A CONSTELLATION OF CHOICES

The foregoing discussions suggest a complex and multifaceted analytical model for collective improvisation: one that examines a constellation of musical and interactional parameters. These include the model's relative specificity and flexibility, its idiomatic realization types, and the practitioners' level of conscious knowledge about it as well as the varying modes of interaction and degrees of direct co-performer influence occurring at any moment in a performance. The previous discussions illustrate how each of these factors, shown in figure 4.11, might influence music analysis.

The full-page figure 4.12 situates broader theories and concepts explored throughout the chapter into this analytical model, offering a visual reminder of the complex processes at play for both improviser and analyst. At the center of the figure, in dark gray ovals and boxes, lies the analytical model from figure 4.11. As we've seen, every improviser's knowledge of her model, whether conscious or unconscious, is shaped by shared knowledge and constraints, and cognitively actualized through mutual entrenched conceptualizations. These interconnected components of collective improvisation comprise the top left corner of figure 4.12. Per the top right corner of the figure, the improviser may be working from a single-voice or multi-voice model—realizing it via the

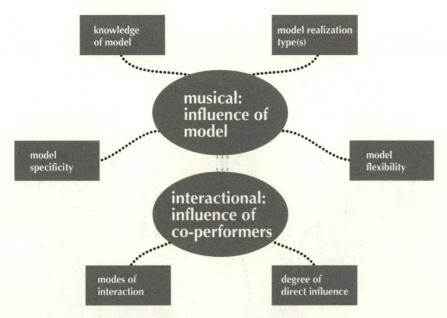

FIGURE 4.11. Analytical model for collective improvisation

many possible textures and approaches in figures 4.5 and 4.6—and ensemble success may be fostered by group flow.

Moving down the figure, we see how the musical model itself, wherever it falls on the continua of specificity shown on the figure's left side and flexibility on its right, should be thought of as a dynamic framework for improvisation, contingent on the interaction of co-performers. Thus, the cloud shape at the center of the figure, emphasizing the "model as dynamic," points to the interconnectedness of these musical considerations with the interactional ones outlined below them. The bottom left of the figure reminds us how performers' various modes of interaction, whether hierarchical or equal, rely on communication codes and the establishment of stable and shifting interactional roles. On the bottom right, we see that while collective performance will be both emergent and intersubjective, the degree of moment-to-moment co-performer influence is determined by the nature of the interactions themselves—whether synchronic or diachronic—and by the ensuing micro, macro, and motivic interactional styles.

I suggest that every collectively improvised practice can be situated within these various continua and oppositions, and that their combination provides a loose framework for understanding how collective improvisation is

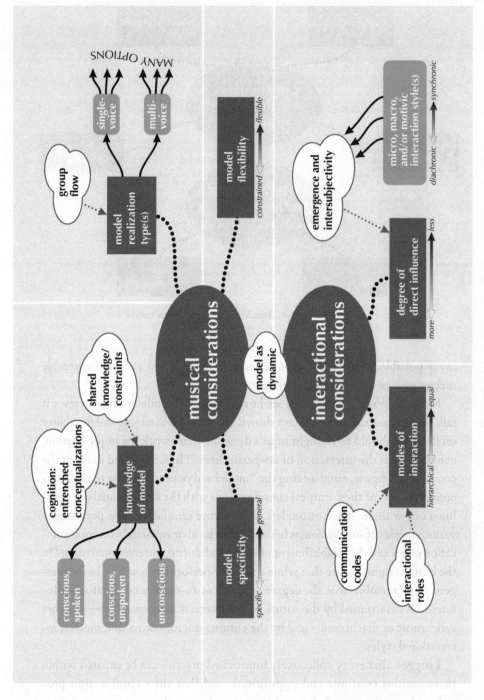

FIGURE 4.12. Factors informing the analytical model in figure 4.11

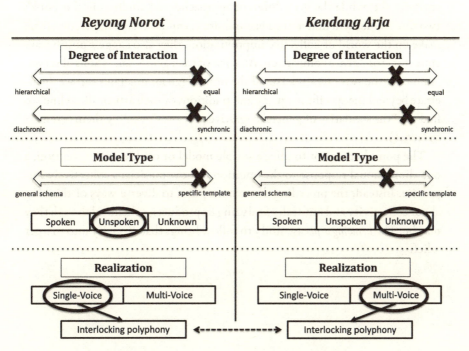

FIGURE 4.13. Comparison: *reyong norot* versus *kendang arja*

constructed (or may be deconstructed) in any practice. Many of the existing resources on collective improvisation have focused on either free improvisation or jazz; Monson, Berliner, Borgo, Hodson, Sawyer, and others have provided excellent models for analyzing these largely Western, relatively turn-based practices with models at the freer ends of the specificity-flexibility spectrum. The two main case studies in this book seek to balance that literature, exploring techniques for analyzing the more synchronic interactions through which musicians extemporize on stricter models in a non-Western, aural music culture. The superficial similarities of the two case studies draw their differences into clearer focus, per figure 4.13. *Reyong norot,* as we've seen, creates equal interlocking polyphony from a very specific, unspoken but explicitly known single-voice model in an almost strictly synchronic, hierarchy-less interaction. By contrast, *kendang arja*'s similar musical texture, as we will see, draws from a less specific, multi-voice model, unknown at the conscious level, and is realized through a mostly synchronic, moderately hierarchical interaction.

The striking contrasts between these two relatively similar practices from within a single music culture highlight the importance of genre-specific analysis. Yet, while the very different approaches and findings in this book's two case studies will hint at the near-infinite permutations of interactions that make up the world of collective improvisation, they also suggest possible avenues for cross-genre comparison. Analysis of each genre can, as Solis observes, "influence the ways we understand the others" (2009, 10). Thus can we "penetrate beyond the specific language and traditions of each artistic discipline" to find the "the similarity of general cognitive processes" guiding them (Pressing 1984, 346).

The point here is not to offer a simple model or cookie-cutter solution, a one-dimensional response to the question of how musicians collectively improvise. Instead, the preceding discussions point to diverse ways of thinking about collectivity and musically analyzing its products, ephemeral though they may be. The *kendang arja* case study to follow brings that diversity into sharper relief.

CHAPTER FIVE

UNRAVELING UNCONSCIOUS MODELS

THE BOUNDARIES OF *KENDANG ARJA*

THE TRADITIONAL "NON-METHOD"

Pak Dewa, father Dewa, is a man with an easy smile. He's always laughing, usually at me and my arja *drumming. But it's never a jeering mockery; it's the laugh of a patient and contented man who is genuinely, wholeheartedly amused by most everything. He says affectionately that my character is* keras, *hard or strong. That I always want to learn more, even if I'm not yet ready; even if my hands still get tired and confused when we play too long or too fast. He's not wrong, of course. His drum improvisations for the Balinese dance drama* arja *are so wild, so utterly delicious, that my brain gets impatient waiting for my hands to catch up. Always.*

Pak Dewa spits out his tobacco and lights up a Marlboro, indicating that it's time for a rest. In his low, scratchy voice he casually starts talking about religion. This happens often,

---

An earlier version of material from chapters 5 and 6 was published as "'The *Lanang* Is the Bus Driver': Intersections of Ethnography and Music Analysis in a Study of Balinese *Arja* Drumming," in *Computational Phonogram Archiving*, Current Research in Systematic Musicology 5, edited by Rolf Bader (Springer International Publishing, 2019), 37–74. Material reproduced with permission from editor and publisher.

a "one-hour" lesson frequently taking three or four. For every drum pattern I've learned from this man, I've gained a hundred insights into his perspectives on Balinese culture, like how the split gate leading into a temple represents the two types of thoughts in a person's mind, good and bad ("baik dan buruk"), and the one shrine we see straight ahead as we enter represents those thoughts becoming one: a single focus on prayer. Today it's about his experience praying in a church in America, knowing that Christianity was far from his Balinese Hindu religion, but feeling deeply that this church was a holy place and believing there was but one god, only many different names for him and varied paths to reach him.[1] I have always thought of Pak Dewa as an intensely spiritual person. This same man, of course, will use the cengceng—one of the many instruments we Western gamelan players are told never to step over, because it is sacred—as an ashtray when there's none other to be found (figure 5.1).

Pak Dewa butts out his cigarette, this time in a makeshift bottle cap ashtray, and plays a few strokes on his drum, kendang. "Ya, lagi," he says. Again. My arms are exhausted from the last hour of repeating in random order, much faster than I can play with any accuracy, the six arja patterns he's taught me. But there's nothing for it; I pick up my kendang and place it in my lap, smaller head on the left, larger head on the right as in the photographs in figure 5.2, and we begin again.

FIGURE 5.1. "Sacred" ashtray. (Photo by Nicole Walker, 2003. Used with permission.)

I've been studying with Pak Dewa for several weeks, and it has not been without its challenges. Although his improvisation on arja's *lower-pitched* wadon *drum is rich and varied, he appears to have conscious awareness of only a small handful of patterns. The six 8- and 12-beat patterns I've learned from him are all rhythmically related. Similar placement of high ringing* kom *strokes, which I notate "o" to represent this Balinese mnemonic, as well as low bass-y Dag (D) strokes in different patterns hint at an underlying grammar.*[2] *Figure 5.3 shows two patterns that Pak Dewa taught for use with a 4-beat cyclic structure. In these and other transcriptions, main strokes* kom *(o) and Dag (D) are shown as round noteheads, high and low respectively. Subsidiary finger taps or "counting strokes," used to kinesthetically maintain running 16th notes, are notated with [x]-noteheads in staff notation and "_" in mnemonic notation.*[3] *Slightly louder left-hand counting strokes, which create a light slap, are notated with triangular noteheads and "l," while the subsidiary bass strokes that often precede Dag (D) are notated with the lowest [x]-notehead and "d." For*

FIGURE 5.2. *Kendang arja* playing position from various angles. Cok Alit of Peliatan (*top left*), Pak Dewa of Pengosekan (*top right*) and Pak Tama of Singapadu (*bottom*). (Photos by Chelsea Edwardson, 2011. Used with permission.)

FIGURE 5.3. Two of Pak Dewa's taught *wadon* patterns

visual clarity, numbers above notations indicate beats in the cycle, dots mark the halfway point of each beat, and dashes delineate the other subdivisions. In the longer Pattern 2, the final note on the first line is shown again in parentheses at the beginning of the second. It is played as a continuous 12-beat pattern.

The two patterns in figure 5.3, with their many off-beat kom (o) strokes and shared "o d" gestures, are clearly connected. But I don't yet really understand how they are constructed, nor how they might either exemplify or illuminate limits in the improvisation of new patterns. What's more, I have little conception of how, in this paired drumming practice, each of Pak Dewa's patterns will complement his partner's on the higher lanang drum. I know that kendang arja *is made to interlock, though like* reyong norot, *its improvisatory nature makes this interlocking less exact than in other paired drum practices. In performance, Pak Dewa's high ringing* kom (o) *strokes dance around his partner Cok Alit's parallel* peng (e) *strokes. Both are played with the left hand on the rim of the drum as in the left photograph in figure 5.4.*

Interlocking, too, are their low bass strokes, the wadon's Dag (D) *and* lanang's *higher-pitched* Tut (T). *Played using the right thumb on the larger head of the* kendang, *as in figure 5.4's right-hand photograph, these strokes almost never coincide in improvised performance. But how is this accomplished?*

At the end of a long day of lessons across south and central Bali, I return to my small guesthouse in Ubud. With a cup of tea in the cool air that night almost invariably brings, I transcribe what I've learned, hoping for some eureka moment. I compare Pak Dewa's wadon *patterns with those of his* lanang *partner Cok Alit, noting how clearly these patterns seem designed to interlock. In figure 5.5, my first* lanang *pattern from Cok Alit is juxtaposed against the first four beats of his partner's* wadon *pattern from the top of figure 5.3.* Tut (T) *strokes never coincide with* Dag (D) *and there is only one collision, circled, of* kom (o) *with* peng (e).

Unlike in reyong norot, however, where precomposed gangsa figuration provides a single model, explicit and specific, any definite models for kendang arja remain unspoken and, I hypothesize, unconscious. In this context, what can each drummer's small collection of taught patterns tell us about his extensive palette of improvised ones? Can taught patterns be considered models for improvisation in and of themselves or are they merely representative samples of patterns made from a looser model of structural and aesthetic guidelines? And is there any way to know for sure? There might be no "there" there.

Walking into the home of an expert drummer like Pak Dewa and asking him to teach me all of his coolest arja *patterns felt something akin to walking into Ella Fitzgerald's*

FIGURE 5.4. Playing technique for *kom* (o)/*peng* (e), played by Cok Alit (*left*), and for *Dag* (D)/*Tut* (T), played by Pak Dewa (*right*). (Photos by Chelsea Edwardson, 2011. Used with permission.)

UNRAVELING UNCONSCIOUS MODELS · 183

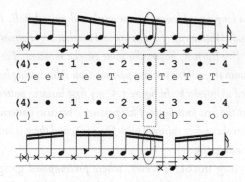

FIGURE 5.5. Comparing Cok Alit's *lanang* with Pak Dewa's *wadon* patterns

home and asking her to teach me how to scat. Both are experts in their practice. Both are improvisers. Yet each would find teaching improvisation in a codified way, the way I hoped to learn it, to be both difficult and strange. They, themselves, learned what they knew in a traditional style of learning-without-teaching that leads to tacit knowledge: a brand of "unpedagogic practice" that Timothy Rice humorously, but fittingly, calls "the traditional non-method."[4] This learning process and the kinds of knowledge it engenders unescapably affect analysis of their improvisations.

"LEVELS OF CULTURE" AND WAYS OF KNOWING

Anthropologist Edward T. Hall (1980 and 1992) has proposed three levels of culture—the formal, the technical, and the informal—levels that, he posits, universally pervade all activities, ideas, and behaviors. The technical and informal levels are particularly relevant to a discussion of the pedagogy of improvisation. The technical level embraces explicit, unambiguous information, transmitted directly from teacher to student, either verbally or through precise system-specific symbols like music notation. Communication is analytical, allowing for a discussion of rules and their underlying theory, and teaching proceeds in a logical, linear progression. Most musicians raised in a Music Conservatory system will be familiar with this methodology. Yet outside the walls of Western educational institutions these pedagogical practices are relatively rare.

Aka musicians learn their intricate polyphonic songs through observation and imitation of their elders. There is little, if any, verbal communication regarding vocal technique or the execution of melodies and melodic improvisation; novices learn through trial and error (see Fürniss 2006, 168). Similar autodidactic practices exist among children across many cultures. A six-year-old boy asked how he learns the complex coordination of breath and melody required to play harmonicas and whistles replies simply: "I figure it out. I listen and figure it out" (Campbell 2001, 220). I Wayan Sudirana (Sudi) describes his learning process for *kendang arja* in similar terms. Although he cites Pak Dewa as a major influence for *wadon* improvisation, he admits he was never *berani*, bold enough to ask for lessons. Instead, he observed Pak Dewa's playing in ceremonies and performances and learned his patterns at speed.[5] As in traditional Javanese "ethnopedagogy,"

> [the learner is] expected to take an active role in "searching" for (*nggolèki*) knowledge. Musical regularities [a]re often not explicitly articulated; students ha[ve] to abstract general features or principles from the compositions and improvisations they hea[r] and infer widely applicable techniques for interpreting or embellishing the models they encounte[r]. (Perlman 2004, 118)

In each of these informal learning situations, playing techniques and patterns are learned through observation and imitation of a master. Rules are never discussed explicitly, as they are in Hall's technical learning environments, but must be discovered independently by each individual learner. These contrasting knowledge acquisition methods have led to the posited existence of several very different ways of knowing:

> intuitively or explicitly, actively or passively, as a way of doing something, as probabilities or immutable facts, and so on. Distinctions of this sort... are manifested in the accessibility of things that we know, in our ability to act on them or talk about them, rationalize and classify them, or trust them to work for us with little or no conscious control. (Brinner 1995, 34–35)

Of particular salience here is the intuitive/explicit dichotomy, which juxtaposes knowledge *of* something with knowledge *about* something.[6] Improvised practices generally rely on both ways of knowing. Most jazz musicians explicitly know the melodies and chord changes of standard tunes. Some can notate the tune; some can talk about its structural details; most are able to play a simplified version or break the tune into smaller sections for pedagogical purposes. Conversely, a musician with intuitive (unconscious) knowledge of the model might only be able to provide another improvised version. Yet while jazz models are often explicitly known, the knowledge base informing their idiomatic performance is as often tacit as explicit.

FIGURE 5.6. *Arja*'s *kendang* and cycle-marking instruments.
(Photo by Chelsea Edwardson, 2011. Used with permission.)

Arja drummers, too, combine explicit with intuitive knowledge of their craft. Each knows explicitly that the higher-pitched *lanang* drum is the leader of the ensemble, a role referenced frequently in lessons and conversation. In this sung-and-danced theatrical form at one time termed "Balinese opera" by Western observers,[7] the *lanang* drummer must pay close attention to the singer-dancers, conveying their cues to the small ensemble of flutes and cycle-marking instruments shown in figure 5.6.

Arja singer-dancers perform the rhythms of their songs independently of the cyclic structures regulating kendang, and the timing of their singing and basic movements has little to no effect on which kendang improvisations are played from one cycle to the next.[8] Yet these performers do command moments of textural change through sudden dance movements called *angsel*, which prompt a disruption in the instrumental accompaniment, generally an increase in volume followed by a break. It is the *lanang* player who transmits *angsel* cues from the singer-dancers to the rest of the ensemble, using patterns featuring a special ringing stroke called *pung* (U). All *kendang arja* players have this explicit knowledge.

Explicitly known by some *arja* drummers but not others are the various cyclic structures accompanying *arja* performance. Different characters in the drama are associated with different moods and personalities, and these are reflected in the speed and beat-count length of various underlying cycles. While distinct from *gamelan gong kebyar*, *arja*'s small ensemble incorporates similar instrument functions. A wooden or bamboo struck idiophone called *guntang* maintains a steady beat every four drum strokes, notated in these chapters as quarter notes. It is from this instrument that the ensemble takes its name: *gamelan geguntangan*. Emphasizing every other beat, or marking the half beat, is a small high-pitched gong called *klenang*. Figure 5.7 shows the *guntang* on the left and the *klenang* on the right.

In figure 5.8 are the ensemble's two sparser cycle-marking instruments. On the left is the *gong pulu*: two large bronze or iron bars strung over a trough resonator. Like the *gong ageng* in *gamelan gong kebyar*, this instrument marks the end of each cycle. The handheld gong *tawa-tawa* in the right-hand photograph generally marks the halfway point between *gong pulu* strokes.

Arja uses four different cyclic structures, or *tabuh*, for different parts of the drama. These are shown in figure 5.9. The slowest is an 8-beat structure, called

FIGURE 5.7. The *guntang* (t), *left*, and *klenang* (n), *right*.
(Photos by Chelsea Edwardson, 2011. Used with permission.)

FIGURE 5.8. The *gong pulu* (G), *left*, and *tawa-tawa* (pu), *right*.
(Photos by Chelsea Edwardson, 2011. Used with permission.)

```
Tabuh Telu (Tabuh Empat)
(8)    1    2    3    4    5    6    7    8
(G)    n         n         pu        n         n         G
(t)    t    t    t    t    t    t    t    t


Tabuh Dua
(4)    1    2    3    4
(G)    n         pu        n         G
(t)    t    t    t    t


Batel
(2)  •    1    •    2
(G)  n    pu   n    G
(t)       t         t


Batel Marah
(2)  •    1    •    2
(G)  n    pu   n    G
(pu)           pu
(t)       t         t
```

FIGURE 5.9. *Arja*'s cyclic structures

tabuh telu ("three") by some drummers and *tabuh empat* ("four") by others. Slightly faster is the 4-beat structure *tabuh dua* ("two"). Reserved for the fastest parts of the performance are the 2-beat gong patterns *batel* and its yet faster cousin *batel marah*, "angry" *batel*.[9] In transcriptions, the beat-keeping *guntang*, often vocalized as "tuk," is notated "t," while the high *klenang* is notated "n." *Gong pulu* like *gong ageng* is notated "G," and the midrange *tawa-tawa*, often vocalized "pung," is shown as "pu." To follow the analyses in these chapters, the reader need not memorize the names or details of these different cyclic structures and instruments; it is enough to understand their general features and functions.

While most *arja* musicians I worked with had explicit knowledge of these different structures, I Ketut Bicuh (Pak Tut), the main *arja* teacher in Apuan of Bangli regency, seemed to have no knowledge of any cyclic structure but the 8-beat one. Because he is the lead drummer for Apuan's relatively frequent *arja* performances, I know that Pak Tut can perform over these different gong patterns, inserting *angsel* cues in the correct locations. His knowledge of cyclic structure, then, is likely intuitive.[10]

Other aspects of the *kendang arja* model and knowledge base, including structural features of their drum patterns and idiomatic ways for creating new ones, appear to be intuitive among all my teachers. This does not affect the fluency of their drumming; in fact, implicit knowledge, lacking the need for conscious effort, may allow easier, faster, and more fluent use of stored patterns in real time.[11] However, without explicit awareness of their art, these very skilled musicians may have trouble communicating that knowledge to others.[12] Rice (1996) found that tacit knowledge of traditional Bulgarian music meant "older men who knew how to play instruments had no way to teach cognitive skills such as the relationship between fingerings and pitches, how tunes were articulated with ornamentation, and how melodies could be remembered" (3–4). Likewise, my Ubud-based teacher I Wayan Pasek Sucipta (Pasek) once warned that Cok Alit would never teach me all his *arja* patterns, in part because he didn't want to give up all his best secrets, but mostly because he did not know them consciously himself.[13] The challenges of this became clear early in my fieldwork.

INTUITIVE KNOWLEDGE AND ITS CHALLENGES FOR THE RESEARCHER

After three lessons with Pak Dewa, I've learned just two short wadon *patterns, and I'm impatient for more.*

"Will you show me the next one?" I ask, as deferentially as possible. He shakes his head, apologizes, and says quite definitively that he cannot; these are the only patterns he uses. Just these two. Having seen Pak Dewa play a dizzying array of arja *patterns, particularly on the* wadon, *his drum of choice, I know this can't be the case. But he's quite convinced. To prove his point, he begins to play, cycling my two patterns, alternating between them, and sometimes combining them, pairing the first half of one with the second half of the other. Eventually, though, I notice him adding unfamiliar patterns. Then, quite suddenly, he stops.*

"Oya!" he says with a crooked grin of recognition, and begins to re-create an improvised pattern to show me. He hasn't been deliberately hiding his patterns, as Pasek might have surmised; he has simply never thought consciously about what they are.

Pak Dewa taught me just five *wadon* patterns the first year I studied with him, adding one more he said he'd remembered when I returned three years later. I had similar experiences with every new guru I sought out. Each was excited and proud to have a Westerner interested in his drumming, each limited in the patterns he could teach.[14]

What does this experience suggest about unconscious models? In this book's first case study, we saw *reyong* players improvising *norot* from a specific model, consciously known if unspoken. Once discovered, the model allowed detailed and directed analysis of the practice. Many other improvised traditions are likewise built on consciously known models. Some, like the tune and chord changes of standard jazz, are overtly stated; others, like the constituent parts of Banda-Linda horn music, or the *balungan* "unplayed melodies" of Central Javanese gamelan pieces (see Perlman 2004), are discoverable through fieldwork. Yet as we saw in the previous chapter, many orally transmitted improvised traditions appear to have no single consciously known model to uncover, even if we ask the right questions. While improvisers who recognize idiomatic and unidiomatic moments in a performance are clearly working from conceptual models, because of the intuitive nature of their knowledge, we may never learn precisely what those models are.

The ability of master *arja* drummers to weave their improvised patterns seemingly effortlessly around one another at high speeds elicits respect and awe among traditional Balinese performing artists. The crowd of top-tier drummers and dancers who always seemed to come out of the woodwork whenever I held a recording session told me that they, too, saw a magic worthy of deeper examination. What allowed my teachers to interlock so seamlessly together? When pressed, most would give some version of Gus Dé's assertion from this book's scene-setting opening: "We just play whatever we want. You can too." My own dismal attempts at improvisation told me the reality was more complicated. But my field research helped draw a clearer picture of the practice. Each of my teachers, as we will see, is a descendant of the Singapadu-village style that dominated the *arja* scene in the early twentieth century. Thus, though all from different villages, they share certain underlying structural and aesthetic guidelines for improvisation.[15] An examination of patterns learned in lessons as well as informal oral music theory will demonstrate what each reveals about intuitive models.

WHAT TAUGHT PATTERNS CAN SAY ABOUT UNCONSCIOUS MODELS

We know that patterns learned from practicing musicians can reveal aspects of explicitly known but unspoken models. The "bare figure" used for didactic purposes in Banda-Linda horn music is considered by the performers to be an "ultimate reference" for each of the music's constituent parts: its "simplest realisation" or àkɔ̄.nɔ̀. This Banda-Linda concept, as we saw in chapter 1, helped corroborate Simha Arom's (1991a) hypotheses about the music, local oral music theory revealing an unspoken but explicitly known model within taught patterns.[16] Lessons with musicians can likewise inform our grasp of unconscious, intuitive models. But with these, we must tread more carefully.

THE DANGERS OF CODIFICATION

From each of my kendang teachers, I learned between one and ten short *arja* patterns per drum. These, each claimed, comprised his full repertoire. Yet transcriptions of improvised sessions revealed many other patterns not taught. Whether these additional patterns were only intuitively known or were considered paradigmatically equivalent to others is unclear.[17] Ascertaining this may be an impossible task, and is not the goal here.

Whatever the reasons for my teachers' assertions about their mental *arja* storehouses, their taught patterns imply a hierarchy of variants, and, I hypothesize, can be a starting point for analyzing their improvisations. That said, the reification of certain patterns as somehow more "fundamental" to a drummer's style is also problematic. *Arja* drumming has not been theorized in a formal institutional context; the social construction of its materials and theory is ad hoc and varies by teacher and place. Would Cok Alit or Pak Dewa present their practice the same way to a different student at another time, or were the specific patterns they chose to teach me based on my drumming abilities and their particular *rasa*, feeling, on a given day? The similarities between Sudi's improvised *lanang* playing and the patterns I learned from Cok Alit, his former teacher, do suggest that Cok Alit might teach a comparable palette to any student who came looking. Further, that Pak Dewa could only think of one additional *wadon* pattern when I returned to his home three years after our initial *arja* encounter implies a division between explicit and intuitive drumming knowledge.

Yet can I consider taught patterns to be models? Does this hierarchy of explicit knowledge also imply a hierarchy of pattern simplicity or centrality? Pedagogically, one might assume that a teacher showing her student only a handful of patterns would choose the most basic, *dasar*, realizations. This was certainly where each of my teachers began, and was perhaps the extent of my lessons with both Pak Tut of Apuan and Pak Tama of Singapadu. Yet I suspect for Cok Alit and Pak Dewa, there was a desire not only to teach the fundamentals of *kendang arja* but also to reveal its more *wayah*, complex or developed, aspects. While their first few taught patterns are relatively *dasar*, I see the later ones as those they were most proud of, the most *wayah* of their consciously known patterns. Sudi, too, taught me several basic 4- and 8-beat *wadon* patterns before then composing a complex 20-beat "improvisation" for me to learn.

This brings us back to the question of codification. In teaching what appears to be all of his explicitly known patterns, both the *dasar* and the *wayah*, Pak Dewa has perhaps unwittingly created a dividing line between "pattern" and "improvisation." What is the status of his taught patterns? Where do they come from? Are they givens from previous generations, passed down directly from his teachers, or has Pak Dewa composed them himself, or borrowed them from other drummers? And in codifying them, does he think of these patterns as precomposed building blocks for improvisation, with identifiable beginnings and endings, or are they simply distillations of previous improvisations meant to represent the limits of his playing style? Further, is there something more fundamental about these patterns than others in his improvisations—much as a V7 chord is more fundamental to a bebop solo than a chromatic cluster chord or quartal harmony—or are they simply a representative sampling? The same questions should be asked in any oral music practice where researchers learn through lessons on their instruments, be they saxophones, mbiras, or kendang. Perhaps these are questions to which we cannot find answers; certainly I do not have them for *kendang arja*. But in choosing to examine improvisation through the lens of taught patterns, and thus further reify those cognitive categories in my own analyses, the questions must at least be asked.

INSIGHTS FROM TAUGHT PATTERNS

Over several research trips to Bali, over several years, I took lessons with musicians in all generations. I began with drummers from the younger generations: skilled musicians in their twenties, thirties, and forties, including Sudi and Pasek in Ubud, Komin in Pengosekan, and Gung Raka in Saba. Once they considered my playing sufficiently *lancar*, fluent, they introduced me to older drummers they admired. Cok Alit of Peliatan and Pak Dewa of neighboring Pengosekan were my first teachers of the older generation, but I also worked with Pak Tama of Singapadu and Pak Tut of Apuan as well as I Wayan Sidja (Pak Sidja) from Bona. In figure 5.10, teachers I worked with extensively on *arja* are shown in black; those who taught just one or two *arja* patterns before deciding they would rather teach something else are shown in gray.

Pedagogical processes differed significantly among these drummers. Each had his own ideas about the best approaches for teaching *kendang arja*: which elements I should learn and in which order. I left the content of my lessons largely in their control, though being of *keras* character, I couldn't help but make requests. Some teachers considered virtuoso specialists largely taught on their favored drum. Cok Alit is a *lanang* player first and foremost, and though he is fluent in *kendang wadon*, he only ever taught me patterns for *lanang*. His longtime partner Pak Dewa, knowing I was studying *lanang* with Cok Alit, mainly

FIGURE 5.10. Tilley's *kendang* teachers

focused on *wadon*. He believed that if I could play what he considered the more complicated *wadon* patterns, learning to play *lanang* would be a breeze.[18] When pressed, Pak Dewa did show me a few of his *lanang* patterns, but our lessons were almost exclusively *wadon*-focused.

By contrast, Pak Tama does not specialize in one of the two drums. As Singapadu's sole active *kendang arja* expert, he generally performs not with other drummers of his generation but with the best of his private students.[19] This makes him a jack-of-all-trades. And as a teacher to troupes in several villages across the island (and perhaps never seeing himself as a great virtuosic drummer, though his playing is impeccable), Tama was more concerned that I understand the larger structure of the drama than that I become fluent in a wide assortment of patterns for improvisation. Thus, he taught me a handful of *lanang* patterns, because the *lanang* is the ensemble leader, but focused mostly on *arja*'s precomposed pieces, the structure of individual songs, and other more general performance concerns. Whenever I asked Tama to show me his *wadon* patterns, he would play a few at speed but never take the time to teach them; that was of secondary importance for a player at my level.

Pak Tut of Apuan was the one teacher who taught his patterns as interlocking composites first, only showing me individual *lanang* and *wadon* parts at my request, and with some difficulty. A student of the late Apuan *arja* expert Pak Patrem, and purportedly the only Apuan resident still fluent in the playing (though Patrem's son, Wardana, could vocalize the patterns), Pak Tut, like Pak Tama, would not have specialized in one of the two drums. While I played exclusively *lanang* in my lessons with him, what was important for Pak Tut was

UNRAVELING UNCONSCIOUS MODELS · 193

Sudi's first pattern (Ubud):

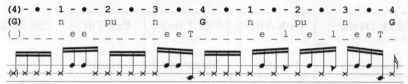

Pak Tama's first pattern (Singapadu):

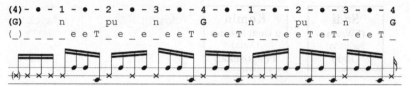

Cok Alit's first pattern (Peliatan):

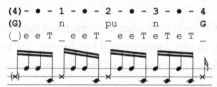

FIGURE 5.11. Comparing *lanang* patterns from different teachers

that I understood the interlocking of the two drums. Individual details of patterns sometimes seemed to be less pertinent for him, and he often simply said of his basic, *dasar* pattern, "and now you can vary it," without really showing me *how*.

Thus, with each teacher, I learned patterns for different drums and focused on different aspects of the art of *kendang arja*. But through these very individualized lessons, several overriding characteristics of the patterns began to emerge. The *lanang* patterns in figure 5.11 will elucidate. They are the first patterns I learned from teachers in three different villages: Sudi in Ubud, Pak Tama in Singapadu, and Cok Alit in Peliatan.

While these patterns are different, three shared features are apparent. First, there seems to be some preference for playing left-hand strokes, either *peng* (e) strokes or subordinate "l" strokes, every other subdivision. Second, patterns from these different teachers all appear to be built from the same motives or building blocks, each peppered with gestures like "e e T," "e T," and "e T e T." Finally, in each of these smaller musical components, final *Tut* (T) bass strokes often directly precede the beat. The second pattern that I learned from Cok

Alit, shown in figure 5.12, gives nuance to these observations. He taught it as a *terbalik*, backward or upside-down, version of the first.

Cok Alit may have meant many things by *terbalik*, and imagining his patterns in a modular way can give some insight. His first pattern, in figure 5.11, is built from three "e e T" gestures and one "e T e T" component, which may also be thought of as two "e T" modules. Single right-hand counting strokes ("_") separate the first three modules as well as aligning with gong. As we can see in figure 5.13, a more complex rearrangement of these components does, in fact, generate his second pattern. Here he has fused the "e e T" and "e T" modules into a longer "e e T e T" gesture not separated by a counting stroke, creating cross-rhythm with the meter in the first three beats of the pattern.

Yet it is not only the individual modules of the pattern that have been shifted. The *terbalik*-ing of these components also engenders a reversal of events coinciding with the beat. In the first pattern, there is a *peng* (e) on beat 3 and counting strokes on beats 1 and 2; in the second pattern the opposite is true. What's more, a different module now prepares the *gong* stroke: "e T e T" as opposed to "e e T." This may suggest that the term *terbalik* is used to signify an exchange

FIGURE 5.12. Cok Alit's second *lanang* pattern, "*terbalik*"

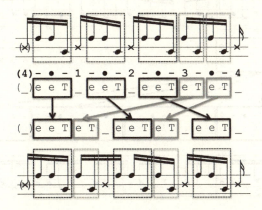

FIGURE 5.13. Transformation from Cok Alit's first pattern (*top*) to his second pattern (*bottom*)

of roles with respect to the gong pattern. Or it may simply refer to the position of the isolated "e e T" gesture, which is shifted from the beginning to the end of the pattern. Thus Cok Alit has created a "backward" version of his first pattern on a number of different levels: in terms of the order of its modules, the gesture chosen to anticipate the arrival of *gong*, and the placement of strokes relative to the beat.

That Cok Alit noticed a *terbalik* relationship in his patterns, though he was not able (or desirous) to express it in such a reductive analytical fashion, raises new questions. Could it be that he recognizes the modular nature of his own patterns? If so, we are given insight into how his ear may segment elements of his patterns while listening and playing, and into his logic for ordering those segments in improvised performance. My lessons with Pak Dewa reinforced this theory of modularity. He had taught me three *wadon* patterns—two 8-beat patterns and a 12-beat one—that I was now cycling while he improvised an interlocking *lanang* part. Once satisfied that I could play these three patterns in sequence for several minutes without faltering, he upped the ante: "*Boleh campur-campur*," he said: "you can mix them up." And he demonstrated, playing pattern 1, then 3, then 2, then 1 again, twice. But then he started mixing them up in more complex ways: taking the first four beats of pattern 2 and tacking them onto the second half of pattern 3; taking the first two beats of pattern 1 and cycling them a few times before moving on to something else, as in figure 5.14.

So there it was. Pak Dewa taught his patterns as 8- and 12-beat units, and he sometimes played them as such. But he conceived of them, and he used

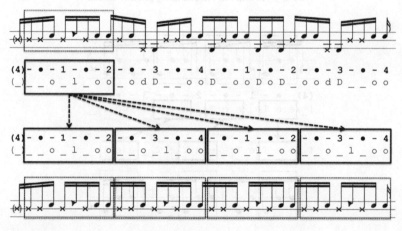

FIGURE 5.14. Cycling a 2-beat module

196 · CHAPTER FIVE

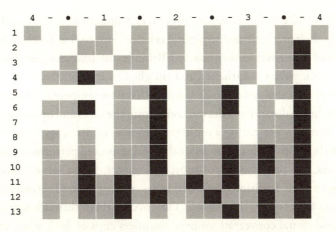

FIGURE 5.15. Visual comparison of *lanang* patterns

them as 2- and 4-beat musical components, to be mixed and matched at will, recombined, or played independently as the basis for improvisation. These smaller units are indeed conceived of as building blocks for longer ones. I hypothesized that, like Cok Alit's *lanang* patterns, they encompassed idiomatic principles, and contained yet smaller modules such as "o d D" and "o o D o D," that might also form the basis for improvisation.

The four *lanang* patterns from figures 5.11 and 5.12 reveal musical gestures and aesthetic principles that appear to cross village boundaries, guiding all of my many teachers' varied *lanang* patterns. The ubiquitous "e e T" and "e T" gestures, for instance, are fiddled with and rearranged to fashion a myriad of different patterns. Figure 5.15 is a visualization of a handful of taught 4-beat *lanang* patterns from various different drummers, arranged by rhythmic similarity. Each square represents one 16th note (or quarter beat) and the patterns move horizontally. The gray squares are *peng* (e) strokes, the black, *Tut* (T) strokes, the white, counting strokes. Although different, just a cursory glance at this chart reveals that the patterns are also, to varying degrees, rhythmically related.[20] This, too, suggests an overarching model for *arja* improvising.

REFINING UNCONSCIOUS MODELS WITH ORAL MUSIC THEORY

While taught patterns can help us make certain hypotheses about the nature of unconscious models, these must then be framed in local music theory. Whether formal or informal, musicians' theories about their own practices can inform our understanding of the roles of different instruments or streams in the model as well as their aesthetic and structural relationships to one another. Monson's analyses of jazz rhythm sections and Brinner's of Javanese gamelan, among many others, were strengthened and enriched by insights from the musicians themselves. My analyses of *kendang arja* are likewise tempered, wherever possible, by Balinese discourse. I draw heavily from the ideas and opinions of teachers and friends representing a multigenerational, multivillage cross section of some of the genre's most knowledgeable and respected performers. While *arja* drummers, like practitioners of most oral musics, have a largely tacit understanding of their tradition, some oral music theory on *kendang arja* does exist: guidelines for playing, or *patokan*.[21] I discovered them through lessons, interviews, and casual conversations over countless cups of *kopi*, while forgotten clove cigarettes slowly smoked themselves down on tile floors.

PERFORMATIVE ROLES: A COLLECTIVE BALANCING OF FREEDOM AND CONSTRAINT

As we saw in the previous chapter, in order for one collectively improvising musician to have ample improvisatory freedom, another must often provide a framework of stability. This need for balance determines each musician's performative role. Standard jazz musicians differentiate soloists from rhythm section performers; in New Orleans jazz it is "first line" and "second line" playing.[22] Many West African drumming ensembles, including Anlo-Ewe and Dagomba traditions, likewise balance lead with supporting drums, the former's scope for improvisation wider than the latter's.[23] Here we see similarities to Balinese paired *batu-batu* drumming, where the relatively fixed playing of the *lanang* gives the *wadon* the freedom to incorporate increasingly syncopated gestures into the texture without fear of disrupting the interlocking (see Bakan 1999, 63, 135–37; Tenzer 2000, 294–96). Arom (1991a) similarly observes of Central African polyphonic traditions:

> Variability in a polyrhythmic substructure may thus be said to be inversely proportional to that observed in the superposed melodic material. For example, the polyrhythmic support provided by the two double bells in Ngbaka "harp songs," where the vocal soloist introduces incessant variations in the melodic theme, is itself invariable.
>
> On the other hand, in the Sabanga *ngbàkè* repertory, a repetitive melody is linked with a xylophone part composed of very short and minimally varied

FIGURE 5.16. Drummers' eyes glued to the dancer. Cok Alit, *lanang* (*left*); Pak Dewa, *wadon* (*right*); Bu Candri, dancer. (Photo by Chelsea Edwardson, 2011. Used with permission.)

periods. The big drum, however, plays nearly free improvisation, while the dancers superpose long and varied cycles on the short voice and xylophone periods. (298–99)

In each case, some of the performers' latitude for improvisation is constrained by their responsibilities to the ensemble as a whole, whether to maintain a meter or groove, lay down a set of chord changes, or preserve the melodic or rhythmic integrity of an ostinato. And the relative fixity of their patterns allows other improvisers more freedom to take risks.

It is generally accepted among *arja* drummers that a *lanang* player's improvisations will be simpler and less varied than his partner's. While differences in constraint between improvising musicians often reflect a hierarchy of soloist and accompanist or background and foreground musician, in *arja*, these differences are instead defined by the performative roles of two equal partners. We know that the *lanang* is *arja*'s lead drum, relaying stylistic changes and structural cues, *angsel*, from the singer-dancers to the ensemble. The photograph in figure 5.16 shows Pak Dewa and Cok Alit playing *kendang* for a recording session with the famous Singapadu singer Ni Nyoman Candri (Bu Candri). While *wadon*-player Pak Dewa (on the right) watches her, and enjoys her performance, Cok Alit's focus on her feet as he waits for her *angsel* cues is intense and unwavering.

Because of this need to concentrate so fully on the singer-dancers, Pak Dewa claims, a *lanang* player has less scope for improvisation than his *wadon* partner.[24] Accordingly, as Sudi asserts, just a few basic *lanang* patterns can be paired idiomatically with virtually any *wadon* pattern, no matter how long or complex.[25] Cok Alit, by contrast, maintains that *lanang* players like himself have more freedom despite their leadership role. He teases gently that a *wadon* player like Pak Dewa simply has more freedom to let his mind wander; while the *lanang* player is diligently watching the dancers, the *wadon* player can be scanning the audience looking for pretty women.[26]

Despite some disagreements, the conventional wisdom is that, as leader, a *lanang* player is more constrained in his improvising. Pak Tama compares this aspect of the *lanang-wadon* relationship to that between *sopir* and *kernet*, the bus driver and the baggage handler. The *lanang* player is the *sopir*; he is in control of the bus. He must constantly be watching the road, following it carefully. He cannot stray off the road, or play around too much lest the bus tip over. The *wadon* player is the *kernet*; he has more freedom to move around the bus, placing bags wherever he finds space and socializing with the passengers. Pak Tama dances his hands back and forth to demonstrate the concept like two performers inside a *barong* costume; the front hand carefully traces a path while the back hand moves around more freely, ducking left and right, coming very close to the front hand then backing away playfully.[27] To Tama, the *wadon* is the drum that makes the sound exciting: "We play like this so that it sounds like the voice of the drums is alive," he says. "The *wadon* is what makes it come alive. Yeah, here," he points to the *lanang* drum, "always continues in the same way.... The *lanang* has some variations too, but far fewer."[28] I have found this to be the case in my analyses as well. Although *lanang* players like Cok Alit and Komin's brother Ketut do play a wide variety of patterns, these are generally shorter, less varied, and less complex than their partners' patterns.

Understanding the relative levels of constraint in each musical strand of a model allows for more faithful analysis of its improvisations. More constrained idioms require a more detailed eye; subtle changes that seem like mild embellishment or interpretation may in fact stem from more radical improvisatory processes, as in Pak Tama's "micro" recombination from chapter 1.

COMPLEMENTARY MUSICAL ROLES

As we saw in the previous chapter, alongside performative roles, many models also dictate specific musical roles for different instruments or musical strands.

These roles, which often overlap with performative ones, are generally complementary, designed to foster the musical give-and-take so central to collective improvisation. In New Orleans jazz, as we saw in figure 0.1, the trumpet or cornet often takes the main melody, interpreting and embellishing it according to both stylistic and personal idiom. The clarinet is generally responsible for improvising a countermelody, together creating a dense polyphony with the cornet. The trombone's idiom is sparser, blending roles of contrapuntal melody making and harmonic support. The keys and rhythm section lay down the meter and chord changes, but they also take advantage of gaps in the melody to insert creative fills. Each performer has a musical role that complements the others; the model is such that concurrent musical streams are likely to interact well.

In Central African polyphonic singing, musical roles are not assigned to specific musicians but rather chosen by individuals in the moment based on the needs of the overall performance. Yet the different musical strands or constituent parts within a model have also been created with an eye to collectivity. Among the Aka, for instance, the main function of the performer who takes on the *mòtángòlè* strand is to enunciate the text of a known song; improvisations are constrained by the need to unambiguously present the melody while also following the general pitch contours of the Aka's tonal language. *Dìyèí*, by contrast, is a textless style of singing that requires a constant alternation between head and chest voice (see Fürniss 2006).

Kendang arja performers, too, are guided in their improvising by preset musical roles, in this case dictating each drum's basic rhythmic function in the ensemble. Among the most specific, yet enigmatic, guidelines for *kendang arja* are the paired concepts of *ngegongin* and *ngematin*. As Hood (2001) states: "The Balinese phrase, '*kendang lanang* ngematin *kendang wadon*' means the *lanang* drum provides the beat for the *wadon*" (86). The term *ngematin* is rooted in the word *mat*, meaning "beat." It refers to the beat stream marked by the *guntang* from figure 5.7, considered the "main beat" and transcribed here as quarter notes.

Hood continues: "the phrase '*kendang wadon* ngegongin *kendang lanang*' means the *wadon* drum player chooses patterns to reinforce the gong cycle. The *wadon* anticipates each repetition of the gong with characteristic phrases" (2001, 86–87). Examination of a handful of taught patterns will show how these complementary musical roles influence *arja* pattern construction.

EMPHASIZING THE BEAT ON *LANANG*: *NGEMATIN*

The concept of *ngematin* is encompassed in the idea, told to me by several of my teachers, that the *lanang* plays on the beat while the *wadon* plays off the beat.

Different drummers revealed this *patokan*, or rule, in quite dissimilar ways. Pak Tama once observed: "If the *lanang* plays on the odd (*ganjil*), *wadon* plays on the even (*genap*). That way . . . no matter how freely they play around they won't run into each other."[29] Cok Alit, though we spoke entirely in Indonesian, actually used the English-language terms "on beat" and "off beat" to refer to these roles.[30] Yet when I asked Sudi, he seemed perturbed by the implication that *arja* improvisation could be boiled down to so basic an idea as "*lanang* is on the beat, *wadon* is off the beat." He told me that such concepts might guide some drummers, and I have heard the same of improvisation on the *reyong*,[31] but that many have never heard the terms *ngegongin* and *ngematin*, and the reality is certainly "not that simple."[32] To Sudi, the concept of *ngematin* is better understood as a general aesthetic guideline encouraging idiomatic interlocking, similar to the complementary beat-marking and cross-metric roles often assumed by interlocking mbira players (discussed in the postlude), or the comparable rhythmic interactions of other African polyphonies:

> *The music is perhaps best considered as an arrangement of gaps where one may add a rhythm, rather than as a dense pattern of sound.* In the conflict of the rhythms, it is the space between the notes from which the dynamic tension comes. . . . A good rhythm, if it is to enhance itself, should both fill a gap in the other rhythms and create an emptiness that may be similarly filled. (Chernoff 1979, 113–14)

Keeping in mind this broader interpretation, can the almost unanimous consensus that the *lanang* plays on the beat while the *wadon* plays off the beat be explained through music analysis? The first hurdle is that, as we have seen, both drummers' hands tend to strike their drums continuously. When asked to clarify the rule, though, most of my teachers would simply play a pattern and triumphantly say, "See?" Clearly they could see something I couldn't. No matter how I phrased the question, or how frequently I tried to steer a conversation to the topic, none of my teachers had a response that satisfied my craving for theoretical understanding. None but I Gusti Nyoman Darta (Komin), a young Pengosekan-based drummer so curious about his music that he had taught himself to play left-handed in order to know explicitly what other drummers implicitly knew (but could not describe) about playing technique. In a lesson one rainy August afternoon, he unceremoniously informed me, completely unsolicited (and to my great delight), that the most basic composite pattern for *kendang arja*, the *dasar*, was conceptually the pattern in figure 5.17.

In this theoretical *dasar*, the *lanang* strikes *peng* (e) "on the beat," aligning with the *guntang* timekeeper as well as the half beat between each *guntang*

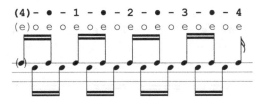

FIGURE 5.17. *Arja*'s most basic composite pattern (*dasar*)

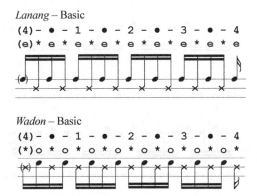

FIGURE 5.18. Basic pattern with right-hand counting strokes

stroke, while the *wadon*'s *kom* (o) strokes occupy the "off-beat" 16th notes (quarter beats) in between. Approaching my analyses with Komin's *dasar* in mind, I found that improvised patterns did often proceed, broadly speaking, with this stroke placement. The "on-beat, off-beat" rule, then, seemed to apply to high rim-stroke use, *arja*'s most basic composite pattern being a strict alternation between off-beat *kom* (o) strokes and on-beat *peng* (e) strokes.

Of course no experienced drumming pair would play a pattern this repetitive for very long. And there are several different ways that drummers vary the *dasar* while still abiding by the "on-beat, off-beat" mandate. We know that *arja* drummers generally prefer to maintain continuous motion, lightly tapping "counting strokes" when not playing one of their main strokes. In the basic *arja* pattern from Figure 5.17, then, where each drummer appears to rest between left-hand rim strokes, he is in fact filling in the spaces with a counting stroke in the right hand. The mnemonic notation in figure 5.18 shows each drummer's right-hand counting strokes as asterisks.

The simplest variation on the *dasar* replaces a main left-hand rim stroke— a *kom* (o) or *peng* (e)—with a counting stroke in the *left* hand, creating variety

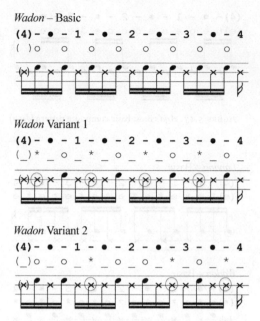

FIGURE 5.19. Counting-stroke variations of the basic *wadon*

while still preserving the one-to-one right-left alternation that makes this pattern so basic. Figure 5.19 shows two common *wadon* variants. In the first, counting strokes replace main strokes symmetrically, every other stroke; in the second—a favored pattern of Pak Tut in Apuan—the combination of counting and main strokes is asymmetrical. Underscores, as in other figures, denote right-hand counting strokes in mnemonic notation; left-hand ones are now circled and marked with asterisks.

Each of these variants creates its own unique composite with the basic *lanang*, per figure 5.20.

Because the *lanang* player, too, can replace any of his *peng* (e) strokes with a counting stroke, we get a total of 65,536 (or 2^{16}) different possible versions of this seemingly simple 4-beat phrase. Exponential growth means at 8 beats long, the same *dasar* has 4,294,967,296 (or 2^{32}) possible realizations! And, while individual drummers generally stick to just a handful of favorites, each of these millions of possibilities can be, and most probably has been, played.

Even in patterns with heavier use of *Dag* (D) and *Tut* (T), drummers still generally follow the "on-beat, off-beat" guideline for *kom* (o) and *peng* (e) placement.[33] Three elucidatory patterns are marked with asterisks and circles in figure 5.21.

FIGURE 5.20. *Wadon* patterns from figure 5.19 paired with basic *lanang*

FIGURE 5.21. "Rule-abiding" "on-beat, off-beat" rim-stroke use

Extending the "On-Beat, Off-Beat" Rule: Double Strokes

If, like Western music theorists Lerdahl and Jackendoff (1983), I consider meter not as a single level of strong and weak pulses but as a metrical grid where "periodicity of beats is reinforced from level to level" (20), I can explore the "on-beat, off-beat" rule at multiple levels. This hierarchical conceptualization of meter in *arja* is most overt in the 2-beat *batel* structures, where each beat level is marked by a phenomenal accent on the cycle-marking instruments, per figure 5.22. The *gong pulu* punctuates the 2-beat level; the beat-keeping *guntang* articulates the main beat and, in combination with the small off-beat *klenang*, also marks the half-beat level (outlined in the rectangle). This leaves the 16th-note or quarter-beat stream for the kendang.

Examining "on-beat, off-beat" placement at different beat levels allows a richer interpretation of the concept. Things become particularly interesting when drummers play two rim strokes in a row, disrupting the regular right-left alternation of the *dasar* with what is conceptually a weaker followed by a stronger rim stroke: "e e" or "o o." This technique may be seen as a kind of embellishment on the model's single-stroke alternation, similar to note-doubling embellishment techniques used in *reyong norot*. When these common double strokes occur, the "on-beat, off-beat" rule suddenly appears to get turned on its head. Where *lanang* lines up with the slower beat levels when using single strokes, as we saw in figure 5.18, when double strokes are used, it is the *wadon* that lands on the beat.[34] Figure 5.23 shows the two theoretical *dasar*, basic patterns, of this more nuanced rule set, their on-beat placement marked with circles and arrows.[35]

Most *arja* drummers seamlessly blend single and double rim strokes in quick succession. In figure 5.24, single *peng* (e) strokes at the end of the *lanang* pattern fall "on the beat," while the *wadon*'s single *kom* (o) strokes before beats 1 and 3 land "off the beat." Yet each pattern also employs double rim strokes that reverse these "on-beat, off-beat" roles at the slower beat level. Together the two patterns create the composite on the bottom of the figure, shown with only

Beats	0	1	2
Gong Pulu	•		•
Guntang (main beat)	•	•	•
Klenang ("off-beat")		•	•
Kendang (16th-notes)	• • • • • • • •

FIGURE 5.22. Metrical hierarchy of cycle-marking instruments, *batel*

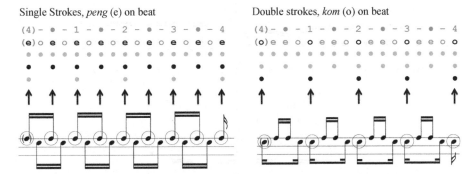

FIGURE 5.23. The "on-beat, off-beat" rule: single versus double strokes

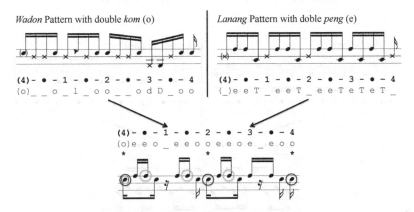

FIGURE 5.24. The "on-beat, off-beat" rule in improvisation.
Wadon (left), lanang (right), composite *(bottom)*

rim strokes for visual clarity. It features the *lanang*'s double *peng* (e) strokes, circled in gray, "off the beat," and the *wadon*'s double *kom* (o), in black, now firmly "on the beat."

Of course this contradictory rule set between single strokes and double strokes creates occasion for like strokes to collide instead of teasing around one another, as we can see in a theoretical combination of the double-stroke *wadon* pattern from figure 5.24 and the basic single-stroke *lanang*. Rim strokes collide in three places aligning with major beats, circled in the composite pattern in figure 5.25.

One might imagine this combination of patterns to be a faux pas in Balinese interlocking, where like strokes are designed to dance around one another, never colliding. But when I asked Cok Alit about it, he laughed and exclaimed, "This isn't *Baris!*"

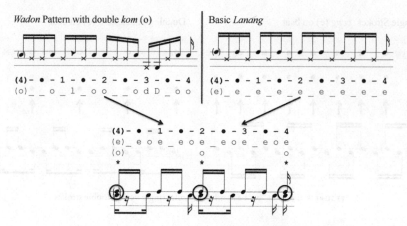

FIGURE 5.25. Contradiction between single and double stroke rules

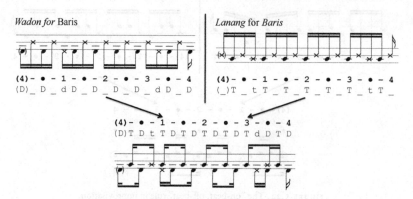

FIGURE 5.26. Interlocking drumming for *Baris* is precomposed

What he meant was that *kendang arja* isn't precomposed, like the drumming for the famous dance piece *Baris* shown in figure 5.26. It's not meant to have perfectly interlocking drumming with no collisions, no *tabrakan*. As long as there weren't too many in quick succession, drummers listening to recordings of their own playing would still be satisfied with a collision here and there. In fact most drummers from the old generation lamented that the *arja* of the young generation had become too "perfect." What was important for these musicians was that the overall impression was one of interlocking; especially at such high speeds, details were sometimes incidental, and small *tabrakan* of *kom* (o) and *peng* (e) could be enjoyed, even wished for. They reminded the listener that the music wasn't precomposed, drawing attention, through their imperfections, to the near perfection of the interaction.

Nuancing the "On-Beat, Off-Beat" Rule: Bass Strokes

The idea that small details of interlocking could be glossed over, and some *tabrakan* tolerated or even looked for in *kom-peng* interactions, seems resonant with most of my teachers' perceptions of *arja*. Details became significantly more important, however, and collisions far less common or seemingly acceptable, when I began looking at the bass strokes: the *wadon*'s *Dag* (D) and *lanang*'s *Tut* (T). This greater attention to detail is hardly surprising; among Balinese musicians and dancers, *Dag* (D) and *Tut* (T) are universally understood to be more structurally significant than *kom* (o) and *peng* (e). Not only in *arja* but also in the famous *legong* and *gamelan gambuh* traditions, these strokes are more often associated with major dance movements, for instance. Thus, the smooth interaction of bass strokes is key to a satisfying performance, even in improvised *arja*. Some drummers will go so far as to make *Dag* (D) and *Tut* (T) placement entirely precomposed, so as to avoid any unwanted collisions. Apuan's *arja* drummers led by I Ketut Bicuh (Pak Tut), for instance, always cycle through the same four patterns, always in the same order. While they use plenty of *kom* (o) and *peng* (e) variation, placement of *Dag* (D) and *Tut* (T)—shown in the mnemonic notation in figure 5.27—is utterly fixed.

While this sort of precise precomposition in *arja* is relatively uncommon, all drummers' placement of *Dag* (D) and *Tut* (T)—whether precomposed or improvised—appears to be significantly more fixed than *kom* (o) and *peng* (e). *Lanang* player Cok Alit, for instance, never places a *Tut* (T) stroke directly on the beat.[36] And only in very rare, controlled situations does he place one on the half beat. As in the two taught patterns in figure 5.28, Cok Alit plays *Tut* (T) strokes on the fourth subdivision of a beat about 75 percent of the time and on the second subdivision about 20 percent.

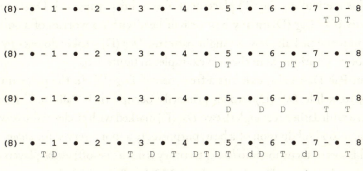

FIGURE 5.27. Pak Tut's fixed *Dag-Tut* interactions, Apuan style

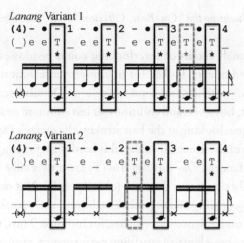

FIGURE 5.28. Cok Alit's *Tut* (T) placement

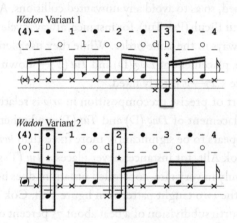

FIGURE 5.29. Pak Dewa's on-beat *Dag* (D) placement

This meticulous *Tut* (T) placement allows his partner Pak Dewa to confidently play *Dag* (D) on any beat or half beat with no worries of a collision. And in many of Pak Dewa's taught patterns, *Dag* (D) strokes do occupy these "on-beat" positions, as in the two examples in figure 5.29.

But Pak Dewa also exhibits a freer use of *Dag* (D). In the pattern in figure 5.30, while *Dag* (D) strokes primarily occupy their "allotted" positions (shown with dashed rectangles), two *Dag* (D) marked with circles and arrows land on the second subdivision of a beat, purportedly a spot reserved for *lanang* use.

This sort of incursion into *lanang* territory is not a one-off; *wadon* players across village styles seem to "break the rules," risking collision in their bass strokes, far more often than *lanang* players. Consistent with the idea that *wadon* drummers should enjoy relative freedom over their *lanang* partners, Pak Dewa's creative license here appears to be supported by yet more suggested constraints on his partner's stroke placement. As in the patterns in figure 5.28, the majority of Cok Alit's *Tut* (T) strokes land not in the second subdivision of the *guntang*'s beat but the fourth. Pak Dewa, then, is still fairly safe in his second-subdivision *Dag* (D) placement in figure 5.30. Further, most of Cok Alit's second-subdivision *Tut* (T) strokes occur in the second half of a pattern, per figure 5.31.

Pak Dewa, who often plays off-beat *Dag* (D) strokes in the early beats of a cycle, is thus still quite unlikely to crash into his partner. The relative rigidity of Cok Alit's *Tut* (T) idioms, and Pak Dewa's familiarity with them, allows Pak Dewa increased *Dag* (D) flexibility. And while this regulatory ambiguity leads to the occasional *tabrakan* between *Dag* (D) and *Tut* (T) strokes in performance—such a collision would occur if the *wadon* pattern in figure 5.30

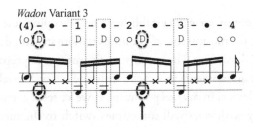

FIGURE 5.30. Pak Dewa's freer use of *Dag* (D) in off-beat positions

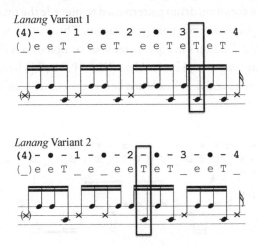

FIGURE 5.31. Cok Alit's 2nd-subdivision *Tut* (T) strokes are often late in a cycle

coincided with the second *lanang* pattern from figure 5.31, for example—these instances are relatively rare.

In every *arja* performance there are moments when the interlocking is considered unsuccessful, and these mostly appear to involve imperfect *Dag-Tut* interactions. Although passages with multiple *kom-peng* collisions are often tolerated, similar passages with one or more *Dag-Tut tabrakan* may be singled out as unsatisfying (*tidak puas*). This is especially the case when those collisions occur just before a *gong pulu* stroke, suggesting that imperfections in interlocking may be more acceptable earlier in a cycle. While "unsatisfying" moments are far less common between seasoned partners like Pak Dewa and Cok Alit, given the improvisatory nature of *arja*, they certainly occur. As Sawyer notes, risk of failure is a central feature of improvisation, and, as we saw in chapter 4, a necessary precursor to group flow (see Sawyer 2007, 54–56).

EMPHASIZING THE CYCLIC STRUCTURE ON *WADON*: NGEGONGIN

While the concept of *ngematin* establishes a beat-keeping role for *lanang*, *ngegongin* states that the musical role of the *wadon* is more structural: to reinforce the gong with special patterns. The use of specific patterns to prepare gong strokes or other important moments in a cyclic structure is a well-established Balinese compositional device. In *gong kebyar* music, as we've seen, a *reyong* player elaborating a melody with *norot* will sometimes switch to the more stable *empat*-style figuration for the two or four beats before a major cyclic marker. Cyclic signposting is also used in precomposed drumming across Balinese genres. Figure 5.32 shows a common drum pattern used to precede the final gong stroke in the long, slow *pengawak* cycles of *legong* dances. This pattern is recognizable to both musicians and dancers and gives a sense of completion at the end of a cycle that might be as long as 256 beats. Here "K," "P," and [x]-noteheads denote loud slap strokes, round noteheads just below the center staff line indicate the

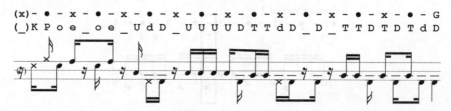

FIGURE 5.32. *Ngegongin* in *legong*

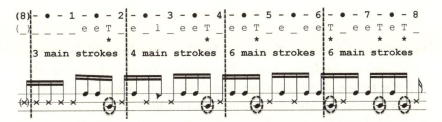

FIGURE 5.33. Increased activity and bass-stroke use leading to gong, 8-beat pattern

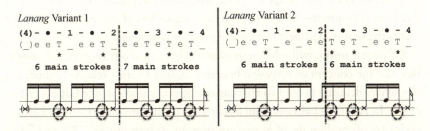

FIGURE 5.34. Increased activity leading to gong in 4-beat patterns

lanang's special cuing stroke *pung* (U), and counting strokes are marked as rests in staff notation.[37]

In *arja*, where shorter 2-, 4-, and 8-beat cycles make such long structure-marking patterns impractical, *ngegongin* takes a different form. Tenzer's study of *gamelan gong kebyar* examines melodies for their kinetic qualities, comparing the *ngubeng* (static) and *majalan* (dynamic) moments within them. He notes that gong strokes and other important cyclic markers tend to "exert 'pull' or 'gravity' on melodic motion, causing the regions that lead up to them to be more *majalan* [more dynamic]" (2000, 179). Many *arja* patterns likewise appear to be built to show increased activity and, particularly important, increased use of *Dag* (D) and *Tut* (T) strokes as a cycle progresses, leading to the gong.

Figure 5.33 shows an 8-beat *lanang* pattern from Pak Tama of Singapadu. Each quadrant of the phrase exhibits an increased use of main strokes: 3, 4, 6, and 6 respectively. Through the second half of the pattern, there is also an increased frequency of *Tut* (T) strokes, marked with circles and asterisks. This densification of main strokes approaching gong exists in shorter *arja* phrases as well. Figure 5.34 shows two 4-beat *lanang* patterns from Cok Alit. In each, the combination of main-stroke use and *Tut* (T) density increases toward the gong.

Structural Signposting

Densification is one type of *ngegongin*, but there are others. While *arja*'s short cycles don't support *legong*'s long cadence gestures, the *wadon* player can achieve a similar feeling of structural signposting simply by playing *Dag* (D) on the beat or half beat directly preceding gong. For further emphasis, this stroke will frequently be followed by soft counting strokes or even rests (which are virtually nonexistent elsewhere). In the mnemonic notation in figure 5.35, we can see that Pak Tut's semicomposed patterns exhibit this placement as do many of Pak Dewa's improvised ones. In each case, regardless of cycle length, *Dag* (D) marks the beat or half beat just before gong; it *ngegongins*.

Of course music will seldom so obediently fit into our theoretical categories, and the concept of *ngegongin* becomes cloudy in *arja*'s relatively short cycles where drummers tend to emphasize not every gong stroke but every few cycles. In Pak Tut's patterns from figure 5.35, for instance, the third and fourth cycles are often thought of as one continuous 16-beat phrase. "*Bersama*," Pak Tama says of these patterns: "together." Alternately, the entire arrangement of four cycles may be thought of as a single sentence, leading through an increased density of *Dag* (D) and *Tut* (T) strokes over each subsequent cycle to a final gong at the end of the fourth cycle. Once again increased activity is evident at this level of hypermeter, with the four cycles featuring 3, 6, 5, and 13 bass strokes

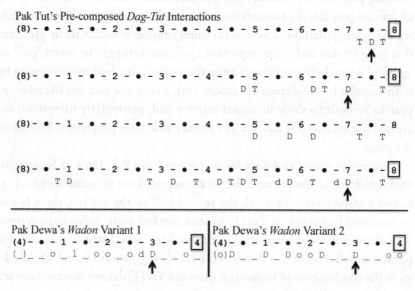

FIGURE 5.35. Signposting *ngegongin* in 4- and 8-beat cycles

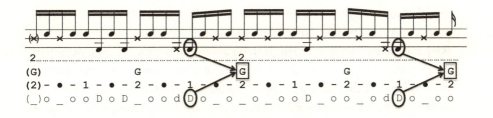

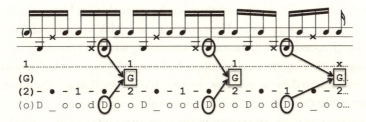

FIGURE 5.36. Signposting *ngegongin* in a 2-beat cyclic structure

respectively. When the player comes back around to the first cycle, the absence of main strokes directly following gong is felt in stark contrast to the increased density of strokes that preceded it.

The compositional logic of this hypermetric structure suggests that articulation of *ngegongin* merits a closer look.[38] Such cycle grouping becomes even more complex in shorter 2- and 4-beat structures, where there does not appear to be any fixed idea about which cycles should feature a final *Dag* (D) in improvised performance. These decisions are shaped neither by the singer-dancer nor by the structure-marking instruments, but appear to be a free choice for the drummer. Figure 5.36 is a short excerpt of improvised *wadon* drumming over a 2-beat cyclic structure, with strong final *Dag*s marked with asterisks and cycles grouped together to show *ngegongin* placement. Pak Dewa does not feel obliged to *ngegongin* before each gong stroke; nor does he attempt to do so at regular intervals; we see *ngegongin* after two cycles, twice, then one, three times in a row, the final one being the strongest. Sometimes he will wait three cycles; sometimes he'll *ngegongin* several cycles in a row. The decision appears to rely on little more than his whim in the moment.

THE BENEFITS OF PARTNERSHIP

The various *patokan*, rules, discussed in this chapter clarify general roles and structural aesthetics for each *arja* drum, offering insight into their unconscious models. However, collective improvisation equally relies on familiarity between partners. As jazz pianist Roland Hanna notes of longtime bass co-performer Richard Davis: "There's a curious thing about musicians. We train ourselves over a period of years to be able to hear rhythms and anticipate combinations of sounds before they actually happen" (quoted in Monson 1996, 49). That *arja*'s *lanang* player leads while the *wadon* follows, that the *lanang* is simple so the *wadon* can be complex, and that each drum plays a role in the *ngegongin/ngematin* and "on-beat, off-beat" dichotomies; these *patokan* provide very basic guidelines to improvisation, nothing more. How *arja* drummers play so seamlessly together at such high speeds, simultaneously improvising without constantly tripping over one another's patterns is accomplished through years of playing with the same musician to develop *pasangan*, partnership. Every Balinese drummer says unequivocally that this is the key to successful *arja* improvising.

On a concrete level, *pasangan* in *arja* involves that same sort of "core of common patterns" or precomposed motives that Berliner (1994, 364) observes in jazz.[39] When Pak Dewa showed me the first *wadon* pattern from figure 5.3, for instance, he taught that his partner Cok Alit would often respond to its series of *Dag* (D) strokes in beats 4–6 with a complementary series of *Tut* (T), together creating the call-and-response in figure 5.37.

This pattern is specific to these two drummers and their students, mutually agreed upon through years of perfecting the art of playing together. Were Pak Dewa to play an *arja* with Pak Sidja of Bona, for instance, the latter would not know how to appropriately respond to these *Dag* (D) strokes. The same is true of other Balinese improvised forms. Komin once told me that he only really enjoyed improvising *reyong norot* with his brother Ketut; they understood each other's styles and tastes so well that the composite was always *wayah*, complex or *memuaskan*, satisfying.[40] Such close relationships are central to collectively improvised music because, as I Ketut Gdé Asnawa notes: "interaction and communication relies upon feeling" (quoted in Hood 2001, 81).

Thus, as we will see in chapter 6, much more than precomposed exchanges, *pasangan* is about the ways in which shared musical influences and opinions

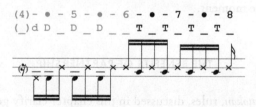

FIGURE 5.37. Beats 4–8 of Pak Dewa and Cok Alit's precomposed interaction

FIGURE 5.38. *Pasangan*: partnership. Pak Dewa (*left*) and Cok Alit (*right*).
(Photo by Chelsea Edwardson, 2011. Used with permission.)

on style and innovation help improvisers develop a compatible grammar of idiomatic playing. And it's about being able to read one's partner's musical, verbal, and nonverbal cues and trusting that that ability is shared. Longtime *arja* partners like Cok Alit and Pak Dewa sit close together and watch each other's faces while they play, interpreting cues through common experience as much as through movement and sound (see figure 5.38). They play together with a mutual joy of shared history that can't be taught, and this depth of connection defines successful collectivity.

IN BROADER SCOPE: MOVING BEYOND THE UNCONSCIOUS MODEL

The analyses in this chapter have explored methods for uncovering elements of unconscious models for improvisation: models transmitted informally and held in the mind and body intuitively. Lessons with practitioners give insight into a genre's aesthetic and structural principles through the snapshot of consciously known taught patterns. While perhaps not a model in and of themselves, these patterns provide a constellation of idiomatic examples of the practice. An analyst can then extract proposed features of its idiom, whether a specific style of jazz, a school (*gharānā*) of Hindustani *alap* performance, or a particular approach to *kendang arja*. Oral music theory, often informal and ad hoc, provides context for connections found between taught patterns, reinforcing hypotheses or, conversely, forcing a reinterpretation. Taught patterns, oral theory, and analyses can thus influence one another in ever-more nuanced ways, reconstructing a picture of the unconscious model, as clear as we can make it. And while not every aspect of such models is knowable, and *pasangan* plays a role in the process, these insights can help frame an analysis of improvised performance.

In chapter 3 I analyzed instances of the four general improvisatory processes of interpretation, embellishment, recombination, and expansion in relation to the *reyong*'s *norot* model. Chapter 6 will do likewise, showing how these processes are differently actualized in the distinct yet related practice of *kendang arja*. But it also aims higher. Understanding how musicians collectively improvise goes beyond looking at notes and the proposed reasons behind them at the local level. Many improvised practices are at least partially shaped by minimally improvised or nonimprovised aspects of musical structure. And individual improvisers each have their own approaches to models and knowledge bases, rooted in regional style as well as personal preference. Thus, analyzing *kendang arja* practice to the fullest possible extent necessitates understanding how improvisers are influenced by larger musical and dramatic structures as well as addressing how each drummer differently stretches the confines of a shared *arja* model to suit both village style and individual taste. These discussions in turn illustrate broader angles from which to analyze collectively improvised musics.

CHAPTER SIX

BEYOND GENERALIZATIONS

THE FREEDOM OF *KENDANG ARJA*

THE ANALYST'S "MOMENT OF TRUTH"

I triumphantly pull off my headphones, breathe an epic sigh of relief, and reward myself with a too-big handful of dark chocolate chips. My eyes wander glassily down to the clock on my computer screen; it's almost 3:00 in the morning. I've been at it for hours . . . for months, actually. For months I have spent every free waking hour (many of which probably should have been sleeping hours) holed up in coffee shops and libraries and living rooms, transcribing. I have developed both a deep appreciation and a strange seething hatred for the slow-down program, which has made possible the accurate transcription of kendang arja *improvisations, especially in the faster* batel *gong structures, but has also introduced a level of microtiming and timbral ambiguity not pertinent to my research questions.*[1] *I have constantly had to remind myself not to get bogged down in details that become smoothed over at full speed, to remember that this is a living, moving, oral tradition. But today, I am done!*

I jack the tempo up to 100 percent and plug in my computer speakers, heedless of my neighbors despite the hour. And I listen, eyes closed, a huge grin of amazed, exhausted affection creeping across my face. This is what I've been doing all these months; I had almost forgotten. I have been documenting one of the coolest genres I know, played by teachers I have grown to love as well as respect. My mind wanders back to the day I recorded this particular track. Pak Dewa was taking a cigarette break and Cok Alit was talking music with Pak Tama (who had stepped in to play one of the incidental percussion instruments for this session) when the singer Bu Candri quietly appeared beside me. In a whisper she confided: "You are capturing the end of an era. I'm getting old and I've spent too much of my life being a dalang, a puppet-master; my voice isn't what it used to be. And Pak Dewa's hand doesn't work as well as it once did.[2] We don't have many years left for this. And there is no generation of great arja artists after us. You are recording history."[3]

I've been longing for this moment when I could look at my files of transcriptions without wondering, "How much longer?" But I've secretly been dreading it too, because this is the moment of truth. This is where the study leads, but what if I'm wrong? What if improvising kendang arja *really does mean "you can play whatever you want" or, worse, what if it's just the taught patterns and nothing more? What if I have nothing to show for this time but a new batch of gray hairs and an unhealthy relationship with the post-midnight hour? Only one way to find out . . .*

In chapter 1, I established four general processes of improvisation employed in most practices: interpretation, embellishment, recombination, and expansion. And I showed through discussions of *reyong norot* improvisation in chapter 3 how aspects of models and knowledge bases discovered through fieldwork could guide analysis of improvised musics, inflecting our understandings of these various improvisational processes at play. It might be tempting to believe that, through this sort of ethnographically informed analysis, generalizations extracted from specific performers and performances will be relevant to any improvisation in the same tradition. Yet it is also vital to look beyond the statements we can make about all *kendang arja* or sitar or *reyong* players, all moments in a performance of bebop or Aka singing or mbira music, to see the more mutable aspects of these practices. Zooming out from a detailed analysis will raise questions expanding our purview to include other dimensions of culture and experience. Particularly salient to a discussion of *kendang arja* are questions of larger musical context, regional style, and individual performer beliefs on the appropriate approach to models of improvisation.

IMPROVISATION IN ITS LARGER MUSICAL CONTEXT

The theory of collaborative emergence, introduced in chapter 4, argues that we cannot fully predict the trajectory of a collective improvisation because the performance of one musician necessarily affects that of the others. The trading solos in South Indian *niraval* and *svara kalpana* improvisations, for instance, are deeply contingent. When soloing, the accompanist must match the general pitch range, rhythmic density, and relative intensity of the soloist who plays before him, keeping pace with her increasingly complex musical offerings without ever outshining her (see Viswanathan and Allen 2004, 65–68). A jazz soloist, either in trading fours or in consecutive improvisations on the tune, may likewise take up a motive or musical suggestion from the previous soloist, expanding, embellishing, or recombining it in his own idiom.

In practices where the needs of note-by-note interlocking leave less room for this kind of imitative interaction, musicians are still affected by their musical context. A second-position *reyong* player hearing her partner in first position shift into more complex off-beat playing might follow suit. Conversely, she may lay down a more straightforward *norot*, emphasizing the beat and staying close to the model, to allow her partner that extended freedom. An Aka polyphonic singer, noticing his neighbor begin to sing in the lyric-driven *mòtángòlè* style, might shift to a *dìyèí* yodel to complement. And an mbira player who hears her partner begin a variant of the melody on the high keys of his instrument might choose to improvise an interlocking high line of her own. Yet each of these musicians will also be influenced by their larger musical contexts. If the women in the mbira performance begin singing in the wailing *kupururudza* style meant to indicate approval or demand more energy from their co-performers, the mbira players can increase the intensity of their playing through bass-ier variants, higher countermelodies, or more complex improvisations. And when a gamelan ensemble increases tempo or dynamics, a *reyong* player may alter the quality of her *norot* improvisations, matching the increase in intensity according to her personal style, be it through more note doublings, more syncopated playing, or particularly dense realizations of the model.[4]

Arja drummers likewise draw influence from co-performers. As we've seen, this sometimes takes the form of special patterns of call and response specific to particular pairs of drummers. Like *reyong* or mbira players though, drum partners will also respond to one another's increases in intensity or complexity. When an *arja* drummer begins to play in a *wayah*—complex—style, he might gaze into the distance to maintain an inward focus. But he will as likely stare directly into his partner's eyes with a wide grin on his face, inviting her to redouble her own efforts. *Pasangan*, partnership, is most satisfying when energy, intensity, and complexity are matched. On top of these interactions, *arja* drummers must also respond to shifts in the larger musical and dramatic context.

HOW MUSICAL CONTEXT INFLUENCES *KENDANG ARJA* IMPROVISATION

The balé banjar is packed to overflowing. It seems that the entire village of Pengosekan has come out to watch tonight's arja *performance. Children clamber to get a good seat at the front of the open-air building, wide awake and rowdy although it's nearly 10:00 p.m. and the show will last several hours. A handful of sarong-clad men have stepped off to the side of the* balé *to smoke their sweet clove cigarettes and exchange pleasantries. What's missing, I suddenly notice, is the young generation: the teenagers and twenty-somethings that I see lounging on their motorbikes offering "transport" to the tourists by day. Their absence is a testament to the decline of* arja*'s popularity in recent decades; thirty years ago, they would all have been here.*[5]

We've been sitting on the floor waiting for the show to begin since just after 8:00 p.m., the planned start time clearly just a loose guideline. None of the Balinese seem perturbed by the wait, however, and the excitement in the crowd is palpable; an arja *in Pengosekan is a rare thing nowadays. Many of my teachers talk fondly of the golden years of* arja*, when a good troupe would have work almost every night of the year in villages across the island. But most of these performing opportunities dried up in the 1980s and '90s.*[6] *Tonight's is part of the* arja revitalisasi, *revitalization, that's been taking place in recent years, as a new generation of performers gains interest in the genre.*

I look up to the stage and see Komin sitting comfortably cross-legged next to Pak Dewa's youngest son I Dewa Putu Rai, cups of half-drunk kopi *at their feet. They're smoking and laughing together as they wait for an indication to begin, Rai gesticulating wildly to emphasize the point of some obviously hilarious story. For tonight's performance, they are* kendang *partners, Rai leading the ensemble on* lanang, *Komin taking Rai's father's traditional place on* wadon. *In many ways, the two make a comical pair. Like his father, Rai is tall and gangly, with wide eyes like the Bhoma demon whose face sits above temple doorways, guarding the entrance from malevolent forces. His enormous, genuine grin isn't quite classically handsome, but you can't help but smile when he laughs, as he's doing now. Komin, by contrast, is a short man, his long curly hair, slowly dreadlocking from neglect, flying out from under his traditional* udeng *headscarf. Below sharp, angular cheekbones, the often-serious appearance of his heavily bearded face (a rarity in Bali) belies a dark, sardonic wit. I've never seen the two of them play together.*

Tonight's is my first arja *performance. While I've been studying the drumming for several months, I've never really given much thought to the dance drama it accompanies. The recent decline in* arja*'s popularity means I've not had the opportunity to see it performed live, and have thus learned the drumming divorced from this setting. But as the performance begins and night arches toward morning, a richer context unfolds before my eyes. Each singer-dancer presents a distinct character type: the ultrarefined princess Galuh and her strong, kind love interest Mantri Manis; the eccentric, mad princess Liku and her overbearing, deep-voiced* mother Limbur (Bali's answer to Wagner's Fricka); the male protagonist's arrogant opposite, Mantri Buduh and his crass, slapstick-clown servants.[7] I've read about these characters, and seen them rehearsing with Bu Candri, but have only just now come to understand that the function of the kendang is to bring their performances to life. Fight scenes are made more intense, romantic moments more sweet, by the choices Komin and Rai make in the course of performance. Like a well-composed film score, their improvising sets the scene, supports the drama, and keeps the audience invested in the story. Until this moment, I have not truly been learning kendang arja... only drumming. And it is no longer enough for me.

We know that an *arja* drummer's latitude for improvisation is limited by the need to rhythmically interlock with his partner. What's more, idiom dictates that each consistently play four drum strokes per beat, performing without the expressive interpretation of moment-to-moment dynamic or timbral shifts. How, then, do these drummers alter intensity to suit the drama?

Central to many aspects of Balinese life is the concept of *ramé*: boisterousness, busy-ness, or fullness. Balinese temple ceremonies are filled with colorful offerings and decorations, multiple gamelan ensembles playing simultaneously, incense and chanted prayers, laughter and liveliness. This *ramé* atmosphere keeps malevolent spirits, who are drawn to emptiness, at bay. Kendang playing is also often described in terms of its level of *ramé*, though emptiness is not considered dangerous! A precomposed pattern or improvised passage can be packed with main strokes, focusing especially on bass-y *Dag* (D) and *Tut* (T) strokes, or it can be sparser, largely made up of counting strokes and a few carefully placed rim strokes. Personal preference sometimes dictates the *ramé*-ness of a drummer's playing. The *lanang* patterns I learned from Cok Alit were all significantly denser than *lanang* patterns learned from my other teachers. As in the bottom three transcriptions in figure 6.1, his taught patterns never have two consecutive counting strokes, often feature several main strokes in succession, and use *Tut* (T) strokes in every rhythmic module. The top three transcriptions in the figure, the first *lanang* patterns I learned from Sudi, Pak Dewa, and Pak Tama respectively, are more typical of taught patterns from my other teachers. While many do use the denser modules Cok Alit favors, these are balanced with sparser rim- and counting-stroke playing.

CYCLIC STRUCTURE AND THE CONCEPT OF *RAMÉ*

Over and above personal preference, the appropriate level of *ramé* in any moment of a performance is suggested by moods, characters, and underlying

FIGURE 6.1. Relative level of *ramé* in taught patterns from different drummers

cyclic structures; the concept of *ramé* thus closely informs *arja* improvising. It is commonly accepted among Balinese drummers that more refined—*halus*—genres, characters, or moments in a piece should most often be accompanied by sparser drumming, while more *ramé* drumming can accompany *keras*—coarse or strong—ones. When I returned to my gamelan group in Vancouver after studying with Cok Alit, and began using his dense *lanang* patterns for the fast *batel* sections of the classic dance style *legong*, Sudi informed me in no uncertain terms that I should not. These patterns, he said, were far too *ramé* for use in this more refined practice, due in particular to their heavy reliance on *Tut* (T). To Sudi, such patterns were suited only to the most intense scenes of an *arja* drama.[8]

It is the different cyclic structures, first seen in figure 5.9, that outline the relative *halus*-ness or *keras*-ness of any moment in an *arja* performance. *Halus* characters and serious situations are generally accompanied by the slower 8-beat *tabuh telu* structure. By contrast, the fastest, shortest, densest structures—*batel* and *batel marah*—are used for fight scenes, comedic acting, and *keras* characters.[9] Four-beat *tabuh dua* cycles accompany characters and action in the middle of the *keras-halus* spectrum. To help create the right mood for these different characters and situations, some *arja* drummers specifically relegate certain patterns for use with certain cyclic structures. Pak Tama teaches *tabuh telu* and *tabuh dua* as separate skills that should not be mixed.[10] Similar to Pak Tut's semicomposed patterns from figure 5.27, Pak Tama's *tabuh telu* playing consists of four patterns always cycled in the same order with purportedly no *Dag-Tut* flexibility. His *lanang* patterns for *tabuh telu* are shown in figure 6.2.

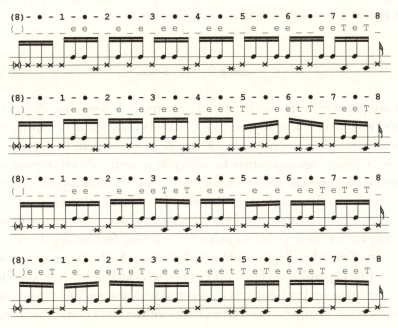

FIGURE 6.2. Pak Tama's taught *tabuh telu* patterns, *lanang*

FIGURE 6.3. Pak Tama's *tabuh dua* patterns are more *ramé*

While *ramé*-ness does increase over the four cycles, because Tama always starts from the first pattern after each dancer-cued break—or *angsel*—he most frequently performs the sparser parts of the collection. This fosters the *halus* atmosphere necessary for serious, dialogue-heavy, or sad moments in the drama. Pak Tama's taught *tabuh dua* patterns, shown in figure 6.3, more closely match the density of his less-used fourth *tabuh telu* pattern.

These denser patterns are appropriate, Tama taught, for any other cyclic structure in *arja*. Yet in his improvisations, he appears to reserve the densest segments of them for use in the fastest structures. The improvised *batel* passage in figure 6.4, first seen in figure 1.1, will elucidate.

Analyzing Ramé-*ness*

A first glance at the passage in figure 6.4 confirms it is denser overall than the *tabuh telu* patterns previously illustrated. The only really sparse parts are the first four beats and the segment labeled "*ngeseh*." The first four beats comprise Tama's standard opening pattern for any cyclic structure; the other sparse segment is the pattern he always uses for the increase in volume, *ngeseh*, that precedes an *angsel* rhythmic break. Otherwise, the passage is relatively *ramé*.

Although the continuum from sparseness to *ramé*-ness is challenging to subdivide and categorize, table 6.1 proposes a typology for assessing the relative density of any 2-beat fragment of *lanang* drumming. A 2-beat segment containing no *Tut* (T) strokes and fewer than six *peng* (e) or audible left-hand counting strokes (l) is considered sparse, as is a segment with just one *Tut* (T) stroke and no *peng* (e) or "l" strokes. Two-beat segments with no *Tut* (T) but at least six *peng*

(e) or "l" strokes, those with two to five main strokes including one *Tut* (T), and those with two *Tut* (T) strokes and no other main strokes are all considered to be of a medium density, "m." Lastly, segments containing more than one *Tut* (T) stroke and at least one *peng* (e) or "l" stroke as well as those containing six or more strokes including one *Tut* (T), I label *ramé*, "R."[11]

FIGURE 6.4. Improvisation for *batel*, Pak Tama

Table 6.1 Criteria for density in a two-beat lanang fragment

LANANG DENSITY, 2-BEAT FRAGMENTS

	SPARSE (S)	MEDIUM (M)	RAMÉ (R)
No *Tut* strokes	and 1–5 left-hand strokes	and 6+ left-hand strokes	n/a
1 *Tut* stroke	and 0 left-hand strokes	2–5 strokes total	6+ strokes total
2+ *Tut* strokes	n/a	and 0 left-hand strokes	and 1+ left-hand stroke(s)

Analyzing the passages from figures 6.2 and 6.4 as simple densities is instructive. In the *batel* improvisation, per the top analysis in figure 6.5, a full half of the passage is of a medium density. Only the required introductory and *ngeseh* patterns are sparse; the rest are *ramé*. Tama's *tabuh telu* patterns, by contrast, are much sparser overall. The bottom analysis in figure 6.5 shows an improvised *tabuh telu* passage that cycles through Tama's four patterns one and a half times before the *angsel*. Over half of its segments are sparse.

Unlike Pak Tama, Pak Dewa and Cok Alit did not teach different variants for different cyclic structures; they led me to believe that any variant could be used in any part of the drama. However, my conversation with Sudi suggested that perhaps not all patterns were wholly appropriate for all cyclic structures. Furthermore, in our lessons Pak Dewa taught that a balance of sparser with more *ramé* patterns was the aesthetic ideal of *kendang arja* improvising. When mixing and matching elements from taught patterns, he instructed, one should always be aware of the more and less *ramé* variants at play and try to maintain balance between them. The patterns I learned from him, four of which are analyzed for their density in figure 6.6, reveal this balance. In constructing taught patterns thusly, Pak Dewa didactically alternates *ramé* with sparse segments, encouraging me to do likewise in my improvisations.

These conflicting ideas left me with many unanswered questions about the concept of *ramé* in *arja* improvising. Was variant use free for each of the four cyclic structures in Cok Alit and Pak Dewa's Peliatan/Pengosekan style, and was this freedom "freer" than in Pak Tama's Singapadu style? Or could one also find in Pak Dewa and Cok Alit's playing a tendency toward more density in the faster cyclic structures, indicating a shared density aesthetic with Pak Tama? If not, how did these drummers differently delineate the shifts in intensity necessary for a satisfying *arja* performance? And how did Pak Dewa's idea of balance play into pattern selection for different cyclic structures? Tables 6.2–6.5 analyze longer excerpts of Cok Alit's *lanang* improvising in each of the four cyclic structures, showing an average density spread over several consecutive passages.

Batel
s-m-R-R-m-R-R-R-m-m / s-m-m-m-*angsel*

Tabuh telu
s-m s-s-s-R s-s-R-R s-R-s-R R-R-R-R s-s-s-R s-s-*angsel*

FIGURE 6.5. Density analysis of *batel* versus *tabuh telu* passages

Pattern 1: s-m-R-m

Pattern 2: s-m-R-s

Pattern 3: s-m-R-R

Pattern 4: s-m-R-R-R-s

FIGURE 6.6. Pak Dewa's taught patterns balance sparseness with *ramé*-ness

These tables indicate the same tendency we saw in Pak Tama's improvising: Cok Alit appears to favor denser playing in shorter structures. Because his taught patterns do not dictate such restrictions, this preference must stem from his wider knowledge base of *arja* improvising. Table 6.6 shows these same numbers in a different way, tallying the total percentage of segments in each density type across Cok Alit's full performance to ensure that segments in shorter passages are not given more weight in the final analysis than those in longer passages. Density differences between the four cyclic structures are just as clear cut in Pak Dewa's improvised *lanang* passages, shown in table 6.7.

BEYOND GENERALIZATIONS · 229

Table 6.2 Density spread for Cok Alit's lanang *improvisations in* batel marah

BATEL MARAH: FASTEST 2-BEAT CYCLIC STRUCTURE

	SPARSE (S)	MEDIUM (M)	RAMÉ (R)
Passage 1	20	20	60
Passage 2	20	20	60
Passage 3	-	-	100
Passage 4	20	20	60
Passage 5	14	29	57
Passage 6	-	14	86
Average	12.5	17	70.5

Table 6.3 Density spread for Cok Alit's lanang *improvisations in* batel

BATEL: FAST 2-BEAT CYCLIC STRUCTURE

	SPARSE (S)	MEDIUM (M)	RAMÉ (R)
Passage 1	-	-	100
Passage 2	18	18	64
Passage 3	-	25	75
Passage 4	-	33	67
Passage 5	-	44	56
Passage 6	23	31	46

(cont'd on next page)

Table 6.3 (Continued)

BATEL: FAST 2-BEAT CYCLIC STRUCTURE

	SPARSE (S)	MEDIUM (M)	RAMÉ (R)
Passage 7	14	29	57
Passage 8	–	15	85
Passage 9	13	60	27
Passage 10	42	23	25
Passage 11	21	36	43
Average	12	29	59

Table 6.4 Density spread for Cok Alit's lanang *improvisations in* tabuh dua

TABUH DUA: MODERATE 4-BEAT CYCLIC STRUCTURE

	SPARSE (S)	MEDIUM (M)	RAMÉ (R)
Passage 1	31	23	46
Passage 2	29	8	63
Passage 3	26	13	61
Passage 4	18	36.5	45.5
Passage 5	42	27	31
Passage 6	17	31	52

(*cont'd on next page*)

Table 6.4 (Continued)

TABUH DUA: MODERATE 4-BEAT CYCLIC STRUCTURE

	SPARSE (S)	MEDIUM (M)	RAMÉ (R)
Passage 7	38	35	27
Average	28.5	25	46.5

Table 6.5 Density spread for Cok Alit's lanang *improvisations in* tabuh telu

TABUH TELU: SLOW 8-BEAT CYCLIC STRUCTURE

	SPARSE (S)	MEDIUM (M)	RAMÉ (R)
Passage 1	46	30	24
Passage 2	30	37	33
Passage 3	73	19	8
Passage 4	40	22	38
Passage 5	53	26	21
Average	48	27	25

Table 6.6 Density spread by percentage in improvised lanang, *Cok Alit*

CYCLIC STRUCTURE	SPARSE (S) %	MEDIUM (M) %	RAMÉ (R) %
Batel Marah	11.5	18	70.5
Batel	12	32	56
Tabuh Dua	30	24	46
Tabuh Telu	26	27	47

Table 6.7 Density spread by percentage in improvised lanang, *Pak Dewa*

CYCLIC STRUCTURE	SPARSE (S) %	MEDIUM (M) %	RAMÉ (R) %
Batel Marah	10.5	34.5	55
Batel	6	34	60
Tabuh Dua	19	39.5	41.5
Tabuh Telu	32	33	35

We can see that Pak Dewa is a slightly less *ramé* player than Cok Alit overall—not surprising, given the relative densities of their taught patterns. However it is also clear that, like his partner, Pak Dewa increases his use of sparser segments for longer gong patterns. Although they do not have the benefit of semicomposed patterns to help determine density, Pak Dewa and Cok Alit are clearly aware of the different *rasa*, feeling, of each cyclic structure and the relative *ramé*-ness that will best support it. And while their penchant for innovation across all cyclic structures means that their passages vary widely, as we will see, these aesthetic requirements, by necessity, limit the use of certain variants in certain structures. Figure 6.7 shows a collection of relatively sparse 4-beat segments from taught *lanang* patterns. While both Cok Alit and Pak Dewa often use these patterns and their variants in improvised performance, they are almost never featured in *batel* structures.

Complicating the Concept of Ramé

Relative density, then, seems to be the primary way that the larger musical and dramatic structure—cyclic gong patterns and characters of differing levels of refinement—shape *kendang arja* improvisation. But the reality is more complicated, and here I return to Pak Dewa's comments on balance. Central to Balinese Hinduism is the idea of finding balance between opposing elements in a duality: a balancing of male and female, dark and light, good and evil, and

FIGURE 6.7. Commonly used taught patterns too sparse for *batel*

so on.[12] Called *rwa bhineda*, literally "two opposites," the ideal also informs aesthetics in the Balinese performing arts. The stock characters presented in each *arja* drama, for instance, represent good and bad archetypes in human society. They play out a story of struggle between the two sides, exploring issues of karma and faith. Good is juxtaposed with evil, but also wealth with poverty, happiness with sadness, coarseness (*keras*) with refinement (*halus*), tradition with modernity, high class with low class, and so on. Duality is also emphasized in specifics of performance and dramatic structure: gravity alongside humor, sung versus spoken dialogue, the alternation of dance and drumming with unaccompanied song and speech, and the mixture of high and low caste languages: Kawi and high Balinese next to everyday Balinese, Indonesian and, these days, occasional English for humor.

As we saw in Pak Dewa's taught patterns in figure 6.6, and in his instructions for mixing and matching pattern elements, a preference for an aesthetic balancing of opposites exists in *kendang arja* also. In Pak Tama's patterns, regardless of relative density, a larger structural logic prizes a balance of more with less *ramé* elements. His *tabuh telu* patterns from figure 6.2 each move from sparser to denser segments approaching the gong stroke. The full metacycle of four patterns also balances sparseness with *ramé*-ness in an end-weighted fashion, each pattern denser than the last. While the *batel* passage in figure 6.4 does not exhibit the same directionality, we still see a balancing of densities. This time, medium-density segments alternate with fully dense ones.

Thus, *arja* improvising appears to require a balance of sparser and denser variants, but the specifics of that balancing are still determined by the underlying cyclic structure. *Tabuh telu* demands lighter, sparser playing to maintain a *halus* feeling; sparse segments usually occupy 25 to 50 percent of any passage of drumming. Yet even in these *halus* moments, the playing cannot be entirely sparse; this would disrupt balance, the lack of rhythmic contrast producing a less musically satisfying performance. Both medium and *ramé* segments, therefore, are used to balance the dominant sparse ones. *Batel* structures, by contrast, allow few sparse segments, instead striking a balance between dense and medium ones. This gives the appropriate *ramé* feel for coarser characters, situations, and emotions, while still maintaining a blend of more with less *ramé* moments.

Alit once told me a story of his first one-on-one encounter with a master musician with whom he hoped to study. As is common, before deciding whether to take him on as a student, the older drummer asked the younger to play for him. Alit recalls pulling out all the stops, playing his densest, most complex improvisations for *kendang tunggal*, solo drum. When he stopped, sweaty and spent, the master looked at him thoughtfully and said simply: "Yeah, I can do that too. But sometimes I don't." While Alit's playing was surely impressive, he lacked the maturity to understand that sparseness and *ramé*-ness, simplicity and complexity work best in opposition.[13] This belief appears to be at the center of *kendang arja*, whether the precomposed interactions of Pak Tut and Pak Tama's *tabuh telu* playing or the improvised patterns of Tama, Cok Alit, and Pak Dewa. Although the desire to balance opposing elements likely informs many musical systems, and is something to look for in the analysis of diverse improvised practices, its particular reflection in Balinese Hindu philosophy is worthy of note in an analysis of *arja*. Yet while certain structural and aesthetic considerations—like this one—may be significant for the majority of *arja* performers, other idioms and priorities are more particularly shaped by individual or regional concerns.

DIFFERENCES IN REGIONAL STYLE

I drop by Sanggar Çudamani, the arts collective launched by Alit and his brothers, whenever I'm in Pengosekan. There are always friends to be seen, not least Pak Dewa, the family patriarch, and very often I'll catch a gamelan rehearsal. Today, Alit's younger brother Rai is teaching one of his new compositions to a group of musicians from north Bali in preparation for the annual gamelan gong kebyar *competition. Komin, who lives just down the street, has also stopped by. He is sitting with half a dozen other musicians, watching the rehearsal and smoking. Several of them gesture me over, and I join them on* balé.

"*Listen to their* norot," *Komin whispers breathlessly as soon as I've sat down. "It's so different from ours. So* keras." *This is the first time I've heard him talk with excitement about someone else's* reyong *improvising.*

I have often heard it said here in the south that people from the north are more keras, *their personalities harder or stronger or louder. But it has never occurred to me that this regional difference might also affect the way they play gamelan. I listen hard, trying to catch a glimpse of their* keras-*ness in action, but it's too fast for me to really break down the idiom.*

"*What are they doing differently?*" *I ask.*

"*I don't know how to explain, exactly,*" *Komin responds. "It's just more* keras. *Not* cocok—*compatible—with my style of playing at all.*" *Then he adds, "You should take lessons with them. Their* norot*'s really cool!*"

Although I never do get the chance to study with the north Bali *reyong* players, who are only in Pengosekan for a couple of days, my conversation with Komin incites a new line of thinking for me. I have been working with the assumption that the model and knowledge base for *reyong norot*, grounded in an explicitly known, fixed *gangsa* figuration style, would be adhered to all over Bali. The rules I have derived allow me to make *norot* that seems acceptable to every *reyong* player I jam or perform with. But it now becomes evident that these have all been south Bali musicians, and regional differences appear to exist even in this relatively constrained practice. That *kendang arja*—with its looser unconscious model—would also differ regionally now seems a given.

Many improvised practices vary by region. In Puerto Rican *bomba*, divergent drumming styles in different areas have stemmed from the innovations of community leaders, who rearrange collections of known songs or use these as the basis for new compositions and rhythmic variants. Ferreras (2005) identifies ten styles or "rhythm categories of bomba performance" (104) in regions across Puerto Rico. Drummers in Loíza with its large Afro–Puerto Rican population, for instance, have developed a style of *bomba* called *seis corrido*, "whose fast tempo and peculiar solo improvisations position it at the African end of the bomba stylistic continuum" (85). A substyle or variant of *seis corrido*, called *bambulé*, draws rhythmic influence from ragtime via New Orleans, Haiti, Cuba, and other former colonies of France and Spain.[14] Regional style likewise dominates the North Indian classical vocal genre *dhrupad*, where several well-established hereditary family traditions, *gharānā*, as well as a number of styles, *bānī*, dictate local models and knowledge bases for improvisation. Similar to *bomba* styles, *gharānā* and *bānī* are regionally based, often associated with individual families and originated by a single master musician who then sets the precedent for a new style.[15] Improvising Cuban *charanga* flute players often cite two preeminent schools of playing, associated with the expert mid-twentieth-century flautists José Fajardo and Richard Egües. While the proliferation of recorded music in Cuba has influenced the interpretation of their idioms in complex ways, both regions and schools play integral roles in the development of improvisational style.[16] Regional stylistic factors, then, must be addressed in discussions of models, knowledge bases, and improvisation. In *kendang arja*, distinct regional styles established by renowned musicians in the early twentieth century draw into question the universality of model elements proposed in chapter 5.

CONTEXTUALIZING REGIONAL VARIATION IN *ARJA*

Although a small island, Bali has almost never been a unified entity, and much of this has to do with its natural topography. The seemingly ubiquitous rice-field expanses of Clifford Geertz's "snug little amphitheatre" (1980, 20), in fact, exist predominantly just in the center-south of the island, with drier climates in the east and some forest still left in the west. Cutting the island in half east to west is a range of volcanic mountains that have, until relatively recently, made travel across Bali arduous. Rivers running off the mountains north to south have forged deep ravines down the face of the island. This means that most major roads in Bali, with the exception of coastal roads, also run north-south. The resulting "difficulty of east–west travel was [historically] conducive to political fragmentation" (Pringle 2004, 5). Although only 2,232 mi.^{2}, about the size of Delaware or Canada's Prince Edward Island, from the seventeenth through the nineteenth centuries Bali supported nine independent states or minikingdoms.

The historically disjointed nature of the island, both politically and topographically, propagated the at-least-partially independent development of arts traditions in villages often only a few miles apart, leading to regional styles in various art forms. In the 1930s, for instance, three regions in south-central Bali—Ubud, Sanur, and Batuan—emerged as preeminent painting centers, each with a distinct style.[17] And before the establishment of standardizing arts academies, regions tended to specialize in music styles as well. Peliatan was known for its *legong* and *janger* performances, Batuan for *gambuh*, Saba for *legong*, Buleleng for *gong kebyar*. In the last half century, better roads, improved communications technology, and centralized arts institutions at the high school and university levels have to some extent negated the individualizing effects of geography and history.[18] However, both top-down and grass-roots movements of *pelestarian*—preservation—and *revitalisasi*—revitalization—have equally pushed back against these standardizing forces (see Tilley 2013, chap. 1). And in traditional practices like *arja*, history looms large. In the early to mid-twentieth century, two south Bali villages—Keramas and Singapadu—emerged as preeminent *arja* regions. Their influence is still felt today, with musicians proudly embracing their musical lineage. Yet while the Singapadu style is relatively well represented across the island, information about the traditional Keramas style is scarce.

COMPETING STYLES OF *ARJA*: KERAMAS AND SINGAPADU

The midday sun bores into my back through my t-shirt as I ride the motorbike through the twisting side roads of Gianyar regency. I am on a quixotic search for kendang arja asli *Keramas, the original* arja *drumming from Keramas. It is an accepted truth among Balinese musicians that Singapadu and Keramas are the two villages most famous for* arja. *The name or location of any drummer still versed in the Keramas style is much less well known, however. I have slowly come to realize that all of my teachers, whether from Singapadu, Peliatan, Pengosekan, Apuan, or Ubud, claim at least a partial lineage to* arja asli *Singapadu. All have opinions about the differences between the Singapadu and Keramas styles. None can direct me to a teacher in Keramas. Some even warn that the traditional style may already have vanished there. Cok Alit asserts:*

> In Keramas, it's already dwindled, because of this: in Singapadu, it's still original, the dance. What's more, Bu Candri is there, you see. My nephew[19] is also an arja dancer there.... Indeed he's still old-style, still original.... In Keramas now, it's already fairly modern.[20]

I don't have very much to go on, just the name of an old dancer living somewhere in town. But I have been successful finding teachers with less information and am feeling cautiously optimistic. Bu Candri has told me that the Keramas dancer Pak Berata studied with her many years ago and hopes that he will know more about the local arja *scene. After many stops, turnarounds, and sometimes-helpful directions, I finally find Pak Berata's home. He is working in the fields, and I am invited in and offered hot* kopi *and snacks while I wait.*

Pak Berata finally joins me, sipping his own coffee, which gives me the unspoken permission to drink mine. After brief introductions and music-related small talk, we get right down to it: a discouraging discussion on the state of arja *in Keramas. There is no one left who still plays the original kendang style, he tells me. In fact, "the* arja *troupe of Keramas dispersed in the late 1970s, with a trend toward individual expertise and professionalism"*

(Kellar 2004, case study 3). There are still a few arja *dancers in the village, many of whom, like Pak Berata and the famous Ibu Latri, have studied with Bu Candri or her father and thus are as much a part of the Singapadu tradition as they are the Keramas one. But all the instrumentalists in Keramas (and there aren't that many anymore) play a newer style of* arja *now: a fusion style learned in arts academies like ISI (Institut Seni Indonesia), the performing arts university in the capital city of Denpasar.*[21] *Pak Berata recommends that I seek out Pak Gobleg in the neighboring village of Medan, the only person that he knows of who still holds in his mind the old Keramas patterns. Unfortunately, unlike most of my other teachers who are musicians by trade, Pak Gobleg works long hours out of town, and I am told that he will likely not have time to meet with me. I head back to Ubud, disheartened, and treat myself to a glass of red wine. Cold, as it always is here, the heat too quickly turning unrefrigerated wine to vinegar.*

Although I was unable to connect with a Keramas-style drummer, conversations with my teachers told a story of regionalism. In a practice where troupes often traveled to perform, and where radio programs through the 1960s, '70s, and '80s brought together musicians and dancers from various regions, many of my teachers had firsthand experience with Keramas-trained *arja* performers. While the regions shared a basic structural framework for the drama, with the same stock standard characters and underlying cyclic structures, there appeared to be several fundamental differences between their styles. Stories from Pak Tama, who had once been invited to play with Pak Gobleg of Medan, as well as Cok Alit, who had performed with troupes in Keramas, indicated that the two styles, in many respects, were mutually unintelligible.

Many of the differences between the Keramas and Singapadu styles seem to stem from the diverse practices that were popular in each area during the genre's development. While Singapadu, drawing inspiration from neighboring Batuan, developed an *arja* colored by dance dramas, Keramas musicians were guided by their expertise in classical singing styles.[22] These contrasting influences led to divergent specializations in *arja* performance practice, with Keramas focusing more heavily on singing while Singapadu more fully developed dance and character idiosyncrasies (see Tilley 2013, chap. 1).[23]

Many Singapadu-trained musicians allege that, in traditional Keramas-style *arja*, elaborate singing became the focus at the expense of the dance elements. Cok Alit remembers playing kendang in the 1970s for a singer-dancer from Keramas. He complains that the dancer's *angsel* cues were so unclear it was almost impossible for him to play a good *angsel* on his kendang. And several of my other teachers, including Pak Tama and Pak Dewa, claim that the drumming in Keramas-style *arja* was closer to *kendang tunggal*, solo drumming, than to the intricately paired kendang practices of the Singapadu style. Thus, they argue, Keramas drummers showed less care for the rhythmic connections between the two drummers, or between drummer and dancer, than did those musicians from a Singapadu lineage.

As for the character of the drumming itself, Cok Alit maintains that Keramas-style *arja* in general was far more *keras*—loud or strong—than *arja* from Singapadu and, by extension, from his own Peliatan:

> It's loud there! Because it's not smooth or soft enough. It's harsh there! Whereas here, in Peliatan, there are patterns of many types: there are loud patterns, soft patterns.[24] It depends on the situation, the character, yeah? But there, indeed just from the drum strokes [he makes a loud busy noise] the character is harsh. It's all strong character there. . . . For example, the *lanang* players use too much *pung* (U).[25]

Cok Alit further asserts that, unlike the Peliatan and Singapadu styles, which have rules or *patokan* governing the rhythmic relationship between *wadon* and *lanang* as we've seen, in Keramas "there are no rules. They don't care."[26] Pak Tama says the same. Yet while it may be true that Keramas musicians, more concerned with excellence in vocals than in dance, would devote less time to developing aspects of drumming, it is as likely that these regional stylistic differences stem from a distinct model and mutually unintelligible knowledge base. It may be not an absence of rules, but rather a different set of them, that makes these drummers incompatible, *tidak cocok*.

Regardless, the aspects of model and knowledge base discussed in chapter 5, rather than being indicative of *arja* as a whole, actually appear to describe a specific regional style of playing developed by two early twentieth-century Singapadu-based musicians: I Cokorda Oka Tublen and I Madé Kredek.[27] Together these partners made a prolific teaching team who, for a quarter of a century, would shape the development of *arja* in villages across Bali.[28] Each of my older generation teachers belongs to this lineage of Singapadu drummers. As we can see in figure 6.8, Cok Alit in nearby Peliatan studied extensively with Cok Oka Tublen, while his Pengosekan-based drum partner Pak Dewa worked briefly with Kredek. Pak Tama, in Singapadu itself, studied with both these masters. And Pak Tut from distant Apuan in Bangli regency learned kendang from his village's late *arja* specialist Pak Patrem, who in turn inherited the practice from Kredek.

Regional style becomes yet more complicated in this next generation of musicians. While Pak Tut and his co-performers in Apuan have only second-hand knowledge of the patterns of one Singapadu master, and thus a relatively

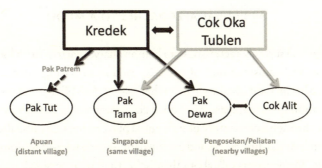

FIGURE 6.8. Family tree of Singapadu *arja*

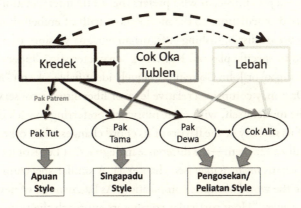

FIGURE 6.9. Complete family tree of second-generation *arja*

limited drumming vocabulary, Pak Tama has considerable firsthand knowledge of both Kredek and Cok Oka Tublen's patterns. Pak Dewa and Cok Alit, through their partnership, are likewise versed in the full *kendang arja asli* Singapadu style. Yet both also worked extensively with another musician: the famous Peliatan-based drummer I Madé Lebah. Because Lebah and other Peliatan drummers did sometimes perform *arja* with Kredek, as well as playing the closely related *legong*-style drumming with Cok Oka Tublen, they would have shaped an acceptably compatible idiom in Peliatan. These *arja* styles, though, still developed largely independently. So the Peliatan/Pengosekan style taught by Pak Dewa and Cok Alit, and played by Komin, Rai, and other younger Pengosekan-based drummers, bears the mark of multiple village styles, each of which separately influenced its model and knowledge base. Thus did three related but independent regional styles evolve from one in a single generation. The more complete, and complicated, family tree of *arja* in my teachers' generation is shown in figure 6.9.

INDIVIDUAL APPROACHES TO A MODEL

While regional style characteristics can help an analyst narrow in on local knowledge bases and idiosyncrasies of models, each improvising musician, in any genre, also has an individual style that is hers alone. As Miller (2014) notes of flute improvisation in Cuban *charanga*, "broad characteristics of the *típica* style can be described through a close study of influential players, but one must also take into account individual differences and personal preference when describing the style as a whole. Many players talk about their '*sello*,' their own personal 'stamp'" (215). Individual style, or *sello*, may mean a partiality to one improvisatory process over others—a jazz musician who prefers the subtle interpretation of timbral shifts or varied articulations to the mordents or trills of embellishment. It may involve the use of distinguishing riffs, ornaments, or versions of a model that become tied to specific players: Kid Ory's "characteristic 'slippery' trombone style" (Israels 1999) or John Coltrane's uniquely identifiable take on "My Favorite Things." Or it may comprise a relative level of liberalism or conservatism with regard to the model itself, with some musicians preferring to stick closer to the contours of its melody or the flavors of its chord changes while others choose to more radically alter them—the difference in degree that Lee Konitz juxtaposed as *variation* versus *improvisation* (see chapter 1). A similar spectrum, of course, also exists in the world of music composition. As Bakan notes of new works for *gamelan beleganjur*: "How particular composers approach the issue of whether or not it is appropriate to employ 'foreign' musical elements in their beleganjur works—and if so, to what degree—reveals much about the range of individual attitudes that shapes the scope of creative production" (1999, 155).[29]

Individual style is mutable, shaped by musical influences over time, shifting personal tastes, and varying degrees of competence as well as by more immediate factors of performance context, inspiration from musical partners, and personal energy or mood in the moment.[30] Thus, when trying to reconstruct models from the performances of individuals or, conversely, to hold up individual performances as exemplars of models, it is important to remember that "we can talk about tendencies but not firm rules when it comes to individual style" (Miller 2014, 226). No musician fits perfectly into the box of a theoretical model.

Longtime co-performers in collective practices develop similar tendencies and attitudes toward improvisation—the heart of any good *pasangan* or partnership. But these shared histories and goals do not fully negate the effects of individual style. Even the two founders of *kendang arja asli* Singapadu, drum partners for years, had their own idiosyncrasies of style, mutually compatible but also distinct. Kredek's son, dancer and scholar I Madé Bandem (and brother to singer-dancer Bu Candri) describes his father's playing style: "My father always told me how to play with the rim, like this." He puts his left fingertips high up on the rim, creating a high, clear *peng* (e) tone. "Instead of this." He moves his fingers down and the tone becomes lower, more *pung* (U) than *peng* (e). "As *krempeng* as I can make it, you know? And then, he always said *arja* should emphasize the left rim. Both *lanang* and *wadon*."[31]

Accordingly, Kredek's patterns were relatively sparse, using mostly rim strokes *kom* (o) and *peng* (e). When playing in the slower 8-beat *tabuh telu* structure, he did incorporate more *Dag* (D) and *Tut* (T). Yet this bass-stroke use was regimented; the fixed *Dag-Tut* interactions we saw in Pak Tut's patterns in figure 5.27 and Pak Tama's in figure 6.2 are legacies of Kredek's playing.[32] The majority of Kredek's patterns for shorter gong cycles, by contrast, were *kom-peng* focused. They were also, as Bandem characterizes, "very simple" and repetitive. In figure 6.10 are several of Kredek's patterns for the 4-beat cyclic structure *tabuh dua*, as played by Bandem. They resemble the most basic, *dasar*, of my other teachers' patterns, combining simple "on-beat, off-beat" rim-stroke work with foundational rhythmic modules like "e e T" and "o d D."

In the wake of decades of influence from *gamelan gong kebyar*, Bandem complains that many of the younger *arja* drummers, even in Singapadu, have lost the subtlety and lightness (and, he believes, the associated freedom of variation) of these more traditional patterns:

> I think the people right now don't pay attention to this kind of *krempeng* for *wadon*, yeah? . . . The last Singapadu *arja* that you saw in the Art Centre at the PKB [the Bali Arts Festival in 2011], that's already more *kebyar*, and with a little bit more *ramé* [busy] style. But you can make interlocking complete with this simpler one. And then, when you play, you can make it *bebas* [free]. It's not really *terikat* [tied], not making a fixed pattern, and you play around listening to the other drummer and can make it more varied. My father played like that.[33]

Cok Oka Tublen, by contrast, preferred more *ramé*, busy patterns; he was purported to use more *Dag* (D) and *Tut* (T) strokes than his partner, used the *pung* (U) strokes generally reserved for cuing throughout his improvising, and even borrowed the full slap strokes *Kap* (K) and *Pak* (P) from large-drum genres like *gamelan gong kebyar*.[34] He is also said to have used fewer counting strokes

FIGURE 6.10. Kredek's patterns for *tabuh dua*

than other *arja* drummers, which likely explains the *ramé* drumming style of his longtime student Cok Alit. Bandem, who interviewed both Singapadu masters before their deaths, reports that their stylistic differences, perhaps predictably, stemmed from outside musical influences. Playing *legong* with musicians in Peliatan, Cok Oka Tublen picked up some of their patterns, purportedly more *ramé* than Kredek's *arja* patterns.[35] But his biggest influence came from *barong melawang*, traveling *barong* dance troupes, from the village of Pinda:

> One of the best *barong melawang* in Bali during that time, in the '30s and '40s, was from Pinda. Pinda has very strong musicians for *barong bangkal* [a pig-shaped *barong*], and also *gamelan gong kebyar*. Pinda has a very strong kind of drumming for *barong*. Very complicated. *Ramé*. More *ramé* than the Singapadu style. Cokorda was always interested in listening to all of these patterns of *barong bangkal* from Pinda. So you know, people picking up different things, improving their style. He developed another style like that.[36]

Thus, despite the fact that he continued to play with Kredek, Cok Oka Tublen also effected his own independent development of Singapadu *arja* in its formative years.

This autonomous development of styles and patterns becomes even more evident in the next generation of musicians, as Cok Alit, Pak Dewa, Pak Tama, and Pak Tut shape their webs of musical influences into the divergent styles of Peliatan/Pengosekan, Singapadu, and Apuan. As with *charanga* flute schools, *bomba* drumming styles, or *dhrupad*'s *gharānā* and *bānī*, *arja*'s regional idioms have largely been molded by the individual preferences of these four men. Central to the differences in their styles are their quite different levels of tolerance for variation on their teachers' idioms. These attitudes are reflected not only in their patterns but also in the way each drummer talks about his teachers and the legacy of their lineage.

As we saw in figure 5.27, Pak Tut never varies *Dag* (D) and *Tut* (T) stroke placement, offering only surface-level interpretation in his rim-stroke use. Conversations and drumming sessions with Bandem and Pak Tama confirm that the patterns Pak Tut teaches are identical to the patterns his teacher Pak Patrem learned from Kredek half a century earlier. When asked if he ever varies his teacher's patterns, Pak Tut responds with absolute incredulity. This is the Apuan style, not meant to be changed.[37] I suspect not only his obvious respect for Patrem but also his restricted vocabulary of patterns, his limited exposure to other styles of *arja*, and his somewhat lower drumming proficiency level all contribute to this more conservative stance (see Tilley 2014). Pak Tut's improvisations, then, stay firmly in the realm of interpretation, where the term "conservative" is not a value judgment but rather an assessment of degree. The interchanging of rim strokes with counting strokes is *bebas*, free, provided the "on-beat, off-beat" rules are adhered to. But Pak Tut does not venture into processes of recombination or expansion in his improvised drumming.

Pak Tama is less conservative with regard to his teachers' patterns, though he still imposes certain explicit limits on improvising. First, he keeps the patterns of his two teachers separate, with Kredek's patterns reserved for use in 8-beat *tabuh telu* structures and Cok Oka Tublen's designated for *tabuh dua* and *batel* structures. Like Pak Tut, he largely varies Kredek's patterns through rim-stroke interpretation and insisted that I do likewise. These four patterns, Tama claims, are designed to be played in the same order every time, always begun again from the first pattern after *angsels* and never altered in their bass-stroke placement. His playing for the other three cyclic structures is less constrained. Taught patterns are varied not just through interpretation but also processes of recombination. What's more, in these structures Tama also appears to work with variants beyond his palette of taught patterns, though these are generally relatively generic in their "on-beat, off-beat" placement and use of familiar modules like "e e T."

Most open to innovation in improvisation are drum partners Cok Alit and Pak Dewa. While both of these drummers speak of their teachers—particularly their local guru Lebah—with respect and awe, each also owns with pride the conscious changes he has made to his drumming style through the years. As previously mentioned, Pak Dewa gleefully admits to "stealing," *mencuri*, patterns from other great drummers he hears. While Cok Alit likewise attributes changes in his drumming to the influence of other musicians, he also claims that he has altered his performance practice as his feeling, *rasa*, and energy levels shift with age. With these drummers we find the most radical approaches to the *arja* model. While they, too, engage processes of interpretation, their techniques for recombination, as we will see, take their improvisations further from the taught patterns than Pak Tama's. What's more, they also employ expansion techniques.

Arja drummers, then, demonstrate a spectrum of tolerance for innovation and pattern reworking, with Pak Tut on the more conservative end and Cok Alit and Pak Dewa on the more liberal end. Understanding their improvisations as versions of a regional model is insufficient without this nuancing of individual attitudes and approaches. Analyses of their improvisations will delineate this spectrum of tolerance and elucidate the effects of personal choice on improvised practice.

INTERPRETATION

As we saw in chapter 1, the shifts in articulation, rhythmic phrasing, dynamics, and accentuation that comprise interpretation in jazz improvisation take a different form in *kendang arja* practice. Here, a similar aesthetic of variable dynamic, articulation, or timbre is created by replacing main strokes with soft counting strokes or, conversely, adding extra main strokes where counting strokes occur in a taught pattern. Figure 6.11 is an 8-beat taught *lanang* pattern from Pak Tama of Singapadu and some of its improvised interpretations. In the mnemonic notation, the lower case "t" indicates a subordinate stroke played with *Tut* (T) technique, similar to the *wadon*'s softer counting stroke "d" and often meant to be all but inaudible. In each transcription, variations on the original taught pattern are outlined with a dashed rectangle.

In the first improvised pattern in figure 6.11, Tama cuts the first *peng* (e); in the second, he adds an extra one. In the third, two *peng* (e) replace counting strokes at the beginning of the pattern. Near the end of that same pattern, Tama replaces one *peng* (e) with an "l" counting-stroke slap. In each

FIGURE 6.11. Interpretation, *lanang*

improvisation, the taught pattern remains structurally and aesthetically intact, but a fresh variant is created through interpretation. This process is ubiquitous among *arja* drummers and the least radical form of improvisation on a taught pattern.

RECOMBINATION

The analyses in chapter 1 also revealed *arja* drummers' extensive use of recombination, which takes a number of different forms in the practice. One common recombination technique involves maintaining the rhythmic identity of a taught pattern in improvisation but shifting the rhythm in relation to the cycle. In the two examples in figure 6.12, the actual drum strokes of the taught patterns remain intact but are displaced by one beat, earlier in Example 1, and later in Example 2. Different rhythmic modules of the patterns are circled in either gray or black to ease visual analysis. Here and in subsequent figures, the taught pattern is notated above the improvised one.

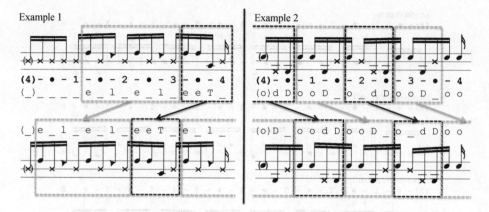

FIGURE 6.12. Recombination: pattern displacement

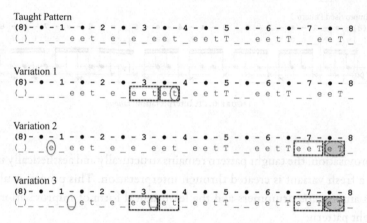

FIGURE 6.13. Increasing recombination of gesture elements

Related to this pattern displacement are instances in which common components of taught patterns, like the *lanang* gestures "e e T" and "e T e T," are reversed or rearranged in improvised performance. In figure 6.13, a taught pattern and three of its improvised variants show a simple, small-scale example of this kind of recombination. For visual clarity in the next several figures, only mnemonic notation is used. The reader need not be overly concerned with the minutiae of each drum stroke in these patterns; rather, most pertinent to the discussion are the improvisational strategies at play. These are shown with arrows, circles, boxes, and the juxtaposition of gray with black text.

In figure 6.13, dotted ovals indicate surface-level interpretation while dashed rectangles show bigger changes of recombination. Leading to the midpoint of Variation 1, Pak Tama takes the "e _" and "e e t" modules from the model and reverses them, adding an extra "t" stroke. This shifts the double *peng* (e) in relation to the beat. In Variation 2, he makes a similar change with full *Tut* (T) strokes, densifying the pattern (circled in gray). Variation 3 combines all these changes with other instances of interpretation. These seemingly small alterations actually give each variation a quite different feeling.

The examples in figures 6.14 and 6.15 show this sort of recombination on a larger scale. In figure 6.14, a simple reversing of the first two beats and the last two beats of a taught pattern creates a brand new pattern using the *campur-campur*, mixing it up technique, that Pak Dewa encouraged in our lessons (discussed in chapter 5).

The improvised pattern in figure 6.15, first encountered in figure 1.5, recombines pattern components in a less symmetrical fashion. Here, the 4-note black module at the taught pattern's end trades places with the six notes of the gray module so that each component now relates differently to the cyclic structure. Add to this a small shifting of the *Tut* (T) stroke at beat 1 (marked with an arrow) and the deletion of another *Tut* (T) stroke in the gray gesture (circled), and Tama has created a very new *lanang* pattern through a blend of interpretation and recombination.

Another kind of recombination sees drummers take components from various different taught patterns and splice them together. Again this can be done symmetrically or asymmetrically. In the middle transcription of figure 6.16 is an improvised *lanang* pattern in which Pak Tama combines the last two beats

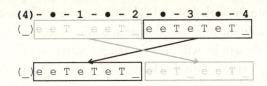

FIGURE 6.14. Larger-scale recombination of pattern elements

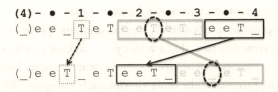

FIGURE 6.15. More complex recombination of pattern elements

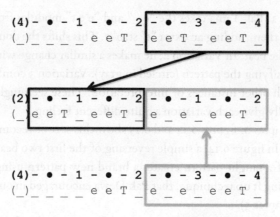

FIGURE 6.16. Recombination of segments from multiple taught patterns

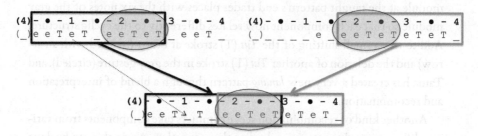

FIGURE 6.17. Recombination through elision of multiple taught patterns

of one taught pattern with the last two beats of another. Together they create a pattern denser in main strokes than either of the original patterns.

Not surprisingly, Cok Alit and Pak Dewa use recombination in yet more inventive ways. In the improvised pattern on the bottom of figure 6.17, Cok Alit begins as though he will play the taught pattern on the top left, varied through interpretation with the deletion of a *peng* (e) stroke (marked with a thin arrow). Yet the passage then dovetails smoothly into the ending of the taught pattern on the top right through the elision of their shared "e e T e T" modules (circled in gray).

Many of the more asymmetric recombinations of pattern elements occur, predictably, in *wadon* improvisation. Because *lanang* playing is bound to the dance and employs simpler patterns, these drummers appear more tightly tied to a grouping structure that aligns with cycle-marking instruments. Thus recombination on *lanang* often occurs in 2- and 4-beat segments. In *wadon* patterns, by contrast, the process can be more rhythmically complex. This is especially true of Pak Dewa's playing. In the first improvised passage in figure 6.18, with thin arrows indicating interpretation, Pak Dewa recombines one beat from the black taught segment with three beats from the gray one. In the second example, two 2-beat segments from taught patterns and a 3-beat one, each altered through interpretation, make up the majority of the new improvised pattern. But here Pak Dewa also recombines small modules from two of the taught patterns: the opening "o d D" module of the pattern segment on the left (circled) and the "o o" module leading to the strong final beat of the pattern segment in the center (in the shaded gray rectangle). These modules he sprinkles in metrically comparable locations throughout the newly improvised pattern.

EXTREME RECOMBINATION AND THE CROSS-RHYTHMIC AESTHETIC

With their more liberal attitudes toward innovation, Pak Dewa and Cok Alit create even more extreme recombinations, where the splicing of diverse taught patterns leads to the creation of new cross-rhythms. A preference toward cross-rhythm is common among many *arja* drummers. In his study of Pak Tama's *arja* practice, Hood (2001) offers up ten interlocking patterns for analysis. Eight of these are 2-beat patterns and contain many of the common modules and

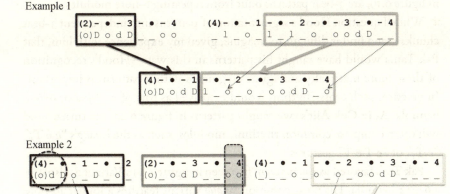

FIGURE 6.18. Asymmetric recombination, *wadon*

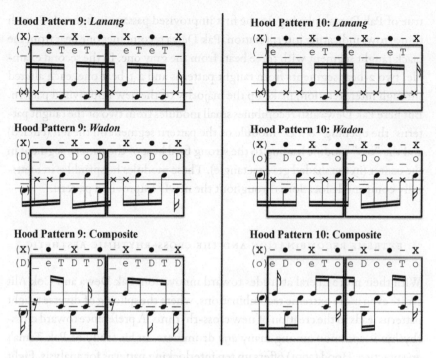

FIGURE 6.19. Cross-rhythmic patterns from Hood's analyses

features discussed in chapter 5. The other two, shown for both *lanang* and *wadon* in figure 6.19, are 3-beat patterns built from repeating 6-note modules.

While I question Hood's segmentation of patterns into independent 3-beat chunks—and find it difficult to imagine, given my experience with him, that Pak Tama would have taught his patterns in this way—Hood's recognition of these more metrically ambiguous segments within patterns is important. In practice, such cross-rhythms would be played as part of a 3+3+2 or 6+6+4 hemiola. As in Cok Alit's two taught patterns in figure 6.20, the turnaround will often comprise common rhythmic modules, such as the *lanang*'s "e e T," "e T," or "e T e T" gestures.

Pak Tut's favored *wadon* pattern, first seen in figure 5.19's Variant 2, also uses a 6+6+4 hemiola. His most common *lanang* variant features a longer 10-note module, which is repeated three times in cross-rhythm to the metrical structure (the third iteration slightly more *ramé*) and followed by a brief 2-note turnaround. Both patterns are shown in figure 6.21.

Only Pak Dewa and Cok Alit, however, appear to generate new cross-rhythms in improvised performance. The mnemonic transcription in the middle of figure 6.22 shows an improvised *wadon* pattern from Pak Dewa, built from elements of three different taught patterns. The combination of the two patterns on the bottom of the figure creates the 6-note motive "o o d D _ _." It gets repeated four times in improvisation (circled), creating a 6-against-4 cross-rhythm with the cycle-marking instruments.

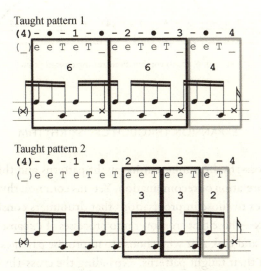

FIGURE 6.20. Cross-rhythm in taught *lanang* patterns

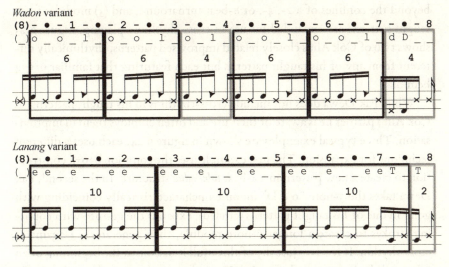

FIGURE 6.21. Cross-rhythm in Pak Tut's favored patterns

BEYOND GENERALIZATIONS · 253

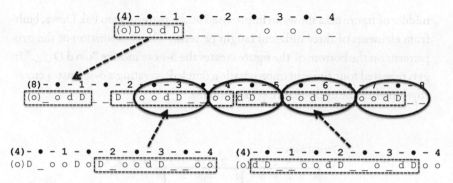

FIGURE 6.22. Recombination creating cross-rhythm

EXPANSION THROUGH CROSS-RHYTHM

We've seen cross-rhythms inherent in taught patterns and those improvised through interpretation or recombination. Yet this common rhythmic aesthetic also contributes to those improvisations that drummers consider their most *wayah*, complex—those that cross over into processes of expansion. Here, again, it is Pak Dewa and Cok Alit who choose to improvise passages more distantly removed from their taught patterns, expanding the cross-rhythmic aesthetic in three main ways: (1) brand new patterns are created that embrace the common 6+6+4 or 3+3+2 rhythmic constructions, (2) cross-rhythms are expanded beyond the confines of a 2-, 4-, or 8-beat turnaround, and (3) modules from taught patterns are expanded for use in cross-rhythmic playing. Figure 6.23 shows two of Cok Alit's closely related improvised patterns, rhythmically different from any of his taught patterns but each featuring that familiar 6+6+4 hemiola.

While Pak Dewa does not include cross-rhythms in his taught patterns, as Cok Alit's partner he is aware of their use and often employs them in improvisation. Three typical examples are shown in figure 6.24; each uses a different technique for expansion. The first example uses the common 6+6+4 construction to create a new pattern in a 4-beat *tabuh dua* structure. In the second, Pak Dewa takes the 3-note "o d D" module uncharacteristically coinciding with gong in one of his taught patterns (circled), expands the gesture with counting strokes to create a longer 6-note module, then generates a 3-against-4 cross-rhythm. It receives just shy of three full iterations at the beginning of an 8-beat *tabuh telu* structure before Pak Dewa moves onto something else. In the last pattern of the figure, improvised over a 2-beat *batel* structure, Pak Dewa

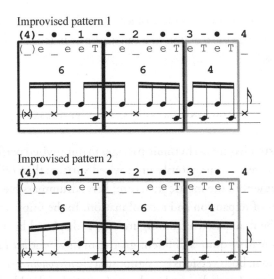

FIGURE 6.23. Cross-rhythm in Cok Alit's *lanang* improvisation

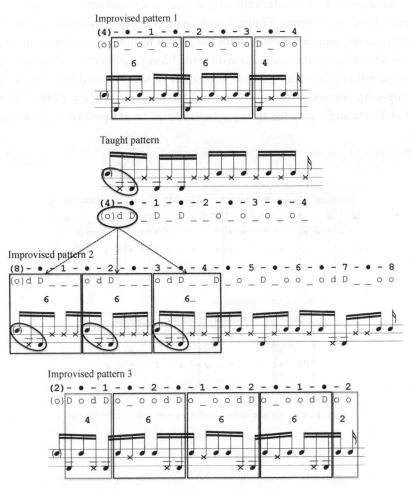

FIGURE 6.24. Cross-rhythm in Pak Dewa's *wadon* improvisation

begins a cross-rhythm in the middle of a cycle and similarly expands it beyond the common 6+6+4 construction to a full 4.5 beats in length, thus creating an offset 6+6+6+6.

COMBINING IMPROVISATORY PROCESSES

Very often, extended cross-rhythmic passages in improvised performance stem from taught patterns or previously improvised variants then offset from their original placement in the metric structure; here, drummers blend improvisatory processes of expansion and recombination. In the improvised pattern in figure 6.25, the final pattern from figure 6.24 is displaced by a half beat and compressed, creating quite a different groove in its 2-beat *batel* structure. Yet the turnaround in both versions is a signpost-style *ngegongin*—a *Dag* (D) stroke anticipating gong (circled)—and each resolves with a double *kom* (o) stroke leading to the gong, consistent with the "on-beat, off-beat" rule.

Seeing the second pattern from figure 6.25 in context reveals the genius of Pak Dewa's improvising. Figure 6.26 shows eight cycles of drumming divided into five segments for analysis, with the pattern from figure 6.25 in segment 2. Pak Dewa begins this sequence with what I like to call a bait and switch. He opens with the first nine notes of a common variant I learned from Pak Tama (top left), altering it through mild interpretation.[38] Yet just when I think Pak Dewa might play the full four beats of this taught pattern, as he does in

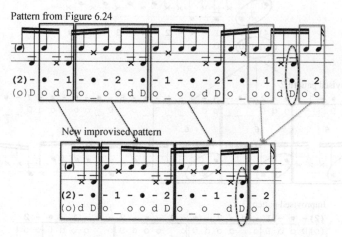

FIGURE 6.25. Cross-rhythm blending expansion and recombination

FIGURE 6.26. Improvised pattern from figure 6.25 in context: interpretation, recombination, and expansion

many other improvisations, he subverts my expectations. Following the halfway point of the pattern, he replaces the second "o o D" with "o o d D," thus retroactively altering my aural analysis; this is not the second half of the taught pattern but rather the beginning of the extended cross-rhythm sequence from figure 6.25 (shown in gray dashed rectangles). Pak Dewa follows up this sequence with four beats of his *dasar*, his most basic taught pattern (top right) first seen in figure 5.14, but with a creative twist of expansion. First, he plays a sparser interpretation of the taught pattern in segment 3, replacing the first two *Dag* (D) strokes with counting strokes and the final double *kom* (o) with softer "l" strokes (all circled). Segment 4 is then a statement of just the first half of the original *dasar*. Only in segment 5 does Pak Dewa finally present the full four beats in their taught form, and here he still replaces the first *Dag* (D) with a *kom* (o) stroke. Thus does he blend interpretation, recombination, and expansion of taught patterns and their associated aesthetics in improvised performance.

WHEN ONE PARAMETER FOR IMPROVISATION CONTRADICTS ANOTHER: *DAG*-ON-GONG

One of the most humbling things I've learned analyzing improvised music is that guidelines discovered through fieldwork, analysis, and performing experience neither can nor do explain everything. Perhaps in these unexplained moments the improviser is, whether consciously or otherwise, playing outside the boundaries of the model; perhaps she is working with an unspoken parameter yet to be discovered; or perhaps, through transformational creativity, she has made something truly new. Often it is the case that two parameters of a model or knowledge base in some way contradict each other, or that multiple parameters must be considered in tandem to discover the underlying principle at play. The improvisation in figure 6.26 presents just such a challenge.

It is commonly understood that a *wadon* player should never let his *Dag* (D) strokes coincide with gong.[39] When playfully teasing *bulé* (non-Balinese) drummers, one of the most widespread musical jokes among Balinese drummers is to play a strong *Dag* (D) directly with gong, mid-improvisation. This will inevitably be followed by peals of good-natured laughter and wide grins in the direction of any *bulé* musician present. But a closer look at the passage from Figure 6.26 shows Pak Dewa aligning a *Dag* (D) stroke with gong (beat 2) in the middle of Segment 2. While this could be a mistake (and mistakes certainly do occur), *Dag* (D) strokes coincide with gong in Pak Dewa's improvisations frequently enough to be of note. And a return to the concept of *ngegongin*—the *wadon*'s anticipation and reinforcement of gong strokes—suggests a more nuanced analysis.

We saw in figure 5.36 that *wadon* drummers do not feel obliged to prepare the gong, to *ngegongin*, in every cycle. This is especially true in the shorter 2-beat *batel* structures, where regimenting placement of *Dag* (D) every other beat would severely limit improvisation on this freer drum. Thus it is useful to consider *ngegongin* at the hypermetric level, recognizing that *wadon* drummers may sometimes think in metacycles rather than single cycles. The transcription in figure 6.27 reimagines the passage from figure 6.26 in terms of its conceptual metacycles, segmenting the improvisation according to the placement of signpost-style *ngegongin*, after three cycles, then two, then three again.

From this new vantage point, the potentially egregious *Dag*-on-gong in the first staff system (circled) is simply an unaccented component of a cross-rhythmic pattern that resolves with an appropriately placed final *Dag* (D) in the following cycle. Were I to consider *ngegongin* in its strictest meaning, as something meant to occur every cycle, the subtlety of this pattern would be lost to my analyses. To offer the most honest possible examination of an improvised

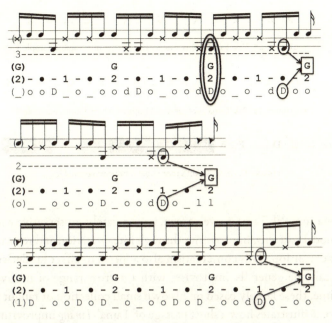

FIGURE 6.27. *Dag*-on-gong and the concept of metacycles

practice, analyses must constantly refer back to taught patterns and oral theory, and may require simultaneous consideration of multiple conflicting concepts.

A LARGER IMPROVISATIONAL LOGIC

We have seen how differing levels of tolerance for divergences from a model can shape improvisation on a moment-to-moment basis, determining which improvisational processes are employed, and how radically. Yet the relative liberalism or conservatism of different improvisers can also affect their playing at a structural level, informing a larger improvisational logic. A more conservative jazz improviser might solo on a small selection of motives from the tune, developing them through embellishment and recombination while never losing sight of their connection to the model; a more liberal approach might see the soloist recombining and expanding a large number of different motives, many of them more distantly related to the original tune, with little if any motivic development or repetition.

Comparing improvised passages from Pak Tama and Cok Alit shows how beliefs about innovation can likewise shape the large-scale structure of an *arja*

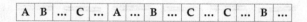

FIGURE 6.28. Pak Tama's conservative improvisational logic, example 1

FIGURE 6.29. Pak Tama's conservative improvisational logic, example 2

FIGURE 6.30. Cok Alit's more liberal improvisational logic

improvisation. Pak Tama, as we've seen, is moderately conservative with regard to his model patterns, improvising through interpretation and recombination but not expansion. This conservatism also appears to affect his decisions on a larger scale; he generally improvises with a narrow range of motives at any given time, these largely based on his own small collection of taught patterns. Figure 6.28 illustrates how a short passage of Tama's *lanang* improvising relates back to his taught patterns. Each box in the figure represents two beats, with two boxes making up a full 4-beat pattern and ellipses indicating a continuation of the pattern in the previous box. In this passage, Tama works with only three main taught patterns at once (labeled A, B, and C), segmenting them, recombining them, and varying them mostly through interpretation.

Even when using a slightly broader spectrum of patterns, Tama still seems to prefer focusing on just two or three of them at once, really taking the time to explore their nuances. Although the passage in figure 6.29 employs elements of five different taught *wadon* patterns, Tama plays mostly with just two, labeled B and C. By varying, segmenting, and recombining these two patterns, and by slowly introducing other variants into the mix (X and Y), Tama keeps the overall structure unpredictable and fresh. The entire passage is flanked by matching bookends (labeled A) that rhythmically contrast the rest of the patterns in the passage. It is an elegant but relatively conservative approach to structure in improvisation.

Through their teachers as well as through their playing experience with diverse musicians for the national radio, Cok Alit and Pak Dewa are versed in a much wider palette of patterns than either Pak Tama or Pak Tut.[40] What's more, their liberal attitudes about innovation in improvisation allow them to push the envelope structurally, freely combining contrasting patterns from their various idioms. Figure 6.30 is a visualization of a segment from Cok Alit's *lanang* improvising, similar in length to Tama's passage from figure 6.29.

Cok Alit appears to base his improvised playing not just on his own taught patterns but also on patterns I learned from teachers in other villages, confirming exposure to a much larger corpus over his lifetime than the small collection he knows consciously and teaches to his students. In figure 6.30, patterns for different village styles are represented by different colors, five in total. The white boxes represent patterns I learned from Cok Alit himself, the light gray, those I learned from Sudi. Dark gray boxes with black text indicate patterns from Pak Dewa's arsenal while dark gray boxes with white text are from Pak Tama. Black boxes with white text indicate patterns that recur frequently in the performance of many drummers but were never explicitly taught to me. Cok Alit explores the full range of available variants in his improvisations—a balanced use of taught patterns from multiple sources. A side effect of this larger and more varied palette of patterns is that there is far less motivic repetition over the course of the passage. While Pak Tama prefers to focus on just a few variants at a time, modifying them through interpretation and recombination and only occasionally incorporating other variants into the mix, Cok Alit uses a large array of variants in quick succession. In this small excerpt of improvising, he plays with thirteen different patterns (A–M), only one of which occurs more than once. This process creates a completely through-improvised passage, without the feeling of familiarity or return implied in much of Pak Tama's playing. While Pak Dewa does tend more toward motivic development than his partner, as we saw in figure 6.26, his improvisations, like Cok Alit's, also display a propensity for pattern diversity throughout.

Because Pak Tut, Pak Tama, Pak Dewa, and Cok Alit are the main *arja* proponents of their villages, and the principal models for the younger generations, their individual approaches and styles have become synonymous with their regions. Thus does personal preference affect regional style, as schools of playing, like North Indian *gharānā* and *bānī*, shape performance practice in collectively improvised aural music cultures.[41]

IN BROADER SCOPE: THE ART OF IMPROVISED INTERLOCKING

Much like the *reyong norot* case study in chapters 2 and 3, the foregoing analyses of *kendang arja* have only indirectly addressed musician interactions. So what do these chapters tell us about collectively improvised interlocking, or about collective improvisation more generally? The taught patterns and oral theory on *arja*, and the idiomatic approaches to improvisatory processes developed by practitioners of the genre, have been fashioned with an eye to generating interlocking rhythms through creative macrointeraction. But in practice, *arja* interlocking is far more capricious. To illustrate its unpredictability, figure 6.31 shows four beats of Pak Dewa's most basic *wadon* pattern, *dasar*, with several improvised pairings from a recording session with Cok Alit. Inherent in this particular *wadon* pattern is a potential collision on the *Dag* (D) stroke directly preceding beat 2. Because the most common placement for a *Tut* (T) stroke in Cok Alit's playing, as we saw in figure 5.28, is the fourth subdivision of a beat, a *Dag-Tut* collision is a risk any time Pak Dewa plays this pattern. In fully precomposed interlocking, the *lanang* pattern would be made to work around this *Dag* (D), as it does in the first example in figure 6.31. Yet this one *Dag-Tut* collision can be acceptable in *kendang arja*, provided the more important signposting-*ngegongin Dag* (D) on beat 3 sounds without a *Tut* (T) collision. That said, some of the pairings in figure 6.31 do contain a less desirable level of collision, marked in the composite patterns with dashed rectangles.

Each of these improvised interactions contains surface-level interpretations that will not be addressed. What's relevant here are the differing levels of *cocok*-ness, compatibility, in each pairing. While the drummers' shared history means

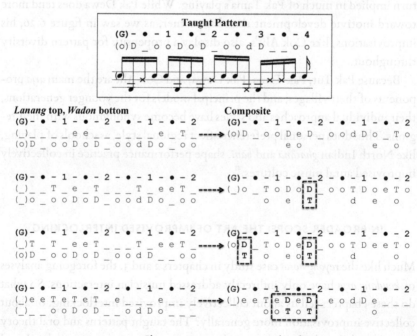

FIGURE 6.31. Chance interactions in improvised performance

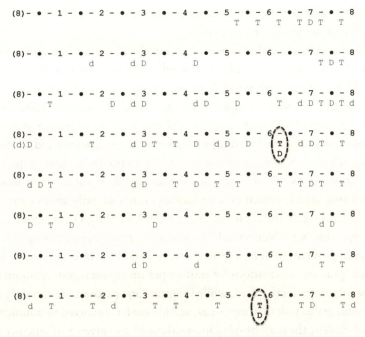

FIGURE 6.32. *Dag-Tut* interactions in improvised performance

that none of these levels of collision is disastrous, the coincidence of each pair of patterns in improvised performance, the more and the less *cocok*, speaks to the controlled arbitrariness of collective interlocking.

Bearing in mind the somewhat random nature of specific pairings, the mnemonic notation in figure 6.32 shows just the more vital *Dag-Tut* interactions of a passage of Pak Dewa and Cok Alit's *arja* improvising. We have seen many of its moment-to-moment choices in the preceding analyses; here I seek to understand how they fit together—the tenor of their interlocking.

While the components of an unconscious regional model and knowledge base—the taught patterns and their rules of engagement—do help drum partners to interlock in improvisation, it's evident from the passage in figure 6.32 that there is nothing guaranteed about their moment-to-moment interactions. Each drummer plays, in no preset order, a large variety of different patterns, both those that are dense with *Dag* (D) or *Tut* (T) strokes and those that are sparse. Sometimes Pak Dewa's *Dag*-heavy patterns line up with Cok Alit's *Tut*-heavy ones as though they had been planned in advance, but more often they don't. And while there are very few instances of *Dag-Tut* collision in this passage, like *kom-peng* collisions, they do exist (circled). Thus neither each individual drummer's exact patterns nor the strict rhythmic relationships between them are predictable or perfect.

I have no wish to reduce *kendang arja* interlocking to the chance combinations of *lanang* with *wadon* that happened on a specific day, with no context for which pairings were *wayah* (complex or great), which acceptable, which questionable, and which simply "oops moments." A more complete study of specific instances of interlocking would benefit from cognitive testing and extensive self-reflexive listening analysis among my teachers and drumming friends. That is not the aim of this study. The examples in these chapters will give the reader a sense of how much the successful execution of *kendang arja*, while being utterly reliant on interlocking, is not actually about controlling the interlocking in the moment. Not really. Like Borgo's ants (2016) jointly solving complex problems while each following an independent agenda, collective improvisation here, as elsewhere, is about how musicians make spaces in their spontaneous creations for another person's spontaneous creations to fit, necessarily imperfectly. And, while longtime *arja* partners are certainly more successful in this task than new ones, and idioms have evolved to minimize the risk of clashes, the play-by-play interactions of any given performance actually involve a great deal of chance. This chance is arbitrated by the nonverbal communication skills of co-performers, the range of model patterns at play within each style, and the idiomatically allowable techniques of interpretation, embellishment, recombination, and expansion. Yet even with seasoned partners, major collisions do occasionally happen. Drummers hearing these moments in recordings of their own playing will invariably pull a sour face or make a self-deprecating remark. The question, then, has become not which pattern fits best with which other pattern in a specific moment of improvisation, but rather how models and knowledge bases of collectively improvised practices are designed to prevent musicians' grimaces . . . 97 percent of the time.

The unpredictability of collective improvisation is part of what draws us to it: the chance of failure, the associated possibility of greatness. Ethnographically informed music analysis can help us understand how, in any collectively improvised practice, musicians are able to mitigate the likelihood of failure while increasing the prospect of greatness, like Alice drinking potions and eating cake in Wonderland. Thus, while any product of collaborative emergence will always be greater than the sum of its parts, the parts can reveal much about the character of the whole.

POSTLUDE

THE IMPLICATIONS OF A COMPARATIVE APPROACH

Throughout this book I have danced around concepts of comparative and cross-cultural analysis. Processes of improvisation proposed in chapter 1 assume cross-genre applicability; chapter 4's parameters of collectivity, outlined for the purposes of nuancing the analysis of individual practices, also look to encourage fruitful comparison. And the book's two case studies, while aiming to present detailed and specific analyses of collective improvisation in Bali, have also taken an outward-looking bearing, seeking connections across practices and suggesting research methods that surpass the limits of single music cultures. Yet what should be the role of comparative and cross-cultural research in music's subdisciplines? While comparison, as Grauer notes, "was once regarded as an essential component of world music research . . . over the last 50 years or so, [it] has fallen into disrepute and disfavor" (2014, 15). Bruno Nettl, one of the founding fathers of modern ethnomusicology, discusses the arguments against comparison at length:

> The many criticisms of comparative work revolve around the difficulty of comparing cultures of which one has varying kinds and degrees of understanding, personal contact, data; and the problem of knowing any culture or music in sufficient depth and breadth to carry out meaningful comparison. There is fear of unwarranted conclusions. There is the allegation that the purpose of comparison is to make value judgments, detrimental to some whose music is being compared. One is in awe of the complexity of musical systems, which itself can make them inherently incomparable. There is suspicion of the quantitative techniques inevitably used in comparative study, and the belief that in a field devoted to this kind of work, data gathering will be prejudicial in favor of materials that lend themselves to comparison. (2005, 66–67)

The current disciplinary skepticism around comparison is rooted in the flaws of late nineteenth-century comparative musicology, which saw as its task the collection, classification, and comparison of all the world's musics, often framing its studies in theories of cultural evolutionism and the search for musical universals. Much has been written about the shortcomings of these early scholars' approaches, not least the inherent racism of their evolutionary theories, their focus on the *sounds* of music at the expense of its behaviors and concepts, and their naïveté in trying to form grand, far-reaching conclusions from just a handful of musical examples—the "one culture = one music" model.[1] As McLean (2006) notes: "no one wants to be tainted with such a brush, and there is irrational distaste for the whole idea of comparison as a result" (315).

Yet more nuanced approaches to comparison have been put forward in the interim (see Savage and Brown 2013; http://www.compmus.org/), as concepts of cultural evolutionism become divorced from "outdated Spencerian notions of progressive evolution" (Savage and Brown 2013, 165) and studies of cultural universals search not for absolutes but rather "statistical universals that occur ... significantly above chance" (Savage et al. 2015, 8987). Savage and Brown (2013) argue that residual resistance to comparative approaches often "appears to be due more to terminological confusion than to theoretical disagreements" (150). In fact, as Nettl points out, many ethnomusicologists use comparative methods in their studies; it is simply that this is often done "without an explicit methodology, and usually without being named" (2005, 63; see also Nettl 2005, 73). But the immediate and emphatic debate that erupted on the SEM-listserv after the fall 2016 announcement of Harvard's (admittedly imperfect) Natural History of Song project, and the apprehension expressed in responses to Grauer's 2006 "Echoes of Our Forgotten Ancestors" and Savage and Brown's 2013 "Toward a New Comparative Musicology," indicate that misgivings about comparison are still alive and well in the field.[2] While many of the complaints lodged against these specific projects cite their more purely quantitative approaches, which risk flattening the "particularities of a culture and the actual experience of encounter in the field" by "abstract[ing . . .] music and people into data" (Clarke 2014, 11–12), these reactions also seem indicative of a larger mindset.

Those wishing to pursue comparative approaches need to be aware of, and explicit about, their limitations. Yet as Nettl argues: "the prescription would seem to be not *avoidance* of comparative study but *more and better* comparative study" (2005, 67, emphasis added). Without trying to downplay the challenges and risks of a comparative approach, particularly one that seeks to be as broad-reaching as Savage and Brown's, I maintain, like Grauer, that "an updated, more methodologically sophisticated and politically sensitive comparative musicology can indeed rise from the ashes of its now outdated ancestor" (2014, 17). Perhaps, as Clarke (2014) argues, the insights we gain won't come in the form of a "grand synthesis," but rather of "fragments and glimpses" of human knowledge and experience (9). Nettl again:

> Of course the concept of comparison is problematic. To note that two things are in one way alike does not mean that they are otherwise similar, spring from the same source, or have the same meaning. There are some respects in which no two creations of humankind can really be compared. On the other hand, I would maintain that even apples and oranges can very well be compared; they turn out to be alike in being fruit, round, and about the same size but different in color, taste, and texture. The fact that, to itself, an apple may not feel the least bit like an orange and doesn't know how it is to feel like an orange may be irrelevant for certain considerations, though crucial for others. The question is whether we can find systematic, elegant, and reliable ways to carry out comparison, and whether, having done so, we find that it has been worth the effort. (2005, 61–62)

The comparative potential that I see in these pages does not involve a search for phylogenetic connections, tracing musical heritage and influence across cultures with goals of historical reconstruction. Nor is it specifically focused on finding phenetic, surface-level similarities between improvised musics, though that may be an inevitable side effect.[3] Instead, the comparison that interests me is one of processes and guiding principles that cross cultures and practices, though they work differently in each. For instance, an *arja* drummer's *recombination*, with his very specific idioms, may look on the surface like a jazz saxophonist's *interpretation*; changes to the taught patterns are often objectively small. But the underlying creative processes more closely parallel the jazz saxophonist's mixing-and-matching and reworking of licks and motives. And while performative roles for the jazz musician delineate soloists and accompanists, for the *arja* drummer they dictate instead a desired level of relative pattern complexity. Comparing these practices through their underlying processes can give insight into ways that both improvisers might in a sense "know how it is to feel like an orange." Although their output differs, and perhaps their intentions also, an exploration of their creative processes, hypothesized through a combination of fieldwork and analysis, can help us touch the heart of how they improvise.

Comparison can be illuminating without being reductive; we can find common processes of interaction and improvisation across multiple music cultures, and these commonalities can actually help us better understand their particularities in each practice. Where a metalanguage exists for talking about collective improvisation across cultures, analysis in one practice might give clues about where to look in another.

CROSS-GENRE COMPARISON IN ACTION

This book's case studies explored the very different actualizations of analogous improvisatory processes in *reyong norot* and *kendang arja*. Yet they also revealed certain parallel guidelines and techniques for improvisation between the two practices, not surprising, given their shared cultural foundation. While recombination and expansion techniques in *reyong norot* differ significantly from those in *kendang arja*, some interpretation and embellishment techniques for *norot* find partial reflection in *arja* improvisation. Each practice, in very general terms, begins with the concept of strict alternation; in *reyong norot*, it is between the core melody note and its upper neighbor, in *kendang arja*, between *lanang* and *wadon* strokes. Performance practice complicates this aesthetic in several ways, as we saw, and some of these, too, can be usefully compared. The primary forms of embellishment in *reyong norot*, for instance, involve a flexible timing aesthetic that produces doubled notes where the model decrees single ones. This finds loose parallels in the paired "on-beat, off-beat" rules of single and double stroke use in *kendang arja*.

Interpretation techniques are also relatively comparable between the two practices, though of course their palettes of note choices differ. In *reyong norot*, model tones can be freely interchanged with *kempyung* harmony tones or rests, while in *kendang arja*, soft counting strokes or louder "l" strokes can replace main strokes, and vice versa. Yet the reality of these parallel rules of interpretation in action also highlights differences between the two practices; while a *kendang arja* player can perform any number of counting strokes between main strokes, a *reyong* player can only rest for a single subdivision of the beat at a time. This difference, as much as anything else, emerges from the playing techniques of each instrument; while counting strokes, though soft, still allow the *arja* drummer to kinesthetically maintain running 16th notes, a *reyong* player cannot perform multiple simultaneous rests without stopping the motion of her hands.[4] Thus, while a kendang player can alternate between right and left counting strokes for as long as he likes before using a main stroke, enabling very sparse pattern construction, a *reyong* player's patterns must remain relatively dense. Here, a comparison of parallel processes brings their differences into sharper relief. Despite Nettl's warning that comparativists "are impressed by similarity, and seek it out" (2005, 68), then, similarity, difference, difference within similarity, and similarity within difference are all in play in comparisons of improvisatory process, and all equally worthy of note. As Clarke argues:

> comparativism, going beyond empiricism and metrics, implies dialectics: not a measuring of similarity based on a subtraction of difference; not a fetishizing of difference so as to become blind to commonality; but a recognition that difference and similarity entirely suppose one another, with now one and now the other in the ascendant, in a tension—a turbulence even—that allows neither term to become assimilated to the other, and that motivates an inquiry that is dynamic and open ended. (2014, 11)

Within-culture comparisons, then, can offer insight into both the similarities and fundamental differences among collectively improvised practices. Yet can comparisons also usefully be drawn between practices from divergent music cultures, not with the goal of proposing a common musical ancestor, nor reducing their nuances down to only the elements they share, but rather as a way to understand improvisatory creativity more broadly? Clarke suggests that "notwithstanding the stylistic differences across cultures, there may be some common territory" in the phenomenology of improvisation. He argues that the generative principles for Western common practice music proposed by Lerdahl and Jackendoff (1983) might likewise be applicable to improvisation in Hindustani classical music, where "unique musical utterances are [also] generated from different realizations of the same set of constraints or deep structures" (Clarke 2014, 11). Here we find parallels to processes of expansion discussed in this book. Yet comparison according to these parameters also

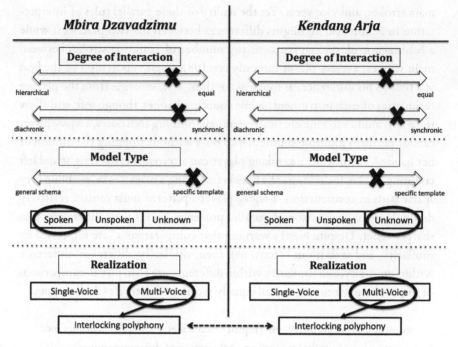

FIGURE 7.1. Comparison: *mbira dzavadzimu* versus *kendang arja*

brings to light differences between the two systems. While Hindustani *khyāl* performances, Clarke notes, share certain melodic and phrase-syntactic models with those in Western common practice music, the more strongly "cyclic, additive principles" of Indian classical music defy the "reticulated, divisive branching structures" of Lerdahl and Jackendoff's model so suited to "Western melodic phraseology" (11).

Rather than being reductive, comparisons on the level of process can actually draw unique aspects of each practice into clearer focus, the premise of commonality elucidating the details of difference. Coming back to the continua of collectivity proposed in chapter 4, we can observe several surface similarities between *kendang arja* and, for instance, the Shona *mbira dzavadzimu* tradition.[5] Although *kendang arja* is based on a somewhat amorphous, unconscious model for improvisation while models for most mbira songs are explicitly known and taught, both result in a multi-voice interlocking polyphony via a relatively equal, largely synchronic interaction. This comparison is shown in figure 7.1.

Thus, while mbira and kendang are from different music cultures, their parameters of collectivity are actually more closely aligned than those of *kendang arja* and *reyong norot* (see figure 4.13). Accordingly, there are also compelling parallels in their general guidelines for improvisation as well as their specific techniques for actualizing improvisatory processes. I will first address some equivalences in performative and musical roles, outlined in figure 7.2.

In chapter 5, we saw how the *lanang*'s leadership role in *arja* performance actually gives his *wadon* partner more scope for innovation in improvisation. *Lanang* players stay closer to taught patterns, which are generally shorter and simpler than their counterparts', so that they can "keep the bus on the road." While both drums employ similar techniques for improvisation, the *lanang*'s creative license is more constrained than his partner's, and inventive *wadon* improvisation is more central to a satisfying performance.

Mbira dzavadzimu playing also sees one of two interlocking instruments take on a performative role of leader—melodic leader in this case—that appears to limit her freedom relative to her partner's. In mbira tradition, the musician playing the melodic strand called *kushaura*, literally "to lead the piece" or "the one that starts," is the player who always begins the performance. Importantly, it is her melodic line that identifies the piece without ambiguity. Her partner on *kutsinhira*, literally "to interweave" or "to exchange parts of a song,"

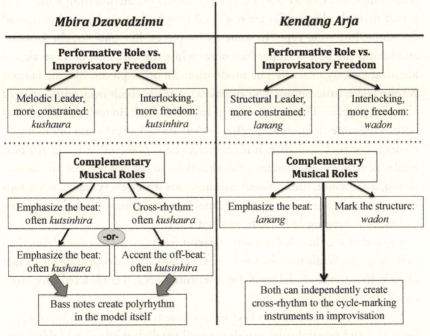

FIGURE 7.2. Parallels and differences in performative and musical roles, *mbira dzavadzimu* versus *kendang arja*

plays a complementary interlocking melody.[6] Because the *kushaura* is the part that sonically identifies the piece, it cannot stray too far from the model for too long in improvised performance. As melodic leader, the *kushaura* player is more constrained. Accordingly, when more and less advanced players perform together—students and teachers for instance—the less experienced musician will almost invariably hold down the basic *kushaura*, leaving the more freely improvised strand for the more experienced player. Like *kendang arja* partners, though both mbira players use similar techniques for improvisation, a performance will still be satisfying if the *kushaura* plays simple variants throughout as long as the *kutsinhira* is free to innovate.[7]

Alongside performative roles, mbira players, like *arja* drummers, also assume complementary musical roles. In both practices, these are largely concerned with the rhythmic qualities of models and their improvisations. In *kendang arja*, as we've seen, the *lanang* emphasizes the beat while the *wadon*'s rhythmic role is more structural, anticipating the arrival of gong with *Dag* (D) strokes. In mbira music, too, complementary musical roles dictate that one melodic strand more closely track the beat, generally through the notes in her lowest range—the bass manual of her instrument. The role of the other strand is not to mark structure as it is in *arja*, but rather to emphasize an off-beat or cross-rhythm with complementary bass-note onsets. A further distinction from *kendang arja* is that these rhythmic roles are not fixed to specific instruments but instead determined by song type. In some mbira pieces, like *Shumba*, the *kushaura* emphasizes the beat with her bass notes while the *kutsinhira* plays an almost identical melody offset by one subdivision. In other pieces, like the famous *Nhemamusasa*, basic *kushaura* and *kutsinhira* models are built from quite different plucking patterns. This compositional approach results in melodic strands that occupy the same "harmonic" pitch space but are melodically and rhythmically distinct. For such melodies, it is generally the *kutsinhira* that tracks the beat while the *kushaura* emphasizes a cross-rhythm. In the basic model for *Nhemamusasa*, for instance, the *kushaura*'s bass notes are struck every four subdivisions in a compound meter, creating a 4-against-3 cross-rhythm to both the *kutsinhira* and the beat-keeping *hosho* rattle, per figure 7.3.[8]

Cross-rhythm, then, holds a very different function in *mbira dzavadzimu* than in *kendang arja*. While for mbira players it is a foundational organizing principle often built into the model itself, for *arja* drummers it is considered a sophisticated expansion technique.

Examining commonalities between diverse traditions through both performative and musical roles can thus reveal parallels while also highlighting difference. The same can be said of comparing improvisatory processes. We

FIGURE 7.3. Cross-rhythm in the *Nhemamusasa* model

know that *kendang arja* and *mbira dzavadzimu* are both paired improvised practices based on multi-voice models that are realized in an equal interlocking polyphony. These surface likenesses suggest the possibility for deeper similarities of improvisatory technique. A handful of observations, outlined in figure 7.4, will clarify connections as well as distinctions.

In *kendang arja*, we saw both *lanang* and *wadon* players interpreting taught patterns through the free interchanging of main strokes, "l" strokes, and counting strokes; mbira players can do likewise with the local pitch class sets of model melodies. Most mbira pieces have relatively triadic (or dyadic) melodic construction, with generally 2–3 different pitch classes used in any small module of music. In *Nhemamusasa*, Berliner proposes, these pitch class sets create a repeating, asymmetrical harmonic rhythm. The first phrase, or measure, of the *kushaura* melody from figure 7.3, with the pitch classes F-A-F-C // E-A-E // D-D-A-D-D, creates a harmonic rhythm of 4+3+5 that recurs in each of the four phrases of the melody. Importantly, the small pitch class sets that define this harmonic rhythm also present possibilities for interpretation. While mbira players will sometimes substitute a "nonharmonic" tone in their improvisations, more often they interchange different pitch classes in the local pitch class set, "giv[ing] rise to new melodic/rhythmic patterns without disturbing the harmonic rhythm of the piece" (Berliner 1993, 98). Other variants see notes replaced with rests, usually in repeating plucking patterns. This loosely parallels the interchanging of main strokes with counting strokes in *arja*.

Mbira Dzavadzimu	Kendang Arja
Interpretation	**Interpretation**
➤ Free exchange of notes in the current pitch set <u>and</u> "non-harmonic tones" ➤ Free exchange of certain notes with rests and vice versa	➤ Relatively free exchange of rim strokes with "l" or bass-strokes ➤ Free exchange of rim strokes with soft counting strokes and vice versa
Recombination	**Recombination**
➤ Relatively free mixing-and-matching of elements from different versions ➤ Alternating basic with complex variants ➤ Different variation types acceptable for different pieces	➤ Free mixing-and-matching of elements from different taught variants ➤ Alternating sparse with dense variants ➤ Different densities acceptable for different cyclic structures
Some Differences	**Some Differences**
➤ Interpretation leads to "inherent rhythms" ➤ Often focus on one version, variation, or type of improvisation at a time	➤ Expansion techniques favoring new cross-rhythms ➤ Free mixing-and-matching of different improvisatory techniques

FIGURE 7.4. Parallels and differences in improvisatory technique, *mbira dzavadzimu* versus *kendang arja*

Yet interpretation has some unique twists in mbira playing, where, unlike on *reyong* or *kendang arja*, improvising musicians can use accents to affect listener perception. Chapter 3 introduced the concept of "inherent rhythms"—melodies or rhythms that arise from a polyphonic texture but are not in fact played as independent entities by any one musician. Such patterns also emerge in mbira performance, yet usually as a result of conscious choice. By accenting some of the notes in her melody, a skilled mbira player can bring certain note combinations to the fore, "creating the effect of variation in [her] performance without actually changing any of the pitches [she is] playing in a particular pattern" (Berliner 1993, 90). A musician can also emphasize connections she hears between her improvised strand and her partner's with this technique, leading to a deeper experience for both musicians and listeners.

Alongside these partial parallels of interpretation, the two practices also have commonalities in their recombination techniques. We know that every *arja* drummer has a collection of consciously known patterns that he varies and recombines each time he plays. Mbira players likewise tend toward mixing-and-matching, *campur-campur*. Many common mbira songs, like *Nhemamusasa*, have multiple known versions—some quite distinct.[9] Like *arja* drummers, mbira players can freely switch between versions of such pieces in improvised performance, commensurate with their experience and the ones they happen to know. What's more, most mbira songs (or versions of songs) are taught not as single entities but rather clusters of possibilities. Students learn the most basic, standard form of the song or version, but are also taught traditional variations passed down through generations, and may even learn new variations that have developed through improvised performance in the current generation (see Berliner 1993, 95). Again, musicians can recombine these different variations and draw upon their idioms to create their own. However, unlike in *kendang arja*, mbira players will often perform the same version or variation many times in succession, perhaps for several minutes, as they slowly explore subtle improvisations. Here I see parallels to *reyong* players who sometimes vary the same improvised pattern over several cycles of *norot*. For mbira players, like *reyong* players, this musical exploration is often approached quite methodically, with only one type of improvisation attempted at a time. A *kushaura* player might first vary just the high notes in the right hand, for instance, then for several cycles perhaps play a variation heavy in bass notes with little activity in the middle register, a technique called *kushaura kwepasi*.[10] Moreover, many longtime mbira co-performers "accommodate each other by playing pairs of *kushaura* and *kutsinhira* parts that they agree are best suited to one another. In such groups, when the *kushaura* player switches to a second *kushaura* part the *kutsinhira* player then changes over to the most appropriate *kutsinhira* counterpart" (Berliner 1993, 103). While this process does happen in a limited way in *kendang arja* through previously agreed-on patterns, moment-to-moment contingency seems to be a more central aspect of mbira performance practice. It is the repetition and methodical improvisation of melodic variants or versions over many cycles that allow this kind of intersubjectivity to shape collectively improvised mbira performance.

Thus, though *kendang arja* and mbira players share certain general approaches to recombination, many of their techniques are in fact quite different. Again, applying a comparative lens—seeking to understand how parallel processes and underlying guidelines for improvisation are differently realized in different practices—offers insight into commonality as well as dissimilarity.

As we've seen in the preceding chapters, analysis of any practice demands contextual insight that only fieldwork, performance experience, and time can provide. Faithful comparative analysis necessarily requires a specialist's understanding of each practice and may benefit from collaboration among multiple researchers and practitioners. The preliminary analyses in this chapter, however—grounded in the work of other scholars as well as my conversations and performing experience with both Shona and Western mbira players—suggest constructive avenues for comparison.[11]

IN BROADER SCOPE: ANALYSIS ON AN EQUAL PLAYING FIELD

In this book, I have proposed a multifaceted analytical model of collective improvisation, putting forward my case studies of *reyong norot* and *kendang arja* as exemplars of the model's potential to frame ethnographically informed analyses across cultures and practices. My hope is that researchers of other improvised genres, whether collective or not, will see the musics they study within these frameworks, much as Michelangelo saw the sculpture in the block of stone. If a common language were adopted for the analysis of improvised practices, just as we have shared terminology to discuss Western compositions across genres, countries, and eras, we could finally engage in a true cross-cultural examination of improvisation.

While not every study of collectively improvised practice need be comparative, there is value in a unifying framework, a metalanguage for thinking and talking about processes of improvisation and parameters of models, knowledge bases, and collectivity. It's not about reducing these practices to their similarities or conversely, as Clarke put it, fetishizing their differences. Nor is it about claiming that there is anything universal in their sounds, behaviors, or associated concepts. Understanding that certain improvisatory processes, model types, and modes of collectivity may be statistically universal, though differently applied in each music culture, nevertheless allows us to assign equal value to improvisation of many stripes. It helps us find productive ways to look at diverse practices through parallel lenses without privileging one kind of improvisation or collectivity over others. By putting all forms of improvisation and modes of collectivity on a level playing field for analysis, we minimize the barriers between ethnomusicology, music theory, jazz studies, and musicology, paving the way for richer, more open dialogue. This in turn will generate a polyphony of voices: an emergent, contingent, and collectively improvised conversation about analysis, improvisation, and the human capacity for creativity.

ACKNOWLEDGMENTS

The questions in this book have been percolating for a long time. They first took root almost two decades ago when I moved to Vancouver to study ethnomusicology at the University of British Columbia and, quite by accident, fell in love with both Balinese gamelan and musical analysis. In the ensuing years, I have learned from, played alongside, and had countless thought-provoking conversations with a wide array of musicians and scholars. If I have managed to provide any insight into the musical processes examined in this book, it is due to their unending generosity; any shortcomings in the book are mine alone.

First, and foremost, I thank my Balinese teachers, most particularly I Dewa Nyoman Sura, I Cokorda Alit Hendrawan, I Wayan Tama, I Dewa Ketut Alit, and I Wayan Sudirana. In their very different ways, each of these men has not only amazed me with his musicianship but also humbled me with his patience, inspired me with his passion for music, continually surprised me with the depth of his knowledge, and warmed me with his abiding generosity. I'm also grateful for other friends, teachers, and musical partners across Bali, too numerous to mention here.

Special thanks goes to Michael Tenzer, a mentor and friend I have been affectionately sparring with for the last nineteen years. Michael introduced me to the world of Balinese music and to the captivating power of music analysis. He showed by example how to aim for the extraordinary, the impeccable blend of analytical rigor, emotional depth, and integrity in his scholarship setting the bar higher than I thought I could reach, while his engaging teaching, respectful collegiality, infectious enthusiasm, and insatiable curiosity invited me to the table without reservation. Michael has read every word of numerous drafts of these chapters, offering the sort of terrifying insights one hopes never to receive but is always grateful for in retrospect. So thank you, Michael, for the friendship, the frankness (always), the extreme mutual nerdiness, and the years of fantastic conversation over dinners, *gangsas*, and glasses of wine. I am a better scholar, musician, thinker, and human being because of you.

This project has benefitted from the invisible collaboration of many minds. I am continually motivated by the scholarship and conversation of my companions in the gamelan community as well as those examining improvisation and applying analytical approaches to world musics. Some are friends with whom I've spent incalculable hours making and nerding out about music, others are simply scholars I have admired from afar; all have deepened my research: Marc Perlman, Ben Brinner, Lisa Gold, Gabe Solis, Richard Widdess, Andy McGraw, Ellen Koskoff, Ingrid Monson, Pat Savage, David Locke, Keith Sawyer, Paul Berliner, David Borgo, Wayne Vitale, Andy Sutton, Michael Bakan, Edward Herbst, Nicholas Gray, Laudan Nooshin, Simha Arom, I Madé Bandem, I Wayan Dibia, I Ketut Gdé Asnawa, Sonja Downing, Pete Steele, Chloe Zadeh, Bruno Nettl, my comrades-in-bronze in Gamelan Gita Asmara, Sanggar Çudamani, and Gamelan Galak Tika, and my beloved AAWM community. Thank you, also, to Nathan Hesselink and John Roeder at UBC for penetrating insights on my *kendang arja* research and generosity with your time, friendship, and expertise. To my colleagues, mentors, and friends in Cambridge, Massachusetts—Patty Tang, Myke Cuthbert, Emily Richmond Pollock, Elina Hamilton, K Goldschmitt, Janet Sonenberg, Evan Ziporyn, Charles Shadle, Marty Marks, Teresa Neff, Fred Harris, and many others—thank you for the easy friendship, the frequent work dates, the useful and encouraging comments on my writing, and the unbending support. And to my dear friends and longtime ethno colleagues Maisie Sum and Deirdre Morgan, you have both inspired me with your tenacity, moved me with your steadfastness, amazed me with your brilliance, and taught me to think in more directions. To me, you are absolute powerhouses, and I love going through this long learning process with you both.

I have been lucky to receive research funding from several sources, including the Canadian Social Sciences and Humanities Research Council, the University of British Columbia, and the Massachusetts Institute of Technology. I'm grateful, too, to the University of Chicago Press, and particularly to my editor Elizabeth Branch Dyson who, when I first pitched this book with a narrower focus, hurled an intellectual curveball: "sounds interesting; now convince me that it's important." The broad lens I've taken in this book, and the new angles into collective improvisation it unearthed for me, are the direct result of that challenge. I'm equally thankful for the careful attention Elizabeth gave to early drafts of several chapters, the quick responses on logistics and edits from Dylan Montanari, Mollie McFee, and Mark Reschke, the detailed copyedits from Dawn Hall, and the series editors' willingness to accommodate the book's many figures. Two other readers, Jay S. Nahani and Alexander Tilley (my brilliant and generous Papa), offered useful comments and suggestions, and two anonymous reviewers provided invaluable feedback and encouragement. Dennis McClendon at Chicago Cartographics helped refine one of the book's gnarlier figures (figure 4.12), and June Sawyers worked closely with me to make a detailed index. Four gamelan compatriots—Emeric Viani, Andreas Liapis, Matt Elkins, and Emma Terrell—braved long hours, broken HVACs, and heat-induced insanity to perform all the demo audio clips for the companion website. And two dear friends, Chelsea Edwardson and Nicole Walker, took most of the book's beautiful pictures. This would be a lesser book without you all, and you're all awesome.

Finally, to my family—the one I lucked into and all the ones I've chosen over the years—thank you for your unfailing love and support. To my grandfather, who instilled in me a love of learning, my parents who supported me musically, emotionally, and intellectually, my sisters who offered true friendship and unabashed honesty, and my chosen families across North America who've held me up with food and hilarity, music and rock climbing, much-needed distractions, irresponsible late-night conversations, and every wonderful thing I didn't even know I needed: Tim and Sue (my irreplaceable Tilleverettey family), Deirdre, Maisie, Paula O, Devin, Kim, Lorne, Kristi, Colin, Andrea, Paula J, Aaron, Chelsea, Nicole, Robert, Kara, K, and many others (not forgetting Captain Jack, Mr. Darcy, and Miss Kitty Fantastico). I'm so grateful for you all.

GLOSSARY OF FREQUENTLY USED TERMS

alap. In North Indian classical music, an unmetered, solo, improvised melody.

angsel. A strongly articulated dance movement in Balinese music, answered by a special drum pattern that cues a sudden increase in volume before a rhythmic break.

arja. A Balinese sung dance drama that tells a love story and balances themes of good and evil (and other opposites). Accompanied by the small *gamelan geguntangan*, which includes paired improvised *kendang arja* drumming.

asli. Original. Thus "*kendang arja asli* Singapadu" means "the original Singapadu style of *arja* drumming."

bass stroke. The lower *Dag* (D) or *Tut* (T) strokes in *kendang arja*.

batel. The shortest cyclic structure in *arja*, at two beats in length.

batel marah. (lit: angry *batel*)   Also called *batel penasar*, this is a more intense variation on the *batel* cyclic structure, usually used for angry or coarse characters or in fight scenes.

calung.   A pair of 5-keyed, one-octave metallophones that play a slow core melody, or *pokok*, in *gamelan gong kebyar*. Usually struck every two beats.

campur-campur.   Mixing it up. Often refers to models or segments of models improvised through recombination.

cocok.   Appropriate, suited to.

collaborative emergence.   See "emergence."

collective improvisation.   Any kind of improvisation where two or more musicians simultaneously improvise. While commonly accepted definitions often assume the different streams are of equal or comparable weight (e.g., New Orleans jazz, free jazz), this book broadens the term to include more hierarchical practices.

combinatorial creativity.   Combining familiar ideas in unfamiliar ways (e.g., visual collage, poetic metaphor).

communication codes.   Musical, verbal, or physical ways that co-performers communicate. Socially constructed.

conceptual elaboration.   Modifying existing concepts within a pre-established conceptual space in order to create something new. Used for exploratory and transformational creativity.

conceptual space.   A structured, culture-based style of thinking, such as the inherent rules of a genre of music. In improvised music, a performer's conceptual space comprises both the model and knowledge base.

conceptual transfer.   Cognitively projecting a familiar concept onto an unfamiliar situation to understand (or create) that new situation. Used for combinatorial creativity.

core melody.   A slow-moving melody that underpins gamelan compositions and on which faster-moving melodic elaborations are built. (See also "*pokok*," "*calung*," "*jegogan*," "*penyacah*," "*ugal*.")

counting strokes. (Compare "main strokes.") Softer drum strokes, sometimes called *anak pukulan* ("child strokes") that are played in between main strokes to kinesthetically maintain running 16th notes (quarter beats) at almost all times in *kendang arja* performance.

Dag **(D).** A low, open bass stroke played with the right thumb on the *wadon*. Often paired with *Tut* (T).

dasar. Basic, foundational.

degree of influence. The degree (in both quality and frequency) to which any one improviser in a collective performance affects the moment-to-moment decisions of any other. May be determined by the nature of the interaction, whether more turn-based or more simultaneous. (See also "macrointeraction," "motivic interaction.")

ding-dong-deng-dung-dang. Balinese solfège. Abbreviated i-o-e-u-a. In *gong kebyar*, these tones approximate C#-D-E-G#-A.

distributed invention. Shared creation across space, time, and multiple innovators.

embellishment. An improvisatory process that often diverges slightly more from the model than interpretation through flexible timing, ornamentation, creative note substitutions, and so on.

emergence. The idea that a collaborative performance does not exist in the mind of one performer but rather emerges out of each performer's actions and interactions. Thus, collective improvisations are inherently unpredictable.

empat. A style of interlocking figuration, played on both *gangsa* and *reyong*, where the composite melody is built from three consecutive scale tones with a fourth higher note used as a parallel "harmony" tone (*kempyung*) to the lowest. (Sometimes more formally called *ubit empat*.)

end-weighted. Referring to both beats within cyclic structures and subdivisions within beats, a metrical conception where the strongest note comes at the end rather than the beginning. End-weightedness in Balinese music influences melody-making, cyclic structures, and improvisation techniques.

entrenched situated conceptualizations. Cognitive structures formed through experience that flexibly guide interaction in similar situations.

expansion. An improvisatory process that involves extending and expanding on elements of known models, and often comprises the most extreme departures from those models.

exploratory creativity. Coming up with new ideas within the confines of existing conventions (e.g., inventing a new recipe in an established style/cuisine).

flow. A feeling of absolute freedom and control, loss of time, ease, ability, and focus, where both optimal enjoyment and optimal performance can occur.

formulaic variation. A kind of improvisation where relatively specific models are reworked through paradigmatic substitutions.

full template. In *reyong norot*, the main note as well as the *kempyung* above and below.

gamelan. An ensemble of instruments from Indonesia, usually built as an inseparable set, and often consisting of various rhythmic and melodic percussion instruments.

gamelan geguntangan. The small gamelan ensemble traditionally used to accompany Balinese *arja* performance.

gamelan gong kebyar. A twentieth-century genre of Balinese gamelan known for its virtuosity and flashy "kebyar" (explosive) aesthetic.

gangsa. Bronze metallophone of the *gamelan gong kebyar*. Often used to play fast, interlocking figuration (*kotekan*).

gong. 1—One of many instruments marking structurally important points in a cyclic structure. 2—Generic term used for the primary gong in any ensemble (e.g., *gong ageng* in *gamelan gong kebyar*, *gong pulu* in *gamelan geguntangan*), which is struck once at the end of each cycle.

gong pulu (G). Two bronze or iron bars strung up over a box resonator, this instrument is struck just once per cycle in *gamelan geguntangan* performance, marking the end/beginning of each cycle.

group flow. (Compare "flow.") Where members of a group achieve a collective flow through a group goal, blending egos, concentrating and listening, communicating, and mutual familiarity.

guntang **(t).** A one-stringed bamboo or wooden tube zither that keeps a steady beat in *gamelan geguntangan*. Vocalized as "tuk."

improvisation. Creation in the course of performance. Broadly defined.

interactional role. In collective improvisation, the often mutable, moment-specific roles of sender/receiver (communicator/communicatee). Connected to concepts of leader versus follower.

interpretation. An improvisatory process that involves small alterations of the model, such as changes in accentuation, dynamics, rhythmic phrasing, and such.

intersubjectivity. The idea that every action in a collective improvisation can only be understood once it has been interpreted and responded to by co-performers. Related to emergence.

jegogan. A pair of 5-keyed, one-octave metallophones that play a slow core melody in *gamelan gong kebyar*. Usually struck every four beats.

kempyung. In *gangsa* and *reyong* figuration, a parallel "harmony" note three scale tones above the main note. *Reyong* also employ *kempyung* three scale-tones below main notes, particularly in *norot* figuration.

kendang. A Balinese drum. (See also "*lanang*," "*wadon*.")

kendang arja. A paired, improvised drumming tradition used to accompany the Balinese sung dance drama *arja*.

keras. Loud, harsh, hard, coarse, or unrefined.

kinetic. In a *pokok*, a moment that shifts between two different tones. (*Majalan*).

klenang **(n).** A small, high, ringing bossed gong that emphasizes an "off-beat" feel in the *gamelan geguntangan*'s cyclic structures.

knowledge base. Additional information and insight that informs idiomatic improvisation on a model. In collective improvisation, a knowledge base must be shared and often emerges through a shared history.

***kom* (o).**   A high ringing stroke played with the fingertips of the left hand on the rim of the *wadon*. Often paired with *peng* (e).

***kotekan*.**   A generic term to describe melodic interlocking parts in Balinese gamelan music, where pairs of musicians create fast melodies by sharing the notes between *polos* and *sangsih*. (See also "*norot*," "*empat*.")

lanang (lit: male).   The higher-pitched of a pair of instruments, particularly drums. In *kendang arja*, the *lanang* is the ensemble leader.

macrointeraction.   (Compare "motivic interaction.") Collectively improvising in a mutually agreed-upon idiom and style, often fulfilling a specific musical and/or performative role, but without necessarily responding to one another's specific musical ideas. Playing simultaneously in a complementary idiom.

main strokes.   (Compare "counting strokes.") In kendang playing, strokes that are played at full strength and make up the rhythmic identity of any pattern. In *kendang arja*, main strokes include *Dag* (D), *Tut* (T), *kom* (o), and *peng* (e), as well as the *lanang*'s cuing stroke *pung* (U).

***majalan*.**   See "kinetic."

***mbira dzavadzimu*.**   A plucked idiophone of the Shona people of Zimbabwe, generally played in pairs (or larger groups). Often called simply "mbira." Its music usually comprises interlocking melodies in a cyclic construction.

metacycle.   A *kendang arja* pattern that does not *ngegongin* at every gong stroke but instead is made up of several cycles leading to a final *ngegongin*. May be any number of cycles in length.

microinteraction.   Subtle shifts in tempo, dynamic, groove, and so on that any good performing group develops together.

model.   Constraints or fixed signposts, learned and agreed on in advance, upon which improvisers base their improvisations.

mode of interaction.   How co-performers interact. Spanning a broad spectrum from cooperation to conflict, most useful to a study of collective improvisation is the interactional spectrum from hierarchical to equal. (See also "interactional role.")

motivic interaction. When the improvisational choices of one musician in a collective performance are imitated, varied, or otherwise responded to by another. Only one of many styles of interaction in collective improvisation. (See also "macrointeraction," "microinteraction.")

multi-voice model. Model for collective improvisation with two or more simultaneous musical strands.

musical analysis. Broadly conceived as analysis of musical particulars closely informed and shaped by ethnographic research.

musical role. (Compare "performative role.") The particular musical function of each performer in an ensemble (e.g., a performative role of "accompanist" might function more specifically to lay down harmony, emphasize the beat, or play a cross rhythm). Linked to performative role.

ngegongin. To reinforce the gong cycle, particularly by anticipating the arrival of the final gong stroke. Theoretically, this is the role of the *wadon* in *kendang arja*.

ngematin. To emphasize the beat (*mat*). Theoretically, this is the role of the *lanang* in *kendang arja*.

ngubeng. See "static."

norot. A style of melodic elaboration or figuration used in *gamelan gong kebyar* that features an oscillation between the current core melody (*pokok*) tone and its scalar upper neighbor, and anticipates each new *pokok* tone with a 3-note pickup gesture. A fixed practice on *gangsa*, *norot* is improvised on *reyong*.

pasangan. Pair, set, or partner. Often used to refer to the long-established partnership required for multiple Balinese musicians to improvise effectively together. A deep connection forged through familiarity and time.

patokan. Rules or guidelines in Balinese music. Also called *pakem*.

pemetit. The fourth (highest) position of the *reyong*.

peng (e). A high ringing stroke played with the fingertips of the left hand on the rim of the *lanang*. Often paired with *kom* (o).

pengenter. The second position of the *reyong*.

penyacah. A pair of 5-keyed, one-octave metallophones that play a slow core melody in *gamelan gong kebyar*. Usually struck every beat.

penyorog. The first (lowest) position of the *reyong*.

performative role. (Compare "musical role.") The function of each musician in an ensemble, e.g., soloist, accompanist, leader, and so on.

pokok. The core melody in *gamelan gong kebyar* from which faster elaborating melodies are derived. Played by the *calung* at the half-note density (every two beats).

polos (lit: basic, simple, direct). Of two complementary elaboration parts played by *gangsa*, *reyong*, and so on, this one more closely tracks the underlying core melody. (See also "*sangsih*.")

ponggang. The third position of the *reyong*.

ramé. Busy, boisterous, full of life. May also refer to a kendang pattern that is particularly dense with main strokes, especially bass strokes.

rasa. Feeling.

recombination. An improvisatory process that involves mixing and matching elements from models.

reyong. A row of tuned gongs (gong chime) played simultaneously by four people. Used in *gong kebyar* and other Balinese gamelan ensembles. Particularly known for its improvisations in the elaborating figuration style *norot*.

rim stroke. The higher *kom* (o) and *peng* (e) strokes in *kendang arja*.

sangsih (lit: different, complementary). Of two complementary elaboration parts played by *gangsa*, *reyong*, and so on, this one either plays parallel *kempyung* "harmony" notes and/or interlocks with the *polos*.

schema. In cognitive studies, a generally unconscious mental structure that creates a set of expectations about how things should look, sound, or occur.

schema for exploration. A broad model for improvisation with sparse and/or flexible or ambiguous signposts.

single-voice model. A model for collective improvisation with just one musical strand.

spoken model. A model for improvisation that is consciously known and overtly referred to, verbally and/or musically. Stems from explicit knowledge.

static. In a *pokok*, a moment where the current tone is repeated. (*Ngubeng*).

tabuh dua. A mid-tempo 4-beat cyclic structure in *arja* performance.

tabuh empat. See "*tabuh telu*."

tabuh telu. The longest and slowest cyclic structure for improvised drumming in *arja* performance, it is eight beats in length. Called *tabuh empat* by some performers.

taught pattern. A *kendang arja* pattern learned directly and explicitly from a teacher.

tawa-tawa (**pu**). In the *geguntangan* ensemble, a medium-sized bossed gong that plays its strokes in regular alternation with the *gong pulu*.

tembang macapat. A collection of poetic forms with fixed structural elements. These forms have become the basis for *arja* songs.

template-abiding. In *reyong norot*, any pattern that contains only basic *norot* tones, *kempyung* above, *kempyung* below, and/or rests.

transformational creativity. Completely altering some aspect of the accepted conventions of a conceptual space in order to create something more radically new. Extremely rare.

Tut (**T**). A midrange, open bass stroke played with the right thumb on the *lanang*. Often paired with *Dag* (D).

ubit empat. See "*empat*."

ugal. The leader of the *gangsas* in *gamelan gong kebyar*. Plays an ornamented core melody, often at the quarter-note density.

unconscious model. A model for improvisation that is not consciously known but may be partially discovered through fieldwork. Stems from intuitive knowledge.

unspoken model. A model for improvisation that is consciously known but not overtly referred to, verbally and/or musically, in traditional contexts. Can often be unearthed through fieldwork.

wadon (lit: female). The lower-pitched of a pair of instruments, particularly drums.

wayah. Deep, great, or complex. Often used to refer to a particularly original or satisfying improvisation.

NOTES

PRELUDE

1. I Wayan Sudirana of Ubud, Gianyar.
2. Usually a word used to describe an open-air public building, *balé* also describes the large open porches often built outside people's homes in Bali.
3. Ida Bagus Madé Widnyana of Tulikup, Gianyar.
4. https://www.press.uchicago.edu/sites/tilley/.
5. *Arja* is generally underscored by one of several different cyclic structures, discussed in chapter 5. It is only the fastest *batel* structures that reach 200 BPM. See Hood 2001, 73–77.
6. Quotes from musicians in this paragraph may be found in other sources, as follows: Wes Montgomery (quoted in Seabrook 2008); Bix Beiderbecke (quoted in Neiwood and English 2012, 32); Miles Davis (quoted in Griffin and Washington 2008, 237); Art Tatum (quote attributed to Tatum on several websites, but not in any scholarly works); Wynton Marsalis (Marsalis 2009, emphasis added).
7. Even in Nettl and Russell's broad-reaching *In the Course of Performance* (1998), a full third of the chapters on the world of musical improvisation focus on the artistry of a single performer.
8. In his 1979 *Gödel, Escher, Bach: An Eternal Golden Braid*, Douglas R. Hofstadter uses the analogy of a colony of ants to describe the ways in which the brain's neurons collaborate to

create a unified mind. See Berliner (1993) on mbira. See Arom (1991a) on Aka singing and other polyphonic group practices in the Central African Republic.

9. On psychology, see Paulus 2000; West 2002. On management science, see Singh and Fleming 2010. On patent law, see Lemley 2012. See also Sawyer (2007) on the psychology and social factors of group genius in music, sport, invention, successful business models, and so on.

10. On the Curies and other scientific collaborators, see John-Steiner 2000, chap. 2. On cubism, see John-Steiner 2000, chap. 3. On the Wright Brothers, see Sawyer 2007, chap. 1. On complementarity, see John-Steiner 2000, chap. 2.

11. A term generally used to describe conversation style, interactional synchrony is a synchronizing of both verbal and nonverbal behaviors at a speed much faster than the conscious mind can create. See Sawyer 2003, chap. 2; Condon and Ogston 1971. Sawyer also relates interactional synchrony to both *entrainment* and *groove*. On improv theater troupes, see Sawyer 2003 and 2007.

12. On brainstorming, see Paulus and Brown 2003; Nijstad, Diehl, and Stroebe 2003; Sawyer 2007, chap. 4; Sawyer 2012, chap. 12.

13. On Gore and other companies embracing an improvisatory collaborative model, see Sawyer 2007.

14. Open-source software, or OSS, is a kind of software whose code, rather than being proprietary, is made available for users to study, alter, add to, and distribute in any way. Notable examples of OSS include the GNU/Linux operating system, the Mozilla Firefox internet browser, and the Apache HTTP server. The advantages of this sort of crowdsourcing approach to invention include quicker turnaround on new innovations, immediate adaptation to new technologies, and a much larger collection of minds working on hard problems and finding and de-bugging errors in code. In a similar spirit, a hackathon (also known as a codefest, hackfest, or hack day) is an event lasting a day or more in which computer programmers, designers, and sometimes project managers get together to work intensively, collaboratively, and often highly experimentally on new software projects.

15. This statement is termed "Linus's Law," and is named in honor of Linus Torvalds, the creator of the Linux kernel that led to the development of the Linux operating system.

16. A term used by Kurt Beyer (2009) to describe Grace Hopper's collaborative development of one of the first commonly used computer programming languages (COBOL). See Lemley (2012) on the implications for patent law.

17. On group improvisation, see Higgins and Campbell 2010; Burnard 2002; Towse and Flower 1993. On *paired improvisation*, see Glazzard and Stokoe 2013, chap. 2; Goodwyn and Branson 2005, chap. 5. On collaborative improvisation, see Monk 2013; O'Neill et al. 2011.

18. Timothy Rice sees this lack of intertextual reference as one of the weaknesses of the field. Rice (2010a) references this lack among researchers on music and identity in a call for its use across the discipline.

19. Note that even the use of the term *improvisation* is problematic and potentially Eurocentric (see Nooshin 2003). In my desire to engage with existing literature on the topic across music genres and subdisciplines, and to find productive points of articulation with scholars in jazz studies, among others, I have elected to use this term despite its limitations.

20. On New Orleans jazz, see Brothers 2009; Schuller 1986.

21. Reproduced from Don Vappie's transcription in Morton (1999).

22. Videos demonstrating this technique can be found at http://academy.jazz.org/what-is-collective-improvisation/ and http://www.pbslearningmedia.org/resource/vtl07.la.ws.style.improv/collective-improvisation/. Accessed March 14, 2017.

23. See Taylor (1998) for an exploration of a similar collectively improvised duet between Louis Armstrong (trumpet) and Earl Hines (piano).

24. Jam bands are rock bands that perform long improvised solos. Some of the original experimental rock bands, like Grateful Dead, are also sometimes called *jam bands*. But the term has gained a life of its own in the last several decades, encompassing genres from folk and progressive rock to acid jazz, hip-hop, bluegrass, blues, country, electronic, and so on. Three examples are the Allman Brothers, Phish, and the String Cheese Incident. Other bands not strictly known as jam bands, such as the Dave Matthews Band, also sometimes play jam-band-style concerts.

25. Free jazz grew up in the midst of the civil rights movement, and many have drawn parallels between the promotion of freedom within the music (and its abolishing of accepted musical structures) and similar desires within society at large. See Henry (2004) on specific albums as social commentary. See Monson (2007) on the historical connections between race, jazz, and social protest.

26. Sindoesawarno (1987) notes: "Artist-performers are *sanggit*, or improvisers, at all times, everywhere. When they play or sing they always search, try, compose, change, invent, and 'play' phrases according to their desires, their feelings, and their ability. The phrases they compose are called *cèngkok*" (378). *Cèngkok* and other processes of in-the-moment creativity in Javanese gamelan are variably termed *improvisation, variation, flexibility, paraphrase, embellishment, elaboration*, and so on. See also Benamou 2010, chap. 5; Brinner 1995; Perlman 2004; Sutton 1993 and 1998; Sutton and Vetter 2006; Vetter 1981.

27. This includes analyses of two paired drum practices (*batel* and *batu-batu*) and a longer discussion of improvisation in *kendang tunggal*, solo drumming.

28. Solo drum practices in Bali are more commonly understood to be improvised. See Sudirana 2009.

29. While not referring specifically to improvisation, this characterization implies a rigidity in all aspects of Balinese life, culture, and by extension, music.

30. Geertz also uses the term "playful" in his discussion of various aspects of Balinese art, society, and personhood, but he frames it in the same limited way: "playfulness is not lighthearted but almost grave" (1973, 400).

31. Buda continues: "If it goes to the west in its improvisation we can go to the north and turn back to the west. For instance, improvising for five beats, they can separate but then the last two must interlock. Three separate and two interlocking—that's good in gendér wayang." Of course, though important and interesting, this statement is still not much more specific than Gus Dé's "we can play whatever we want."

32. On the paired drumming of the *gamelan gambuh*, believed by many to be the precursor to *kendang arja*, see Asnawa 1991. On drumming in *gamelan gong kebyar*, see Tenzer 2000, chap. 7.

33. On some of the arguments for and against music theory and analysis in ethnomusicology, see Solis 2012b; Tilley 2018. On the history and diverse directions of the field, see Nettl 2010 and 2005; Myers 1992. On the anthropology/musicology divide, see Tilley 2003.

34. On the original model, see Merriam 1964. On its remodeling to forefront Geertzian formative processes of historical construction, social maintenance, and individual creation and experience, see Rice 1987. On the incorporation of the many participants of Small's (1998) musicking (audience, performer, composer, and so on) into the Rice-Merriam model, see Mendívil 2016.

35. Molino identifies three dimensions of symbolic analysis for "objects" from the social sciences (for example, language, religion, music). In terms borrowed from semiotics, *poietic analysis*

refers to processes of creation, *aesthetic analysis* refers to processes of reception, and *neutral analysis* analyzes the nature of the object itself. See Arom 1991a, 157–59.

36. There almost invariably is. For a close examination of local music theory among the Kaluli, for instance, see Feld 1981.

CHAPTER ONE

1. This concert took place on October 15, 2015.
2. I Dewa Nyoman Sura of Pengosekan, Gianyar.
3. I Cokorda Alit Hendrawan of Peliatan, Gianyar.
4. This phenomenon is termed *content addressability*. See Gabora and Ranjan 2013.
5. Also termed *analogic thinking*. See Perlman 2004, chap. 1; Sawyer 2007, 110–12.
6. On these three types of creativity, see Boden 2004 and 2013.
7. Boden (2013) notes that some innovators, like Picasso, can generate multiple new transformations over the course of their careers. Yet for most creators, she says, combinatorial and exploratory creativity are the norm. "That's abundantly clear," she continues, "when one visits a painter's retrospective exhibition, especially if the canvasses are displayed chronologically: one sees a certain style being adopted, and then explored, clarified, and tested. It may be superficially tweaked (a different palette adopted, for example). But it's only rarely that one sees a radical transformation taking place." The same is true of scientific creativity, Boden asserts: "the list of a scientist's research papers rarely includes a transformative contribution: mostly, scientists explore the implications of some already accepted idea. Even if that idea is itself transformative, and relatively recent, it normally prompts exploration rather than further transformation" (8).
8. Note that Sawyer (2007) also identifies a cognitive process called *conceptual combination*, which informs many acts of combinatorial creativity (for example, the creation of Reese's candies through the once-radical combination of chocolate and peanut butter). However, I find the concept of *conceptual transfer* to more closely describe the combinatorial creativity involved in most musical improvisation. It is likely that the concept of *conceptual combination* will be particularly relevant when discussing fusion genres, where the mapping of properties and structures across domains of knowledge is central. It will not be discussed here.
9. Conversation with I Dewa Nyoman Sura, July 2011.
10. Conversation with Anak Agung Raka, July 2008. Paraphrased.
11. Eitan Wilf's provocative *School for Cool* (2014) examines how this process occurs in academic jazz programs, grappling with the conceptual tension between institutionalization and spontaneous creation.
12. See Pressing (1984) for several examples of referents.
13. Arom also looks at a musical system as a *code* with "two essential parts: a set of elements and a set of rules defining how these elements operate and combine" (Ruwet quoted and translated in Arom 1991a, 157). See Arom 1991b and 1991a, 157–69, 225–26, 250–72 on the model concept and modelization.
14. Richard Widdess (2013), with the benefit of nearly four decades of perspective, raises some concerns about this potentially "one-dimensional concept of performance," which suggests that performers need only consider one thing at a time: "mak[ing] decisions about how to

get to the next 'structural point' at the beginning of each 'block' " (197). His worry is that this view potentially whitewashes the complex process of "multiple parameters in play at any one time, and decisions being made at many moments along the way between structural points" (198). Yet, despite its potential weaknesses, Nettl's article presents an important blurring of the line between "improvisation" and "composition"—radical for the time—allowing for improvisation to have organization and pre-planning while composition embraces chance and spontaneity.

15. On this testing out of different musical ideas in the performance of composed works see Benson 2003, chap. 2.

16. Nooshin continues: "Such processes of line-drawing and category-making relate directly to the self-other binaries evoked by Lawrence Kramer . . . and they raise important questions about how musical difference is both imagined and articulated through the dominant discourses that come to frame musical practices" (216).

17. On music as a "process" as well as a "work" (or "product") see Cook 2013; Cook and Everist 1999; Redhead and Hawes 2016. Nettl (1974) dichotomizes Beethoven's arduous, meticulous composition method with Schubert's "quick, spontaneous creation of lieder" (6) as two ends of a continuum: rapid and slow versions of the same process. He likewise places the musics of three different American First Nations—Pima, "Eskimo" (Inuit), and Plains—on right, left, and center points of the same continuum. This approach seems much truer to the processes of both improvisation and composition than a simple opposition. In his 2013 "Improvisational Fictions," though, Paul Steinbeck cautions: "When we say that improvisation is like composition, our analyses tend to valorize the things we seek out in composed music, particularly relatedness and complexity" (para. 5). He argues, borrowing a theory from Marion A. Guck (1994), that scholars create analytical *fictions*: "carefully crafted 'stories of [their own] involvement' with music. . . . Through these fictions," Steinbeck continues, "analysts encourage their readers to have particular musical experiences, revealing in turn their own beliefs about music, listening, and the practice of analysis" (para. 3). Yet despite these potentially damning words, Steinbeck's article does not seek to disprove this and other "fictions" about improvisation. Its aim is rather to make readers and scholars aware of their biases (as self-reflexive ethnomusicologists attempt to be), and to encourage scholarship that comes from many interdisciplinary perspectives, including looking to seemingly distant fields such as organizational studies (see, e.g., Weick 2002). Steinbeck's argument is that, as with many theories, the idea that improvisation is like composition must be approached with caution. It is not untrue; it is just not that simple. That said, I agree with Nettl and others that looking at improvisation and composition as bedfellows rather than opposites provides interesting insights into the processes of both.

18. Also termed *varied realizations*. See Berkowitz (2010) on varied realizations (which he generally terms simply *variation*) and other improvisatory techniques. See Turino (2009) for a discussion of *formulaic variation* in several participatory practices including mbira and string-band music. Note that for Turino, formulaic variation appears to include only "paradigmatic substitutions I have made before" (104). Yet my analyses will show that potential idiomatic substitutions for many models are almost endless and, as simple rule-based reworkings of those models, will still be formulaic variation whether or not they have been previously played.

19. Patterns for the lower-pitched *wadon* would rhythmically contrast those of the lanang, with a mind to interlocking.

20. In later chapters, an alternate notation system is used for *kendang arja* transcriptions. Because this system requires some explanation, I have opted to use only Western notation for the examination of general improvisatory concepts in this chapter.

21. It is important to note that the techniques I categorize as combinatorial do require some basic knowledge of the conceptual space of the genre: within-system equivalences, idiom-appropriate ornamentation, and so on. That said, unlike those techniques that I consider exploratory, these combinatorial techniques are closer to poetic metaphor or visual collage, requiring cognitive processes of conceptual transfer rather than conceptual elaboration. An effective work of combinatorial art only emerges through an understanding of the basic elements being combined and their diverse meanings, yet the artist is still working with existing materials, objects, and concepts, not creating new ones within her conceptual space. It may be, though, that these improvisatory techniques straddle the line between creativity types, or use elements of more than one in different moments. As Perlman says of his categories for the cognitive processes of creative thinking: "the boundaries between them can often be blurry, but there is no need for us to patrol these borders. In any particular case of creativity it may be impossible to say which of these processes is primarily responsible" (2004, 34). The science of creativity is still relatively new, and much more research is necessary.

22. Most of my *kendang arja* teachers will use the term *improvisasi* or *improv* when referring to their *arja* playing, despite the fact that the loanword *variasi* also exists in the Indonesian language.

23. Association for the Advancement of Creative Musicians.

24. On the concept of overlapping schemas in Indian improvisation, see Widdess 2011a, 2011b, and 2013. On schema theory for inherent patterns in Bugandan interlocking polyphonies, see Wegner 1993. On oral poetry, see Rubin 1995. On country and hip-hop, see Shevy 2008.

25. While these processes are more often used in solo practices like *alap*, they are also seen in collective styles, particularly those more hierarchical practices where musicians are afforded varying levels of creative license.

26. Widdess defines the *alap* as "a 'manifestation' or 'making clear' (*prakaṭīkaraṇa*) of the *rāga*" (Widdess 2011a, 188).

27. In combination, these parameters help evoke appropriate extramusical associations for a given raga.

28. Figures 1.8, 1.9, and 1.10 are reproduced from Widdess 2011a, with permission.

29. The tonic has already been introduced in the first 20 seconds of the improvisation through a characteristic opening sequence that involves the strumming of the sitar's drone strings and sympathetic resonator strings. See Widdess 2011a, 194–96.

30. On pedagogical lineage (*gharānā*) and other concepts relating to individual style, see Karnani 2005; Sanyal and Widdess 2004.

31. See Widdess 2011a, 195, for the full schema.

32. Also termed *conceptual extension*.

33. Nettl observes similar levels of play in Persian improvisatory systems, where "various degrees of 'improvisatoriness' or departure from a PoD [point of departure]" are both recognized and encouraged (Nettl 2009a, 194).

34. Berkovitz takes these definitions from Gleason and Ratner 2009, 19–22 and 465–83. He also proposes analogies between the knowledge bases of language and music (see Berkowitz 2010, 101–8).

35. On the acquisition of a knowledge base in both language and music, see Berkovitz 2010, 108–18.

36. On various aspects of this learning process in academic settings, see Wilf 2014, chaps. 5–6.

37. On the systems model of creativity, see Csikszentmihalyi 1988 and 1990.

CHAPTER TWO

1. I Dewa Ketut Alit of Pengosekan, Gianyar.

2. On these techniques, called *kecekan* and *ocak-ocakan* respectively, see Gold 2005, 64–67.

3. Often generically called *kotekan*, in different musical contexts, these characteristically Balinese interlocking techniques are variably termed *kilitan, candetan, reyongan,* and so on (see Bakan 1999, 53). The terms vary by instrument, technique, region, and generation. In the current case study, I generally avoid an overarching term, preferring to refer to specific techniques by name (*norot, empat, noltol,* etc.); this is the commonly accepted approach among most Balinese musicians (I Dewa Ketut Alit, personal communication April 2017).

4. While there are many different versions of the *Baris reyong* melody, each is built from the same strict principles of *empat* interlocking.

5. For those unfamiliar with gamelan, this small range lacking both phrasing and rhythmic variety might not look like a typical melody. However, it is often sung by Balinese musicians for pedagogical purposes and, though formulaically composed, is indeed considered "melodic."

6. On the effects of familiarity and experience (as well as age and tempo) in detecting melodic alterations, see Dowling et al. 2008. Closely related studies on the cognition and psychology of musical expectation include Meyer 1957; Huron 2006. Pearce and Wiggins (2012) extend these studies to include computational and probabilistic modeling.

7. On *partimento*, see Sanguinetti 2012. On *pagode*, see Stanyek and Oliveira 2011.

8. The knowledge base of each of these traditions is much more detailed and nuanced; here I am only concerned with the basic model.

9. Most of the musical examples in this chapter and the next stem from recording sessions I did with I Dewa Ketut Alit in Vancouver, British Columbia, in the winter and spring of 2002. (See Tilley 2003 for full transcriptions and more detailed analyses.) In these sessions, Alit improvised *norot* for several pieces, both traditional and newly composed, at each position of the *reyong*. He then taught me a handful of patterns for each and we discussed their interlocking qualities. This research has been supplemented by lessons and conversations with Alit and other musicians in the interim, observation of performances in Bali, and a 2016 video recording session of a full *reyong* complement in Pengosekan, Gianyar. Thus contextualized, examining Alit's earlier improvisations at the cellular level can offer insight into the unspoken rules that guide them. Yet no single study provides a complete picture, and research in other regions would doubtless yield additional results.

10. This ordering is partially inspired by challenges I faced in my *reyong norot* research. Coming to Step 5 far too early, I struggled with comprehension and interpretation of many basic musical facts that the order of events suggested here could have mitigated.

11. Baily (2001) outlines some of the weaknesses of this term, and Hood himself noted that "musicality" is more far-reaching.

12. This scale, *selisir*, is a mode of the Javanese 7-tone *pélog* scale. In notating gamelan thusly, I join a tradition going back to McPhee (1966). Yet the actual pitch distribution of *selisir* varies significantly among villages and gamelan makers.

13. Gamelan makers tune pairs of instruments to be slightly "out-of-tune," so that the difference tones between their frequencies create a beating effect. This is done exactingly across the ensemble so that every note in every pair pulsates at the same rate.

14. Blake (2010) discusses the benefits of various kinds of listening, from background listening to analytical dissection. See also Borgo (2005, 26–30) on different listening styles.

15. Bakan extensively explores the value of "learning to play" in his research on *gamelan beleganjur* (1999). I originally adapted the phrase from Baily's (2001) "learning to perform" as a more all-encompassing replacement for the term *bi-musicality*. Another good option, used by Monson (1996, 131), is *poly-musicality*.

16. This is true whether physically performing or simply moving and gesturing while listening. See also Gibbs 2006; Leman 2007; Godøy and Leman 2009.

17. One may argue that too much embodied solidarity with musicians could lead to a loss of objectivity, but the general consensus is that the benefits of performance far outweigh its potential pitfalls.

18. It may also have cognitive benefits. Recent research in linguistics has found improved divergent and creative thinking, greater mental elasticity and metalinguistic awareness, and heightened communicative sensitivity among bilinguals (see Cummins 1998; Lazaruk 2007; Bialystok 2001). I propose that musicians with performing proficiency in multiple musical systems have likewise honed the mental elasticity needed to find patterns and understand structure in unfamiliar genres, to read musicians' physical and aural cues, and to recognize multiple options for musical success. These skills can then be brought to new musical systems, increasing the potential for subtle and sensitive cross-cultural analysis.

19. Many researchers of Balinese music, after Jaap Kunst, term cyclic music punctuated by fixed patterns of gong strokes *colotomic*. In an effort to encourage cross-cultural observation, I prefer the broader term cyclic, and see the gongs' strokes as part of a stratified polyphony.

20. This common gong structure is called *Gilak*.

21. On insights into diverse apprenticeship styles gleaned through practical studies in Afghani *dutâr* and *rubâb*, see Baily 2001.

22. Interestingly, students in Study Abroad programs showed less improvement in a number of fluency factors than those in Intensive Domestic Immersion programs. The authors credit this difference to the latter group's dedication to consistently speaking, listening to, reading, and writing French outside of class.

23. Note: because both *gangsa* and *ugal* range from *dong* (D) to the *ding* (C#) two octaves above, their full range is transcribed O-E-U-A-I-o-e-u-a-i, with lower octave pitches notated using uppercase letters. Range is not differentiated, however, in *reyong* transcriptions. A *ding* (i) in the lower octave is considered functionally equivalent to one in the higher octave, and *reyong* players can actualize the same figuration regardless of contour or octave placement in *ugal* and *gangsa* melodies.

24. See Ellingson 1992; Marian-Bălașa 2005; Seeger 1958; Stanyek. 2014; Tilley 2018. See England et al. (1964) for a revealing demonstration of the subjectivity and creativity of both transcription and analysis.

25. On microtiming, individual musical roles, and ensemble entrainment, see Polak, Jacoby, and London 2016.

26. Most scholars attempting staff notation of Balinese music use a similar system, but as previously mentioned, its beaming is problematic. Lisa Gold attempts a novel approach to the

end-weightedness of cycles if not of beats, placing the full beat of the gong tone before the repeat sign (e.g., Gold 2005, 61). Yet Balinese musicians do not consider the three 16th-notes following the gong tone to be part of the old cycle; they are the beginning of the new one. Staff notation thus seems incapable of being bent to an end-weighted conception. This is further complicated by gamelan's rhythmic stratification. Where different instrument groups move at different rhythmic densities, each group could be said to "begin the new cycle" independently, when first articulating a pitch not belonging to the old cycle. While the music is not felt in this divided way, these density strata create notational complications: Gold is forced to tie the *calung* and *jegogan*'s gong tones over the bar line at an artificial point. Every notational approach has both benefits and intrinsic representational challenges. I hope that the breadth of approaches throughout this book will demonstrate their relative strengths and weaknesses.

27. Tenzer (2000) examines these musical relationships in depth. Here, only the details relevant to an analysis of *reyong norot* are discussed.

28. One may argue that, because each instrument derives its part from the same melody, the music is technically heterophonic. However, both perceptually and experientially it is polyphonic.

29. True to an end-weighted conception, the *penyacah* track the *ugal* every other beat (at the *calung* density), then anticipate each of these structurally important tones with the scale degree either above or below (compressed into a single octave), thus playing every beat. On this and other compositional techniques, see Tenzer 2000, chap. 6.

30. The imperfect alignment of the "A" in *penyacah* and *calung/ugal* represents a composer's choice to sacrifice vertical convergence for a smoother, more interesting melody line in all instruments.

31. Also termed *nyok cok* (sometimes spelled *njok tjok*). On this and other interlocking techniques, see Gold 2005, 58–64; Tenzer 2000, 213–31; Vitale 1990.

32. On tacit versus explicit knowledge and its effect on learning and teaching, discussed in more detail in chapter 5, see Han and Ellis 1998; Hall 1980; Brinner 1995.

33. Monson owns that this technique was more successful with some musicians than others.

34. These and other note choices will be made clear in subsequent sections. Octave equivalence can be seen following the *klentong* (t) stroke: Alit stays in the low octave on *reyong* while the *gangsas* go high.

35. Conversation with I Dewa Ketut Alit, April 2017.

36. Sometimes a composer will opt for more static *norot* realizations, tracking the slower-moving core melody instrument *jegogan* (discussed in chapter 3). Tracking the *calung*, however, is the norm.

37. Interlocking melodies can be played at slower tempi, particularly in slower-moving sections of a piece or in older, more classical styles. In these instances, the choice between parallel and interlocking figuration is stylistic.

38. Note that *sangsih* players fall into unison with *polos* on the top three pitches of the instrument, where *kempyung* tones are unavailable.

39. Although *gangsa norot* in parallel figuration features two voices, because the same compositional model is used for interlocking, I consider it a single-voice model.

40. "Les divers elements . . . une fois dissociés, peuvent perdre leur sens et jusqu'a leur identité. Il apparaît donc nécessaire d'avoir constamment sous les yeux une *image globale* du document sonore destiné à l'étude" (Arom 1969, 172).

41. Interview with I Dewa Ketut Alit, February 15, 2002.
42. Conversation with I Dewa Ketut Alit, April 2017.
43. See Titon 2009, 125, for an image of the mbira with keys labeled.
44. Of course this is something of a chicken-and-egg theory; we don't know whether melodic preferences influenced the structure of the instrument or vice versa, and it is as likely some combination of the two.
45. For other techniques, like *empat*, it is not uncommon for *reyong* players to go outside these ranges; the *penyorog*, for instance, frequently plays *dong* (o). This flexibility is not employed in *norot*.
46. See Locke 1998, 48–68 on response drum improvisation and 74–123 on lead drum improvisation.

CHAPTER THREE

1. See Tenzer 2009.
2. Personal communication with Michael Tenzer, spring 2017, referring to a lesson with Loceng in 1979.
3. See video at https://www.youtube.com/watch?v=yl5WSlSHtK8—Komin (I Gusti Nyoman Darta), Ketut, and their nephew playing together with a family friend in 4th position.
4. The first position *penyorog* musician can play *deng, dung, dang, ding*, and a dyad of *deng* and *ding*, or she can rest, making six options for each of eight subdivisions (though when *ding* is used by her partner she has just four options). Mathematically this is 6^8 or 1,679,616 different combinations. The fourth position *pemetit* player controlling four notes and a rest has 5^8 or 390,625 options. The other players have 4^8 or 65,536 possible realizations with the 3rd position *ponggang* often working with 3^8 or 6,561 options.
5. On mbira, see Berliner 1993. On Aka singing, see Fürniss 2006; Arom 1991.
6. Herndon, in this statement, was referring to the linguistics-based structural analyses in vogue through the 1970s.
7. I borrow the idea of a plural "views" from Gerd Grupe: "If we want to understand musics of various cultures more thoroughly, and I think as ethnomusicologists we should, we need to do so by aiming at a kind of analysis that includes emic views on the subject in order to make sure that our findings are not mere artifacts of our own thinking but actually relate in a meaningful way to the cultural practices and musical concepts of the people who have created them. The plural 'views' is not to be ignored" (2016, 45).
8. I have taken the concept of a polyphony of voices from McGraw; he cites it as "Foucault after Bakhtin" (2005, xvii).
9. In other words, musicians can create the effect of pitch variance in a nonvariable pitch instrument by either changing its timbre or removing the note altogether, substituting it with silence. This limited set of options relates to the four ways Tenzer (2011b) posits rhythm is created: tone change, duration change, accent change, and punctuation.
10. There are exceptions, but they are few and will not be explored here.
11. These, of course, are compressed into a single octave to accommodate the *reyong* players' limited ranges.

12. Conversations and hands-on demos with several experienced mbira players, both North American and Shona (2016 to present), revealed several such interpretive options.

13. Note that Central Javanese gamelan is generally composed and learned using cipher notation: a series of numbers from either 1 to 6 or 1 to 7 indicating the notes of the scale from lowest to highest. See Gitosaprodjo (1984) chap. 4 on notation, chap. 2 on the different scale (*laras*) types. See Becker (1988) for cipher notation of various gamelan works.

14. Personal communication and hands-on demo, Jody Diamond, December 2017. For an example, see http://www.gamelanbvg.com/gendhing/gamelanGlossary.pdf, 13. Accessed February 25, 2019.

15. While this term could also be applied to *reyong norot*, my sense is that these musicians are not thinking of such patterns simply as full patterns with notes taken away (though of course on paper this is precisely what is happening) but rather as more mature variants of simpler patterns. I thus prefer the broader concept of interpretation, and a free interchanging of many options, one of which is a rest.

16. On mbira, see Berliner 1993. On Bugandan and other traditions, see Kubik 1962 and 1960.

17. Cognitive research suggests humans are more likely to hear interleaved melodies as independent when other musical features, such as relative pitch, timbre, or dynamics, also differ. By contrast, listeners are generally unable to cognitively separate interlocking melodies in similar ranges, dynamics, and timbres; they will be heard as a single stream of notes (see Dowling and Harwood 1986, 125–27).

18. See Sanguinetti 2012, 99–164 for rules, 167–341 for analyses.

19. Conversation with I Dewa Ketut Alit, April 2017.

20. As Borgo notes, "improvising music certainly requires focused listening, quick reflexes, and extreme sensitivity to the group flow, but it equally demands individual fortitude and tenacity not to be overwhelmed by the speed of interaction and the availability of musical options" (2005, 81).

21. More experienced musicians generally occupy first and second positions. Notes at these positions are naturally louder and their players are often considered leaders. That said, because of the fourth position *pemetit*'s expanded range and freedom to use its high *dung* (u) in "inhospitable tonal situations," experienced musicians also enjoy playing *pemetit*; Alit once told me it was his favorite position to play. He would never play there, however, if it meant having a weak player in first position.

22. This is not a hard and fast rule. I have seen players strike all eight notes of a two-beat cell, but it is relatively uncommon.

23. Although this preference guides *reyong norot* improvisation on all core melody tones, *dong* (o) appears to be the note most consistently played in this way.

24. Conversation with I Dewa Ketut Alit, January 2002.

25. On wavelike tempo (*ombak*) and other temporal qualities of gamelan, including concepts of microtiming not addressed here, see McGraw 2013, 166–73.

26. Note that in most of this chapter's figures, cells are notated without their initial gong/core melody tone in the *reyong*. These will only be shown, as in this figure, where relevant to the analysis.

27. Lesson with I Dewa Ketut Alit, February 2002.

28. Lesson with I Dewa Ketut Alit, March 2002.

29. Personal communications, 2011.

30. While the two *dong* (o) at the beginning of Example 1 are both technically template tones, it is likely that Alit feels this pattern as a delayed unison, making the first *dong* (o) experientially a nonstandard tone.

31. Another common variant is suspending the 1st subdivision upper neighbor into the 2nd. This is most commonly followed by an anticipation, creating a note-doubling pair, for example, //3-3-2-2/ instead of //3-2-3-2/.

32. This shift from /0-0-1-0// to /0-1-1-0// parallels variants in interlocking drumming where the two drums' bass strokes *Dag* (D) and *Tut* (T) may likewise interlock using either /D-D-T-D// or /D-T-T-D//. That the flexible shifting between single-note alternation and asymmetrical note-doubling crosses instrument idioms is noteworthy. On drum idioms in *gamelan gong kebyar*, see Tenzer 2000, chap. 7.

33. Personal communication, 2012.

34. Note that in the template-abiding pattern in Example 2, a desire to stay as close to the improvised pattern as possible has led to three consecutive *dang* (a) followed by three consecutive *dung* (u). I have placed one of each in parentheses, indicating a possible place for a rest.

35. The great Karnatak composer Tygaraja often precomposed his *sangati* for a more systematic unraveling of these characteristics in performance.

36. Alit often employs the same technique when anticipating the upper neighbor tone of pickup gestures.

37. It is noteworthy that most of these note-doublings are end-weighted, beginning on a weak subdivision and ending on a strong one, regardless of which is the nonstandard tone. A delayed unison has the nonstandard note in the 1st subdivision repeated in the 2nd, while an anticipation often occurs between the 3rd and 4th subdivisions. A suspension also occurs in these subdivisions, but the first is the template-abiding tone. The upper-neighbor suspension in the pickup gesture has the template-abiding tone in the 7th subdivision repeated in the 8th. The one exception to this end-weightedness is the anticipation of the pickup gesture's upper neighbor (metrically different from the rest, even in the model). Here, an anticipation in the 6th subdivision is resolved through repetition in the weaker 7th.

38. In the past I proposed a theoretical category of "reverse *norot*" for such nonstandard tones (see Tilley 2003). However, recent conversations with Alit have convinced me that this category does not resonate within the music culture. Openness to reassessing and even rejecting our hypotheses must be a central component of fieldwork-based analysis. Thus, I maintain the broader designation of "creative pitch substitutions" for this category, without the tidier explanation of my own outmoded theory.

39. Conversation with I Dewa Ketut Alit, April 2017.

40. Conversation with I Dewa Ketut Alit, April 2017.

41. Pages 67–69 address the concept cross-culturally.

42. The former is more common than the latter. Note that this static-kinetic switch does not alter the pitch content of the pattern's first half, only its pickup gesture.

43. Lesson with I Dewa Ketut Alit, February 2003.

44. These rising three-note gestures leading to the core melody tone may also be shared between partners, as in a *dong-deng-dung-deng* (o-e-u-e) gesture shared between 2nd and 3rd position.

45. Lesson with I Dewa Ketut Alit, winter 2001.

46. Although *ding* (i) is a template note here, the consistency with which Alit rests in the *penyorog* figuration after a-u-a, thereby turning listener attention to the *pengenter*'s *ding*, points to its importance and hints at a temporary core melody intensification.

47. Conversation with I Dewa Ketut Alit, April 2017. That said, studies have shown that the human brain processes auditory stimuli faster than visual stimuli, connecting to the cerebral cortex in 8–9 milliseconds and producing an auditory, kinesthetic, or tactile reaction in 100–160 milliseconds. Kinesthetic error correction (EC) happens even more quickly: 50–60 milliseconds. "EC times are important for improvisation because it may reasonably be argued that they reflect minimum times for decision-making that is expressive or compositional" (Pressing 1988, 136–37, quote on 137). This cognitive speed does suggest some potential for reactions in close collective improvisation, like *reyong norot*, to happen in real time.

CHAPTER FOUR

1. Located in the majority-Chinese Strathcona neighborhood of Vancouver, BC.
2. See Flores 2008.
3. From *rematar*, "to end or conclude," *remate* can conclude a series of movements or otherwise enhance the song. Most often, beginning flamenco dancers first learn to place them between sung phrases.
4. On these metaphors of performance interaction, see Borgo 1996, 27–28; Monson 1996. On reflective versus reactive processes, see Al-Zand 2008.
5. Coined to describe interactive processes in Western improvised contemporary art music, but applicable to most collective practices, the term uses the prefix *hetero* rather than *poly* to "emphasize the *separateness* of the contributing members" and their distinct contributions to the music (9).
6. On the various ways music scholars have examined improvisation, beginning with Ernst Ferand in 1938, see Nettl 1998, 1–4.
7. As discussed in chapter 1, each has elements of improvisation; their difference lies in *degree*.
8. Such parameters are often established in advance. Shifts between them may happen naturally or, in the case of techniques like *conduction* (Morris 2017), be coordinated during performance.
9. On ways of knowing, discussed in chapter 5, see Brinner 1995, 34–39.
10. This process characterizes much Southeast Asian music. While often called "heterophonic," "polyphonic stratification seems a more precise description, since each of the 'layers' is not just a close approximation of the main melody, but also has distinct characteristics and a style of its own" (Morton 1976, 21).
11. I borrow the idea of "support" as opposed to "accompaniment" from Brinner 1995, 173.
12. On agent systems, see Gloor, Oster, and Fischbach 2013; Pelz-Sherman 1998, chap. 4.
13. On elastic coordination, see Harrison and Rouse 2014. Berliner juxtaposes this as a tension between the "rights of the individual" and the "welfare of the group" (1994, 417).
14. Harrison and Rouse note: "Often, under conditions of complete freedom to explore, people revert to 'tried and true' responses to alleviate the cognitive complexity of too many options" (2014, 1260). This view contradicts many studies that consider constraints an impediment to creativity. For a literature review, see Harrison and Rouse 2014, 1260. For a case study where constraints increase creativity, see Sawyer 2007, 120–25.
15. Interview with I Cokorda Alit Hendrawan, summer 2011.
16. Some models of creativity subdivide this stage into two steps. Finke, Baylis, and Ward's 1992 Geneplore model includes *generative* and *exploratory* phases; Sawyer's (1992) model includes

ideation and *selection*. Csikszentmihalyi's (1996) five-stage model of *preparation, incubation, insight, evaluation,* and *elaboration* also reflects processes of model acquisition and fluency.

17. Scholars of embodiment and enactive cognition examine how the body actively contributes to these cognitive processes. See Borgo 2005, chap. 3.

18. On automaticity and its importance to fluency, see Pressing 1988, 139–41; Thomson and Jaque 2017, 14.

19. Cognitive load theory suggests that our capacity for the cognitive processing of tasks is finite. See Kenny and Gellrich 2002, 121.

20. In a study of the motor-performance effects of embodiment-cognition compatibility, Chen and Bargh (1999) asked tests subjects to either push or pull a lever whenever a word appeared on a screen. Those subjects instructed to pull responded more quickly to positive words while those instructed to push responded more quickly to negative words. This suggests that "embodiment-cognition compatibility affect[s] performance efficiency" (Barsalou et al. 2003, 57).

21. On interactional synchrony in improvised music, see Sawyer 2003, 37–39.

22. Harvey gives the example of Pixar's production teams.

23. The concept of *taksu* has close equivalents in many cultures, including *duende* in flamenco. While some consider *taksu* a birthright, other Balinese performers pray to the spirit of *taksu* before a performance, hoping to attain it.

24. Others would disagree. I Wayan Tama often spoke of the special shrine in his village that he and other Singapadu performers prayed to for *taksu*.

25. I Wayan Sudirana, personal communication, October 2018.

26. On these factors of flow, see Biasutti 2017, 2.

27. Pearce (2016) sees *flow* as paralleling Goffman's (1961) concept of *engrossment*.

28. While flow states are often reported in group activities, most research on flow focuses on the individual. Recent work by Sawyer (2003, 2007), Hart and Di Blasi (2015), Pearce (2016), Gaggioli et al. (2017), and Seddon (2005) addresses the concept they respectively term *group flow, shared* or *combined flow, intersubjective flow, networked flow,* and *empathetic attunement*. Note that group flow is different from individual flow within groups; the group flows as a unit, with a unified goal.

29. Thus, sufficient experience in a practice is a precursor to group flow. See Seddon 2005, 58.

30. On collective versus private intention, see Hagberg 2016.

31. Gaggioli and colleagues (2015) term this mutual awareness *social presence*.

32. Sawyer notes that riskier genres of improvisation, like free jazz, are harder to market because they *do* sometimes fail (2003, 57–58). Experienced audiences, however, learn to appreciate this heightened risk.

33. As Bakan poetically observes: "only when we learn to trust one another, to dissolve in the realization of our shared humanity, will the music finally play" (1999, 133). Improv theater troupes often play games designed to hone listening skills, cohesion, and mutual trust. See Sawyer 2003, 64–65. But see also Sawyer 2003, 63 and 65 on the dangers of "over rehearsing."

34. On common versus interpersonally shared histories, see Bastien and Hostager 1992. On microdomain as localized domain (model and knowledge base), see Sawyer 2003, 125. See Pressing (1988, 155) for a mathematical equation tracing the creation of a microdomain.

35. On the closely related theory of *symbolic interactionism*, see Blumer 1967.

36. Figures 4.8 and 4.9 are reproduced from Monson 1996, 141–42 and 159–60, with permission.

37. Note that the level and nature of musical competence varies across musical communities, and that such distinctions influence different performers' improvisational choices (see Brinner 1995). For this study, I assume high-level competence as a precondition to successful collective improvisation in order to focus on how successful collectivity is achieved.

38. This concert took place on February 1, 2018, at the Somerville Theater in Somerville, Massachusetts.

39. See Harvey (2014) on conflict and creative synthesis; Harrison and Rouse (2014) on de-integration as a catalyst for creative re-integrations; Corbett (2016, 59–62) on the Consensus/Dispute dichotomy.

40. Linell (2001) says the same of verbal interactions, but prefers the term *co-ordination* as a "weaker form of cooperation" (13).

41. Social conventions also include interpersonal behavior, performance etiquette, and expectations. See Bastien and Hostager 1992, 94–96.

42. On these modes of verbal interaction see Seddon 2005. Seddon also suggests three parallel modes of nonverbal interaction.

43. On *bèlè* cuing, see Gerstin 1998, 137–52. On Garcia's cues, see Pettengill 2013, 44.

44. While such interaction is often intentional, the relationship between call and response causative, it may also be nondirected, the relationship referential. See Brinner 1995, 177.

45. In his study of nonverbal communication in music pedagogy, Kurkul (2007) suggests subcategories for such cues.

46. Speaker overlap, stutters, and pauses help people determine intent in conversational interaction (see Sawyer 2003, 18–21). Musicians are more constrained in their communication by the musical needs of the performance as well as the physical requirements of playing an instrument. However, Pelz-Sherman found that people watching videotaped performances with no sound could consistently discern leaders and followers, for instance, through body position and movement alone.

47. On jazz roles, see Monson 1996, chap. 2. On *pagode*, see Stanyek and Oliveira 2011.

48. On attentional loading, see Pressing 1988, 155.

49. On this spotlight metaphor, see Hagberg 2016, 490–91.

50. On prioritized integrative attention and other forms of attention, see Keller 2008.

51. Interestingly, tabla players watched sitarist's hands more frequently if they did not have previous performing experience together. This suggests watching hands may be a more active way to receive but may also occupy a larger portion of the cognitive load.

52. Bastien and Hostager (1992) found the same in jazz ensembles, where mutual attention was highest around points of change.

53. Gaggioli and colleagues (2017) term this an "interaction of dependence."

54. Solis notes: "The drawback of a disciplinary ghettoization of the study of improvisation to those musical situations where it is marked as the central activity is that it has limited our understanding of musical improvisation in general" (2009, 7). The same could be said of degrees of collectivity.

55. Chernoff (1979) and Arom (1991) both bring up this point several times.

56. On these and other characteristics, see Sawyer 2003, 4–13; Hsieh 2012, 152–53; Hsieh 2009, 45–48.

57. Sawyer addresses this in several sources (1997, 2000, 2003, 2007). Of course the physical aspects of improv theater can engage simultaneous improvisation.

58. https://www.ucbtheatre.com/show/741. Accessed March 5, 2018.

59. https://www.youtube.com/watch?v=P4HTxmqNTCY&feature=youtu.be. Accessed February 26, 2018. The transcribed excerpt begins at 4:07; the monologue runs 1:45–4:05.

60. Much improv comedy pushes the boundaries of off-color and inappropriate humor. While the humor in this statement lies in the ludicrousness of the suggestion, it is also important to recognize how often women and girls are sexualized, essentialized, and disempowered in comedy tropes.

61. On these aspects of emergence, see Sawyer 2003, 10–13.

62. Figure 4.10 is reproduced from Bunk 2011, 239, with permission.

63. On the dialectical model, see Benson 1977.

64. Sawyer and DeZutter propose that "interactions among group members often become a more substantial source of creativity than the inner mental processes of any one participating individual" (2009, 83).

65. On the "yes, and" rule, see Sawyer 2003, 36. Corbett (2016, 20) argues, by contrast, that this rule need not always apply in improvised music, and that at times it may be a detriment to the performance.

66. See Wiedemann (1975) for an analysis of a far less mutually determined example of this process, between Miles Davis and Thelonius Monk, in Davis's iconic 1954 version of "The Man I Love."

67. For other examples, see Brinner 1995, 177–78. I differentiate this dichotomy from the weak and strong senses of sharing described by Hagberg (2016), where the weak sense has no aspect of collective intentionality: "The husband says, 'I know it's important to keep the romance alive, so we go out two nights every week. I go on Monday and Wednesday and my wife goes on Tuesday and Thursday'" (484).

68. Microinteraction is related to musical *entrainment* (see Clayton, Sager, and Will 2005) as well as to concepts of embodiment, embodied mimicry, and mirror neuron circuits (see Barsalou et al. 2003). Walton and colleagues (2015) term this process *microscopic interaction*, noting that coordinated up-and-down head movements in particular "play a large role in performance expressivity" (6). Gloor, Oster, and Fischbach (2013) found that when musicians are experiencing group flow, their body movements oscillate in parallel. These so-called honest signals, they hypothesized, indicate parallel energy levels. (On honest signals, see also Pentland 2008.)

69. Both Pelz-Sherman (1998) and Corbett (2016) differentiate macrointeraction from completely "independent simultaneous action" (Corbett 2016, 54–58), where what emerges is "a presentation of co-existing rather than inter-relating streams" (Pressing 1984, 351). Independent simultaneous action creates the *swarm* effect proposed by Borgo (2005). Here, however, we are largely concerned with *cooperative* interaction, whether synchronic or diachronic, resulting in Borgo's *sync*.

CHAPTER FIVE

1. Lessons with I Dewa Nyoman Sura, summer 2008.

2. In this chapter and the next, kendang patterns are notated in Western staff notation, as in chapter 1, as well as with letters representing Balinese mnemonics. Staff notation will ease

comprehension for Western-trained music scholars while the mnemonics, I hope, will allow Balinese musicians not versed in Western notation to enter the dialogue. Again, meter is end-weighted and transcriptions use parentheses to show that conception.

3. These are sometimes termed *anak pukulan*, child strokes (see Hood 2001). They parallel ghost strokes used in Western drumkit as well as Mande and Northern Sotho drumming traditions (see Weinberg 1994, 20; Charry 2000; Mapaya 2014).

4. On "unpedagogic practice," see Lortat-Jacob 1995, 13. On "the traditional non-method," see Rice 1996, 4.

5. Conversation with I Wayan Sudirana, May 2007.

6. Knowledge *of* something comprises what Dennett (2017) terms "competence without comprehension." On ways of knowing in music, see Brinner 1995, chaps. 1–2; in language, see Han and Ellis 1998.

7. On *arja* in general, see Dibia 1992; Widjaja 2007; Tilley 2013, chap. 1. On the singing (*tembang*), see Herbst 1997.

8. Lessons and interviews with all my teachers corroborate this assertion.

9. While both *batel* structures are reserved for intense moments in the drama, I Wayan Tama of Singapadu names the faster one *batel marah* because it is more often used for very intense fight scenes and angry or unrefined characters. I Gusti Nyoman Darta (Komin) in Pengosekan, by contrast, refers to this structure as *batel penasar*, referencing the clown (*penasar*) characters it often accompanies.

10. It might instead entail a distinction between active and passive knowledge. See Brinner 1995, 35.

11. On this phenomenon in language, see Paradowski 2008, 524.

12. As Brinner (1995) notes, "explicitness of knowledge enhances a musician's performance capabilities chiefly in instructional situations . . . allow[ing] a person to convey aspects of competence to others" (66).

13. Conversation with I Wayan Pasek Sucipta, June 2008.

14. This does not prove that my teachers couldn't communicate all their patterns. However, the ubiquity of their seeming inability is noteworthy.

15. Taught patterns and oral theory likely differ among drummers descended from contrasting styles (discussed in more detail in chapter 6).

16. Similar terminology exists among the Aka, though again it is rarely used and must be uncovered through fieldwork. For instance, *kpókpó*, literally "straight on," describes an unvaried realization of a melody, while *kété bányé* means to vary it. See Fürniss 2006, 176–77.

17. Arom notes of paradigmatic equivalence in Central African polyphonic improvising: "All the possible realisations of a given rhythmic figure are culturally speaking identical. . . . Any realisation of a given part in a polyrhythmic ensemble can thus be superposed on any realisation of any other part, *provided the conditions of interweaving . . . are respected*" (1991a, 299).

18. Lesson with I Dewa Nyoman Sura, June 2008.

19. For our recording session, Tama chose his student I Ketut Buda Astra to be his partner. An accomplished drummer, Buda is not yet a master and still occasionally struggles, particularly in faster gong structures where the difference between his and Tama's proficiency levels becomes clear.

20. The same may be said of taught *wadon* patterns, though these, for reasons addressed further on, are somewhat more varied. See Tilley 2013.

21. While Hood (2001, 87) uses the term *uger-uger*, this was not a term I heard during my fieldwork. Whenever a teacher referred to performance rules of any kind (which was not often), they always used the terms *patokan* or *pakem*, both of which translate roughly as "standard."

22. On standard jazz, see Berliner 1994; Monson 1996. On connections between second line playing in New Orleans jazz and funk, see Doleac 2013.

23. On Ghanaian traditions, see Chernoff 1979; Locke 1998.

24. Conversation with I Dewa Nyoman Sura, August 2008.

25. This is reflected in Hood's (2001) concept of "variable pattern pairs."

26. Conversation with I Cokorda Alit Hendrawan, June 2007.

27. *Barong* is a mythical lion-shaped benevolent demon, featured in, among other things, the famous *Calonarang* story. Like a Chinese dragon, the character is played by two dancers in a single costume.

28. "Kita main begitu supaya kedengaran suara kendang itu hidup. Wadon yang hidupnya. Ya di sini tetap jalan. . . . Lanangnya ada juga variasi sedikit, tapi lebih sedikit disini" (conversation, June 2011).

29. "Kalau kendang lanang itu di ganjil . . . wadon, genap. Supaya tetap bisa jatuh itu [lanang] di ganjil, disini [wadon] tetap genap, biar dimana dia main-mainkan, tak tabrakan" (conversation, June 2011).

30. This theorizing—both the use of English-language terms in Indonesian conversation and the verbalized concept of patterns built of odd and even parts—is likely a product of long-term contact with Western students versed in music theory, like myself, who have asked their teachers to think and talk about *kendang arja* in these ways. None of my more geographically isolated teachers spoke thusly about their practice, nor were they familiar with the terms when asked. Yet the relative ubiquity of the concepts is noteworthy, and worthy of investigation.

31. Several of my teachers, including Sudi and Alit, have told me that, when improvising *reyong norot*, the first position *penyorog* player should emphasize the off-beats while the second position *pengenter* plays more "on-the-beat." Although my analyses of *norot* have shown that this is sometimes the case, as Sudi would say, it's never "that simple."

32. Conversation with I Wayan Sudirana, January 2010.

33. Exceptions often occur in patterns from the older *klasik* (classic) style. Here, *lanang* players place some *peng* (e) off the beat and their *wadon* partners are afforded less creative license. See Tilley 2013, 237–40.

34. Exceptions in Pak Tut's *lanang* patterns, where double *peng* (e) strokes indiscriminately land on the beat or the half beat, can be explained through the rigidity of his *wadon* idiom, which appears to employ no double rim strokes. See Tilley 2013, 241.

35. Of course even within these larger confines, drummers still "break the rule."

36. Exceptions occur in special cuing patterns.

37. There are many variants of this classic cadential motive, this one from Anak Agung Raka's Saba-village style. The beats are marked as "X" because the drumming pattern stays the same regardless of cycle length, which will vary by piece.

38. Note that structure at this hypermetric level is not articulated by the singer-dancer, who pays no heed to specific kendang patterns and may place an *angsel* in any cycle.

39. While Hood (2001, 79–81) calls these *rumus*, I did not encounter this term in my fieldwork, not even from Pak Tama, who was Hood's main teacher. When asked, none of my teachers had a sense of the term as it related to *arja*.

40. Conversation with I Gusti Nyoman Darta, June 2008.

CHAPTER SIX

1. In this research, I made extensive use of the Seventh String Software program "Transcribe!" Better designed to deal with melodies and harmonies than drum sounds with complex overtones, the program was something of a misnomer in my case. While not useful for transcription, it was invaluable for slowing down a sound file without changing its pitch. I found I could slow recordings to about 60 percent of their original speed before they became too distorted, though I often found 70–85 percent better for hearing the details without losing sight of the full patterns. One of the drawbacks of such a program is that it often introduces a level of timbral or rhythmic detail not relevant at full speed. Listening to passages I had transcribed on slow-down again at full speed helped me check my work.

2. Between my 2008 and 2011 trips to Bali, Pak Dewa suffered a stroke. Although he is mostly recovered, he still feels numbness in one hand, and this, unfortunately, affects his playing.

3. Paraphrase of a conversation with Ni Nyoman Candri in Singapadu, August 2011.

4. On Aka singing, see Fürniss 2006. On mbira, see Berliner 1993. Conversations and playing experience with both mbira and *reyong* players corroborate these ideas.

5. On the reasons for *arja*'s decline, see Tilley 2013, chap. 1; Mashino 2011.

6. Interview with I Dewa Nyoman Sura, August 3, 2011.

7. On these and other details of the *arja* drama, see Dibia 1992; Tilley 2013, chap. 1.

8. Conversation with I Wayan Sudirana, fall 2008. Cok Alit would disagree in principle, though it's true that he intersperses sparser with denser patterns for more refined characters or moments in *arja* performance (discussed further on).

9. The most *halus* moments of all are not accompanied by improvised drumming, which by nature is always somewhat *ramé*. Sparse precomposed drumming is used instead.

10. Note that Pak Tama actually calls the *tabuh telu* (tabuh three) structure "*tabuh empat*" (tabuh four). I use *tabuh telu*, the term preferred by Pak Dewa and Cok Alit, to maintain consistent terminology throughout.

11. I have chosen to mix languages here for purely practical reasons. The term "dense" would be abbreviated "D," a letter already in use for *Dag* strokes. And the Balinese term for sparse, *langah*, would require the "l" used for left-hand counting-stroke slaps.

12. This dichotomy is similar to that of *yin* and *yang*.

13. Conversation with I Dewa Ketut Alit, winter 2002.

14. On this and other regions, styles, and substyles of *bomba* drumming, see Ferreras 2005, chaps. 2–3.

15. On *gharānā*, see Karnani 2005. On *bānī* and other aspects of *dhrupad*, see Sanyal and Widdess 2004.

16. On the two schools of *charango* flute playing and other components of style, see Miller 2014, 215–16.

17. On the darker painting style unique to Batuan, see Geertz 1995. For a broad overview, see Vickers 2012.

18. Many of the younger-generation musicians I work with attended the government-sponsored high school for the performing arts, SMKI (Sekolah Menengah Karawitan Indonesia, formerly KOKAR) as well as the performing arts university, ISI (Institut Seni Indonesia, formerly STSI and ASTI).

19. Here he is not referring to an actual nephew but a relative by caste: a Cokorda, or prince, like him.

20. "Kalau di Keramas, udah agak berkurang. Karena itu dah: kalau di Singapadu, masih original itu ya, tari-tari. Apa lagi ada Bu Candri, itu lah. Keponkan saya juga kan dia penari *arja* yang di sana.... Memang beliau masih stil kuno, masih asli, original, itu.... Di Keramas sekarang, sudah agak moderen" (interview with I Cokorda Alit Hendrawan, August 13, 2011).

21. There was a young *arja* troupe from Keramas that performed in the annual Bali Arts Festival (PKB) while I was there in 2011. This group, however, did not perform in the *arja asli* Keramas style but rather in the newer academy-trained (ISI) style. According to Anak Agung Wiyat, the son of the old Keramas *arja* master Anak Agung Putu Gelgel, the last time *arja* Keramas was really active was in 1984, when they were performing the *Cupak Gerantang* story. As Balinese dancer and scholar I Madé Bandem notes, "right now they are being not very active. You wait, maybe next year they'll be active again [laughs]" (interview, August 3, 2011).

22. Batuan was famous for *gambuh* as well as *topeng* and *calonarang*; Keramas specialized in *kidung* and *kekawin* (interview with I Made Bandem, August 19, 2011). Many of the early *arja* musicians in Singapadu also performed *topeng*, *calonarang*, and *Sisia* (interview with I Wayan Dibia, August 15, 2011).

23. Interviews with both I Wayan Dibia and I Madé Bandem corroborate this information.

24. This relates back to concepts of *ramé*.

25. "Keras di sana! Karena lembutnya kurang. Keras di sana!... Kalau di sini, di Peliatan, ada polanya gimana, ada pola keras, pola mana, pola lembut. Tergantung situasi, karakter, ya. Kalau di sana, memang dari pukulan aja sudah [makes loud busy noise]—karakternya keras. Semua keras karakter di sana.... Misalnya, terlalu banyak pakai *pung*" (interview with I Cokorda Alit Hendrawan, August 13, 2011).

26. "Tidak patoknya. Tidak peduli dia" (interview with I Cokorda Alit Hendrawan, August 13, 2011).

27. I Madé Kredek is I Madé Bandem and Ni Nyoman Candri's late father. On his life and work, see Widjaja 2002.

28. I Wayan Dibia's father I Wayan Griya was also an important early figure in *arja asli* Singapadu, but he did not travel to teach as Kredek and Cok Oka Tublen did (interviews with I Madé Bandem, August 3, 2011, and I Wayan Dibia, August 15, 2011).

29. See Bakan 1999, chaps. 3–4, on individual approaches to *kreasi beleganjur*, with specific examples from well-known composers.

30. Harker (2008) explores the impact of collaborations with dancers in the late 1920s on Louis Armstrong's approach to rhythm.

31. Interview with I Madé Bandem, August 18, 2011.

32. A *kendang arja* jam session with Bandem and Pak Tama confirmed this connection.

33. Interview with I Madé Bandem, August 18, 2011.

34. In *arja*, these more *keras* (hard, strong) strokes are generally reserved for marking the end of an *angsel*. They are not used in improvised patterns. One exception is in *batel marah*, where Pak Tama sometimes replaces rim strokes with slap strokes for a more *keras* sound. This choice likely reflects his time studying with Cok Oka Tublen.

35. Interview with I Madé Bandem, August 18, 2011. Many musicians likewise observe that Peliatan-style *kendang arja* is more *ramé* than the current Singapadu style.

36. Interview with I Madé Bandem, August 18, 2011.

37. Pak Tut does not appear to be aware of the lineage of his patterns beyond his teacher, Pak Patrem; thus, the patterns in his mind belong to Apuan. But interviews with Bandem about

his father's various students confirm Patrem's direct connection to Kredek, and Pat Tut's drum patterns tell the same story.

38. Given the shared pedagogical lineage of the two drummers, it is not surprising that Pak Dewa shares common patterns with Pak Tama.

39. The one exception to this rule is the very last gong in a piece, which will almost invariably be articulated with a *Dag* (D) stroke.

40. The national radio, RRI (Radio Republik Indonesia), held live *arja* broadcasts on Sunday mornings, originally organized by Kredek, from the late 1950s into the 1980 and '90s (interview with I Madé Bandem, August 19, 2011). See Tilley 2013 on the diverse performing experiences of all drummers in this study.

41. On aspects of the cultural evolution of music through transmission, variation, and selection—both vertically (between generations) and horizontally (peer to peer)—see Savage and Brown 2013, 164–71.

POSTLUDE

1. On the "one culture = one music" model, see Savage and Brown 2014. On the history, strengths, and weaknesses of comparative musicology, see Nettl 2005, chap. 6; Seeger 1992; Toner 2007; Tilley 2018.

2. On accessing the listserv and its archives, see http://www.ethnomusicology.org/general/custom.asp?page=Resources_EListsSI. On the Natural History of Song project see https://www.naturalhistoryofsong.org/. On Grauer, see Stock 2006; Leroi and Swire 2006. On Savage and Brown, see Clarke 2014. Clarke's hesitations, though strong, are not absolute: "I wouldn't see a return to forms of comparative musicology whose roots lie in the nineteenth century as in itself necessarily heralding 'a bright future' that will transform ethnomusicology, or even musicology more widely. But I certainly would want to agree that comparativism can usefully have a place in our thinking" (12).

3. On phenetic versus phylogenetic connections and classifications, see Savage and Brown 2013, 153–54. This dichotomy parallels Blacking's (1971) distinction between surface and deep structures.

4. Her damping motion will allow one rest—the equivalent of a right-hand counting stroke following a *Dag* (D) or *Tut* (T) for instance—but were she to rest for a second subdivision, her hands would stop moving.

5. Shona musicians generally call this instrument simply mbira. While there are many kinds of mbira among the Shona, the *mbira dzavadzimu* (mbira of the ancestors) is the most internationally known—a side effect of the research of Paul Berliner (1993) as well as the efforts of Western teachers and promoters like Erica Azim (1999; see also mbira.org). See Perman 2015 on the perhaps unbalanced popularity of *mbira dzavadzimu*.

6. Berliner (1993, 73) and conversations with Erica Azim confirm these details.

7. Conversations, lessons, and workshops with several mbira performers seem to corroborate this idea. Berliner, too, says: (1) because mistakes can be detrimental to performance in an important ceremony like a *bira* (spirit possession ceremony), "students should play only basic *kushaura* parts at a *bira*," and (2) the *kutsinhira* player "has the same, *or a greater*, range of possibilities

for variations available to him during a performance" (1993, 95 and 101, emphasis added). Note, though, that different songs and performance contexts allow different levels of improvisation overall.

8. There are many different versions of a piece like *Nhemamusasa* and, even within a single version, many different ideas about where "the beginning" of its cyclic melody lies. While this version is the same as the one in Berliner (1993, 93), my interpretation of its start point differs, based on the way the melody was taught to me in mbira workshops and on my own embodied learning experience of that basic model. My transcription begins in the middle of Berliner's phrase III.

9. These versions are often overtly associated with specific musicians.

10. On this and other kinds of variation, see Berliner 1993, 95–103.

11. While I rely heavily on Berliner 1993, also useful were Perman 2015, Tracey 2015, and Scherzinger 2010.

REFERENCES

Agawu, Kofi. 2003. *Representing African Music: Postcolonial Notes, Queries, Positions*. New York: Routledge.

Agawu, V. Kofi. 1990. "Variation Procedures in Northern Ewe Song." *Ethnomusicology* 34, no. 2: 221–43.

Al-Zand, Karim. 2008. "Improvisation as Continually Juggled Priorities: Julian 'Cannonball' Adderly's 'Straight, No Chaser.'" *Journal of Music Theory* 49, no. 2: 209–39.

Armstrong, Alayne C. 2008. "The Fragility of Group Flow: The Experiences of Two Small Groups in a Middle School Mathematics Classroom." *Journal of Mathematical Behavior* 27, no. 2: 101–15.

Arom, Simha. 1969. "Essai d'une notation des monodies à des fins d'analyse." *Revue de Musicologie* 55, no. 2: 172–216.

———. 1991a. *African Polyphony and African Polyrhythm: Musical Structure and Methodology*. Cambridge: Cambridge University Press.

———. 1991b. "Modélisation et modèles dans les musiques de tradition orale." *Analyse musicale* 22: 67–78.

Asnawa, I Ketut Gdé. 1991. "The *Kendang Gambuh* in Balinese Music." Master's thesis, University of Maryland.

Azim, Erica. 1999. "On Teaching Americans to Play Like Zimbabweans." *African Music* 7, no. 4: 175–80.

Baily, John. 2001. "Learning to Perform as a Research Technique in Ethnomusicology." *British Forum for Ethnomusicology* 10, no. 2: 85–98.

Bakan, Michael. 1999. *Music of Death and New Creation: Experiences in the World of Balinese Gamelan Beleganjur*. Chicago: University of Chicago Press.

Baker, Colin. 2001. *A Parents' and Teachers' Guide to Bilingualism*, 2nd ed. Clevedon, UK: Multilingual Matters.

———. 2006. *Foundations of Bilingual Education and Bilingualism*, 4th ed. Clevedon, UK: Multilingual Matters.

Barsalou, Lawrence W. 1999. "Perceptual Symbol Systems." *Behavioral Brain and Sciences* 22: 577–600.

Barsalou, Lawrence W., Paula M Niedenthal, Aron K. Barbey, and Jennifer A. Ruppert. 2003. "Social Embodiment." In *The Psychology of Learning and Motivation: Advances in Research and Theory*, edited by Brian H. Ross, 43–92. Amsterdam: Academic Press.

Bastien, David T., and Todd J Hostager. 1992. "Cooperation as Communicative Accomplishment: A Symbolic Interaction Analysis of an Improvised Jazz Concert." *Communication Studies* 43, no. 2: 92–104.

Bateson, Gregory. 1970. "Bali: The Value System of Steady State." In *Traditional Balinese Culture*, edited by Jane Belo, 384–402. New York: Columbia University Press. First published 1949.

Becker, Howard S. 2000. "The Etiquette of Improvisation." *Mind, Culture, and Activity* 7, no. 3: 171–76. DOI: 10.1207/S15327884MCA0703_03.

Becker, Judith. 1988. "Appendix 2: Javanese Cipher Notation (*Titilaras Kepatiahan*) of Musical Pieces Mentioned in the Texts." In *Karawitan: Source Readings in Javanese Gamelan and Vocal Music*, vol. 3, edited by Judith Becker and Alan H. Feinstein, 47–427. Ann Arbor: University of Michigan, Center for South and Southeast Asian Studies.

Benamou, Marc. 2010. *Rasa: Affect and Intuition in Javanese Musical Aesthetics*. Oxford: Oxford University Press.

Benson, Bruce Ellis. 2003. *The Improvisation of Musical Dialogue: A Phenomenology of Music*. Cambridge: Cambridge University Press.

Benson, J. Kenneth. 1977. "Organizations: A Dialectical View." *Administrative Science Quarterly* 22: 1–21.

Berkowitz, Aaron L. 2010. *The Improvising Mind: Cognition and Creativity in the Musical Moment*. Oxford: Oxford University Press.

Berliner, Paul F. 1993. *The Soul of Mbira: Music and Traditions of the Shona People of Zimbabwe*. Chicago: University of Chicago Press. First published 1978.

———. 1994. *Thinking in Jazz: The Infinite Art of Improvisation*. Chicago: University of Chicago Press.

Beyer, Kurt. 2009. *Grace Hopper and the Invention of the Information Age*. Cambridge, MA: MIT Press.

Bialystok, Ellen. 2001. *Bilingualism in Development: Language, Literacy, and Cognition*. Cambridge: Cambridge University Press.

Biasutti, Michele. 2017. "Flow and Optimal Experience." In *Reference Module in Neuroscience and Biobehavioral Psychology*. http://dx.doi.org/10.1016/B978-0-12-809324-5.06191-5. Accessed March 15, 2018.

Blacking, John. 1971. "Deep and Surface Structures in Venda Music." *Yearbook of the International Folk Music Council* 3: 91–108.

Blake, Ran. 2010. *Primacy of the Ear: Listening, Memory, and Development of Musical Style*. Brookline, MA: Third Stream Associates.

Blumer, Herbert. 1967. *Symbolic Interactionism: Perspective and Method*. Englewood Cliffs, NJ: Prentice-Hall.

Boden Margaret A. 2004. *The Creative Mind: Myths and Mechanisms*, 2nd ed. London: Routledge.

———. 2013. "Creativity as a Neuroscientific Mystery." In *Neuroscience of Creativity*, edited by Oshin Vartanian, Adam S. Bristol, and James C. Kauffman, 3–18. Cambridge: MIT Press.

Borgo, David. 1996. "Emergent Qualities of Collectively Improvised Performance." *Pacific Review of Ethnomusicology* 8, no. 1: 23–40.

———. 2005. *Sync or Swarm: Improvising Music in a Complex Age*. New York: Continuum.

———. 2016. "The Ghost in the Music, or the Perspective of an Improvising Ant." In *The Oxford Handbook of Critical Improvisation Studies*, vol. 1, edited by George E. Lewis and Benjamin Piekut, 91–111. New York: Oxford University Press.

Brick, Howard. 2000. *Age of Contradiction: American Thought and Culture in the 1960s*. Ithaca, NY: Cornell University Press. First published 1998.

Brinner, Benjamin. 1995. *Knowing Music, Making Music: Javanese Gamelan and the Theory of Musical Competence and Interaction*. Chicago: University of Chicago Press.

———. 2008. *Music in Central Java: Experiencing Music, Expressing Culture*. Oxford: Oxford University Press.

Brothers, Thomas. 2009 "Who's on First, What's Second, and Where Did They Come From? The Social and Musical Textures of Early Jazz." In *Early Twentieth-Century Brass Idioms: Art, Jazz, and Other Popular Traditions*, edited by Howard T. Weiner, 14–34. Studies in Jazz 58. Lanham, MD: Scarecrow Press.

Brown, Lee B. 2000. "'Feeling My Way': Jazz Improvisation and Its Vicissitudes—A Plea for Imperfection." *Journal of Aesthetics and Art Criticism* 58, no. 2: 113–23.

Bunk, Lou. 2011. "Timbre-and-Form: The BSC and the Boston Improvising Community." In *Analytical and Cross-Cultural Studies in World Music*, edited by Michael Tenzer and John Roeder, 225–62. Oxford: Oxford University Press.

Burnard, Pamela. 2002. "Investigating Children's Meaning-Making and the Emergence of Musical Interaction in Group Improvisation." *British Journal of Music Education* 19, no. 2: 157–72.

Burrows, Jared B. 2004. "Musical Archetypes and Collective Consciousness: Cognitive Distribution and Free Improvisation." *Critical Studies in Improvisation* 1, no. 1: 1–15.

Camilleri, Frank. 2008. "Collective Improvisation: The Practice and Vision of Ingemar Lindh." *TDR: The Drama Review* 52, no. 4: 82–97.

Campbell, Patricia S. 2001. "Unsafe Suppositions? Cutting across Cultures on Questions of Music's Transmission." *Music Education Research* 3, no. 2: 215–26.

Carson, Ciaran. 1996. *Last Night's Fun: In and Out of Time with Irish Music*. New York: North Point.

Charry, Eric. 2000. *Mande Music: Traditional and Modern Music of the Maninka and Mandinka of Western Africa*. Chicago: University of Chicago Press.

Chen, Mark, and John A. Bargh. 1999. "Consequences of Automatic Evaluation: Immediate Behavioral Predispositions to Approach or Avoid the Stimulus." *Personality and Social Psychology Bulletin* 25, no. 2: 215–24.

Chernoff, John Miller. 1979. *African Rhythm and African Sensibility: Aesthetics and Social Action in African Musical Idioms*. Chicago: University of Chicago Press.

Clark, John. 2010. "Mercedes-Benz History: The Route to the Riding Car." *Mercedes Benz*, August 10, http://www.emercedesbenz.com/autos/mercedes-benz/classic/mercedes-benz-history-the-route-to-the-riding-car/attachment/mercedes-benz-history-451858_759091_3592_2422_647106c38343a/. Accessed January 23, 2017.

Clarke, David. 2014. "On Not Losing Heart: A Response to Savage and Brown's 'Toward a New Comparative Musicology.'" *Analytical Approaches to World Music* 3, no. 2: 1–14.

Clayton, Martin, Byron Dueck, and Laura Leante. 2013. "Introduction: Experience and Meaning in Music Performance." In *Experience and Meaning in Music Performance*, edited by Martin Clayton, Byron Dueck, and Laura Leante, 1–16. Oxford: Oxford University Press.

Clayton, Martin, and Laura Leante. 2013. "Embodiment in Music Performance." In *Experience and Meaning in Music Performance*, edited by Martin Clayton, Byron Dueck, and Laura Leante, 188–207. Oxford: Oxford University Press.

Clayton, Martin, Rebecca Sager, and Udo Will. 2005. "In Time with the Music: The Concept of Entertainment and Its Significance for Ethnomusicology." *ESEM Counterpoint* 11: 3–75.

Coltrane, John, and Don DeMichael. 1960. "Coltrane on Coltrane." *Downbeat: Jazz, Blues, and Beyond.* http://www.downbeat.com/default.asp?sect=stories&subsect=story_detail&sid=1034. Accessed August 2, 2016.

Condon, William S., and William D. Ogston. 1971. "Speech and Body Motion Synchrony of the Speaker-Hearer." In *Perception of Language*, edited by David L. Horton and James J. Jenkins, 150–73. Columbus, OH: Charles E. Merrill.

Cook, Nicholas. 2013. *Beyond the Score: Music as Performance*. Oxford: Oxford University Press.

Cook, Nicholas, and Mark Everist, eds. 1999. *Rethinking Music*. Oxford: Oxford University Press.

Corbett, John. 1995. "Ephemera Underscored: Writing around Free Improvisation." In *Jazz among the Discourses*, edited by Krin Gabbard, 217–40. Durham, NC: Duke University Press.

———. 2016. *A Listener's Guide to Free Improvisation*. Chicago: University of Chicago Press.

Couch, Carl. 1986. "Elementary Forms of Social Activity." In *Studies in Symbolic Interaction: The Iowa School*, edited by Carl J. Couch, Stanley L. Saxton, and Michael A. Katovich, 113–29. Greenwich, CT: JAI Press.

Cowdery, James. 1984. "A Fresh Look at the Concept of Tune Family." *Ethnomusicology* 28, no. 3: 495–504.

Csikszentmihalyi, Mihaly. 1975. *Beyond Boredom and Anxiety: Experiencing Flow in Work and Play*. San Francisco: Jossey-Bass.

———. 1988. "Society, Culture, and Person: A Systems View of Creativity." In *The Nature of Creativity*, edited by Robert J. Sternberg, 325–39. New York: Cambridge University Press.

———. 1990. "The Domain of Creativity." In *Theories of Creativity*, edited by Mark A. Runco and Robert S. Albert, 190–212. Newbury Park, CA: Sage.

———. 1996. *Creativity: Flow and the Psychology of Discovery and Invention*. New York: Harper Perennial.

Cummins, Jim. 1998. "Immersion Education for the Millennium: What Have We Learned from 30 Years of Research on Second Language Immersion?" In *Learning through Two Languages: Research and Practice; Second Katoh Gakuen International Symposium on Immersion and Bilingual Education*, edited by M. R. Childs and R. Michael Bostwick, 34–47. Shizuoka, Japan: Katoh Gakuen.

Davidson, Jane W. 2009. "Movement and Collaboration in Music Performance." In *The Oxford Handbook of Music Psychology*, edited by Susan Hallam, Ian Cross, and Michael Thaut, 364–76. Oxford: Oxford University Press.

Davis, Miles. 1996. "Miles Davis." In *Reading Jazz: A Gathering of Autobiography, Reportage, and Criticism from 1919 to Now*, edited by Robert Gottlieb, 243–61. New York: Pantheon Books.

Dennett, Daniel. 2017. *From Bacteria to Bach and Back: The Evolution of Minds*. New York: W. W. Norton.

Diamond, Jared M. 1999. *Guns, Germs, and Steel: The Fates of Human Societies*. New York: Norton.

Dibia, Wayan. 1992. "*Arja*: A Sung Dance-Drama of Bali: A Study of Change and Transformation." PhD diss., University of California, Los Angeles.

Doleac, Benjamin. 2013. "Strictly Second Line: Funk, Jazz, and the New Orleans Beat." *Ethnomusicology Review* 18. https://ethnomusicologyreview.ucla.edu/journal/volume/18/piece/699. Accessed April 19, 2018.

Dowling W. Jay, James C. Barlett, Andrea R Halpern, and Melinda W. Andrews. 2008. "Melody Recognition at Fast and Slow Tempos: Effects of Age, Experience, and Familiarity." *Perception and Psychophysics* 70, no. 3: 496–502.

Dowling, W. Jay, and Dane L. Harwood. 1986. *Music Cognition*. Orlando, FL: Academic Press.

Ellingson, Ter. 1992. "Transcription." In *Ethnomusicology: An Introduction*, edited by Helen Myers. London: Macmillan.

England, Nicholas M., with contributions by Robert Garfias, Mieczyslaw Kolinski, George List, Willard Rhodes, and moderated by Charles Seeger. 1964. "Symposium on Transcription and Analysis: A Hukwe Song with Musical Bow." *Ethnomusicology* 8, no. 3: 223–77.

Eteläpelto, Anneli, and Jaana Lahti. 2008. "The Resources and Obstacles of Creative Collaboration in a Long-Term Learning Community." *Thinking Skills and Creativity* 3, no. 3: 226–40.

Feld, Steven. 1981. "'Flow Like a Waterfall': The Metaphors of Kaluli Musical Theory." *Yearbook for Traditional Music* 13: 22–47.

———. 1982. *Sound and Sentiment: Birds, Weeping, Poetics, and Song in Kaluli Expression*. Philadelphia: University of Pennsylvania Press.

Fernando, Nathalie. 1999. "Patrimoines Musicaux de la Province de l'Extrême-Nord du Cameroun: Conception Classification Vernaculaires Systematiques." PhD diss., Université de Paris IV (Paris-Sorbonne).

———. 2010. *Patrimoines Musicaux de l'Extrême-Nord du Cameroun*. Paris: SELAF.

Ferreras, Salvador E. 2005. "Solo Drumming in the Puerto Rican Bomba: An Analysis of Musical Processes and Improvisational Strategies." PhD diss., University of British Columbia.

Finke, Ronald. 1990. *Creative Imagery: Discoveries and Inventions in Visualization*. Hillsdale, NJ: Erlbaum.

Finke, Ronald A., John Baylis, and Thomas B. Ward. 1992. *Creative Cognition: Theory, Research, and Applications*. Cambridge, MA: MIT Press.

Flores, Eva Ordóñez. 2008. "Dance Improvisation Rules and Practice in the Cuadro Flamenco." *World of Music* 50, no. 1: 33–47.

Freed, Barbara F., Norman Segalowitz, and Dan P. Dewey. 2004. "Context of Learning and Second Language Fluency in French: Comparing Regular Classroom, Study Abroad, and Intensive Domestic Immersion Programs." *Studies in Second Language Acquisition* 26: 275–301.

Frisch, Lara. 2016. "Improvised Music and the Improbability of Communication." In *Researching Improvisation—Researching by Improvisation: Essays about the Exploration of Musical Improvisation*, edited by Reinhard Gagel and Matthias Schwabe, 204–23. Bielefeld: Transcript.

Fürniss, Susanne. 2006. "Aka Polyphony: Music, Theory, Back and Forth." In *Analytical Studies in World Music*, edited by Michael Tenzer, 163–204. Oxford: Oxford University Press.

Gabora, Liane, and Apara Ranjan. 2013. "How Insight Emerges in a Distributed, Content-Addressable Memory." In *Neuroscience of Creativity*, edited by Oshin Vartanian, Adam S. Bristol, and James C. Kauffman, 19–44. Cambridge, MA: MIT Press.

Gaggioli, Andrea, Alice Chirico, Elvis Mazzoni, Luca Milani, and Giuseppe Riva. 2017. "Networked Flow in Musical Bands." *Psychology of Music* 45, no. 2: 283–97.

Gaggioli, Andrea, Elvis Mazzoni, Luca Milani, and Giuseppe Riva. 2015. "The Creative Link, Investigating the Relationship between Social Network Indices, Creative Performance, and Flow in Blended Teams." *Computers in Human Behavior* 42: 157–66.

Geertz, Clifford. 1973. *The Interpretation of Cultures*. New York: Basic Books.

———. 1980. *Negara: The Theater State in Nineteenth-Century Bali*. Princeton, NJ: Princeton University Press.

Geertz, Hildred. 1995. *Images of Power: Balinese Paintings Made for Gregory Bateson and Margaret Mead*. Honolulu: University of Hawai'i Press.

Gerstin, Julian. 1998. "Interaction and Improvisation between Dancers and Drummers in Martinican Bèlè." *Black Music Research Journal* 18, no. 1/2: 121–65.

Gibbs, Raymond W., Jr. 2006. *Embodiment and Cognitive Science*. New York: Cambridge University Press.

Gitosaprodjo, Sulaiman, comp. 1984. "*Ichtisar Téori Karawitan dan Teknik Menabuh Gamelan* (Summary of the Theory of Karawitan and Technique of Playing the Gamelan)." Translated from Indonesian by Judith Becker. In *Karawitan: Source Readings in Javanese Gamelan and Vocal Music*, vol. 1, edited by Judith Becker and Alan H. Feinstein, 335–87. Ann Arbor: University of Michigan, Center for South and Southeast Asian Studies. First Published as *Ichtisar Téori Karawitan dan Teknik Menabuh Gamelan*. Malang: Keluarga Karawitan RRI Malang, 1970.

Givan, Benjamin. 2016. "Rethinking Interaction in Jazz Improvisation." *Music Theory Online* 22, no. 3 (September). http://mtosmt.org/issues/mto.16.22.3/mto.16.22.3.givan.html. Accessed February 20, 2019.

Glazzard, Jonathan, and Jane Stokoe. 2013. *Teaching Systematic Synthetic Phonics and Early English*. Northwich: Critical Publishing.

Gleason, Jean Berko, and Nan Bernstein Ratner. 2009. *The Development of Language*, 7th ed. Boston: Pearson Education.

Gloor, Peter A., Daniel Oster, and Kai Fischbach. 2013. "JazzFlow—Analyzing 'Group Flow' among Jazz Musicians through 'Honest Signals.'" *Künstl Intell* 27: 37–43.

Godøy, Rolf Inge, and Marc Leman. 2009. *Musical Gestures: Sound, Movement, and Meaning*. New York: Routledge.

Goffman, Erving. 1961. *Encounters: Two Studies in the Sociology of Interaction*. Indianapolis: Bobbs-Merrill.

Gold, Lisa. 1998. "The *Gender Wayang* Repertoire in Theater and Ritual: A Study of Balinese Musical Meaning." PhD diss., University of California, Berkeley.

———. 2005. *Music in Bali: Experiencing Music, Expressing Culture*. Oxford: Oxford University Press.

Goldberg, Joe. 1965. *Jazz Masters of the 50s*. New York: Macmillan.

Goodwyn, Andrew, and Jane Branson. 2005. *Teaching English: A Handbook for Primary and Secondary School Teachers*. London: Routledge.

Grauer, Victor. 2006. "Echoes of Our Forgotten Ancestors," *World of Music* 48, no. 2: 5–58.

———. 2014. "Toward a New Comparative Musicology: Some Comments on the Paper by Savage and Brown." *Analytical Approaches to World Music* 3, no. 2: 15–21.

Gray, Nicholas. 2010. "Of One Family: Improvisation, Variation, and Composition in Balinese Gendér Wayang." *Ethnomusicology* 54, no. 2: 224–56.

———. 2011. *Improvisation and Composition in Balinese* Gendér Wayang: *Music of the Moving Shadows*. Farnham: Ashgate.

Griffin, Farah Jasmine, and Salim Washington. 2008. *Clawing at the Limits of Cool: Miles Davis, John Coltrane, and the Greatest Jazz Collaboration Ever*. New York: St. Martin's Press (Thomas Dunne Books).

Grupe, Gerd. 2016. "Culturally Informed Analysis and Ways to Disclose Local Musical Knowledge." In *World Music Studies*, edited by Regine Allgayer-Kaufmann. Berlin: Logos.

Guck, Marion A. 1994. "Analytical Fictions." *Music Theory Spectrum* 16, no. 2: 217–30.

Gumperz, John J. 1982. *Discourse Strategies*. New York: Cambridge University Press.

Hagberg, Garry L. 2016. "Ensemble Improvisation, Collective Intention, and Group Attention." In *The Oxford Handbook of Critical Improvisation Studies*, vol. 1, edited by George E. Lewis and Benjamin Piekut, 481–99. New York: Oxford University Press.

Hall, Edward T. 1980. *The Silent Language*. Westport, CT: Greenwood Press. First published in 1959.

———. 1992. "Improvisation as an Acquired, Multilevel Process." *Ethnomusicology* 36, no. 2: 223–35.

Han, Youngju, and Rod Ellis. 1998. "Implicit Knowledge, Explicit Knowledge, and General Language Proficiency." *Language Teaching Research* 2, no. 1: 1–23.

Harker, Brian. 2008. "Louis Armstrong, Eccentric Dance, and the Evolution of Jazz on the Eve of Swing." *Journal of the American Musicological Society* 61, no. 1: 67–121.

Harrison, Spencer H., and Elizabeth D. Rouse. 2014. "Let's Dance! Elastic Coordination in Creative Group Work: A Qualitative Study of Modern Dancers." *Academy of Management Journal* 57, no. 5: 1256–83.

Hart, Emma, and Zelda Di Blasi. 2015. "Combined Flow in Musical Jam Sessions: A Pilot Qualitative Study." *Psychology of Music* 43, no. 2: 275–90.

Harvey, Sarah. 2014. "Creative Synthesis: Exploring the Process of Extraordinary Group Creativity." *Academy of Management Review* 39, no. 3: 324–43.

Hayes-Roth, Barbara, Lee Brownston, and Robert van Gent. 1998. "Multiagent Collaboration in Directed Improvisation." In *Readings in Agents*, edited by Michael N. Huhns and Munindar P. Singh, 141–47. San Francisco: Morgan Kaufmann.

Heimarck, Brita Renée. 2003. *Balinese Discourses on Music and Modernization: Village Voices and Urban Views*. Current Research in Ethnomusicology 5. London: Routledge.

Henry, Lucas Aaron. 2004. "Freedom Now! Four Hard Bop and Avant-Garde Jazz Musicians Musical Commentary on the Civil Rights Movement, 1958–1964." Master's thesis, East Tennessee State University.

Herbst, Edward. 1997. *Voices in Bali: Energies and Perceptions in Vocal Music and Dance Theater*. Hanover, NH: University Press of New England.

Herndon, Marcia. 1974. "Analysis: The Herding of Sacred Cows?" *Ethnomusicology* 18: 219–62.

Higgins, Lee, and Patricia Shehan Campbell. 2010. *Free to Be Musical: Group Improvisation in Music*. Plymouth, UK: Rowman and Littlefield.

Hodson, Robert. 2007. *Interaction, Improvisation, and Interplay in Jazz*. New York: Routledge.

Hofstadter, Douglas R. 1979. *Gödel, Escher, Bach: An Eternal Golden Braid*. New York: Basic Books.

Hood, Made Mantle. 2001. "The Kendang Arja: Improvised Paired Drumming in Balinese Music." Master's thesis, University of Hawai'i.

Hood, Mantle. 1960. "The Challenge of 'Bi-Musicality.'" *Ethnomusicology* 4, no. 2: 55–59.

Hsieh, Su-Ching. 2009. "Cognition and Musical Improvisation in Individual and Group Contexts." PhD diss., Institute of Education, University of London.

———. 2012. "Cognition and Musical Improvisation in Individual and Group Contexts." In *Musical Creativity: Insights from Music Education Research*, edited by Oscar Odena, 149–64. Farnham, Surrey: Ashgate.

Hugill, Andrew. 2012. *The Digital Musician*, 2nd ed. New York: Routledge.

Huron, David. 2006. *Sweet Anticipation: Music and the Psychology of Expectation*. Cambridge, MA: MIT Press.

Hutchins, Edwin. 1995. *Cognition in the Wild*. Cambridge, MA: MIT Press.

Israels, Chuck. 1999. "Performance Notes." In *Black Bottom Stomp: Composed by Ferdinand "Jelly Roll" Morton*. Essential Jazz Editions Set #1: New Orleans Jazz, 1918–27: n.p. Smithsonian Institution and Jazz at Lincoln Center. Miami: Warner Bros. Publications.

John-Steiner, Vera. 2000. *Creative Collaboration*. Oxford: Oxford University Press.

Johnson-Laird, Philip. 2002. "How Jazz Musicians Improvise." *Music Perception* 19: 415–42.

Karnani, Chetan. 2005. *Form in Indian Music: A Study in Gharanas*. Jaipur: Rawat Publications.

Katz, Dick. 1958. "Review: Recordings, Mile Davis." *Jazz Review* 1, no. 1: 28–31.

Kellar, Natalie. 2004. "Beyond New Order Gender Politics: Case Studies of Female Performers of the Classical Dance-Drama *Arja*." *Intersections: Gender, History, and Culture in the Asian Context* 10. http://intersections.anu.edu.au/issue10_contents.html. Accessed June 15, 2012.

Keller, Peter E. 2008. "Joint Action in Music Performance." In *Enacting Intersubjectivity: A Cognitive and Social Perspective on the Study of Interactions*, edited by Francesca Morganti, Antonella Carassa, and Guiseppe Riva, 205–21. Amsterdam: IOS Press.

Kenny, Ailbhe. 2014. "'Collaborative Creativity' within a Jazz Ensemble as a Musical and Social Practice." *Thinking Skills and Creativity* 13: 1–8.

Kenny, Barry J., and Martin Gellrich. 2002. "Improvisation." In *The Science and Psychology of Music Performance: Creative Strategies for Teaching and Learning*, edited by Richard Parncutt and Gary E. McPherson, 117–34. New York: Oxford University Press.

Kernfeld, Barry. N.d. "Improvisation, §III: Jazz." In *Grove Music Online*, edited by Laura Macy. *Oxford Music Online*. http://www.oxfordmusiconline.com.libproxy.mit.edu/subscriber/article/grove/music/13738pg3#S13738.3. Accessed August 28, 2016.

———. 1995. *What to Listen for in Jazz*. New Haven, CT: Yale University Press.

Kippen, James. 1985. "The Dialectical Approach: A Methodology for the Analysis of Tabla Music." *Bulletin of the International Council for Traditional Music (UK Chapter)* 12: 4–12.

———. 1992. "Tabla Drumming and the Human-Computer Interaction." *World of Music* 34, no. 3: 72–98.

Kubik, Gerhard. 1960. "The Structure of Kiganda Xylophone Music. *African Music* 2, no. 3: 6–30.

———. 1962. "The Phenomenon of Inherent Rhythms in East and Central African Instrumental Music." *African Music* 3, no. 1: 33–42.

Kurkul, Wen W. 2007. "Nonverbal Communication in One-to-One Music Performance Instruction." *Psychology of Music* 36, no. 2: 215–45.

Labov, William. 1972. *Sociolinguistic Patterns*. Philadelphia: University of Pennsylvania Press.

Lazaruk, Walter Andrew. 2007. "Linguistic, Academic, and Cognitive Benefits of French Immersion." *Canadian Modern Language Review* 63, no. 5: 605–27.

Leman, Marc. 2007. *Embodied Music Cognition and Mediation Technology*. Cambridge, MA: MIT Press.

Leman, Marc, and Pieter-Jan Maes. 2014. "The Role of Embodiment in the Perception of Music." *Empirical Musicology Review* 9, no. 3–4: 236–46.

Lemley, Mark A. 2012. "The Myth of the Sole Inventor." *Michigan Law Review* 110, no. 5: 709–60.

Lerdahl, Fred, and Ray Jackendoff. 1983. *A Generative Theory of Tonal Music*. Cambridge, MA: MIT Press.

Leroi, Armand M., and Jonathan Swire. 2006. "The Recovery of the Past." *World of Music* 48, no. 3: 43–54.

Lieberman, Fredric. 1967. "Relationships of Musical and Cultural Contrasts in Java and Bali." *Asian Studies* 5, no. 2: 247–81.

Lindh, Ingemar. 2010. *Stepping Stones*. Translated by Benno Plassmann and Marlene Schranz with the assistance of Magdalena Pietruska. Holstebro: Routledge.

Linell, Per. 2001. *Approaching Dialogue: Talk, Interaction, and Contexts in Dialogical Perspectives*. Philadelphia: John Benjamins.

Littleton, Karen, Sylvia Rojas-Drummond, and Dorothy Miell. 2008. Introduction to the special issue "Collaborative Creativity: Socio-Cultural Perspectives." *Thinking Skills and Creativity* 3, no. 3: 175–76.

Locke, David. 1998. *Drum Gahu: An Introduction to African Rhythm*. Tempe, AZ: White Cliffs Media.

Lortat-Jacob, Bernard. 1995. *Sardinian Chronicles*. Chicago: University of Chicago Press.

Mapaya, M. G. 2014. "Dinaka/kiba: A Descriptive Analysis of a Northern Sotho Song-Dance Performative Compound." *African Journal for Physical, Health Education, Recreation and Dance (AJPHERD)* 20, no. 2: 426–38.

Marchetti, Emanuela, and Kristoffer Jensen. 2010. "A Meta-Study of Musicians' Non-Verbal Interaction." *International Journal of Technology, Knowledge, and Society* 6, no. 5: 1–11. http://www.Technology-Journal.com.

Marian-Bălaşa, Marin, ed. 2005. "Notation, Transcription, Visual Representation." Special issue, *World of Music* 47, no. 2.

Marsalis, Wynton. 2009. *Marsalis: Racism and Greed Put Blues at the Back of the Bus—CNN Political Op-Ed, Social Commentary*, October 24. http://www.cnn.com/2009/OPINION/10/24/wynton.marsalis.blues.race/. Accessed August 2, 2016.

Mashino, Ako. 2011. "Between Classic and Modern: The Aesthetic and Social Evolution of Balinese *Arja* from the 1990s to the 2010s." Paper presented at ICTM World Conference, St. John's, Newfoundland.

Matusov, Eugene. 1996. "Intersubjectivity without Agreement." *Mind, Culture, and Activity* 3, no. 1: 25–45.

McAdams, Stephen, and Daniel Matzkin. 2003. "The Roots of Musical Variation in Perceptual Similarity and Invariance." In *The Cognitive Neuroscience of Music*, edited by Isabelle Peretz and Robert J. Zatorre, 79–94. Oxford: Oxford University Press.

McGraw, Andrew Clay. 2005. "*Musik Kontemporer*: Experimental Music by Balinese Composers." PhD diss., Wesleyan University.

———. 2008. "Different Temporalities: The Time of Balinese Music." *Yearbook for Traditional Music* 40: 136–62.

———. 2013. *Radical Traditions: Reimagining Culture in Contemporary Balinese Music*. Oxford: Oxford University Press.

McLean, Mervyn. 2006. *Pioneers of Ethnomusicology*. Coral Springs, FL: Llumina.

McPhee, Colin. 1966. *Music in Bali: A Study in Form and Instrumental Organization in Balinese Orchestral Music*. New Haven, CT: Yale University Press.

Meer, Wim van der. 1980. *Hindustani Music in the Twentieth Century*. The Hague: Martinus Nijhoff.

Mendívil, Júlio. 2016. "The Battle of Evermore: Music as a Never-Ending Struggle for the Construction of Meaning." In *World Music Studies*, edited by Regine Allgayer-Kaufmann, 67–91. Berlin: Logos.

Merriam, Alan P. 1964. *The Anthropology of Music*. Evanston, IL: Northwestern University Press.

Meyer, Leonard. 1957. "Meaning in Music and Information Theory." *Journal of Aesthetics and Art Criticism* 15, no. 4: 412–24.

Miller, Dan E., Robert A. Hintz, and Carl J. Couch. 1975. "The Elements and Structure of Openings." *Sociological Quarterly* 16: 479–99.

Miller, Sue. 2014. *Cuban Flute Style: Interpretation and Improvisation*. Lanham, MD: Scarecrow Press.

Monk, Augusto. 2013. "Symbolic Interactionism in Music Education: Eight Strategies for Collaborative Improvisation." *Music Educators Journal* 99, no. 3: 76–81.

Monson, Ingrid. 1996. *Saying Something: Jazz Improvisation and Interaction*. Chicago: University of Chicago Press.

———. 1997. "What's Sound Got to Do With It?: Jazz, Poststructuralism, and the Construction of Cultural Meaning." In *Creativity in Performance*, edited by Keith Sawyer, 95–112. Greenwich, CT: Ablex.

———. 1999. "Riffs, Repetition, and Theories of Globalization." *Ethnomusicology* 43, no. 1: 31–36.

———. 2007. *Freedom Sounds: Civil Rights Call Out to Jazz and Africa*. New York: Oxford University Press.

Moran, Nikki. 2013. "Social Co-regulation and Communication in North Indian Duo Performances." In *Experience and Meaning in Music Performance*, edited by Martin Clayton, Byron Dueck, and Laura Leante, 40–61. Oxford: Oxford University Press.

Morris, Lawrence D. "Butch." 2017. *The Art of Conduction: A Conduction Workbook*. New York: Karma.

Morris, Robert. 2001. "Variation and Process in South Indian Music: Some *Kritis* and Their *Sangati*." *Music Theory Spectrum* 23, no. 1: 74–89.

Morton, David. 1976. *The Traditional Music of Thailand*. Berkeley: University of California Press.

Morton, Jelly Roll. 1999. *Black Bottom Stomp: Composed by Ferdinand "Jelly Roll" Morton*. Essential Jazz Editions Set #1: New Orleans Jazz, 1918–27. Smithsonian Institution and Jazz at Lincoln Center. Miami: Warner Bros. Publications.

Myers, Helen, ed. 1992. *Ethnomusicology: An Introduction*. New York: Norton.

Neiwood, Kay, and Christianna English. 2012. "Jazz at Lincoln Center." In *Insights and Essays on the Music Performance Library*, edited by Russ Girsberger and Laurie Lake, 32–36. Galesville, MD: Meredith Music Publications.

Nettl, Bruno. 1974. "Thoughts on Improvisation: A Comparative Approach." *Musical Quarterly* 6, no. 1: 1–19.

———. 1987. "Transplantation of Musics, Confrontation of Systems, and Rejection Mechanisms." *Miscellanea Musicologica: Adelaide Studies in Musicology* 12: 100–108.

———. 1998. "Introduction: An Art Neglected in Scholarship." In *In the Course of Performance: Studies in the World of Musical Improvisation*, edited by Bruno Nettl and Melinda Russell, 1–23. Chicago: University of Chicago Press.

———. 2005. *The Study of Ethnomusicology: Thirty-One Issues and Concepts*, new ed. Urbana: University of Illinois Press.

———. 2009a. "On Learning the Radif and Improvisation in Iran." In *Musical Improvisation: Art, Education, and Society*, edited by Bruno Nettl and Gabriel Solis, 185–99. Urbana: University of Illinois Press.

———. 2009b. "Preface." In *Musical Improvisation: Art, Education, and Society*, edited by Bruno Nettl and Gabriel Solis, ix–xv. Urbana: University of Illinois Press.

———. 2010. *Nettl's Elephant: On the History of Ethnomusicology*. Urbana: University of Illinois Press.

Nettl, Bruno, and Ronald Riddle. 1973. "Taqsim Nahawand: A Study of Sixteen Performances by Jihad Racy." *Yearbook of the International Folk Music Council* 5: 11–50.

Nettl, Bruno, and Melinda Russell, eds. 1998. *In the Course of Performance: Studies in the World of Musical Improvisation*. Chicago: University of Chicago Press.

Nettl, Bruno et al. "Improvisation." *Grove Music Online*, edited by Laura Macy. www.oxfordmusiconline.com.libproxy.mit.edu/subscriber/article/grove/music/13738?q=improvisation/. Accessed March 14, 2016.

Nijstad, Bernard A., Michael Diehl, and Wolfgang Stroebe. 2003. "Cognitive Stimulation and Interference in Idea-Generating Groups." In *Group Creativity: Innovation through Collaboration*, edited by Paul B. Paulus and Bernard A. Nijstad, 137–59. Oxford: Oxford University Press.

Nooshin, Laudan. 2003. "Improvisation as 'Other': Creativity, Knowledge, and Power; The Case of Iranian Classical Music." *Journal of the Royal Musical Association* 128, no. 2: 242–96.

———. 2017. "(Re-)imagining Improvisation: Discursive Positions in Iranian Music from Classical to Jazz." In *Distributed Creativity: Collaboration and Improvisation in Contemporary Music*, edited by Eric F. Clarke and Mark Doffman, 214–35. Oxford Scholarship Online. DOI: 10.1093/oso/9780199355914.003.0019. Accessed October 17, 2018.

Olivier de Sardan, Jean-Pierre. 2015. *Epistemology, Fieldwork, and Anthropology*. Translated by Antoinette Tidjani Alou. New York: Palgrave Macmillan.

O'Neill, Brian, Andreya Piplica, Daniel Fuller, and Brian Magerko. 2011. "A Knowledge-Based Framework for the Collaborative Improvisation of Scene Introductions." In *Interactive Storytelling: Fourth International Conference on Interactive Digital Storytelling, ICIDS 2011, Vancouver, Canada, November 28–1 December, 2011; Proceedings*, edited by Mei Si, David Thue, Elizabeth André, James C. Lester, Joshua Tanenbaum, and Veronica Zammitto, 85–96. Berlin: Springer.

Onishi, Hideaki, and Pamela Costes-Onishi. 2010. "Improvisation in the Philippine Kulintang: An Analysis on Creativity in the Process of Imitation." Paper presented at the First International Conference on Analytical Approaches to World Music. University of Massachusetts, Amherst, February 19–21.

Ornstein, Ruby Sue. 1971. "Gamelan Gong Kebyar: The Development of a Balinese Musical Tradition." PhD diss., University of California, Los Angeles.

Paradowski, Michał B. 2008. "Corroborating the Role of L1 Awareness in FL Pedagogy." In *33rd International LAUD Symposium: Cognitive Approaches to Second/Foreign Language Processing; Theory and Pedagogy*, 515–80. Essen: Linguistic Agency University of Duisburg-Essen.

Paulus, Paul B. 2000. "Groups, Teams, and Creativity: The Creative Potential of Idea Generating Groups." *Applied Psychology: An International Review* 49: 237–62.

Paulus, Paul B., and Vincent R. Brown. 2003. "Enhancing Ideational Creativity in Groups." In *Group Creativity: Innovation through Collaboration*, edited by Paul B. Paulus and Bernard A. Nijstad, 110–36. Oxford: Oxford University Press.

Paulus, Paul B., and Bernard A. Nijstad. 2003. "Group Creativity: An Introduction." In *Group Creativity: Innovation through Collaboration*, edited by Paul B. Paulus and Bernard A. Nijstad, 3–11. Oxford: Oxford University Press.

Paulus, Paul B., and Bernard A. Nijstad, eds. 2003. *Group Creativity: Innovation through Collaboration*. Oxford: Oxford University Press.

Peal, Elizabeth, and Wallace E. Lambert. 1962. "The Relation of Bilingualism to Intelligence." *Psychological Monographs* 76: 1–23.

Pearce, Celia. 2016. "Role-Play, Improvisation, and Emergent Authorship." In *The Oxford Handbook of Critical Improvisation Studies*, vol. 2, edited by George E. Lewis and Benjamin Piekut, 445–68. New York: Oxford University Press.

Pearce, Marcus T., and Geraint A. Wiggins. 2012. "Auditory Expectation: The Information Dynamics of Music Perception and Cognition." *Topics in Cognitive Science* 4: 625–52.

Pelz-Sherman, Michael. 1998. "A Framework for the Analysis of Performer Interactions in Western Improvised Contemporary Art Music." PhD diss., University of California, San Diego.

Pentland, Alex "Sandy." 2008. *Honest Signals, How They Shape Our World*. Cambridge, MA: MIT Press.

Perlman, Marc. 1998. "The Social Meaning of Modal Practices: Status, Gender, History, and Pathet in Central Javanese Music." *Ethnomusicology* 42, no. 1: 45–80.

———. 2004. *Unplayed Melodies: Javanese Gamelan and the Genesis of Music Theory*. Berkeley: University of California Press.

Perman, Tony. 2015. "A Tale of Two Mbiras." *African Music* 10, no. 1: 102–26.

Pettengill, Richard. 2013. "Performing Collective Improvisation: The Grateful Dead's 'Dark Star.'" In *Taking It to the Bridge: Music as Performance*, edited by Nicholas Cook and Richard Pettengill, 37–69. Ann Arbor: University of Michigan Press.

Polak, Rainer, Nory Jacoby, and Justin London. 2016. "How West African Drummers Keep Time Together: Musical Roles and Individual Behavior in Ensemble Entrainment in Jembe Music from Mali." Paper presented at the Analytical Approaches to World Music Conference, the New School, New York.

Pressing, Jeff. 1984. "Cognitive Processes in Improvisation." In *Cognitive Processes in the Perception of Art*, edited by Ray Crozier and Anthony Chapman, 345–63. Amsterdam: North Holland.

———. 1988. "Improvisation: Methods and Models." In *Generative Processes in Music: The Psychology of Performance, Improvisation, and Composition*, edited by John A. Sloboda, 129–78. Oxford: Clarendon Press.

———. 1998. "Psychological Constraints on Improvisational Expertise and Communication." In *In the Course of Performance: Studies in the World of Musical Improvisation*, edited by Bruno Nettl and Melinda Russell, 47–67. Chicago: University of Chicago Press.

Pringle, Robert. 2004. *A Short History of Bali: Indonesia's Hindu Realm*. Crows Nest, NSW: Allen and Unwin.

Puterbaugh, Parke. 1997. "Phresh Phish." *Rolling Stone* 754: 42–47. http://www.rollingstone.com/music/features/phresh-phish-19970220. Accessed August 29, 2016.

Radano, Robert M. 1992. "Jazzin' the Classics: The AACM's Challenge to Mainstream Aesthetics." *Black Music Research Journal* 12, no. 1: 79–95.

Raymond, Eric S. 2001. *The Cathedral and the Bazaar: Musings on Linux and Open Source by an Accidental Revolutionary*, rev. ed. Sebastopol, CA: O'Reilly Media. First published in 1999.

Redhead, Lauren, and Vanessa Hawes, eds. 2016. *Music and/as Process*. Newcastle upon Tyne: Cambridge Scholars Publishing.

Reich, Steve. 2000. Foreword to *Gamelan Gong Kebyar: The Art of Twentieth-Century Balinese Gamelan Music*, by Michael Tenzer, xv–xviii. Chicago: University of Chicago Press.

———. 2002 "Postscript to a Brief Study of Balinese and African Music (1973)." In *Writings on Music, 1965–2000*, edited by Steve Reich, 69–71. New York: Oxford University Press.

Rice, Timothy. 1987. "Toward the Remodeling of Ethnomusicology." *Ethnomusicology* 31, no. 3: 469–88.

———. 1996. "Traditional and Modern Methods of Learning and Teaching Music in Bulgaria." *Research Studies in Music Education* 7, no. 1: 1–12

———. 2010a. "Disciplining Ethnomusicology: A Call for a New Approach." *Ethnomusicology* 54, no. 2: 318–25.

———. 2010b. "Ethnomusicological Theory." *Yearbook for Traditional Music* 42: 100–134.

Ricoeur, Paul. 1981. *Hermeneutics and the Human Sciences: Essays on Language, Action, and Interpretation*. Cambridge: Cambridge University Press.

Rinzler, Paul. 1988. "Preliminary Thoughts on Analyzing Musical Interaction among Jazz Musicians." *Annual Review of Jazz Studies* 4: 153–60.

Rubin, David C. 1995. *Memory in Oral Traditions: The Cognitive Psychology of Epic, Ballads, and Counting-Out Rhymes*. New York: Oxford University Press.

Ruwet, Nicolas. 1966. "Methodes d'analyze en musicology." *Revue Belge de Musicologie* 20: 65–90. Later translated by Mark Everist as: Ruwet, Nicolas. 1987. "Methods of Analysis in Musicology." *Music Analysis* 6, no. 1–2: 11–36.

Sanguinetti, Giorgio. 2012. *The Art of Partimento: History, Theory, and Practice*. Oxford: Oxford University Press.

Sanyal, Ritwik, and Richard Widdess. 2004. *Dhrupad: Tradition and Performance in Indian Music.* Aldershot: Ashgate.

Savage, Patrick E., and Steven Brown. 2013. "Toward a New Comparative Musicology." *Analytical Approaches to World Music* 2, no. 2: 148–97.

———. 2014. "Mapping Music: Cluster Analysis of Song-Type Frequencies within and between Cultures." *Ethnomusicology* 58, no. 1: 133–55.

Savage, Patrick E., Steven Brown, Emi Sakai, and Thomas E. Currie. 2015. "Statistical Universals That Reveal the Structures and Functions of Human Music." *PNAS (Proceedings of the National Academy of Sciences of the United States of America)* 112, no. 29: 8987–92.

Sawyer, Keith. 1992. "Improvisational Creativity: An Analysis of Jazz Performance." *Creativity Research Journal* 5, no. 3: 253–63.

———. 2007. *Group Genius: The Creative Power of Collaboration.* New York: Basic Books.

———. 2012. *Explaining Creativity: The Science of Human Innovation,* 2nd ed. New York: Oxford University Press.

———. 2015. "Group Flow and Group Genius." *NAMTA Journal* 40, no. 3: 29–52.

Sawyer, R. Keith. 1997. "Improvisational Theater: An Ethnotheory of Conversational Practice." In *Creativity in Performance,* edited by R. Keith Sawyer, 171–93. Greenwich, CT.

———. 2000. "Improvisational Cultures: Collaborative Emergence and Creativity in Improvisation." *Mind, Cultures, and Activity* 7, no. 3: 180–85.

———. 2003. *Group Creativity: Music, Theater, Collaboration.* Mahwah, NJ: Lawrence Erlbaum Associates.

Sawyer, R. Keith, and Stacy DeZutter. 2009. "Distributed Creativity: How Collective Creations Emerge from Collaboration." *Psychology of Aesthetics, Creativity, and the Arts* 3, no. 2: 81–92.

Scherzinger, Martin. 2010. "Temporal Geometries of an African Music: A Preliminary Sketch." *MTO* 16, no. 4. http://www.mtosmt.org/issues/mto.10.16.4/mto.10.16.4.scherzinger.html. Accessed April 30, 2018.

Schuller, Gunther. 1986. *Early Jazz: Its Roots and Musical Development.* Oxford: Oxford University Press.

Seabrook, Andrea. 2008. *All Things Considered,* NPR News, July 19. http://www.npr.org/templates/story/story.php?storyId=92710979. Accessed August 21, 2016.

Searle, John. 1990. "Collective Intentions and Actions." In *Intentions in Communication,* edited by Phillip R. Cohen, Jerry Morgan, and Martha E. Pollack, 401–16. Cambridge, MA: MIT Press.

Seddon, Frederick A. 2005. "Modes of Communication during Jazz Improvisation." *British Journal of Music Education* 22, no. 1: 47–61.

Seddon, Frederick, and Michelle Biasutti. 2009. "A Comparison of Modes of Communication between Members of a String Quartet and a Jazz Sextet." *Psychology of Music* 37, no. 4: 395–415.

Seeger, Anthony. 1992. "Ethnography of Music." In *Ethnomusicology: An Introduction,* edited by Helen Myers, 88–109. New York: Norton.

———. 2002. "A Tropical Meditation on Comparison in Ethnomusicology: A Metaphoric Knife, a Real Banana, and an Edible Demonstration." *Yearbook for Traditional Music* 34: 187–92.

Seeger, Charles. 1958. "Prescriptive and Descriptive Music Writing." *Musical Quarterly* 44: 184–95.

Shevy, Mark. 2008. "Musical Genre as Cognitive Schema: Extramusical Associations with Country and Hip-Hop Music." *Psychology of Music* 36, no. 4: 477–98.

Shumays, Sami Abu. 2013. "*Maqam* Analysis: A Primer." *Music Theory Spectrum* 35, no. 2: 235–55.

Sindoesawarno, Ki. 1987. "*Ilmu Karawitan* [Knowledge about Gamelan Music], Volume I." Translated from Indonesian by Martin Hatch. In *Karawitan: Source Readings in Javanese Gamelan and Vocal Music*, vol. 2, edited by Judith Becker and Alan H. Feinstein, 311–87. Ann Arbor: University of Michigan, Center for South and Southeast Asian Studies. First Published as *Ilmu Karawitan*. Surakarta: Konservatori Karawitan Indonesia, 1955.

Singh, Jasjit, and Lee Fleming. 2010. "Lone Inventors as Sources of Breakthroughs: Myth or Reality?" *Management Science* 56, no. 1: 41–56.

Small, Christopher. 1998. *Musicking: The Meanings of Performing and Listening*. Middletown, CT: Wesleyan University Press.

Smith, Christopher J. 1999. "'I Can Show It to You Better Than I Can Explain It to You': Analyzing Procedural Cues in African-American Musical Improvisations." PhD diss., Indiana University.

Solis, Gabriel. 2009. Introduction to *Musical Improvisation: Art, Education, and Society*, edited by Bruno Nettl and Gabriel Solis, 1–17. Urbana: University of Illinois Press.

———. 2012a. "Recent Trends in the Study of Musical Improvisation: Training the Interactive Musical Mind." Presented to the Japanese Association for the Study of Musical Improvisation, September 22–23. http://jasmim.net/2012The%20State%20of%20Research%20 in%20Musical%20Improvisation1.doc. Accessed January 10, 2017.

———. 2012b. "Thoughts on an Interdiscipline: Music Theory, Analysis, and Social Theory in Ethnomusicology." *Ethnomusicology* 56, no. 3: 530–54.

Spector, Stanley J. 2016. "The Grateful Dead and Friedrich Nietzsche: Transformation in Music and Consciousness." In *Countercultures and Popular Music*, edited by Sheila Whiteley and Jedediah Sklower, 157–70. London: Routledge.

Stanyek, Jason, ed. 2014. "Forum on Transcription." *Twentieth Century Music* 11: 101–61.

Stanyek, Jason, and Fabio Oliveira. 2011. "Nuances of Continual Variation in the Brazilian Pagode Song 'Sorriso Aberto.'" In *Analytical and Cross-Cultural Studies in World Music*, edited by Michael Tenzer and John Roeder, 98–146. Oxford: Oxford University Press.

Steele, Peter M. 2013. "Balinese Hybridities: Balinese Music as Global Phenomena." PhD diss., Wesleyan University.

Steinbeck, Paul. 2008. "'Area by Area the Machine Unfolds': The Improvisational Performance Practice of the Art Ensemble of Chicago." *Journal of the Society for American Music* 2, no. 3: 397–427.

———. 2013. "Improvisational Fictions." *MTO: A Journal of the Society for Music Theory* 19, no. 2.

Stock, Jonathan P. J. 2006. "Clues from Our Present Peers? A Response to Victor Grauer." *World of Music* 48, no. 2: 73–91.

Sudirana, I Wayan. 2009. "*Kendang Tunggal*: Balinese Solo Drumming Improvisation." Master's thesis, University of British Columbia.

Sum, Maisie. 2011. "Staging the Sacred: Musical Structure and Processes of the Gnawa Lila in Morocco." *Ethnomusicology* 55, no. 1: 77–111.

Sumarsam. 1984. "Inner Melody in Javanese Gamelan." In *Karawitan: Source Readings in Javanese Gamelan and Vocal Music*, vol. 1, edited by Judith Becker and Alan H. Feinstein, 245–304. Ann Arbor: University of Michigan, Center for South and Southeast Asian Studies.

First Published as "Inner Melody in Javanese Gamelan." Master's thesis, Wesleyan University, 1975.

Sutton, R. Anderson. 1982. "Variation in Javanese Gamelan: Dynamics of a Steady State." Ann Arbor, MI: University Microfilms.

———. 1993. *Variation in Central Javanese Gamelan Music: Dynamics of a Steady State*. Center for Southeast Asian Studies, Monograph Series on Southeast Asia, Special Report no. 28. DeKalb: Northern Illinois University.

———. 1998. "Do Javanese Gamelan Musicians Really Improvise?" In *In the Course of Performance: Studies in the World of Musical Improvisation*, edited by Bruno Nettl and Melissa Russell, 69–92. Chicago: University of Chicago Press.

Sutton, R. Anderson, and Roger R. Vetter. 2006. "Flexing the Frame in Javanese Gamelan Music: Playfulness in a Performance of *Ladrang Pankur*." In *Analytical Studies in World Music*, edited by Michael Tenzer, 237–72. Oxford: Oxford University Press.

Sweet, Jeffrey. 1978. *Something Wonderful Right Away: An Oral History of the Second City and the Compass Players*. New York: Avon Books.

Tanner, Jeremy. 2006. *The Invention of Art History in Ancient Greece: Religion, Society, and Artistic Rationalisation*. Cambridge Classical Studies. Cambridge: Cambridge University Press.

Taylor, Jeffrey. 1998. "Louis Armstrong, Earl Hines, and 'Weather Bird.'" *Musical Quarterly* 82, no. 1: 1–40.

Tenzer, Michael. 2000. *Gamelan Gong Kebyar: The Art of Twentieth-Century Balinese Music*. Chicago: University of Chicago Press.

———. 2006a. "Introduction: Analysis, Categorization, and Theory of Musics of the World." In *Analytical Studies in World Music*, edited by Michael Tenzer, 3–38. Oxford: Oxford University Press.

———. 2006b. "*Oleg Tumulilingan*: Layers of Time and Melody in Balinese Music." In *Analytical Studies in World Music*, edited by Michael Tenzer, 205–36. Oxford: Oxford University Press.

———. 2009. *Let Others Name You*. Performed by Genta Buana Sari collective, Sanggar Çudamani collective, OSSIA ensemble. New World Records. CD.

———. 2011a. *Balinese Gamelan Music*, 3rd ed. Tokyo: Rutland; Singapore: Tuttle Publishing.

———. 2011b. "Generalized Representations of Musical Time and Periodic Structures." *Ethnomusicology* 55, no. 3: 369–86.

———. 2018. "Polyphony." In *The Oxford Handbook of Critical Concepts in Music Theory*, edited by Alexander Rehding and Steven Rings. New York: Oxford University Press. DOI:10.1093/oxfordhb/9780190454746.013.32. Accessed October 26, 2018.

Tenzer, Michael, ed. 2006. *Analytical Studies in World Music*. Oxford: Oxford University Press.

Tenzer, Michael, and John Roeder, eds. 2011. *Analytical and Cross-Cultural Studies in World Music*. Oxford: Oxford University Press.

Theiner, Georg, and John Sutton. 2014. "The Collaborative Emergence of Group Cognition." In "*Commentary*/P. E. Smaldino: The Cultural Evolution of Group-Level Traits," 277–78. *Behavioral and Brain Sciences* 37: 243–95.

Thomas, Margaret E. 2014. "Conlon Nancarrow, 'Hot Jazz,' and the Principle of Collective Improvisation." *MTO: A Journal of the Society for Music Theory* 20, no. 1.

Thomson, Paula, and S. Victoria Jaque. 2017. "Understanding Creativity in the Performing Arts. In *Creativity and the Performing Artist*, edited by Paula Thomson and S. Victoria Jaque. A

Volume in Explorations in Creativity Research. London: Academic Press. https://doi.org/10.1016/B978-0-12-804051-5.00001-9. Accessed March 2, 2018.

Tilley, Leslie. 2003. "*Reyong Norot* Figuration: An Exploration into the Inherent Musical Techniques of Bali." Master's thesis. University of British Columbia.

———. 2013. "*Kendang Arja*: The Transmission, Diffusion, and Transformation(s) of an Improvised Balinese Drumming Style." PhD diss., University of British Columbia.

———. 2014. "Dialect, Diffusion, and Balinese Drumming: Using Sociolinguistic Models for the Analysis of Regional Variation in *Kendang Arja*." *Ethnomusicology* 58, no. 3: 481–505.

———. 2018. "Analytical Ethnomusicology: How We Got out of Analysis, and How to Get Back In." In *Springer Handbook of Systematic Musicology*, edited by Rolf Bader, 953–77. Berlin: Springer.

———. 2019. " 'The *Lanang* Is the Bus Driver': Intersections of Ethnography and Music Analysis in a Study of Balinese *Arja* Drumming." In *Computational Phonogram Archiving*. Volume 5 of Current Research in Systematic Musicology Series, edited by Rolf Bader, 37–74. Springer International Publishing.

Titon, Jeff Todd, ed. 2009. *Worlds of Music: An Introduction to the Music of the World's People*, 5th ed. Belmont, CA: Schirmer Cengage Learning.

Toner, P. G. 2007. "The Gestation of Cross-Cultural Music Research and the Birth of Ethnomusicology." *Humanities Research* 14, no. 1: 85–110.

Towse, Esmé, and Claire Flower. 1993. "Levels of Interaction in Group Improvisation." In *Music Therapy in Health and Education*, edited by Margaret Heal and Tony Wigram, 73–81. London: Jessica Kingsley Publishers.

Tracey, Andrew. 2015. "The System of the Mbira." *African Music* 10, no. 1: 127–49.

Tuedio, James A. 2013. Abstract for "Forces Torn Loose from the Axis: Collective Common Sense as a Strategic Factor in Successful Group Improvisation" for the Fifteenth Annual Meeting of the Grateful Dead Scholars Caucus, Albuquerque, NM, February 8–11, 2012. In *Studying the Dead: The Grateful Dead Scholars Caucus, An Informal History*, edited by Nicholas G. Meriwether, 251. Lanham, MD: Scarecrow Press.

Turino, Thomas. 2009. "Formulas and Improvisation in Participatory Music." In *Musical Improvisation: Art, Education, and Society*, edited by Bruno Nettl and Gabriel Solis, 103–16. Urbana: University of Illinois Press.

Vetter, Roger. 1981. "Flexibility in the Performance Practice of Central Javanese Music." *Ethnomusicology* 25: 199–214.

Vickers, Adrian. 2012. *Balinese Art: Paintings and Drawings of Bali, 1800–2010*. Tokyo: Tuttle Publishing.

Viswanathan, T., and Matthew Harp Allen. 2004. *Music in South India: The Karṇāṭak Concert Tradition and Beyond: Experiencing Music, Expressing Culture*. New York: Oxford University Press.

Vitale, Wayne. 1990. "*Kotekan*: The Technique of Interlocking Parts in Balinese Music." *Balungan* 4, no. 2: 2–15.

Walton, Ashley E., Michael J. Richardson, Peter Langland-Hassan, and Anthony Chemero. 2015. "Improvisation and the Self-Organization of Multiple Musical Bodies." *Frontiers in Psychology* 6: 1–9.

Wegner, Ulrich. 1993. "Cognitive Aspects of Amadinda Xylophone Music for Buganda: Inherent Patterns Reconsidered." *Ethnomusicology* 37, no. 2: 201–41.

Weick, Karl E. 2002. "Improvisation as a Mindset for Organizational Analysis." In *Organizational Improvisation*, edited by Ken N. Kamoche, Miguel Pina e Cunha, and João Vieira da Cunha, 49–70. London: Routledge.

Weinberg, Norman. 1994. "Guidelines for Drumset Notation." *Percussive Notes* 32, no. 3: 15–26.

Weisberg, Robert W., and Joseph W. Alba. 1981. "An Examination of the Alleged Role of 'Fixation' in the Solution of Several Insight Problems." *Journal of Experimental Psychology: General* 110, no. 2: 169–92.

West, Michael A. 2002. "Sparkling Fountains or Stagnant Ponds: An Integrative Model of Creativity and Innovation Implementation in Work Groups." *Applied Psychology: An International Review* 51: 355–87.

Widdess, Richard. 2011a. "Dynamics of Melodic Discourse in Indian Music: Budhaditya Mukherjee's *Ālāp* in *Rāg Pūriyā-Kalyān*." In *Analytical and Cross-Cultural Studies in World Music*, edited by Michael Tenzer and John Roeder, 187–224. Oxford: Oxford University Press.

———. 2011b. "Implicit *Raga* Knowledge in the Kathmandu Valley." *Analytical Approaches to World Music* 1, no. 1: 73–92.

———. 2013. "Schemas and Improvisation in Indian Music." In *Language, Music, and Interaction*, edited by Ruth Kempson, Christine Howes, and Martin Orwin, 197–209. London: College Publications.

Widjaja, N. L. N. Suasthi. 2002. "I Madé Kredek, 1906–1979: Kehidupan, Karya, dan Pemikirannya." Master's thesis, Universitas Gadjah Mada.

———. 2007. "Dramatari *Gambuh* dan Pengaruhnya pada Dramatari Opera *Arja*." PhD diss., Universitas Gadja Mada.

Wiedemann, Erik. 1975. "Une Minute Mystique de Jazz: Some Remarks on the Conditions of Collective Improvisation." *Musik & Forsknig* 1: 95–106.

Wiggins, Jacqueline H. 1999/2000. "The Nature of Shared Musical Understanding and Its Roles in Empowering Independent Musical Thinking." *Bulletin of the Council for Research in Music Education* 143: 65–90.

Wilf, Eitan. 2014. *School for Cool: The Academic Jazz Program and the Paradox of Institutionalized Creativity*. Chicago: University of Chicago Press.

Wise, David Burgess. 1974. "Lenoir: The Motoring Pioneer." In *The World of Automobiles*, edited by Ian Ward, 1181–82. London: Orbis Publishing.

Wolfram, Walt, and Ralph Fasold. 1974. *The Study of Social Dialects in American English*. Englewood Cliffs, NJ: Prentice-Hall.

Zadeh, Chloe. 2012. "Formulas and the Building Blocks of Ṭhumrī Style—A Study in Improvised Music." *Analytical Approaches to World Music* 2, no. 1: 1–48.

INDEX

Page numbers in italics refer to illustrations.

acid jazz, 293n24
acid rock, 35, 143
Afghanistan, fieldwork in, 63
Agawu, Kofi, on music analysis, 16
agent systems, 147, 166
Aka music, 307n16; constituent parts, 48; *dìyèí*, 201, 221; improvisation, 4, 48, 92, 166; *kònzàlémbò* (master of the song), 48; learning, 184; models for, 48; *mòtángòlè*, 201, 221; polyphonic singing, 4, 48, 92, 166, 220, 221
alap, 28, 43, 59, 90, 92, 102, 142, 296n25, 296n26; contour schemas, 37–38; embellishment techniques in, 37–38, *37*; expansion techniques in, 38–40, *39*, *40*; exploratory creativity, 38; and *gharānā*, 218; pitch schemas, 37–38, *37*; and raga, 37–38, 55; recombination techniques in, 38; and schemas for exploration, 36–40; *vistār*, as organizational principle of, 38, 123. *See also* Hindustani classical music
Alit. *See* Alit, I Dewa Ketut
Alit, I Dewa Ketut, 56, 57, 64, *66*, 67, 72, 81, 82, 86, 89, 94, 297n9, 302n38, 308n31; balance, on importance of, in improvisation, 235; conceptual space for *norot*, 54; core melody, flexible interpretation of, in *norot* improvising, 126–32; core melody, on importance of, in *norot* improvising, 116–17; creative pitch substitution, in *norot* improvising, 115–17; embellishment techniques, in *norot* improvising, 103–17; *empat*, in *norot* improvising, 119–20; expansion techniques, in *norot* improvising, 123–32; flexible timing, in *norot* improvising, 102–14; improvisation techniques for *reyong norot*, summary, 132–33; improvising *norot* for static core melody, 124; on individual agency and interaction in collective improvisation, 134–35; interpretation techniques, in *norot* improvising, 97–98, 99–101; on *norot* model ("base"), 74–77, 98; ornamentation, in *norot* improvising, 114–15; recombination techniques, in *norot* improvising, 118–23; teaching style, 51–54; on *wayah*, 104, 105–6, 108–12
Allen, Geri, and partnership, 155

Allman Brothers, as jam band, 293n24
Amadinda, Bugandan, and schema theory, 36
American folk revival music, realizations of a model, 145
Ammons, Gene, influence of, 26
Anak Agung Putu Gelgel, on *arja*, in Keramas, 310n21
Anak Agung Raka, 17, 192, 308n37; invisible collaboration, 25
Anak Agung Wiyat, on *arja*, in Keramas, 310n21
anak pukulan, 307n3. *See also* counting strokes
analytical approaches. *See* music analysis
analytical fictions, 295n17
analytical frameworks. *See* analytical models/frameworks
analytical models/frameworks, 15–16, 55, 74; for collective improvisation, broadly defined, 140–41, 158, 160, 174–77, 175, 176, 276; for improvisation, broadly defined, 28, 41–43, 42; and modelization, 26–27; for *reyong norot*, as broadly inclusive, 84–86, 85, 86; and typologies, 8–9, 13–14, 28, 140, 145
Anastasio, Trey, on mimicry, 36
angsel, 162, 186, 188, 199, 226, 228, 239, 245, 310n34
Anlo-Ewe dance-drumming, 8, 198. *See also* Ewe dance-drumming
Apuan: *arja*, 188, 191, 192, 193–94, 204, 238, 240, 241, 245, 310n37; *kendang arja* patterns, 209, 209
Arini, Ni Ketut, 65
arja, 2, 65, 73, 75, 179, 308n39; as Balinese opera, 186; characters in, 222–23; cyclic structures (*tabuh*) of, 187–88, 188; decline in popularity, 3, 222; defining of, 12–13; explicit vs. intuitive knowledge in, 186–90; *halus*, 224–26; improvised dialogue, 13; instrumentation, 12–13, 186–87; *keras*, 224–25, 240; pedagogical lineages, 240–41, 241; radio broadcasts of, 311n40; regional styles, 237–41; revitalization of, 222, 238; structure of performance, 12–13, 222–23
arja drumming. *See kendang arja*
Armstrong, Louis: improvisation, 3, 47, 293n23; influence from dancers, 310n30
Arom, Simha: on analysis, 18, 80; on equivalence, 307n17; on freedom and constraint, in improvisation, 198, 305n55; on models and modelization, 26, 49, 55, 190; on musical systems as codes, 294n13
Arsawijaya, Sang Nyoman, on improvisation, 10
ars combinatoria, 117
Art Ensemble of Chicago, interaction in collective improvisation, 149, 154, 161
ashtray, "sacred," 180
Association for the Advancement of Creative Musicians (AACM), free improv, 35–36, 143

Astra, I Ketut Buda, 11, 293n31, 307n19
attention: of analyst, 164; attracting of, 162, 163, 208; cognitive load, 150, 165, 305n51; commanding of, 159, 171; and communicative state, 165; to detail, in *arja* improvising, 209, 243; dividing of, 166–67; focusing of, 163, 166–67, 186; of listener, 89, 97, 208, 302n46; and need, 165; placing of, 165; prioritized integrative, 165
Azim, Erica, 311n5; on acquiring knowledge base, in mbira, 46

Bach, Johann Sebastian, 61
Baily, John: on bi-musicality, as term, 297n11, 298n15; on performing, as fieldwork, 63
Bakan, Michael: on familiarity and partnership, 154, 304n33; on "foreign" elements, in *beleganjur* compositions, 242; on improvisation, in Balinese drumming, 9–10; on learning to play, as research technique, 60, 298n15
balance: of creativity vs. control, 13; duality, of opposing elements in, 234–35; of established vs. new, 149; of fixed vs. flexible, 11; of individual vs. group, 8, 134, 135, 148, 153; of musical/performative roles in improvisation, 167, 198–201; of skill level vs. challenge, 152, 153–54; of sparse vs. dense, 228–29, 235
Bali, 29, 54, 89, 139, 144, 154, 235, 236, 240, 265; Batuan region of, 237, 239, 310n22; Buleleng region of, 237; fieldwork in, 58, 60, 61, 63–65, 71–74; as historically disjointed land, 237; immersion, experience of, 64–65, 67; improvisation, lack of in, 9; improvisation in, as neglected, 10; independent development of arts in, 237; interlocking, aesthetic of, 2, 11, 53; music, improvisation in, 10–11; nonverbal communication in, 161, 162–64; north, as *keras*, 236; paired drum traditions in, 1–2, 12–13; Pinda village, 244; preservation of arts in, 238; presumed rigidity in, 293n29; recording sessions in, 71–72; regional variation of arts in, 237–38; revitalization of arts in, 222, 238; rhythmic and melodic precision, praise of, 9; Saba village, 17, 25, 192, 237, 308n37; Sanur region of, 237; as spontaneous and flexible, 10; static and unchanging, stereotyped as, 10. *See also* Apuan; Keramas; Peliatan; Pengosekan; Singapadu; Ubud
Bali Arts Festival (PKB), 243, 310n21
Balinese Hinduism: balance, central to, 234; duality in, 234; *rwa bhineda* (two opposites), 234
Balinese performing arts: balance in, 234; coarseness (*keras*), 234; duality in, 234; preservation and revitalization in, 222, 238; refinement (*halus*), 234; regional variation in, 237–38

Balinese theater, as improvised, 10–11
balungan, 91, 190
Banda-Linda horn music, models for improvisation, 49, 190
Bandem, I Madé: on *arja asli* Singapadu, 243–45; on *arja* in Keramas, 310n21; on *wayah*, 104
bānī, 236–37, 245, 261
Baris: *empat* technique in, 52–53, *53*, 76; end-weighted beats in, *62*; end-weighted meter in, 61–62, *62*; gong structure in, 61; interlocking drumming in, 207–8, *208*
barong melawang, influence on *kendang arja*, 244
Barsalou, Lawrence W., on simulators, 150
"Bass-ment Blues," 156, *157*, 158
bass strokes: in *kendang arja*, 12, 27, 61, 161. See also *Dag* (D) strokes; *kendang arja*; *Tut* (T) strokes
Bastien, David T., nonverbal communication, 162
batel, 188, 206, 219, 245, 254, 256, 291n5, 293n27; density of drumming in, 226–27, 228, *230–31*, *232*, *233*, *233*; improvised drumming for, *227*; as *keras*, 225; and *ngegongin*, 258; vs. *tabuh telu*, drumming for, *228*; taught patterns, too sparse for, 234
batel marah, 188, 307n9, 310n34; density of drumming in, *230*, *232*, *233*; as *keras*, 225
batu-batu drumming, 9–10, 198, 293n27
bebop, 192, 220
Becker, Howard: on balancing autonomy with constraint, 148; on shared interest in improvisation, 160
Beethoven, meticulous composition technique, 295n17
Beiderbecke, Bix, on improvisation, 2
bèlè (Martinican): macrointeraction in, 174; musical communication in, 160–61; partnership in, 154–55; *réciprocité*, 151; shared knowledge and, 148
Bellson, Louis, on nonverbal communication, 163
Berata, I Dewa Putu, 52, 82, 135–36
Berata, Pak (dancer from Keramas), 238, 239
Berkowitz, Aaron: on constraint in improvisation, 26; on knowledge base, 296n34; on recombination, 31
Berliner, Paul: analyses of jazz improvisation, 3, 87, 177; on conceptual space, in jazz, 46; on embellishment, 100–101, 114; on harmonic rhythm in mbira music, 273; influence on popularity of *mbira dzavadzimu*, 311n5; on interpretation, 93; on levels of intensity in improvisation, 28, 87; on relationships in fieldwork, 63; on relative freedom of *kutsinhira* in mbira performance, 311n7; on stasis, freedom of, in improvisation, 124
Bicuh, I Ketut (Pak Tut), 235; conservative approach to improvisation, 209, 245–46, 260; cross-rhythm in *kendang arja*, 204, 252, 253; cyclic structure, intuitive knowledge of, 188, 209; *Dag-Tut* interactions, 209, 243; improvised patterns, 204; *ngegongin*, 214, *214*; "on-beat, off-beat" rule and, 209, 308n34; pedagogical lineage, 240–41, 261, 310n37; *ramé* and, 225; second-hand *arja* knowledge, 240–41, 245; teaching, 191, 192, 193–94
bi-musicality, 58, 298n15; basic musicianship and, 60
Bishop, Walter, Jr., recombination techniques, 118
"Black Bottom Stomp," collective improvisation in, 6–7, *7*
Blake, Ran, on kinds of listening, 298n14
bluegrass, 293n24
blues, 293n24
Boden, Margaret A., on creativity types, 294n7
"Body and Soul," 47
bomba, 91, 245; regional variation, 236
Borgo, David: analyses of improvisation, 177; on individual agency in collective improvisation, 134, 264; sync or swarm, 147, 306n69
Bowie, Lester, collective improvisation, 161
brainstorming techniques, 4
Braque, Georges, collaboration, 4
Brick, Howard, on AACM's collective improvisation, 36
Brinner, Benjamin: analyses of improvisation, 3, 198; on explicit knowledge, 307n12; on Javanese *imbal* variation techniques, 96; on musical competence and interaction, 3, 6; on roles in interaction, 164
Brown, Steven, on comparative analysis, 266–67
BSC (free improv group), 169, *170*, 171
Bu Candri. *See* Candri, Ni Nyoman
Buda. *See* Astra, I Ketut Buda
bulé, 258
Bulgarian music, tacit knowledge of, 189
Bunk, Lou, analyses of collective improvisation, 169, *170*

cadences, 75–76; of *legong*, 214; marked by change, 119–20, 127; signposting of, 214; *tihai* and *mora*, 127. See also *ngegongin*
calung, 66, 69, 77–79, 85, 99, 104–5, 108–9, 114–15, 125. *See also* core melody
campur-campur, 32, 196, 249, 275. *See also* recombination
Candri, Ni Nyoman, 10–11, 199, *199*, 220, 223, 238–39, 243
Carter, Ron, partnership in improvisation, 154–55
Carvin, Michael, on roles in improvisation, 166–67
Central African polyphonic improvising, 198–99, 307n17; singing, 201. *See also* Aka music

Central Javanese gamelan, 3, 9, 90, 91, 124, 190, 198; *gendér*, flexible timing, 102; *imbal* techniques, 96; *rebab*, embellishment, 37; scales, 297n12, 301n13; traditional pedagogy of, 185; variation/improvisation in, 38, 47, 123–24, 145. See also *balungan*

charanga: regional styles, 237, 245; *típica* style, 242

Clarke, David, on comparative analysis, 267, 269–70, 276, 311n2

cocok (suited), 16, 236; collective interlocking and, 262–63; and *pasangan*, 155; and *rasa*, 134; *tidak cocok* (incompatible), 240

cognitive processes, 14–15, 19, 147, 153, *176*, 178, 189, 264; and attention, 165; as basis for analysis, 17–18, 20, 135; cognitive load, 150, 165, 305n51; compatibility effect, 150; and creativity types, 23–25; distributed cognition, 151; entrenched situated conceptualizations, 150, 155, 174; improvisatory processes, influence on, 39, *41*; and improvisatory processes, overlapping of, *41*; information processing models, 149; simulators and, 150

cognitive schemas, 296n24; in Hindustani classical music, 36–38

cognitive studies: on familiarity and expectation, 56; on familiarity and recognition, 55–56; on links between gesture and perception, 59; on problem solving, 44–45

Cok Alit. *See* Hendrawan, I Cokorda Alit (Cok Alit)

Cok Oka Tublen. *See* Tublen, I Cokorda Oka

Coleman, Ornette, collective improvisation, 7–8

collaboration, 3–4; and creativity, 5; emergence, 168, 220, 264; group genius, 24–25; hackathons, 5; invisible, 24–26; original inventions and, 24. *See also* collective improvisation

collaborative emergence. *See* emergence

collaborative webs: as collective learning, 5; Route 128 vs. Silicon Valley, 4–5

collective creativity. *See* collective improvisation; creativity

collective improvisation, 3–4, 43, 58; and agency, 134; analysis of, 64, 71, 74, 92, 135, 140, 143, 166–67, 171–78, 228, *270*; analytical model of, 174–75, *175*, *176*, 177–78; attention and, 165–66; avant-garde, 7; as balance of individual creativity and group need, 8, 134, 135, 148; in Bali, 11, 12–13; blending of egos in, 153; in Central Javanese gamelan, 96; close listening in, 153; and *cocok*, 155; cognitive processes for, 149–51; as collaborative emergence, 167–69, 171, 220–21; and collective intention, 153, 172; communication codes, 158–59, 160–66; comparative analysis and, 5, 13–14, 16, 177–78, *177*, 265, 268–76; complete concentration, as necessary, 153; concept of, 5–9; as confrontational or competitive, 36; constraints and, 29; control in, 153; cooperative interaction, 160; creativity types and, 24–26; defining of, 6, 138–41; definition of, extended, 8–9; degrees of co-performer influence in, 171–74; as distributed invention, 5–9; as dynamic interaction, 138–40; effective communication in, 153; emergence, 167, 169–72, *170*, 220–21; equal participation in, 153; equal vs. hierarchical, 145–46, 166–67, 175, 177, 199, 296n25; experimental, 7; familiarity among co-performers, 154, 216–17; and flow, 151–53; formulaic variation and, 29; free jazz, 7–8, 35–36; give-and-take, as central to, 201; as group flow, 153–55, *153*; group goals in, 153; inherent rhythms and, 96–97; interaction, modes of, 159–60; interactional roles, 164–67; interaction and, 15, 50, 134, *135*, *141*, 147, 157, 158–74, *175*, *176*, 177–78, *177*, 216, *270*, *271*; intersubjectivity, 136, 167, 169–72, *170*; in jam bands, 7, 35–36; in jazz, 6, 7–8, 74, 91, 139, 145–46, 147, 148, 151, 156–58, 157, 166–67, 171, 172–73, 216; in *kendang arja*, 2, 5–6, 8, 11, 12, 261–64, *270*, *271*; in mbira music, *270*, *271*; microinteractions, 173; models, as designed to interact, 201; models, knowledge of, 144–45, *144*; models, realization of, 145–47, *146*; models, specificity and flexibility of, 142–44, *142*, *143*; models and knowledge bases, as dynamic, 155–56, *157*, *158*; motivic vs. macrointeractions, 171–74; musical considerations of, 141–58, *141*, *175*, *176*; musical roles in, 8, 91, 139, 164, 167, 172–74, 200–201, 272; and mutual trust, 154–55, 216–17; in New Orleans jazz, 6–7, *7*, 8; nonverbal communication, 161–66; nonverbal communication, as marker of interactional roles, 164–66; as participatory music, 6; partnership and, 154–55, 215–17, 242; performative roles in, 164, 198–200; potential for failure in, 153–54, 264; psychedelic, 7; recording of, for analysis, 71–72; reflective vs. reactive processes, 6; in *reyong norot*, 11–12, 14–15, 57, 90, 92, 143, 172, 177–78, *177*; risk and, 33; as shared knowledge, 147–51; sharing and not-sharing, alternating between, 172; terminology, as unstandardized, 6; in theater arts, 8; typology of, 8, 19, 140–41, 145; unpredictability of, 136, 148, 262–63, 264. *See also* creativity; improvisation; jazz; *kendang arja*; knowledge base; model; *reyong norot*

collectivity. *See* collective improvisation

colotomic music, 288n19

Coltrane, John: conceptual space for improvisation, 46; individual approach, 242 combinatorial creativity: conceptual combination and, 294n8; conceptual transfer and, 23; defining of, 23; embellishment and, 37; vs. exploratory creativity, 33, *33*, 37, 41–43, *42*; formulaic variation and, 31; in improvisation, 23, 24, *24*, 33, *33*; interpretation and, 31, 43; in *kendang arja*, 31–33; recombination and, 31, 33, 41, 43. *See also* creativity

combined flow, 304n28. *See also* group flow

communication, 15, 50, 72, 141; analysis, influence on, 18, 160; codes of, 160–61, 175; and collective improvisation, 147, 158–59; competence in, 45–46; and constraints, setting during performance, 156; exercises of, 35–36; group creation and, 136, 166; and group flow, 153; and interaction, 136, 158–59; interactional roles and, 165–66; of knowledge, 55–56; learning and, 184–85, 189; levels of culture and, 184–85; and listening, 8, 153; mimicry, as basic level of, 36; modes of interaction, 159–60; musical, 160–61; mutual gaze, 163–64; nonverbal (physical), 161–66, 264; between players, 124, 134, 136; sensitivity of, and bilingualism, 288n18; of speakers vs. musicians, 305n46; states of, 165–66; uptake, 164; verbal, 160, 161, 162, 184

communication codes. *See* communication

comparative analysis, 19; vs. comparative musicology, nineteenth century, 265–67; criticisms of, 266–67; cross-cultural comparisons, 16, 178, 140, 265, 268–76, *270*, *271*, *274*; frameworks for, 8, 14–15, *42*, 174–75, *175*, *176*; implications of, 265–68; of improvisation, 5–6, 14–15; models for, 140–41; to refine typologies, 28, 93–94, 141; reliance on broadly applicable categories, 114, 140; similarity and difference, as identifying, 268–69, 275; of underlying processes, 267–68; as unifying framework, 6, 276; within-culture, 177–78, *177*; within-genre, 57, 84–86, 101, 194, *197*, 259–61

comparative musicology: flaws of, 266; vs. New Comparative Musicology, 266–67; updated, 266–68

compatibility effect, 150

competence: communicative, in language, 45; without comprehension, 307n6; degrees of, 242, 305n37; individual style and, 242; musical, 3, 45–46; as precondition to collective improvisation, 305n37; shared, necessity of, 147

complex systems, 147, 167, 266

composition, 18; in Bali, 10, 12, 23, 52, 209, 212, 242, 299n29; creativity in, 23, 236, 242; and improvisation, as continuum, 26–28; mbira, 272, *273*

conceptual combination, 294n8; combinatorial creativity, informing of, 294n8

conceptual elaboration: and conceptual expansion, 38; and creativity, 23, *24*, 37; embellishment and, 37; expansion and, 38–39; and improvisation, 24; interpretation and, 43

conceptual expansion, 38, *41*. *See also* conceptual elaboration

conceptual space: combinatorial creativity and, 296n21; creativity and, 23; defining of, 23, 46; for improvisation, 46, 47, 50, 54–58; and improvisatory processes, 33; knowledge base and, 44–47; models and, 54–58; of *reyong norot*, 57, 85; unraveling, 54–75; as unspoken, 48–50, 54, 56. *See also* knowledge base; model

conceptual transfer, 22, 294n8; and creativity, 23, *24*, 37; embellishment and, 37; and improvisation, 24; interpretation and, 43

constraints, 269; cognitive, 26; in collective improvisation, 8, 12, 13, 148; creativity within, 26, 38, 43, 143; emotional, 26; freedom, enabled by, 148–49, 198–200, 211, 271–72; group/shared, 148–49, 155–56, 174; as impediment to creativity, purported, 303n14; in *kendang arja*, 36, 245; models for improvisation and, 26, 29, 201; musical, 26; perceptual, 26; and performative roles, 198–200; physical, 26; physiological, 26; of raga, 43; in *reyong norot*, 56, 94, 98–99, 143, 236; stylistic, 26

Corbett, John: on free jazz models, 55; on "yes, and . . ." rule, 306n69

core melody, 71, 100; ambiguity in, 129–31, *130*; analytical numbering, 84–86, *85*; as central to *reyong norot*, 65; defining of, 69; density and, 68–69, 77, 124–27; *empat* substitution and, 119–20; as end-weighted, *68*; and expansion, 123–32; function in gamelan, 65–67, 69; *gangsa norot* and, 76, 77–79; gong tone, 68, 69, 77–78, 81, 103; instruments of, 66, *68*, 69, 77, 99, 125; interpretation of, in Javanese gamelan, 96; kinetic quality of, 77–78, 118–20, 123–24, 124–27; parallels in, 131–32, *131*; *pokok*, 65; *reyong norot* and, 72, 76, 83, 92, 94, 103–4, 105–6, 108, 125–28, 129–32; shifts between tones, *85*; stratified polyphony and, 68–69, *68*, 298n26; as structurally important, 78, 99, 103, 116–17, 121, 122, 127

counting strokes, 195, 197, 213, 214, 243; in *dasar* (basic) pattern, 203–4; defining of, 181; and density, 223, 226; interpretation and, 246–47, 247, 268–69, 273–74; variation of, 203–4, 244–45, 257, 268–69, 273

country music, 293n24

Crawford, Kevin, communication in improvisation, 158–59

creativity, 9, 16, 54, 84, 276, 293n26, 298n24; boundaries of, 19–20, 22–24; cognitive processes of,

creativity (cont.)
  20, 296n21; as collaborative process, 3–5; collective/group, 24–26, 143–44, 160, 167; combinatorial, 23–24, 31, 33, 37, 41, 42, 42; conceptual combination and, 294n8; conceptual elaboration and, 23; conceptual spaces, grounded in, 23; conceptual transfer and, 22–23; and constraint, 8, 12, 13, 26, 143, 148, 156, 303n14; as cumulative and imitative process, 25; as derivative, 26; dialectal model of, 169; different types of, 23–24, 24, 27, 33, 42–43, 42, 296n21; distributed invention and, 5; exploratory, 23–24, 33, 33, 35, 37, 41, 42, 42; and familiarity, 22–23; and flow, 151–52; and group genius, 4–5, 24; and improvisatory processes, 33, 38, 42–43, 269; individual vs. group, 3–4, 13, 134, 135–36, 143–44, 148–49, 306n64; invisible collaboration and, 24–26; in larger groups, 4; models of, 303–4n16; patent law, rethinking of, 5; spontaneous, 3, 26; studies of, 14, 15; systems model of, 48, 156; transformational, 23–24, 258; See also collective improvisation; conceptual space; flow; improvisation; knowledge base; model
cross-rhythm, 21, 60; in empat, 122; in kendang arja improvisation, 251–57, 253, 254, 255, 256, 257, 271, 272, 274; in kendang arja taught patterns, 195, 252, 253, 256; in mbira music, 271, 272, 273; in reyong norot, 84. See also expansion
Csikszentmihalyi, Mihaly: on flow, 152–53; models of creativity, 156, 303n16
Cuba: bongo, improvisation in, 94; charanga, improvisation in, 237, 242
cubism, collaboration and, 4
Çudamani, Sanggar, 16–17, 81–82, 89, 235
cultural evolutionism, 266
Curie, Marie, collaboration, 4
Curie, Pierre, collaboration, 4
cycle-marking, 13, 103, 127, 212–15, 250, 253, 271; instruments for, 61–62, 71, 186–87, 186, 187; metrical hierarchy of instruments for, 206, 206. See also cadences; ngegongin

Dag (D) strokes, 181–83, 183, 204, 209–16, 223, 243, 245, 256–58, 262–63, 272. See also bass strokes; kendang arja; Tut (T) strokes; wadon
Dagomba drumming traditions, 198
Daimler, Gottlieb, internal combustion engine, as collaborative invention, 24
"Dark Star" (Grateful Dead), 163; as intertextual mass, 149
Darta, I Gusti Nyoman (Komin), 52, 192, 222–23; on batel marah, 307n9; on dasar, 202–3, 203; kendang arja style, 241; and Ketut, brother, 90,

134, 216; on regional style, 236; reyong norot style, 134
dasar (basic), 22, 27, 191, 194, 202–4, 206, 243, 257, 262. See also kendang arja
Dave Matthews Band, 293n24
Davis, Miles, 29, 47; on improvisation, 3, 109–10
Davis, Richard, partnership in improvisation, 155, 216
degrees: of collectivity, 305n54; of competence, 242; of creative license, 18; of freedom, 28, 34–35, 34, 43, 80; of influence, from co-performers, 171–74; of interaction, 15, 140, 171–74
deLisle Nelson, Louis, interpretation in jazz, 93
density. See ramé
Dewa, Pak. See Sura, I Dewa Nyoman (Pak Dewa)
dhrupad. See Hindustani classical music
distributed cognition, 151
distributed invention, 5; defining of, 138

Edison, Thomas, lightbulb, as collaborative invention, 24, 117
Egyptian classical music, heterophony in, 145
elastic coordination, 148
electronic music, 293n24
embellishment, 6, 36, 54, 80, 84, 91, 118, 124, 132, 167, 218, 220, 264, 293n26; in alap performance, 37–38, 37; in American folk revival music, 145; combinatorial creativity in, 37; conceptual transfer in, 37; creative pitch substitution as, 115–17; as cross-culturally applicable concept, 101–2; defining of, 37, 98, 101–2; vs. expansion, 38, 41; exploratory creativity in, 37; flexible timing as, 102–14, 113; idiomatic use, 98; as improvisatory process, 28, 37, 41, 42; in Javanese music, 37, 185; in jazz, 28, 37, 39, 43, 87, 98, 101–2, 201, 231, 242, 259; in kendang arja, 43, 206, 268; as level of intensity, 28, 87; ornamentation as, 114–15; recombined, 38, 111; in reyong norot, 101–17, 119, 132, 206, 268; on trompong, 43; in various genres, 39, 43, 87, 102, 145
embodiment, 90, 306n68; and analysis, 59–60; and competence, 147; embodied cognition, 59; embodied experience, of improvisation, 54, 57, 99; embodied solidarity vs. objectivity, 298n17; embodiment-cognition compatibility, 304n20; performance and, 59–62, 148; understanding and, 47, 59–60, 148
emergence, 15, 264; collectivity and, 167–74, 176; defining of, 167–69, 220; degrees of influence and, 171–74; in improv theater, 167–69, 171; in musical improvisation, 169–71, 170; music analysis and, 171–74; as partial, 171–74. See

also collective improvisation; interaction; intersubjectivity
empat, 53, 54, 188, 297n3, 300n45; aesthetic of, 122, *123*, 297n3, 300n45; defining of, 53, 120–21; extrapolating aesthetic of, in *reyong norot*, 122, *123*, 136; *rasa* (feeling) of, 119–20; as recombination technique, 119–20; as structural marker, 121, 212; substitutions, in *reyong norot*, 120–22, *121*, 126, 127, 130, *130*, 134, 136, 212; vs. *ubit telu*, 76
empathetic attunement, 304n28. *See also* group flow
enanga harp (Baganda), inherent rhythms, 96–97
end-weighted meter. *See* meter
entrenched situated conceptualizations, 150–51, 155, 174, *176*
equivalence, 142; as culturally bound concept, 56; formulaic, 111; in *kendang arja* patterns, 29–30; in *kendang arja* vs. mbira improvisation, 271–76; musical, 29–30, 56; octave, 53, 82, 84, 298n23; paradigmatic, 29, 56, 191, 307n17; between *reyong* and *gangsa norot*, 76; in *reyong norot* improvisations, 56–57, *56*, 113; as system-specific, 56, 296n21
ethnography: ethnographically informed analysis, 9, 16–20, 76–77, 87, 91–92, 118, 135, 220, 264, 276; ethnographic methods, 58–75. *See also* ethnomusicology; fieldwork; music analysis; oral music theory
ethnomusicology, 14, 58, 59, 62, 63, 64, 70, 89, 276, 300n7; analytical, 2, 16–20, 49, 67, 92; vs. comparative musicology, 265–67; dialectical, 73–74; Merriam's tripartite model for, 17–19; self-reflexive, 295n17. *See also* comparative analysis; comparative musicology; ethnography; music analysis
ethnopedagogy. *See* pedagogy
Ewe dance-drumming, 92, 117, 134, 145–46, 166; improvisation in, 76, 87, 94, 96, 111. *See also* Anlo-Ewe dance-drumming
expansion, 54, 84, 91, 101, 167, 218, 221, 264, 269; in *alap* performance, 38–39, *39*, *40*; ambiguity in model, using, 129; in combination, 256–57, *257*; and conceptual expansion, 38; contradictions in, 258–59; through cross-rhythm, 254, 256–59, 272; vs. embellishment, 38, 41; as exploratory, 43; as improvisatory process, 38, 43; individual pieces and, 129–32; individual style and, 245–46; in jazz, 39, 123; in *kendang arja*, 245–46, 254–61, 268, 272; and larger improvisational logic, 259–61; as liberal approach to improvisation, 259–61; motives, developing and extending of, 124; particularities of model, playing on, 129–32; as piece-specific, 123, 129–32; vs. recombination, 122; in *reyong norot*, 80, 116, 117, 122, 123–32, *133*, 268; stasis,

relative freedom of, 124–25; of taught patterns, 257; underlying structure, playing with, 124–27; in various genres, 43, 87, 124; *vistār*, 38–39, 123
expectation, 297n6; and anticipation, 150; channeling of, in social interactions, 164; and cognitive load, 150–51; compatibility affect and, 150; and improvisation, 43, 55–56, 91–92, 148, 154–55, 164; and listening, 55; nonverbal communication and, 161–62; performances, guiding of, 164; schemas as, 36; shared, 149, 154–56; subverting of, in improvisation, 109, 118, 256–57; unconscious, 36
experimental music, collective improvisation in, 7, 35–36
explicit knowledge, 14, 15, 49, 189, 202; defining of, 184; impact on analysis, 144–45, *144*; vs. intuitive knowledge, 185, 191; in *kendang arja*, 186–89, 191; in mbira, 270; of models for improvisation, 48, 50; in *reyong norot*, 77, 177, 183, 236; taught patterns and, 190; and technical learning, 184
explicit models, 49, 50, 177, 183, 185; analysis and, 144, *144*; in *gangsa norot*, 77, 236; in jazz, 14, 48; in mbira, 270. *See also* explicit knowledge; spoken models; unconscious models; unspoken models
exploration: as degree of improvisation, 34–35, 41–43, *42*, *142*; and exploratory creativity, 34–35; general schemas for, as models, 35–41, 55, 124, 142–43; mental structures of, 36
exploratory creativity: vs. combinatorial creativity, 33, *33*, 37, 41–43, *42*; conceptual elaboration and, 23, 37; conceptual expansion and, 38; defining of, 23; embellishment and, 37; expansion and, 38, 43; and exploration, 34–35; formulaic changes and, 41; in improvisation, 23, 24, *24*; recombination and, 33, 41, 43. *See also* creativity

Faber, Ann, on constraints in free improvisation, 156
familiarity, 261; for analysis, necessity of, 54, 55, 124–25; collective improvisation, reliance on, 154–55, 211, 215–17; and group flow, 154–55; in improvised traditions, as vital, 46, 59, 118; influence on recognition and expectation, 55, 56; listening and, 59; *pasangan* and, 154–55, 211, 215–17; performance, as fostering, 71
Favors, Malachi, collective improvisation, 161
Feld, Steven, ethnographically informed analysis, 91
Ferreras, Salvador E., on *bomba*, 91
Fey, Tina, improv comedy, 168

fieldwork, 15, 102, 189, 258; analysis, as complementary, 19, 49, 55, 57, 91–93, 220, 268; and contextual insight, 275; immersion as, 64–67; interviews as, 72–74; knowledge bases, to uncover, 50; knowledge of model and, 144–45, 220; lessons as, 74–75; listening as, 58–59; models, to uncover, 49, 55, 190; performing as, 59–64; playing experience, as useful, 62–63; recording sessions as, 71–72; techniques, 49, 58–75; transcription and, 67–70

Fitzgerald, Ella, 183–84

fixed playing: of *angsels*, 13; balanced with flexible, 11, 27–28, 43, 117, 125, 137, 139, 141, 146, 148, 198, 243; of gamelan compositions, 52, 54, 102; of *gangsa norot*, 12, 48, 70, 75, 77–79, 81, 236; of kendang, 12; in *kendang arja*, 198, 209, 243; liquid and solid relationships, 146; made flexible on *reyong*, 80–82, 125; as model for improvisation, 12, 48, 70, 75–76, 77, 81

flamenco, 27, 140, 147, 158; *duende*, 304n23; embellishment in, 102; improvisation in, 137–38; interactional roles, 166; *llamada*, 138, 139; models for, 35, 36, 141, 142, 143, 145; performative roles, 164; *remate*, 138–39; shared knowledge and, 148

flow: defining of, 151, 152; factors of, 152; as group phenomenon, 153; in improvisation, 151–54; as shared, 304n28; and *taksu*, 152. See also group flow

formulaic variation, 36, 132, 137, 295n18; combinatorial creativity and, 31, 42; defining of, 29, 34–35; vs. exploration, 34–35, 42, 57, 92, 124, 142–44, 142, 143; exploratory creativity and, 33, 42; as improvisation, 29, 34–35; interpretation and, 31, 43; in *kendang arja*, 28–34, 92; levels of improvisational freedom, 31; in mbira, 82, 92, 111; as paradigmatic substitution, 295n18; recombination and, 31–33, 41; in *reyong norot*, 57, 92, 96, 166; techniques for, 29–33; templates for, as models, 28–34, 55

free jazz, 28; civil rights movement, 293n25; collective improvisation in, 7, 8; failure and, 304n32; interactional roles in, 166; models for improvisation, 35–36, 55, 143, 177

Free Jazz (Coleman), 7–8

Freeman, Bud, nonverbal communication, 162

gamelan, 16, 223, 235, 293n26; compositional ingenuity, celebrated for, 10; as cyclic, 12; drumming in various genres of, 9–10, 12, 209; flexible timing, at ensemble level, 102; improvisation in various genres of, 9–11; makers of, 298n13; notation of, 298n26; as precomposed, 9, 52; rote, learning by, 52; spontaneous improvisation, purported lack of, 52–53. See also *gamelan gong kebyar*

gamelan beleganjur, 60, 298n15; *batu-batu* drumming, 9–10; composition in, 242; drum improvisation in, 9

gamelan geguntangan, 12; cycle-marking instruments, 186–87, *186*, *187*; naming of, 186–87

gamelan gong kebyar, 63, 89–90, 92, 186, 212, 237; analytical numbering, 84–86, *85*; annual competition of, 235–36; close player interaction, 9; cyclicity, centering on, 12, 59, 61; end-weighted meter and beats, 61–62, *62*, *68*; five-tone scale, use of, 57–59, *59*, 115; *gong ageng*, 61–62, 187; hanging gongs, 61; improvisation, downplaying of, 9–10, 52; improvisation in, 9, 11–12; influence on *arja*, 243–44; kinetic qualities of, 127, 213; *kotekan*, 12; *majalan* (dynamic), 213; melodic building blocks of, *68*, 69, 125; *ngubeng* (static), 213; nonimprovisatory, seen as, 9–10, 52, 53; paired tuning, 59; rote, learning by, 52; solfège, 58, *59*, *68*; stratified polyphony of, *68*, 69, 125; teaching of, 51–52, 65–67, *66*; transcription of, 67–69, 298n26; tuning system, 58–59, *59*. See also core melody; *gangsa*; *gangsa norot*; interlocking patterns; *reyong*; *reyong norot*

Gamelan Sekar Jaya, 65, 67, 75, 77

gangsa, 67, 81, 89–90, 116; defining of, 65; as fast elaborating instrument, 12, 69, 136; figuration styles, 70, 76, 94; interlocking melodies, 69–70, *70*, 78–79; *kempyung* tones, 94; learning, traditional pedagogy, 66, *66*; melodies, as fixed, 12, 48, 83, 236; as model for *reyong norot*, 14; *nyog cag* technique, 76; *polos*, 69–70, *70*, 78–79; *sangsih*, 69–70, 78–79, 94, 299n38; *ubit empat*, 76; *ubit telu*, 76. See also *gangsa norot*

gangsa norot, 67, *70*; *calung* core melody and, 77, 125; as fixed, 48, 106, 183, 236; interlocking figuration, 78–79, 94; *kempyung* (harmony tones), 79; model for, 77–79; as model for *reyong norot*, 14, 48, 75–77, *75*, 80, 98, 236; *ngubeng* vs. *majalan*, 77–78; vs. *noltol*, 77, 81; parallel figuration, 79, *79*, 94; *polos*, 69–70, *70*, 78–79; vs. *reyong norot*, 12, 14, 75, 81, 83–84, 96, 98, 183; *sangsih*, 69–70, *70*, 78–79

Garcia, Jerry: musical communication, 161; nonverbal communication, 163

Geertz, Clifford, Balinese tropes, 10–11, 237, 293n30

gendér wayang, improvisation and creativity in, 11, 23, 92

Gestalt psychology, nine-dot problem, 44

Getz, Stan, on improvisation, 43

gharānā, 236–37, 261

Gillespie, Dizzy, influence of, 47

Givan, Benjamin, on styles of interaction, 173

Gnawa *lila* performances, intent, 91
Gobleg, Pak (*arja* drummer from Medan), 239
Goffman, Erving, impression management, 162
Gold, Lisa, notation of gamelan music, 298n26
gong, in gamelan, function of, 61
gong ageng, 187–88
gong pulu, 187–88, 206, 212
Gordon, Dexter, influence of, 26
Gordon, Franklin, flow in improvisation, 151
Grateful Dead, 293n24; collective improvisation, 149; musical communication codes, 161; nonverbal communication, 163–64
Grauer, Victor, on comparative approaches, 265–67
Gray, Nicholas: on *gendér wayang* improvisation, 92; on improvisation, in Bali, 10–11
Griya, I Wayan, 310n28
group creativity. *See* collective improvisation; creativity
group flow, 15, 174–75, *176*, 301n20; body movement and, 306n68; collective improvisation as, 153–55; conditions for, 153–55, *153*; honest signals, 306n68; vs. individual flow within groups, 304n28; and models for improvisation, as dynamic, 155–58; and *pasangan*, 155–56; risk of failure and, 212. *See also* flow
group genius: vs. brainstorming, 4; collaboration and, 4–5; defining of, 4; group flow, 153–55; invisible collaboration and, 24–26; vs. lone genius, 4; unpredictability and, 147
group improvisation, 6. *See also* collective improvisation
Grupe, Gerd, on plural views, in ethnomusicological research, 300n7
Guck, Marion A., on analytical fictions, 295n17
Gung Raka. *See* Anak Agung Raka
guntang, 186–87, *187*, 188, 201, 202, 203, 206, 211
Gus Dé. *See* Widnyana, Ida Bagus Madé

hackathons, 292n14
Hagberg, Garry L.: on attention, 165; on weak and strong sharing, 306n67
Hall, Edward T., on levels of culture, 184–85
Hall, Jim, mutual trust in improvisation, 154–55
halus: defining of, 224; vs. *keras*, 224, 225, 226, 234; precomposed drumming and, 309n9; and *ramé*, 309n9; for *tabuh telu*, 225, 235
Hanna, Roland, on partnership in improvisation, 155, 216
hard bop, 45–46
Harris, Barbara, on flow, 151
Hawkins, Coleman, influence of, 26, 46–47
Hendrawan, I Cokorda Alit (Cok Alit), *181*, 199, *199*, 220, 245; cross-rhythm, 252, *253*, 254, *255*; *Dag-Tut* interactions, 262–63; denser playing, preference for, 223–25, *224*, 229, 233, 243–44; density in *kendang arja*, 228–29, *230–32*, 309n8; on improvisation, 28–29; influences, 240–41; on Keramas-style *arja*, 239–40; on *lanang* as leader, 200; on *lanang* freedom, 200; *lanang* improvising, *230*, *231*, *232*, 260–61; *lanang* patterns, *184*, *194*, *195*, 197, 200; liberal approach to improvisation, 228, 246, 250, *250*, 251, 254, 259–61, *260*; modularity of *arja* patterns, 194–96, *195*; musical interactions, *arja*, 161, 182–83, *184*, 216, *216*, 262–64, *262*, *263*; *ngegongin*, 213, *213*; nonverbal communication, 162; on "on-beat, off-beat" rule, 202; *pasangan*, 154, 155, 212, 216–17, *216*, *217*; pedagogical lineage, 240–41, *241*; on practice, 22, 28–29; precomposed interaction, *216*; recombination, use of, 250–51; on regional styles, 105–6, 238–40; on shared knowledge, 148; on *tabrakan* (collisions), 207–8; taught patterns, 191, 229, 252; taught patterns, as designed to interlock, 182–83, *184*; teaching, 63–64, 189, 191–93; *terbalik*, 195–96; *Tut* (T) stroke placement, 209–11, *210*, *211*
Herbst, Edward, on improvisation in Balinese theater, 10
heterophony, 13, 140; in *arja*, 13; as simultaneous variation, 145; vs. stratified polyphony, 303n10, 308n28
heteroriginal music, 140
Hindustani classical music, 55, 109; comparative analysis and, 269–70; *dhrupad*, 236–37, 245; interactional roles in, 165–66; *khyāl*, 270; models for, 57, 118; rag/raga, 3, 37–38, 109, 111; realizations of models, 145; tabla, 82, 98, 305n51; tala, 118. *See also alap*; *bānī*; *gharānā*
hip-hop, and schema theory, 293n24
Hodes, Art, nonverbal communication, 162
Hodson, Robert, analyses of jazz improvisation and interaction, 123, 177
Hofstadter, Douglas R., 291n8
Hood, Madé Mantle: cross-rhythmic patterns in *arja*, 252, *252*; interlocking *arja* patterns, 251–52, 308n25; on *ngegongin* and *ngematin*, 201; on *rumus*, 308n39; on *uger-uger*, 308n21
Hood, Mantle, on bi-musicality, 58, 60, 297n11
Hopper, Grace, collaborative development of COBOL, 292n16

immersion, as research tool, 64–67
improv comedy, 167–69, 171, 173; pushing boundaries, 306n60; sexist tropes in, 306n60. *See also* collective improvisation; emergence; improvisation; improv theater; intersubjectivity
improvisation: analysis of, 16–20, 54–55, 60, 64, 86–87, 91–92, 101, 166–67, 174–78, 191, 258,

INDEX · 339

improvisation (*cont.*)
267–76; balance in, 8, 11, 13, 134, 135, 148, 149, 167, 198, 228, 235, 261; in Balinese music, 10–13, 54, 67; in Balinese music, downplaying of, 9–10; in Balinese music, significance of, 10; as codified, 184, 191–92; cognitive processes of, 24–26, *41*, 149–51; cognitive schemas and, 36; collaboration and, 3–4; combinatorial creativity and, 23–26, *24*, 31; and composition, as continuum, 26–28; as concept, 22; and conceptual space, 46–50, 54–58; definitions of, 26–29, 34–35; degrees vs. processes of, unpacking, 28; as distinctive human practice, 28; as dynamic communication process, 159; as dynamic interaction, 138–40, 155–58; ensemble type, as shaped by, 91–92; equivalence and, 56–57; as Eurocentric term, 292n19; in Ewe music, 86–87; as exploration, 35–40; exploratory creativity and, 23–26, *24*; fixed models for, 12; in flamenco, 137, 141, 148; as flow, 151–55; as formulaic variation, 28–33; as free, 2–3, 143, 166, *170*, 198–99; guidelines, transcending of, 98; individual approaches to, 242–46, 259–61; individuality vs. collaboration, 2–3; as inspiring more improvisation, 105; instrument construction, influence of, 82–84; knowledge base, reliance on, 14, 44–47, 98–99, 236; larger musical context, influence of, 220–29, 233–35; level of freedom in, 2–3, 42–43, *42*, 80, 132, 199–200; "levels of intensity," 28, 37, 87, 93, 123; model, as based on, 14, 26–28, 54–55, 75–76, 141–47, 189–90; models, finding, 58–75; modular approach to, 117, 194–95; musicology of, 3, 5; phenomenology of, 269; practice, importance of, 3; processes of, 14, 28–33, *33*, 35–43, *41*, *42*, 91, 123, 220; regional styles, differences in, 235–41; risk of failure in, 212; spoken, as turn-based, 167; spontaneity, myth of, 21–22; spontaneity vs. preparation, 2–3; as spontaneous creativity within constraints, 26; stasis and, 122–23; structure marking in, 127; subverting expectations, 109, 118, 256–57; teaching of, 74–75, 179–85, 190–92; terminology for, as unstandardized, 6, 34–35, *34*; as umbrella term, 34; vs. variation, 28, 34–35. *See also* collective improvisation; creativity; embellishment; expansion; interpretation; jazz; *kendang arja*; knowledge base; mbira; model; recombination; *reyong norot*

improvised variations, 87. *See also* formulaic variation; improvisation

improviser: as creative genius, 2–3; as existential hero, 3; individuality vs. collaboration, 3; spontaneity vs. preparation, 3. *See also* collective improvisation; improvisation

improv theater, 8, 28–29; and chemistry, 155; dangers of over-rehearsing, 304n33; interactional synchrony and, 4; mutual trust, honing of, 304n33; as turn-based, 167, 173; "yes, and . . ." rule, 171. *See also* improv comedy; improvisation

Indian classical music. *See* alap; Hindustani classical music; Karnatak music improvisation

individual style, 15, 310n29; conservative, 245–46, 247, 259–61; improvisational logic and, 259–61; in *kendang arja*, 242–46, 250–54, 259–61; knowledge base and, 45, 47, 136; liberal, 245–46, 250–51, 252–53, 254, 259–61; model and, 45, 47, 54; as mutable, 242; and personal preference, 82, 150, 218, 220, 242, 245; reasons for, 244; regions, as synonymous with, 236–37, 245, 261; *sello* (personal stamp), 242

informal oral music theory. *See* oral music theory

inherent rhythms, 96–97, 274

Institut Seni Indonesia (ISI), 239, 309n18

interaction, 18; accommodation, 160; analysis of, 160, 162, 166–67, 268; autocratic action, 159–60; bodily cues, 161–64; as capricious, 262–64; chase, 160; in collective improvisation, 135, 139, 141, 158–69, 171–75, 177–78; common processes of, 268; communication codes, 160–66; competition, 160; complexity of, in improvisation, 50, 136; conflict, 160; conversational, 161–62; cooperative, 160, 306n69; with co-performers' musical ideas, 91; *Dag-Tut*, 212, 214, 243, 262–63, *263*; of dance with drummer, various genres, 16, 148; degrees of, 15, 140, 171–74; diachronic, 173–75, 306n69; distributed cognition and, 151; as dynamic, 139–40, 155–58, 157; elastic coordination, enabling of, 148; emergence and, 167–74; environmental considerations, 59; ethnographic, 9; factors of, in improvisation, 140–41, 158–69, *170*, 171–78, *175*, *176*; feeling, reliance on, 216; frameworks of, in Art Ensemble of Chicago, 149; in *gamelan gong kebyar*, 9; hierarchies of, 166, 177; human, forms of, 159–60; human-computer, 6; imitative, 221; as imperfect, 136; in improvisation, various practices, 3–4; of intentions, 167; interactional analysis, 162; intersubjectivity and, 167–74; vs. introspection, 163–64; in jazz, 3, 91, 123, 139–40, 148, 157, 162–63, 164, 166, 172–73, 216, 221; in *kendang arja*, 177, 208, 221, 271; *kom-peng*, 209–10; levels of, 163–64; macrointeraction, 173–75, 261–62; in mbira, 270, *271*; microinteraction, 173, 175; modes of, 140, 159–60, 174–75; moment-to-moment, 7, 134–36, 263; motivic, 173–75; musical, 139–40, 141–42, 145–47, 155–59, 157, 160–61, *170*, 202, 208, 220–21; musical vs.

conversational, 305n46; mutuality, 160; nature of, and international style, 173; in New Orleans jazz, 6–7; nonverbal communication, 161–66; openings, 160; with past performances, 91; precomposed, *216*, 235; of researcher, one-on-one, 70–75; in *reyong norot*, 94, 134–36, 177, 221; roles in, 164–67, 172–75, 177, 261; shared history of, 147–49, 262–63; sharing vs. not sharing, 172; social, 19; social panic, 160; in social situations, 150–51; studies of, musical, 3–4, 6; styles of, 172–74; synchronic, 173–75, 177, 270, 306n69; turn-based vs. simultaneous, 173–74; unpredictability of, and group genius, 147; widespread patterns of, 162. *See also* collective improvisation; interactional roles; interactional synchrony

interactional roles: analysis, informing of, 166–67; collective improvisation and, 167–69, 171, 174, 175; as communication states, 164; improvisational options and, 166–67; in jazz, 166–67; as mutable, 164–65; nonverbal communication and, 164–66; in various genres, 164–65

interactional synchrony, 4, 150–51; entrainment, 292n11; groove, 292n11

interlocking patterns, 46, 102, 198, 293n31; in Balinese precomposed drumming, 2, 10, 208, *208*, *212*, 302n32; in Banda-Linda horn music, 49; in Central Javanese gamelan, 96; cognition and, 301n17; on *gangsa*, 12, 69–70, *70*, 76, 77, 78–80, 84, 89, 99–100, 299n37; in *kendang arja*, 2, 13, 15, 29, 33, 71–72, 146, 148, 154, 173–74, 182–83, 193–94, 196, 202, 207, 209–12, 223, 243, 251–53, 261–64, 270, 272–73, 295n19; *kotekan*, 12, 297n3; in mbira, 50, 92, 146, 173, 221, 270, 271–73; polyphony, as subcategory of, 140, 145; on *reyong*, precomposed, 52–53, *53*, 54, 61; in *reyong norot*, 12, 14–15, 54, 70, 83, 84, 116, *116*, 120, 121, *121*, 128, *127*, 134–35, 136, 139, 143, 145, 166, 172, 177, 182, 221, 297n9. See also *gangsa norot*; *kendang arja*; mbira; *reyong norot*

interpretation, 27, 35, 54, 84, 91, 118, 122, 167, 218, 220, 264, 301n15; in *alap* performance, 36–37, *37*; in combination, 41, 43, 122–23, 249, 256–57, *257*; combinatorial creativity and, 33, *33*; conceptual elaboration and, 43; conceptual transfer and, 43; as cross-culturally applicable concept, 93–94; cross-rhythms, 254; defining of, 31, 93–94; idiomatic guidelines for, in *reyong norot*, 98–101; as improvisatory process, 28, *41*, 86; interchanging notes and rests as, 94–97; interchanging of notes as, 94–97; in jazz, 31, 93, 267–68; in *kendang arja*, 31, *31*, 33, 43, 80, 93–94, 200, 223, 245–47, *247*, 248, 249, 250, 251, 254, 256–57, 260, 262, 268–69, 273–74; in

mbira, 273–74; of nonverbal communication, 161–66; vs. recombination, 33, *33*; in *reyong norot*, 93–101, 113, 115, *132*, 268–69; as small-scale formulaic variation, 43; as variation, 34; in various genres, 43, 87, 93, 242

intersubjective flow, 304n28. *See also* group flow

intersubjectivity, 136, 275, 304n28; collectivity and, 167–74, *176*; defining of, 167–69; degrees of influence and, 171–74; in improv theater, 167–69, 171; musical analysis and, 171–74; in musical improvisation, 169–71, *170*; as partial, 171–74. *See also* collective improvisation; emergence; interaction

intertextuality, 6

intuitive (tacit) knowledge, 13, 46, 71, 74, 161, 198, 217; and challenges for research, 189–90; defining of, 185; vs. explicit knowledge, 185, 191; impact on analysis, 144–45, *144*; informal learning and, 184–85; in *kendang arja*, 186–89. *See also* explicit knowledge

Inuit, 295n17; singing games, 145

invisible collaboration, 24–26

Jackendoff, Ray: generative principles of music, 269–70; on meter, 206

Jaki Byard Quartet, 156, *157*, 158, 171

jam bands, 35, 143, 293n24

Jauk, improvisation and interaction, 16

jazz, 6, 17, 59; agent systems in, 147, 166; analysis of, 14, 156–58, 217–18; attention and, 305n52; chemistry, 155; cognitive simulators in, 150; collectivity and, 8, 139, 177; conceptual space of, 46–47; conservatism vs. liberalism, 259; as conversation, 91; embellishment techniques, 37, 43, 98, 101–2, 242; equivalence and, 56; expansion techniques, 39, 43, 123; explicit vs. intuitive knowledge, 185; flexible timing, as embellishment, 102; flow and, 151; improvisation, 3, 14, 25, 43, 86, 105, 109, *157*, 242; individuality vs. collaboration in, 2–3; institutionalization of, 294n11; interaction, 166–67, 172–74; interactional roles, 166–67; interpretation techniques, 31, 43, 93, 242, 246, 267–68; invisible collaboration and, 25–26; knowledge base, 48, 74, 185; "levels of intensity" in improvisation of, 28, 87, 93; macrointeraction, 173; models, 26, 35, 48, 55, 57; models, as dynamic, 156, 169–71; models, as explicit, 14, 48, 49, 144, 190; models, as flexible/relatively free, 7, 35, 90, 92, 143–44, *143*; models, as multivoice, 145; mordents, 37, 98, 114; motivic interaction, 139, 173, 221; musical interaction, *157*; musical roles, 91, 139, 164, 166–67, 172–73; nonverbal communication, 162–64; ornaments,

jazz (cont.)
    as embellishment, 114; partnership and familiarity, 155, 216; performative roles, 164, 166, 198, 268; recombination techniques, 118, 268; research in, 63, 73, 74, 91, 177, 198; scatting, 92; shared knowledge, 148; sharing vs. not sharing, 172; specificity-flexibility spectrum, 143; spontaneity vs. preparation in, 2–3; stasis, freedom of, 124; trading fours, 139, 173; tune and chord changes, as overtly stated, 190; verbal communication in, 160. *See also* collective improvisation; improvisation; New Orleans jazz
jazz studies, 6, 276, 292n19
Jean-Baptiste, Etienne, on partnership, 155
jegogan, 66, 69, 103, 116–17, 121, 125
Jelly Roll Morton, collective improvisation of, 6–7, *7*, 8

Karnatak music improvisation, 111; *alapana*, 43; *kriti*, 39, 43, 86, 127; *mridangam*, 82; *niraval*, 43, 127; *svara kalpana*, 39, 127; *tanam*, 43
Kebyar Jaya Semara, 127–28, *127–28*
kempyung, 80, 98, 116, 118–21, 126, 131; above model tones, *79*; analytical marking, *95*, 100; below model tones, 94, *95*; defining of, 79; in *gamelan gong kebyar*, 94; idiomatic use, in *reyong norot*, 99; in improvised *reyong norot*, 106, *107*, 110, 111, *112*, 113, *113*, 118, 119, 120, 122, *123*, 126, 131, *132*, 134–35, *136*; as interpretation, in *reyong norot*, 94–97, 100–101, *100*, *101*, 268–69
kendang (drum), 1; as ensemble leader, 12; as interlocking, 12; playing as precomposed, 2, 9–10, 12. See also *kendang arja*
kendang arja, 5, 7, 11, 16, 38, 44–45, 63, 72, 74, 80, 86, 117, 127, 140, 158, 162, 171–72, 178; *angsel*, 186, 199, 310n34; balanced roles in, 216; as balance of creativity and control, 13; as balance of freedom and constraint, 198–200; balancing of opposites, 234; balancing sparse and dense, 228, *229*, 233–35; collective creativity and, 25; as collective improvisation, 6, 8; as complex and subtle, 13; conservatism vs. liberalism, 245–46, 259–61; contradictions in rules, 258–59; co-performers, influence from, 221; counting strokes, 181, 203–4, 214, 246–47; as creativity with control, 13; cross-rhythm in, 251–56, 272–73; *Dag* (D) and *Tut* (T) strokes, 33, 182, *183*, 204, 209–12, 213, 243; *Dag* (D) strokes, placement of, 209–11, 214–15, 245; *Dag* on gong, 258–59; *Dag-Tut* interaction, 182, 209, *209*, 212, 214, 216, *216*, 243, 262, *263*; *dasar* (basic pattern), 22, 27, 202–3, *203*; density in, 75, 226–29, *227*, *228*, *229*, *232–35*, 233–35;

as designed to interlock, 2, 3, 183, *184*, 201, 261–62; embellishment techniques, 43, 206, 268; expansion techniques, 254–59; explicit knowledge, 186; as formulaic variation, 28–33; freedom in, 3; *gamelan gong kebyar*, influence on, 243; improvisation, as limited, 34, 223; improvisational logic, large-scale, 259–61; incompatible styles, 239; individual approaches, 242–46, 259–61; influence between drummers, 25, 185; innovation in, 25, 245–46, 259–60; interactional roles in, 165–66; interlocking, limits on improvisational freedom, 223; interlocking, reliance on, 15, 209, 221, 261–64; interlocking, unpredictability of, 262–64; interlocking ability of, 33, 71, 190; interpretation techniques, 31, *31*, 93–94, 246–47; intuitive knowledge, 186; Keramas style, 238–40; *keras* strokes, 310n34; knowing, different ways of, 15, 184–90; knowledge base, 50, 188–89, 197–215, 229, 240–41; *kom* (o) and *peng* (e) strokes, 181, *183*, 243; *kom-peng* interaction, 182, 203–4, 206–7, 209, 212, 263–64; *lanang*, 206–7; *lanang* player's improvisations, as simpler, 199–200; larger musical context, influence on improvisation, 222–35; larger musical context of, 220, 221–23; learning process of, 179–84, 185; left-hand strokes, 194; main vs. counting strokes, 93–94; *mbira dzavadzimu*, comparison, 270–76, *270*, *271*, *274*; model, 13, 15, 28–30, *30*, 35, 36, 49, 50, 92, 142, 145, 146, 177, 183, 188, 191, 197, 217–18, 270; model, as storehouse of patterns, 29; model, as unconscious, 183, 215–16, 217–18, 236, 263; model, individual approaches to, 242–46; as modular, 33, 195–97, 243, 245–54; motivic development in, *257*, 259–61, *260*; musical communication codes, 160; musical roles in, complementary, 200–15, 272; *ngegongin*, 212–15; *ngematin*, 201–12; *ngeseh*, 226; nonverbal communication, 163–64; note-doubling, 206; "on-beat, off-beat" rules, 202–4, *205*, 206–7; "on-beat, off-beat" rules as contradictory, 206–7, *208*; oral music theory, 19, 190, 191, 197–215; *pasangan* (partnership) in, 154, 215–17; *patokan* (rules), 198, 215–16; performative roles in, 198–200; precomposition in, 209; *pung* (U) stroke, 186; and *ramé*, 223–29, 233–35; *ramé*, analysis of, 226–33; recombination techniques, 31–32, 247–53, *251*; recording sessions of, 72, *73*; regional styles, differences in, 235–41; regional styles as incompatible, 148, 239–40; vs. *reyong norot*, 177–78, *177*; rhythmic building blocks, 33; rhythmic independence from singer, 13, 186; rhythmic rigidity of, 43; Singapadu style, 190, 228, 238, 239, 240–46;

spontaneity and nuance, reliance on, 13; structure-marking in, 212–15; as subtle and complex, 13; synchronic interactions of, 173; *tabrakan* (collisions), 183, 207–12, 262–63, 264; taught patterns, 191, *194*, 274; taught patterns, as models for improvisation, 29–30, 49–50, 183, 190–97, 217–18, 245–47, *247*, 259–63, 267–68, 271; teachers, *193*; *terbalik*, 195–96; traditional pedagogical practices, 179–84; transcription of, 68–69, 181, 188, 191, 219–20, 295n20, 306n2; *Tut* (T) strokes, placement of, 209–11; unpredictability of, 262–64; unsuccessful interactions in, 211–12; *wadon*, 206–7, 212; *wadon*, freer improvisation of, 199–200, 210–11, 258; *wayah* playing, 2, 191, 216, 221; younger players, lack of subtlety of, 243. *See also* Bicuh, I Ketut (Pak Tut); collective improvisation; counting strokes; Hendrawan, I Cokorda Alit (Cok Alit); improvisation; interlocking patterns; *lanang*; Sudirana, I Wayan (Sudi); Sura, I Dewa Nyoman (Pak Dewa); Tama, I Wayan; taught patterns; *wadon*

kendang arja asli Keramas. *See kendang arja*
kendang arja asli Singapadu. *See kendang arja*
kendang tunggal, 235, 239–40, 293n28
Keramas: *arja*, 238–40, 310n22; rules, purported lack of, in *kendang arja*, 240
keras: as character, 179, 192, 234, 236; vs. *halus*, 234, 240; in music, 224–26, 236, 240
khyāl. See Hindustani classical music
kinesthetic error correction (EC), 303n47
kinetic. *See majalan* (kinetic/dynamic)
klenang, 187–88, 206
knowledge: acquisition, 184–85; as explicit, 14, 48, 50, 58, 144, 174, 184–86, 188, 190–91, 236; independent, within a collective, 172; as intuitive/implicit/tacit, 19, 46, 49, 71, 74, 161, 174, 184–86, 188–91, 198, 202; of model, 144–45, *144*; as passive, 75; passive vs. active, 185, 207n10; as shared, 136, 147–49, 155; taught patterns and, 191–92; ways of knowing, 15, 184–89. *See also* explicit knowledge; intuitive (tacit) knowledge; knowledge base; shared knowledge
knowledge base, 136, 220, 242, 276; communication codes, 160; conceptual space, 44–47; defining of, 45–47; as domain, 48, 156; as dynamic, 155–56, 158; for *gangsa norot*, 78–79, *79*; instrument construction, influence of, 82–84; for jazz, 14, 46–47, 48, 74, 87, 98, 144, 160, 185; for *kendang arja*, 50, 188–89, 197–215, 229, 240–41; for language, elements of, 45; and microdomain, 156; as multifaceted, 45; regional styles and, 237; for *reyong norot*, 55–56, 57, 80–84; shared, 147–48; structural vs. social conventions of, 160. *See also* collective improvisation; conceptual space; creativity; improvisation; model

kom (o) strokes, 181–83, 202–4, 206–9, 243, 256–57, 263
Komin. *See* Darta, I Gusti Nyoman (Komin)
Konitz, Lee, 87, 98, 123, 242; on embellishment, 37; on improvisation, 34; on interpretation, 31; on levels of intensity in improvisation, 28, 93; on variation, 34
kotekan, 9, 11–12. *See also empat*; *gangsa norot*; interlocking patterns; *norot*; *nyog cag*; *reyong norot*
Kramer, Lawrence, on self-other binaries, 295n16
Kredek, I Madé, 240–42, 245, 310n28, 310n37, 311n40; *arja* drum patterns, 243–44, *244*
kulintang ensemble, interaction in, 139
Kunst, Jaap, on colotomy, 288n19
Kurkul, Wen W., on nonverbal communication, 305n45
kushaura, 271–73, 275, 311n7
Kuti, Fela, 21
kutsinhira, 271–72, 275, 311n7

lanang, 222, 226; beat, emphasis on, 201–4, 272; defining of, 12; density in, *227, 228, 230, 231, 232, 233*; improvisation on, 29–33, *30*, 227, 260–61; individual style in, 191, 223–25, *224*, 240, *244*; interpretation techniques, *31*, 246–47, *247*; as leader of ensemble, 186, 199, *199*, 216, 271; *ngematin* and, 201–2; "on-beat, off-beat" rules (bass strokes), 209–12; "on-beat, off-beat" rules (double strokes), 206–8; "on-beat, off-beat" rules (left-hand strokes), 202–5; *pung* (U) stroke, 186, 212–13; recombination techniques, 32, 248, 250; relative difficulty/scope for improvisation, 192–93, 198–200, 216, 250; rhythmic modules, 33, 194–96, 248, 249, 252; strokes, 182–83, *183*, 246; taught patterns, *30*, 194–95, *194, 195*, 197, *197*, 224, *253*; *wadon*, rhythmic relationship with, 12, 183, *184*, 198–200, 206–7, *207, 208*, 209–12, 240, 243, 252, 262–64, 268, 271–73, 295n19. *See also kendang arja*; *wadon*
language learning, 58; and competence, 45; intensive immersion and, 64; and music, comparison, 43, 46
language variation, 107–8, 124
Latri, Ibu (dancer from Keramas), 239
layālī, 3
learning, 9, 137, 278; in academies, 184, 239, 297n36; autodidactic practices, 184–85; dialogue and, 74; fundamentals, through performance, 60–61; gamelan, 51–52, 58–59, 61–62, 65–67, *66*, 70, 301n13; informal, 184–85;

learning (*cont.*)
kendang arja, 192–94; knowledge bases, 44, 46–47, 98; language, 58, 64; to listen, 35–36; mbira, 274–75, 312n8; models for improvisation, 35, 43, 49, 55, 141, 144; of musical systems, 58–59; oral, 51–52; partnership and, 154–55, 161; playing/performing for, 59–64, 192, 298n15; *reyong norot*, 51–52; as social process, 4–5; technical, 184, 185; traditional pedagogies, 61–62, 179–85; and ways of knowing, 15, 184–85. *See also* lessons; pedagogy

Lebah, I Madé, 241, 246

legong, 17, 244; *lanang* patterns, 224–25; *Legong Lasem*, 2; *pengawak* ending, for *kendang*, 212–13, 212

Lerdahl, Fred: generative principles of music, 269–70; on meter, 206

lessons, 1, 25, 29, 63, 70, 71, 131, 161, 182, 185, 186, 198, 249, 297n9, 307n8; dialogue during, 74–75; musicians' thought processes, as insight into, 74, 103, 125–26, 190–97, 217–18, 228, 311n7; oral music theory and, 15; pedagogical approach in, *kendang arja*, 189; pedagogical approach in, *reyong norot*, 76–77; as research technique, 19, 49–50, 64, 65, 74–75, 99, 189–90; and transcription, 68–69. *See also* learning; pedagogy

levels of culture: formal, 184; informal, 184–85; technical, 184, 185; and ways of knowing, 184–89

lightbulbs, innovation for, 24–25

Lindh, Ingemar, and collective improvisation, 8

lineage, pedagogical: in Hindustani classical music, 38; in *kendang arja*, 238–40; legacy of, 245

Linell, Per, on verbal interactions, 305n40

linguistics, and bilingualism, 288n18

Linus's Law, 292n15

listening: attentive, 59; close, and group flow, 153, 156; and competence, 45; as embodied experience, 99; and familiarity, 55; and immersion, 64–65; in improvisation, 8, 35–36, 136, 138, 139, 159, 163, 168, 171, 196, 304n33; insider's experience of, 89–90; intense, 61; in interviews, 73; and learning, 46–47, 61, 74, 76, 185, 244; nuanced, 64; in recording sessions, 72, *73*, 208; repeated, 59; as research tool, 16, 17, 29, 58–59, 64, 69, 71, 99, 236, 264, 309n1; self-reflexive, 264; styles of, 298n14; thoughtful, 59, 66–67

local oral music theory. *See* oral music theory

Loceng, I Wayan, on difficulty of *reyong*, 90

Locke, David, analyses of Ewe drum improvisation, 87, 92, 96

lone genius: vs. distributed invention, 5, 138; eureka moment, as overhyped, 4; legend of, 4

Lúnasa, improvisation and communication, 158–60, 164

macrointeraction, 173–74, 262; vs. independent simultaneous action, 306n69

majalan (kinetic/dynamic): in core melodies, 78, 213; in *norot*, 78, *78*, 118. *See also ngubeng* (static)

Marsalis, Wynton, on improvisation, 3

mbira, 3–4, 16, 29, 50, 92, 134, 192, 220, 311n5; collective improvisation, as egalitarian realization, 146; cross-rhythm, 272–73; field research and, 63; formulaic variation in, 82; inherent rhythms in, 96–97, 274; interlocking, 146, 202; interpretation techniques, 95–96, 273–74; *kendang arja*, comparison, 270–76, *270*, *271*, *274*; knowledge base, 46, 48–49; *kupururudza* singing, 221; *kushaura*, 271–73; *kutsinhira*, 271–72; musical context, and improvisation, 221; musical roles, 272; *Nhemamusasa*, 48, 272–73, *273*, 274; performative roles, 271–72; playing technique, 82; recombination techniques, 32, 117–18, 274–75; *Shumba*, 272; synchronic interactions of, 173, 270; versions of songs, 48–49, 111

mbira dzavadzimu, unbalanced popularity of, 311n5. *See also* mbira

McBee, Cecil, on collectivity, 139

McGraw, Andrew Clay, on *musik kontemporer*, improvisation in, 10

McLean, Mervyn, on comparative musicology, 266

McPhee, Colin: on improvisation in Bali, 9, 52; notation of gamelan, 297n12

Merriam, Alan, tripartite model, of ethnomusicological research, 17–18

meter, 139, 195, 199, 201; end-weighted, 62, *68*, 307n2; hierarchical conception of, 206; hypermeter, 214–15; unmetered music, 37, 102

Michelangelo, 276

microdomain, 156

microinteraction, 173; entrainment, related to, 306n68

microscopic interaction, 306n68

microtiming, 68, 219

Mingus, Charles, improvisation, 28–29

Mitchell, George, collective improvisation of, 6–7, *7*

model, 259–60; as analytical tool, 26–27; as broad concept, 27–28; as composed parts, 27; as contextualizing performance, for listener, 54–56; as continual feedback loop, 47; contradictory elements of, 258; *dasar*, 27; definitions of, 26–27, 48–49; as domain, 48; as dynamic, 149, 155–56, *157*, 158; explicitly known, 48, 77, 144–45, *144*, 185, 190; for exploration, general schema, 35–40; field, identifying of, 48; finding, as researcher, 58–75; flexibility of, 27, 41, 142–44; for formulaic variation, specific template, 28–33; for free jazz, 35; for *gangsa norot*, 77–79; as general schema, 35–40; importance to analysis and understanding, 54–57; improvisation on, 26; improvisatory processes, 41–43; individual approaches to, 242–46; as influenced by other models, 75–77; in jazz, 14, 26, 43, 48, 49, 55, 57, 92, 143, 144, 145–46, 177, 185, 190; for *kendang arja*, 13, 15, 28–30, *30*, 35, 36, 49, 50, 92, 142, 145, 146, 177, 183, 188, 191, 197, 217–18, 270; knowledge of, 144–45; multi-voice, 15, 145–46, *146*, 174–75, 177, 270, 272–73; as musical macro-units, 26; and musical roles, 201; for *Nhemamusasa*, 272, *273*; performance, contextualizing of, 54–56; realization of, 145–47, *146*; regional styles, 237; for *reyong norot*, 13, 14, 32, 48, 54, 56–58, 65, 67, 70, 74–79, 80, 86, *86*, 92, 94, 95–97, 106, 142–43, 177, 183, 189, 236, 268; as shared knowledge, 147–49; single-voice, 14, 145, *146*, 174–75, 177; spaces between, as improvised parts, 27; specificity of, 27–28, 41, 142–43; as specific template, 28–33; spoken, 48, 86–87, 144–45; as system of potentialities, 117; as umbrella term, 34; unconscious, 15, 55, 217–18; unspoken, 14, 48, 49, 54, 55–56. *See also* collective improvisation; conceptual space; creativity; improvisation; knowledge base

modes of interaction, 15, 50, 140, 159, 174–75; communication codes, 160–61; nonverbal communication and, 161–66

Molino, Anthony, symbolic analysis, 18, 293n35

Monk, Thelonious, 150; and collectivity, 306n66; influence, 47

Monson, Ingrid: on collective improvisation in jazz, 3, 6, 156, *157*; on liquid and solid musical elements, 146, 166; on music analysis as crucial, 17; poly-musicality, use of term, 298n15; research on jazz improvisation, 63, 73–74, 91, 177, 198, 299n33

Montgomery, Wes, on improvisation, 2

mora, 127

Moran, Nikki, on co-regulation and communication, 165

Morton, Jelly Roll, collective improvisation of, 6–7, *7*, 8

motivic interaction, 175, 261; in jazz, 173, 259; vs. macrointeraction, 173–74

mountain bikes, invisible collaboration and, 25

Moye, Don, collective improvisation, 161

Mukherjee, Budhaditya: *alap* of, 37–40; embellishments techniques, 37, *37*; expansion techniques, 38–39, *39*, *40*, 123

multi-voice models, 15, 145–46, *146*, 174; for *kendang arja*, 177, 270, 272–73; for mbira, 270, 272–73, *273*. *See also* model

musical roles, 8, 159; complementary, 200–201, 272; ensemble cohesiveness, contribution to, 167; equivalences in, 271; as fixed, 139; interactional roles and, 172–74; in jazz, 91, 139, 164, 166–67, 172, 201; in *kendang arja*, 173–74, 200–15, 216, 272; in mbira, 173, 272; nonverbal communication and, 164–66; practice-specific, 173–74; as predetermined, 174, 201; in various genres, 164, 201

music analysis: approaches, as diverse, 17–20, 49, 50, 58–75; cellular vs. global, 80, 90–91, 124, 124–25, 143–44, 220; challenges of, 14, 49, 67, 258; cognitive schemas and, 36; and comparison, 84–85, 114, 177–78, *177*, 265, 267–68, 269–70, *271*, *273*, 275–76; as concept, 16–19; constraint of model, as informing, 200; cross-cultural approaches to, 28, 140–41, 177–78, 265, 269–70, *271*, 272, *273*, 275–76, 288n18; cultural analysis, as complementary, 17–18, 19–20; defining of, 16–19; degrees of co-performer influence, as informing, 171–74; embodiment and, 59, 99; emergence and, 167; ethnographically informed, 5–6, 9, 15, 16–20, 86–87, 91–92, 118, 135, 198, 268, 275–76; familiarity and, 59, 60–61, 124–25; frameworks for, 15, 16, *42*, 174–75, *174*, *176*; genre-specific, 13–14, 177–78; immersion, as informing, 64–67; of improvisation, existing studies, 3–4, 5–6, 9–11, 177; individual approaches to improvisation and, 242–46; of interaction, 134–36, *135*, 156–58, *157*, 160–61, 164, 169, *170*, 171–74, 261–64, *262*, *263*; interactional roles and, 166–67; interviews, as informing, 72–74; knowledge, intuitive vs. explicit, as influencing, 144–45, *144*, 184; lessons, as informing, 74–75; listening to music, as informing, 58–59; Merriam's model and, 17–19; models for improvisation and, 26–27, 54–55, 58, 141–47, 220; as multimodal, 18, 141; musicians and, 16–17, 196, 264, 300n7; as "neutral," 18; oral music theory, as informing, 14–15, 197–98, 258–59; paradigmatic, 49; performance experience, as informing, 59–64, 99; piece-specific, 90, 123; recording sessions and, 71–72; rejecting hypotheses, 302n38; scale of, 80; shortcomings of, 135, 191–92; taught patterns, as informing, 190–92, 218, 258–59; traditional pedagogies and, 61–62; transcription and, 67–70; of unconscious models, 14, 55, 144–45, 189–90, 217–18; uses, as diverse, 19; zoom, differing levels in, 124, 143–44, 220. *See also* analytical models/frameworks; comparative analysis; oral music theory

musicology, 14, 276

music theory, 276, 293n33, 308n30. *See also* oral music theory

Myers, Helen, on performance, as shared experience in fieldwork, 62–63
"My Favorite Things," 150, 242

Natural History of Song project, 266
Nettl, Bruno: on comparative approaches, 265–67, 269; on composition vs. improvisation, 26, 295n17; on improvisation, 22, 26–27, 34; on models, 26, 296n33
networked flow, 304n28. *See also* group flow
New Orleans jazz, 201; as collective improvisation, 6–8, 7; musical roles, 201; performative roles, 198. *See also* collective improvisation; jazz
ngegongin, 202, 212, 216, 262; defining of, 212; as densification, 213; as increased activity, 213; metacycles and, 258–59, 259; vs. *ngematin*, 201; signposting, 214–15, 214, 215, 256; as structure-marking, 212; as *wadon*'s role, 212–15
ngematin, 216; defining of, 201–2; as *lanang*'s role, 201–2; vs. *ngegongin*, 201; as "on-beat, off-beat" rule, 201–12; *wadon*, off the beat, 201–2
ngeseh, 226, 227, 228
ngubeng (static): in core melodies, 77–78, 213; freer improvisation and, 124, 125; in *norot*, 77–78, 78, 118. See also *majalan* (kinetic/dynamic)
Nhemamusasa, 48, 272–74, 273, 312n8
nine-dot problem, 44, 44
niraval, 43, 127, 220–21
noltol, 297n3; vs. *norot*, 77, 81
nonverbal communication: communication states, 165; defining of, 161; impression management, 162; in improvisation, 162–64; interactional analysis and, 162; interactional roles, as marker of, 164–65; interaction and, 161–62; and *pasangan*, 216–17, 264; prioritized integrative attention, 165; uptake, 164
Nooshin, Laudan, on improvisation, 27, 295n16
norot, 12, 64, 68; defining of, 77–78; on *gangsa*, 75–77; *kempyung*, 79, 79; knowledge base, 82; *majalan* (kinetic), 78, 78; as *manis* (sweet), 122; "movability" of contour, 84–86, 85; *ngubeng* (static), 77–78, 78; pick-up gesture (3-note anticipation), 78–79; on *reyong*, 80–82; *reyong-gangsa* connection, 76–77; *reyong* players, improvising in, 54, 56, 56, 221. See also *gangsa norot*; *reyong norot*
Northern Ewe songs, variation in composition, 43
notation, 184, 295n20; Balinese mnemonic, 181–82, 203–4, 212–13, 246, 306n2; Balinese solfège, 62, 95; Javanese cipher, 301n13; limitations of, 67–68; staff, of Balinese genres, 62, 67–68, 102, 181–82, 212–13, 298n26, 306n2; systems, choice among, 67. *See also* transcription

Notre Dame Cathedral, thirteenth century consonance rules, 23
nyog cag, 76

octave equivalence, 52–53, 82, 94, 298n23, 299n34
old-time string-band music, formulaic variation in, 29
Oleg Tumulilingan, 51, 65, 69; alternate core melody, 129–31, 130, 131; core melody, 66, 68, 68, 77–78, 85–86, 85; core melody instruments, 68; *gangsa* melody, 70, 75, 78–79, 79, 95; *reyong norot* "base," 75, 75; *reyong norot* for, 83–84, 99, 104
openings, 160
open-source software (OSS), 292n14
oral music theory, 14, 87, 91, 190, 218; formal, 197–98; informal, 197–98; in *kendang arja*, 197–215
ornamentation, 102, 117, 139, 145, 189, 296n21; in Ewe drumming, 111; in jazz, 37; in *reyong norot*, 114–15, 114, 115. *See also* embellishment
Ory, Kid: characteristic style of, 242; collective improvisation of, 6–7, 7

pagode, 55, 75–76, 127; cadential variations, 121; *chamadas*, 129; performative roles in, 164; *roda* events, 127
paired improvisation, 2, 6. *See also* collective improvisation; *kendang arja*
Pak Dewa. *See* Sura, I Dewa Nyoman (Pak Dewa)
Pak Sidja. *See* Sidja, I Wayan
Pak Tama. *See* Tama, I Wayan
Pak Tut. *See* Bicuh, I Ketut (Pak Tut)
paradigmatic analysis. *See* music analysis
paradigmatic equivalence. *See* equivalence
Parker, Charlie, 3; influence, 26, 47
partimento, improvisation, 55, 98
partnership. *See pasangan* (partnership)
pasangan (partnership), 4–5, 86, 156, 241; defining of, 154; and improvisation, 215–18, 217, 221, 242; mutual trust, developing of, 60, 154–55, 217; as precomposed interactions, 216, 216. See also *cocok* (suited)
Pasek. *See* Sucipta, I Wayan Pasek
patent law, and collaborative process, 4, 5
patokan, 198, 202, 215–16, 240
Patrem, Pak (late *arja* drummer from Apuan), 193, 245, 310n37
pedagogy, 6, 305n45; autodidactic practices, 184–85; didactic practices, 49, 190, 228; ethnopedagogy, in Java, 185; in flamenco, 137–38; of improvisation, 15, 74, 184; "learning-without-teaching," 184; lineages of, 38, 238–41, 241, 245–46, 311n38; traditional, 60, 61, 118, 184, 272; traditional Balinese, 29–30, 53–54, 61–62, 65–67, 66, 74–75, 76–77, 98, 179–81, 191, 192–

94, 202, 225, 228, 297n5; ways of knowing and, 15, 29–30, 184–85, 188–89. *See also* learning; lessons
Peliatan, 17, 237; *arja*, 63, 192, 194, 228, 238, 240–41, 245
Pelz-Sherman, Michael: on communication states, 165; on heteroriginal music, 140; on interactional styles, 165, 172, 305n46, 306n69
pemetit, 83, 114–15, 124
peng (e) strokes, 182–83, 194–97, 202–4, 206–9, 226–27, 243, 246–47, 250
pengenter, 83–84, 97, 116, 128, 134, 301n21
Pengosekan, 16, 202, 235, 236; *arja*, 26, 32, 192, 222, 228, 238, 240–41, 241, 245
penyacah, 66, 69, 127–28; relationship to *calung*, 299n29
penyorog, 83–84, 94, 96, 114, 116, 130–31, 134
performance: cognitive benefits of, 288n18; embodied cognition, 59; embodiment and, 47, 57, 59–60, 62, 99, 158, 298n17; fundamentals, embodying through, 27, 60–61; for learning, 59–62; lessons, 74–75, 99; *rasa* (feeling), developing of, 60–61; as research tool, 9, 19, 27, 58, 59–64, 142–45, 258, 275–76; social connections, gaining through, 62–64; traditional pedagogies, learning through, 61–62; as unique/temporary model, 35–36, 147–49, 155–58
performative roles, 167; analysis and, 174; complementary, 272; equivalences in, 271; interactional roles and, 165; in jazz, 164, 198, 268; in *kendang arja*, 198–200, 201, 268, 271; in mbira, 271–72; as practice-specific, 164, 174, 200–201; in various genres, 164, 198
performing. *See* performance
perkembangan, 10
Perlman, Marc: on benefits of music analysis, 17; on cognitive categories, 296n21; use of Javanese oral music theory, in research, 91
Peterson, Ralph, on partnership, 155
Phish, 293n24; collective improvisation of, 36; Including Your Own Hey exercise, 35–36
Picasso, Pablo: collaboration, 4; transformational creativity, 294n7
pickup basketball, group genius in, 4
Pliny, on recombination in Greek tragedy, 117
plural "views," 92
pokok. *See* core melody
polos: as interlocking with *sangsih*, 11; for *norot*, 69–70, 70, 78–79
poly-musicality, 298n15
polyphony, 202, 300n8; Central African, various, 4, 26, 48, 49, 55, 166, 184, 198–99, 201, 221, 307n17; inherent rhythms and, 96–97, 274; interlocking, 14, 143, 145, 172, 177, 270; New Orleans jazz, 6–7, 7, 201; stratified, 68, 69, 145, 288n19, 299n28, 303n10; typologies of, 140, 145–47
polyphony of voices, 92, 276
ponggang, 83–84, 90, 124, 134
post-bop, 173
postjazz, 148
Pressing, Jeff: on knowledge base, 45; on referent, 26
process, vs. product, 28
product, vs. process, 28
progressive evolution, Spencerian notions of, 266
psychedelic rock, 35–36, 143

radioactivity, 4
Radio Republik Indonesia (RRI), *arja* broadcasts, 311n40
raga, 109, 111; and *alap*, 37–38
Rāg Pūriyā-Kalyān, 38
Rai, I Dewa Putu, 52, 222–23, 235–36, 241
ramé, 252, 310n24; analyzing of, 226–29, 227, 230, 231, 232, 233–35, 233; and balance, 233–35; as Balinese aesthetic, 223; concept of, 223–24, 233–35; cyclic structures and, 225–28; defining of, 223; in *kendang arja*, 223–35; and *keras*, 224; and personal preference, 223, 224–25, 224, 233, 243–44
rasa, 92, 102, 191; defining of, 54; group, 134; improvisation, as guiding, 103, 119–20, 150, 233, 246; internalizing of, 60–61
Rastocle, Paulo, partnership, 155
recombination, 36, 54, 84, 91, 101, 115, 116, 167, 200, 218, 220, 264; *campur-campur* (mixing it up) as, 32, 249; in combination, 38, 110, 111, 119, 256, 257; combinatorial creativity and, 31, 33, 41; commonalities of, 274; cross-figuration borrowing as, 120–22; cross-rhythms and, 251–54, 254; defining of, 31; and *empat*, 119–20; in exploration, 35; exploratory creativity and, 33, 41; as flexible concept, 33, 41, 43; as formulaic, pejoratively, 34; formulaic variation and, 41; idiomatic use, 98; as improvisatory process, 31, 41; inherent rhythms, as perceptual recombination, 96–97; vs. interpretation, 33, 33; in jazz, 117–18, 221, 259, 268; in *kendang arja*, 31–33, 32, 43, 117–18, 196–97, 245, 246, 247–54, 260, 261, 267–68, 274, 275; in mbira, 117–18, 274–75, 274; micro-recombination, 32–33, 32; pattern displacement as, 247, 248; in *reyong norot*, 80, 117–24, 132, 268; of stasis and motion, 118–20; in various genres, 43, 86–87
recording sessions, for research, 49, 64, 71–72, 74, 106, 191, 297n9

Red Hot Peppers, collective improvisation of, 6–7, 7, 8
reflective vs. reactive processes, 139
regional style, 19; in Balinese arts, 237–38; individual approaches to, 242–46, 261; in *kendang arja*, 235–41, *241*, 261, 263; models and, 236, 240; personal preference and, 15, 218, 220, 261; reasons for, in *arja*, 239–41, 242–44; in various genres, 91, 236–37, 242, 245
reyong, 48, *52*, 65, 69, 158, 220; as cellular, 2-beat units of sound, 80, 82, 99, 101; *empat* figuration, 52–53, *53*, 54, 76, 121, *121*, 212; fixed pitches of, 94; flexible pairings, 84, *84*; vs. *gangsa* figuration, 76, 79; improvisation, 11–12, 67, 80–82, *81*; interactional roles, 165; interlocking melodies, 52–53; *kempyung*, 94–97, 99, 106, 110–12, 122; numbering for analysis, 84–86, *85*, *86* octave equivalence, 52–53, 82, 94, 298n23, 299n34; *pasangan*, 154; playing as fixed, 52–53; playing positions of, 83, *83*; ranges of, 83–84, *83*; sharing of, 83. See also *pemetit*; *pengenter*; *penyorog*; *ponggang*; *reyong norot*
reyong norot, 50, *81*, 86–87, *135*, 144, 147, 171, 218, 220, 261, 276, 301n15; anticipation, as embellishment, 106–12, *108*, *110*, *112*; aural and visual experience of, 80–82, 89–90; "the base," 74–75, *75*; conceptual space of, 54, 55–56, 57, 80; continuous motion, 81; core melody, ambiguity in, for expansion, 129; core melody, as central to, 65, 69, 77, 84–85, 100; core melody, parallels in, for expansion, 131–32; core melody anticipation, as embellishment, 106, *107*, 108, 110, *110*, 112–13, 119, 126, 141; creative pitch substitution, as embellishment, 115–17; cross-figuration borrowing, as recombination, 120–22; delayed unison, as embellishment, *103*, 104–6, *104*, 110, 122; effects of resting on gong, *103*; embellishment techniques, 101–17, 268; *empat* aesthetic in, 122, *123*; *empat* substitution, as recombination, 120–21, 130, *130*, *131*, 136; end-weightedness and, 85, 103, 302n37; equivalence in, 56–57, *56*; expansion techniques, 123–32; flexible approach to *gangsa* model, 80–84; flexible timing, and *wayah*, 111–12; flexible timing, as embellishment, 102–14, *113*; *gangsa norot*, as model for, 12, 14, 74–77, 79; gong tone and, 81; group creativity, 143; group *rasa*, 134; immersion into, 64–67; improvised cells, comparison of, *86*; improvised cells, with nonstandard tones, *101*; individual agency and, 134–35; individual pieces and, 129; insider's listening experience of, 89–90; instrument construction, influence of, 82; interactional roles, 165, 166; interaction and, 15, 94–95, 134–35, 136, 139, 140, 158, 221; interchanging stasis and motion, as recombination, 118–19, 122; interpretation, idiomatic guidelines for, 98–101; interpretation techniques, 93–101; intersubjectivity, 172; *kempyung*, 94–100, 135, 268; *kempyung* below, 94–95; vs. *kendang arja*, 177, 268–71; knowledge base, 80–84, 98; larger-scale improvisational logic, 111–12, 275; learning to play and, 59–64; lessons, 74–75; limited ranges, influence of, 83–84; listening and, 58–59; model, as storehouse of paradigmatic variations, 32; model, as unspoken, 60, 189; model, from *gangsa norot*, 77–79; model for, 13, 14, 32, 48, 54, 56–58, 65, 67, 70, 74–79, 80, 86, *86*, 92, 94, 95–97, 106, 142–43, 145, 177, 183, 189, 236, 268; musical communication codes, 161; *ngubeng* vs. *majalan*, 77–78; nonstandard tones, 92, 101, *101*; note-doubling, as embellishment, 106, 122, 206, 221, 268; ornamentation, as embellishment, 114–15; partnership, 216; perceived structural motion, decreases in, 125–26; perceived structural motion, intensification of, 127–29; performing to experience traditional pedagogies, 61–62; performing to learn fundamentals, 60–61; pick-up gesture (3-note anticipation), 78–79, 106, 109, 118, 122, 128; Pinda style, 244; *rasa* (feeling), 54, 92, 102; recombination techniques, 117–23; recording sessions of, 71–72; regional style differences, 235–36; rests in, 56–57, 80, 82, 96–100, 118, 135, 269; reverse *norot*, 302n38; rhythmic flexibility, as structure marking, 103–10; rhythmic flexibility and variety, 81, 96, 102; as simultaneous improvisation, 12, 136, 166, 172; stasis, freedom of, 122–23; structural flexibility, as expansion, 124–27; structurally important notes, rests on, 99; structure marking, as embellishment, 106–10; suspension, as embellishment, 105–12, *105*, *106*, *109*, *112*, *113*; techniques for improvisation, summarized, *132–33*; transcription of, 67–70; and *wayah*, 92, 102–3, 105–9, 111–12. See also Alit, I Dewa Ketut; collective improvisation; *gangsa norot*; improvisation; interlocking patterns; *reyong*

Rice, Timothy, 184; on intertextuality, 292n18; on tacit knowledge, 189
Ricoeur, Paul, theory of narrative, 171
Rinzler, Paul, on styles of interaction in jazz, 172–73
rock, nonverbal communication, 163
roles in improvisation. *See* interactional roles; musical roles; performative roles
Rollins, Sonny, influences on, 25–26
Route 128, lack of collaboration in, 4–5
rwa bhineda, 234

Sakura, I Dewa Madé, 52
sangati: improvisation of, 43, 111; precomposition of, 302n35
sangsih, 94, 299n3; as interlocking with *polos*, 11; for *norot*, 69–70, *70*, 78–79
Sanguinetti, Giorgio, on *partimento* improvisation, 98
Savage, Patrick E., on comparative analysis, 266–67
Sawyer, R. Keith, 177; on conceptual combination, 294n8; on group flow, 153–54; on jazz knowledge base, 48; on model specificity and flexibility, 142; on risk of failure, in improvisation, 212, 304n32
schema for exploration. *See* exploration
schema theory, 296n24
Schubert, Franz, quick composition style, 295n17
Searle, John, on we-intentions, 172
Seeger, Anthony, on "theoretical cuts," 67
Sekolah Menengah Karawitan Indonesia (SMKI), 309n18
selisir, 297n12
Seventh String Software program, 309n1
Sevillanas, 137
shared flow, 304n28. *See also* group flow
shared knowledge, 136, 162; and collectivity, 147–49; and familiarity/partnership, 154–55, 216–17; vs. individual style, 218, 242–46; and shared constraints, 174; and shared expectations, 149, 155–56; and shared history, 147, 149, 155–56, 217, 262–63; shared history, as unique model, 149; shared *rasa*, 134
Shona *mbira dzavadzimu*. *See* mbira
Sidja, I Wayan, 192, 216
Silicon Valley, collaboration in, 4–5
Simeon, Omer, collective improvisation of, 6–7, *7*
simulation, entrenched situated conceptualizations, 150
Sinatra, Frank, nonverbal communication, 163
Singapadu, 29, 72, 199; *arja*, 190, 191, 192, 193, 194, 213, 228, 238–41, *241*, 242–46, 307n9, 310n22, 310n28, 310n35; *taksu* in, 304n24
single-voice model, 14, 145–46, *146*, 174–75, 177; for *reyong norot*, 78–80. *See also* model
Smith, Christopher J., on nonverbal communication, 162
Smith, Tab, influence of, 46
Soleá, improvisation in, 137
Solis, Gabriel: on benefits of music analysis, 17, 178; on disciplinary ghettoization, in study of improvisation, 305n54
specificity-flexibility spectrum, 27, 41, 142–44, *142*, *143*, 174, 175, 177; zoom, differing levels in analysis, 143–44. *See also* model
spoken models, 55, 144. *See also* explicit models; unconscious models; unspoken models

static. *See ngubeng* (static)
Steinbeck, Paul, on improvisational fictions, 295n17
String Cheese Incident, as jam band, 293n24
Subandi, I Madé, 65–67, 69
Sucipta, I Wayan Pasek, 189, 192
Sudi. *See* Sudirana, I Wayan (Sudi)
Sudirana, I Wayan (Sudi), 1–2, 63, 192, 194, 223, 261; Cok Alit, similarities in *lanang* patterns, 191; on *lanang*, relative simplicity of, 200; *lanang* patterns, 194, 224; on *ngematin*, 202; Pak Dewa, influence on, 185; on *ramé*, 224–25, 228; on *reyong*, "on-beat, off-beat" playing, 308n31; on *taksu*, 152; on *wayah*, 109
Sum, Maisie, on improvisation, in Gnawa *lila* performance, 91
Sundanese *suling*, embellishment, 102
Supasta, I Madé, 82, 135
Sura, I Dewa Nyoman (Pak Dewa), 22, 89–90, *181*, *183*, 199, *199*, 220, 222, 223, 235, 309n2; on balance, 228, *229*, 233–34; on *campur-campur*, 32, 196–97, 249; *cocok* and, 155; cross-rhythm, 252–53, 254, *254*, *255*, 256; *Dag*-on-gong, 258, *259*; *Dag*-Tut interactions, 262–63; on *dasar*, 27, 262; density, in *kendang arja*, 233, *233*; expansion techniques, 254–57; influence of, 185; influences, 25; intuitive knowledge, 189, 191; on Keramas-style *arja*, 239–40; on *lanang*, relative simplicity of, 200; *lanang* passages, density differences, 233; *lanang* patterns, 224, 262; liberal approach to improvisation, 228, 246, 250, 251, 254–57, *256*, 260; modularity of *arja* patterns, 196, *196*; musical interactions, *arja*, 161, 182–83, *184*, 216, *216*, 262–64, *262*, *263*; *ngegongin*, 214, *214*, 215, *215*; nonverbal communication, 162, 163–64; "on-beat, off-beat" rule, 210–11, *210*, *211*; and *pasangan*, 154, 155, 212, 216, *216*, 217; pattern vs. improvisation, dividing line between, 191–92; pedagogical lineage, 240–42, *241*, 311n38; pre-composed interaction, 216; and *ramé*, 228, *229*, 233, *233*; recombination techniques, 250–54, *251*, *254*; regional style, *241*, 245, 261; taught patterns, *182*, *184*, 224, 229, 234, 256–57; taught patterns, as designed to interlock, 182–83, *184*; teaching, 179–81, 189, 191–93, 228; *wadon*, relative freedom, 200, 210–11, *210*, *211*
Sutton, R. Anderson, on improvisation, in Central Javanese gamelan, 6, 91–92, 123–24, 132
svara kalpana, 39, 127, 220–21
swing, 45–46, 59
symbolic analysis, 293n35
system of potentialities, 117
systems model of creativity: domain, 48, 156; field, 48; for jazz improvisation, 48; microdomain, 156

INDEX · 349

tabla, 82, 98, 305n51
tabuh dua, 188, 225–26, 243, 245, 254
tabuh empat, 187–88, 309n10. See also tabuh telu
tabuh telu, 187, 188, 225, 226, 228, 234, 243, 245, 254; halus, maintaining of, 235
tacit knowledge. See intuitive (tacit) knowledge
taksu, 152, 304n23
tala, 117–18
Tama, I Wayan, 34, 72, 73, 181, 220, 223, 229, 256, 307n19, 308n39; batel, improvisation for, 227, 235; on batel marah, 307n9; combinatorial creativity and, 31; conservative approach to improvisation, 228, 245–46, 259–61, 260; cross-rhythm, 251–52, 252; on cyclic structures, drumming for, 225, 225–26; exploratory creativity, 33; improvisation, 29, 30; interpretation techniques, 31, 31, 246–47, 247; keras strokes, use of, 310n34; lanang patterns, 194, 224, 225–26, 260; model patterns, 30, 32–33; ngegongin, 213–14; on "on-beat, off-beat" rule, 202; pedagogical lineage, 240–41, 241, 243, 245, 311n38; ramé and, 225–27, 228, 234–35; recombination techniques, 31–33, 32, 117, 248–50, 248, 249, 251–52; on regional styles, 239, 240; on roles of drums, 200; tabuh dua patterns, 225, 226, 226; tabuh empat, 309n10; tabuh telu patterns, 225–26, 225, 228, 234–35; on taksu, 304n24; taught patterns, 30, 260; teaching, 191, 192, 193; wadon patterns, 260
taqsim, 3, 27, 36, 102
Tatum, Art, on improvisation, 3
taught patterns, 201, 220, 223, 229, 234; codification, dangers of, 30, 191–92; cross-rhythms in, 254, 255, 256; expansion of, in kendang arja, 254–59; insights from, 192–97; interpretation of, 246–47, 273; for lanang, 210, 224, 225, 226; mixing-and-matching of, 228, 245; as models for improvisation, 29–30, 49–50, 183, 190–97, 217–18, 245–47, 247, 259–63, 267–68, 271; as modular, 195–97, 243; oral music theory and, 197–98; as precomposed building blocks, 192; rasa (feeling) of, 233; recombination of, 247–54, 274–75; sparse, 234; status of, 183, 191–92; unconscious models, 190, 197; visual comparison of, 197; for wadon, 182, 210, 229. See also kendang arja
tawa-tawa, 187–88
teaching. See pedagogy
tembang macapat, 10–11, 23, 93
Tenzer, Michael, 89; on benefits of music analysis, 19; on improvisation, in Bali, 9; on kinetic quality, in gamelan gong kebyar, 213; on rhythm creation, 300n9; on typologies, 140, 213
tertian harmony, 61

Teruna Jaya, 81–82, 81, 84, 96, 120, 135, 135
tihai, 127
Torvalds, Linus, 292n15
traditional Irish music, 102, 117, 158–59; nonverbal communication in, 163–64
transcription: challenges of, 67, 71–72; for confirmation and detail, 69–70; for context, 69; embodiment and, 59; of end-weightedness, 68; as research tool, 3, 49, 67–70, 71, 87, 99, 102, 191; slow-down programs and, 219. See also notation
transformational creativity, 258; conventions, altering of, 23; defining of, 23; preexisting knowledge, based on, 24; as rare, 24, 25. See also creativity
Tublen, I Cokorda Oka: individual kendang arja style, 243–45, 310n34; and Singapadu-style arja, 240–41, 310n28
Turino, Thomas, 6; on formulaic variation, 29, 34, 295n18; improvisation, definition of, 34; on interaction in improvisation, 50
Tut, Pak. See Bicuh, I Ketut (Pak Tut)
Tut (T) strokes, 182–83, 183, 194, 197, 204, 209–14, 216, 223, 225–27, 243, 245, 246, 249, 262–63. See also bass strokes; Dag (D) strokes; kendang arja; lanang
Tygaraja, 302n35
typology: categories, when not a good fit, 114–15; of collective improvisation, 140–41, 142, 143, 144, 145, 146, 174–78, 175, 176; criterion, 140; of improvisation, 28, 29, 31, 34–35, 34, 37, 38, 41, 42; parameter, 140; trait, 140. See also analytical models/frameworks

ubit empat. See empat
ubit telu, 76
Ubud, 182, 189, 192, 237, 239; arja, 194, 238
ugal, 9, 65–66, 69, 72, 76, 139
unconscious models, 36, 58, 136, 174; analysis and, 14, 15, 50, 55, 144–45, 144, 189–92, 217–18; dangers of codification, 191–92; and intuitive knowledge, 189–90; in kendang arja, 15, 177, 183, 190–215, 236, 263; lessons and, 74; oral music theory and, 197–98, 217–18; partnership, benefits of, 215–17; as regional, 236, 263, 270; taught patterns and, 190–97; ways of knowing and, 184–89
unspoken models, 87, 258; analysis and, 48–50, 55, 144–45, 144, 176, 189–90; finding, as researcher, 58–75; in Java, 185; in kendang arja, 183; in reyong norot, 14, 54, 55–56, 57, 58, 70, 74–75, 177, 189, 297n9
Upright Citizens Brigade: emergence, 167–69, 171; improvisation, transcribed, 168; intersubjectiv-

ity, 167–69, 171; pushing boundaries, 306n60; sexist tropes in, 306n60; "yes, and . . ." rule, 171

Vallely, Cillian, 159

variation, 6, 23, 87, 242, 295n18; in Central Java, 91–92, 124, 293n26; defining of, 34; as degree of improvisation, 28; and equivalence, 56; in Irish music, 158, 159; in mbira, 46, 48, 111, 275, 311n7; paradigmatic, 32; regional, 235–41. *See also* formulaic variation; improvisation

vistār, as expansion, 38, 123

wadon, 222, 246, 260; counting-stroke variations, *204*; *Dag*-on-gong, 258–59; improvisation on, 196–97; individual style in, 185, 243, *244*, 308n34; as *kernet*, 200; *lanang*, rhythmic relationship with, 12, 183, *184*, 198–200, 206–7, *207*, 208, 209–12, 240, 243, 252, 262–64, 268, 271–73, 295n19; *ngegongin* and, 201, 212–15; "on-beat, off-beat" rules (bass strokes), 209–12; "on-beat, off-beat" rules (double strokes), 206–8; "on-beat, off-beat" rules (left-hand strokes), 202–5; recombination techniques, 250–51, *251*; relative difficulty/scope for improvisation, 192–93, 198–200; relative freedom of, in *arja*, 199–200, 210–11, 216, 250–51, 271, 307n20, 308n33, 308n34; rhythmic modules, 182, 252–53; role of, as structural, 212, 214–15, 272; strokes, 181, *183*; taught patterns, 189, 191, 196. See also *kendang arja*; *lanang*

Washington, DC, speech patterns, 107–8, 124–25

wayah, 2, 17, 92, 115, *119*, 136, 216, 244, 264; defining of, 104, 109; flexible timing as, 103–12; in *kendang arja*, 191, 221, 254; in *reyong norot*, 103–6, 106–10, 111–13

Webster, Ben, influence of, 46

we-intentions, 172

Western contemporary art music, improvisation in, 148, 303n5

Widdess, Richard: on Nettl's model concept, 292n14; on schemas for *alap* performance, 37–39, *37, 39, 40*, 123

Widnyana, Ida Bagus Madé, 1–3, 190

W. L. Gore and Associates, collaboration and experimentation, 4

Wright Brothers, collaboration, 4

Young, Lester, influence of, 26, 46

zoom, differing levels in analysis, 143–44